A-Z

227053

KU-183-586

...TH

Key to Map Pages	2-3	Postcode Map	112-113
Large Scale Bristol City Centre	4-5	Index to Streets, Towns, Villages, Stations & selected Places of Interest	114-166
Large Scale Bath City Centre	6-7		
Map Pages	8-111	Index to Hospitals & Hospices	167-168

REFERENCE

Motorway	**M5**	Cycleway (selected)	🚲
Primary Route	**A4**	Bristol Ferry Waterbus Stop	**F**
		Fire Station	■
A Road	**A36**	Hospital	**H**
B Road	**B4055**	House Numbers Selected roads	13 8 3
Dual Carriageway		Information Centre	**i**
One-way Street Traffic flow on A Roads is also indicated by a heavy line on the driver's left.	→ →	National Grid Reference	³60
		Park & Ride	Ashton Vale **P+**
Restricted Access		Police Station	▲
Pedestrianized Road		Post Office	★
City Centre Loop		Safety Camera with Speed Limit Fixed cameras and long term road works cameras Symbols do not indicate camera direction	③⓪
Track & Footpath	- - - - -		
Residential Walkway	··············	Toilet: without facilities for the Disabled with facilities for the Disabled	▽ ▽
Railway	Station / Tunnel / Level Crossing / Heritage Sta.	Viewpoint	🔆
Built-up Area	SMALL ST.	Educational Establishment	▢
		Hospital or Healthcare Building	▢
Local Authority Boundary	— · — · —	Industrial Building	▢
Posttown Boundary		Leisure or Recreational Facility	▢
Postcode Boundary within Posttown	— — — —	Place of Interest	▢
Map Continuation	**40** Large Scale City Centre **4**	Public Building	▢
Car Park (selected)	**P**	Shopping Centre or Market	▢
Church or Chapel	†	Other Selected Buildings	▢

SCALE

Map Pages 8-111 1:15,840

0   ¼ Mile

0   250   500 Metres
4 inches (10.16 cm) to 1 mile   6.31 cm to 1 km

Map Pages 4-7 1:7,920

0   ⅛ Mile

0   100   200   300 Metres
8 inches (20.32 cm) to 1 mile   12.63 cm to 1 km

Copyright of Geographers' A-Z Map Company Limited

Fairfield Road, Borough Green, ...
Telephone: 01732 781000 (Enqu...
01732 783422 (Reta...
www.a-zmaps.co.uk
Copyright © Geographers' A...
Edition 5 2009
Every possible care has bee...
at the date of publication. How...
inaccuracies, we do not accept any responsibility for loss or damage resulting from reliance on information contained within this publication.

...apping data licensed from
...he permission of the Controller
...ry Office.
...ved. Licence number 100017302
...www.PocketGPSWorld.com
...right 2008 © PocketGPSWorld.com
...ned in this atlas is accurate

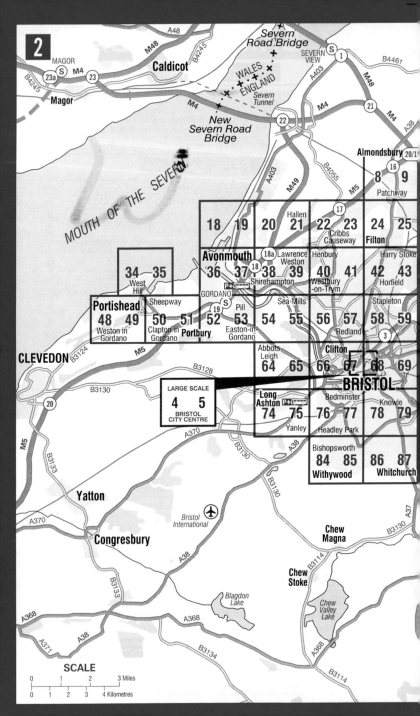

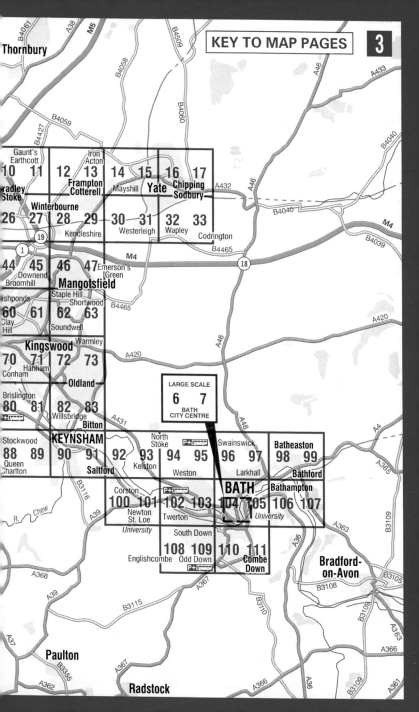

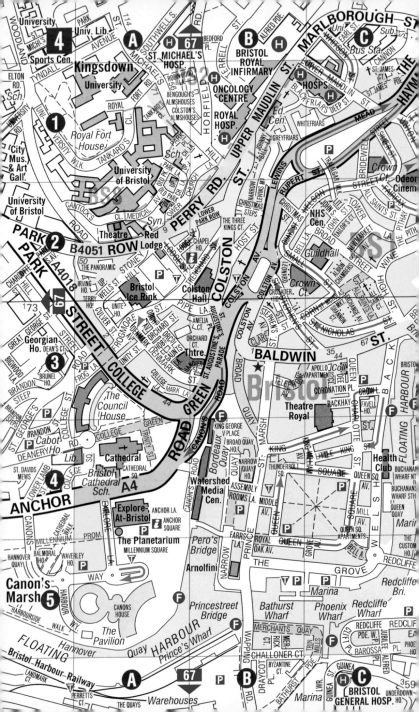

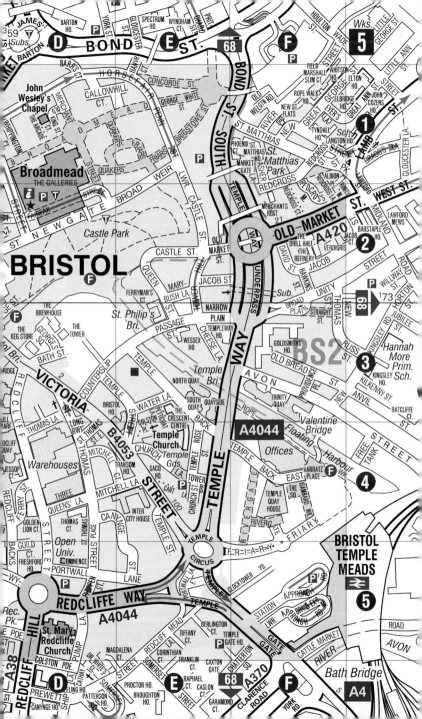

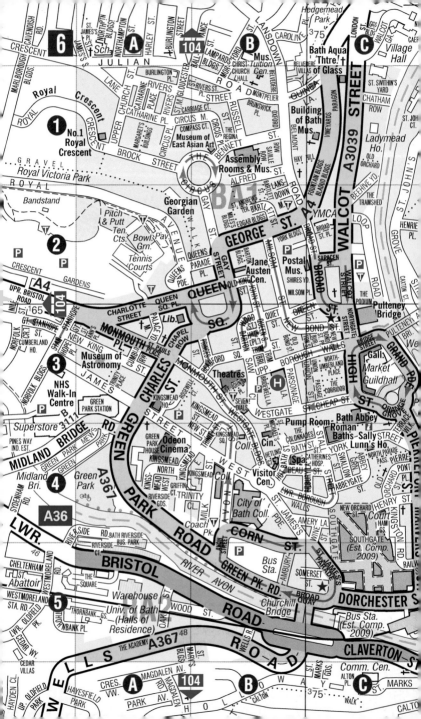

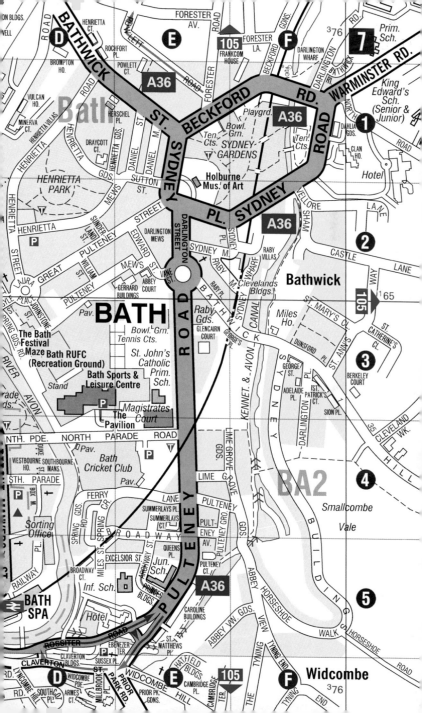

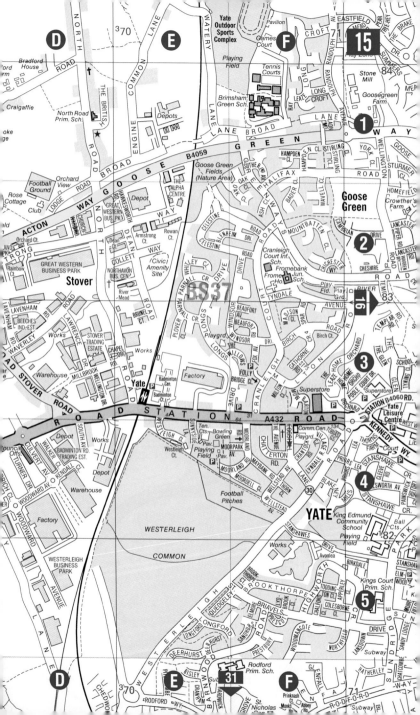

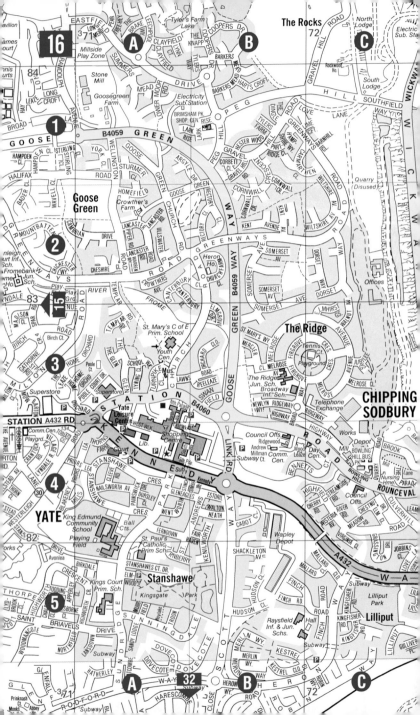

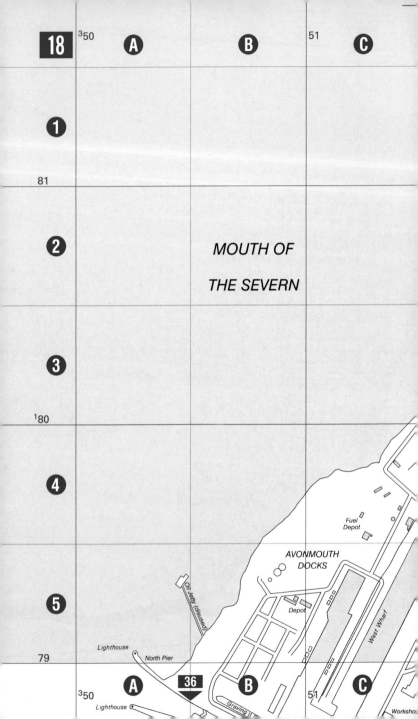

18 ³50 **A** **B** 51 **C**

1

81

2 *MOUTH OF*

THE SEVERN

3

¹80

4

Fuel
Depot

5 AVONMOUTH
DOCKS

Oil Jetty (disused)

Depot

West Wharf

Lighthouse   North Pier

79

A **36** **B** **C**

³50

Lighthouse   Graving   51

Worksho.

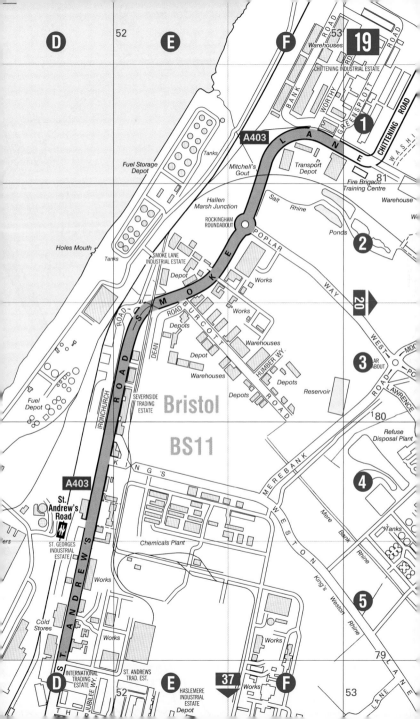

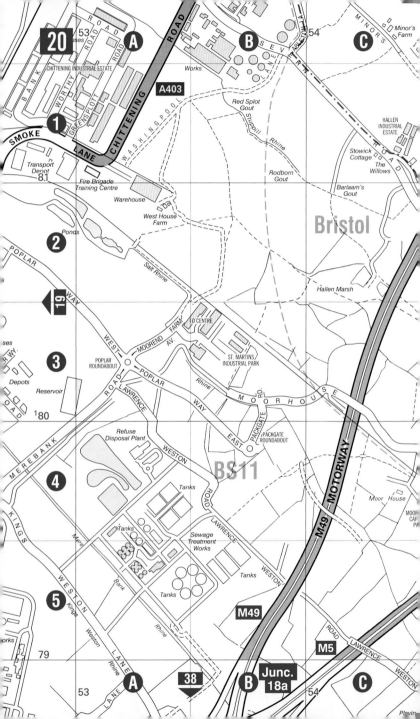

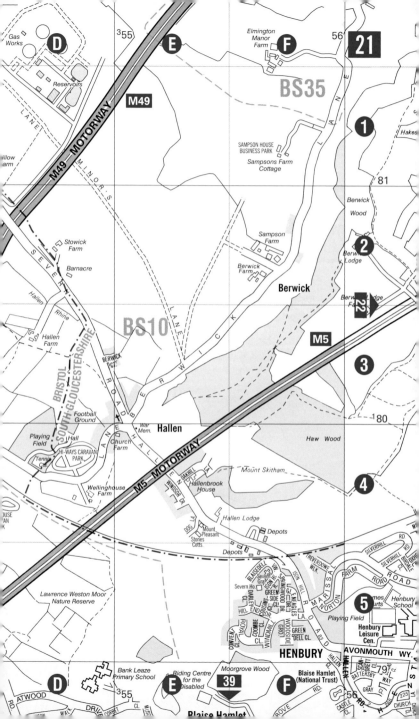

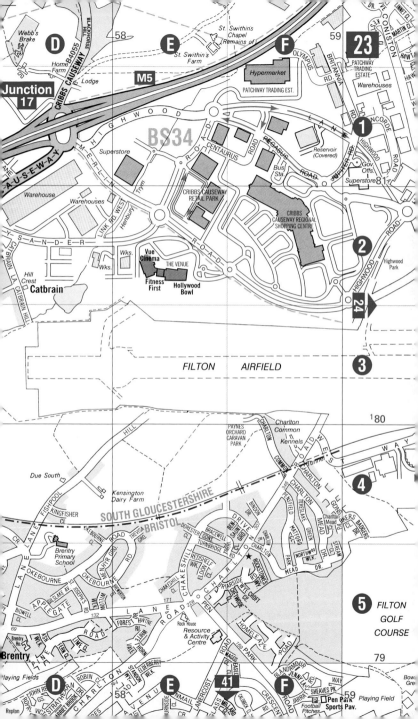

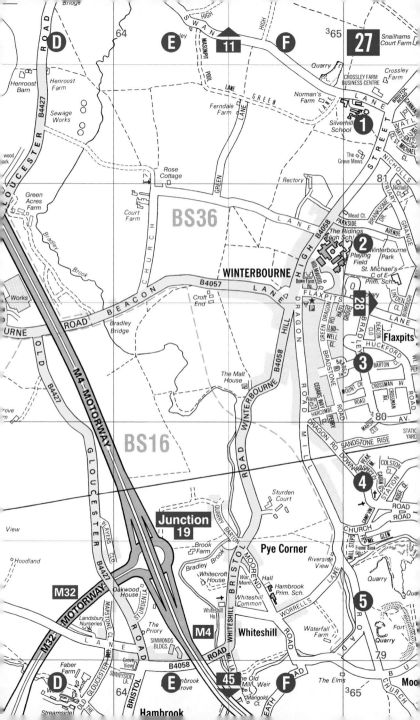

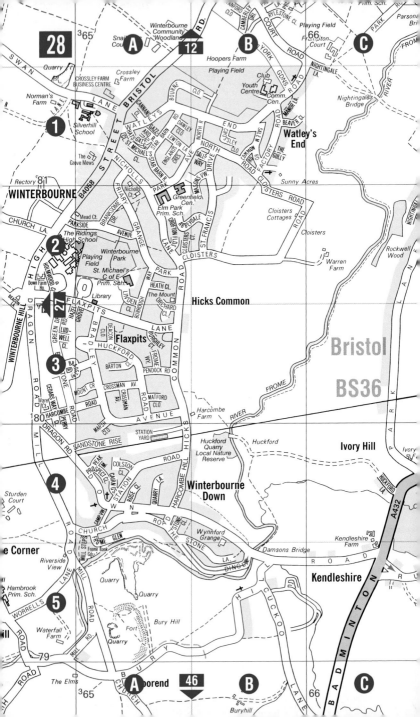

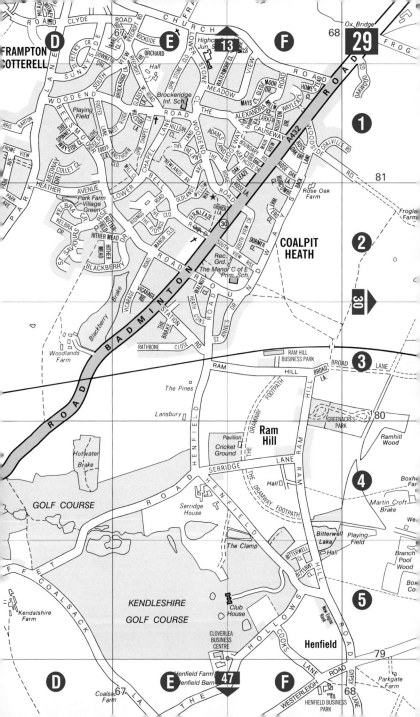

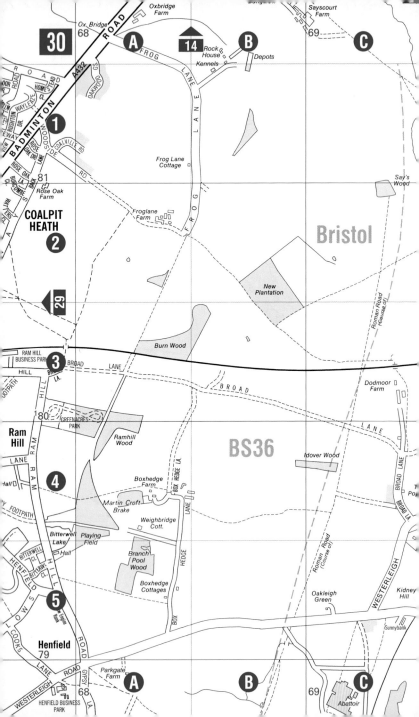

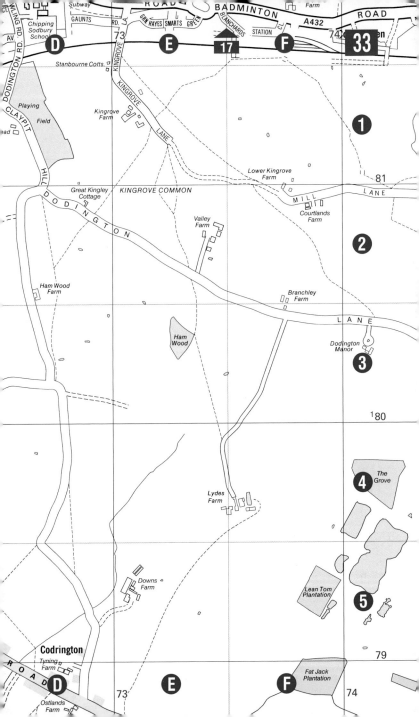

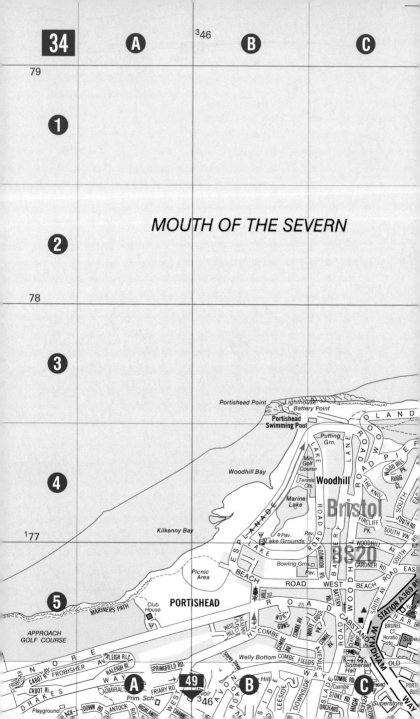

34

A ³46 **B** **C**

79

1

MOUTH OF THE SEVERN

2

78

3

Portishead Point
Lighthouse
Battery Point
**Portishead
Swimming Pool**
Putting
Grn.
WOODLAND
ROAD
PIER
WOOD HILL
PK.
RUGG
CL.
SOUTH
THE KNOLL
Min.
Golf
Course
Woodhill
Woodhill Bay
Tennis
Cts.
Marine
Lake
Bristol
FIRCLIFF
PK.
SOUTH RD.
SOUTH VW.
Kilkenny Bay
Pav.
Pav.
Lake Grounds
BS20
WOODHILL
AV.
SOUTH
Bowling Grns.
GARDNER RD.
ROAD EAST
Pav.
Picnic
Area
BEACH
ROAD WEST
BEACH
SOUTH AV.
STATION A369 RD.
BRUNEL
CT.
Horatio
Ho.
Supe
PORTISHEAD
MARINERS PATH
Club
House
32
HILL
25
NORE
GDNS.
WHITE LODGE
COMBE AV.
COMBE
BATTERY ROAD
WOODHILL
Youth
Cen.
Somerset
Hall
PORT
BU.
4

5

APPROACH
GOLF COURSE
NORE
CABOT RISE
FROBISHER
AV.
LEIGH RI.
RALEIGH RI.
SPRINGFIELD RD.
WAY
ADMIRAL'S
FRIARY RD.
WEST CHANNEL RD.
Resr.
³46
Welly Bottom
COMBE FIELDS
Hill
LEESIDE
DOWNSIDE
SLADE ROAD
STOKE RD.
HIGH ST.
Coombe
ORCHARD
Precinct
Superstore
B3124
WAY
CABOT RI.
DRAKES
FROBR. RI.
Playground
ACK-
DOWN RD.
QUANTOCK RD.
HIGHLANDS
A Prim. Sch.
49 ³46
B Hill
C

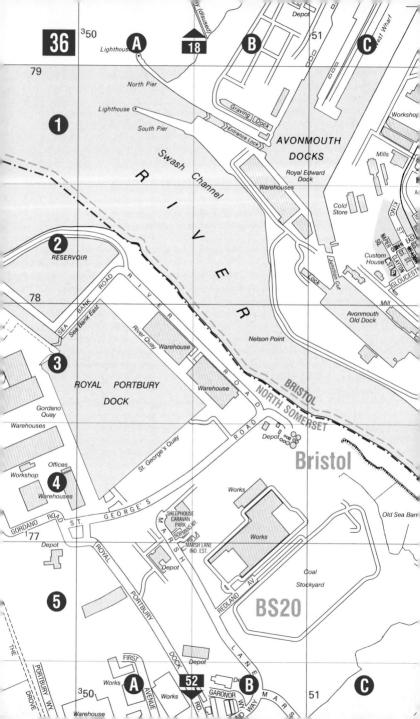

79

1

Lighthouse

North Pier

Lighthouse

South Pier

Swash Channel

R I V E R

2
RESERVOIR

3

78

SEA BANK ROAD

Sea Bank East

R I V E R

ROYAL PORTBURY DOCK

Gordano Quay

Warehouses

4
Offices
Workshop
Warehouses

River Quay

Warehouse

Warehouse

St. George's Quay

ROAD

ROAD

GORDANO ROAD

77

Depot

5

THE PORTBURY WY.

DRIVE

FIRST

Works

Warehouse

350

ST.

S T.

GEORGE'S

ROYAL

PORTBURY

DOCK

RD.

AVENUE

Works

A

52

Depot

GARDNOR RD.

Sheephouse
Caravan Park
NORMANS WY.

MARSH
MARSH LANE
IND. EST.

Depot

Works

Works

REDLAND AV.

MARSH LANE WY.

Coal
Stockyard

BS20

B

51

West Wharf

C

Depot

18

Graving Dock

Entrance Lock

AVONMOUTH DOCKS

Royal Edward Dock

Warehouses

Workshop

Mills

Cold Store

KING

ST.

QUEEN
ST. EAST

CLINTON
ST. EAST

MEAD ST. EAST

Custom House

GLOUCEST

Mill

Avonmouth
Old Dock

Nelson Point

Junction Cut

Lock

BRISTOL

NORTH SOMERSET

Depot

Bristol

Old Sea Ban

B

C

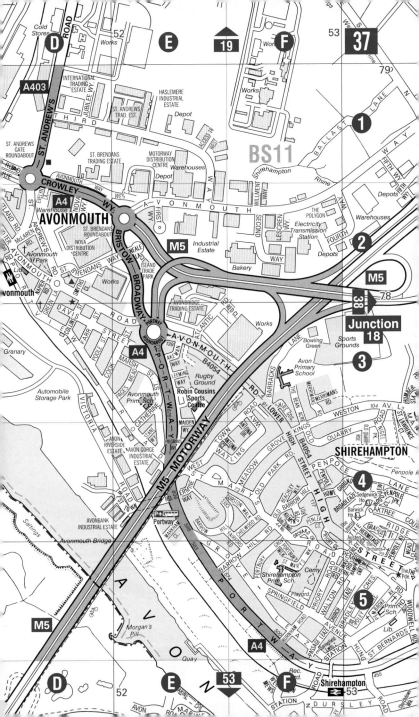

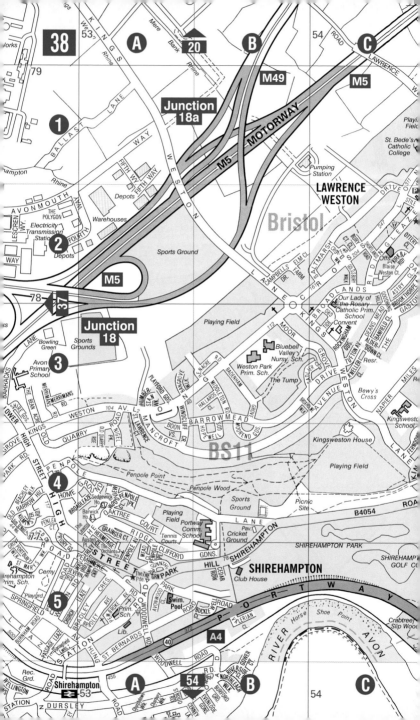

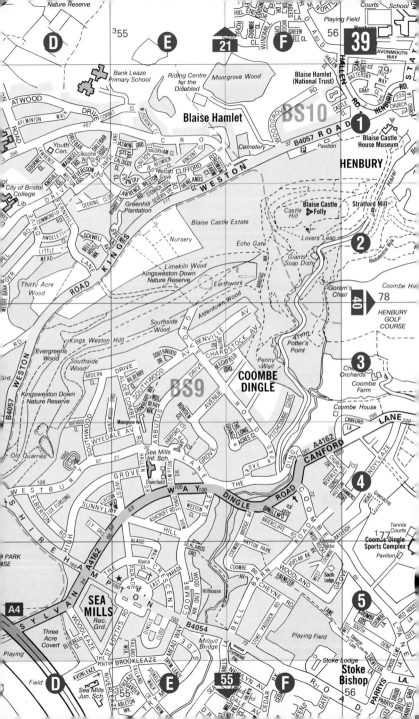

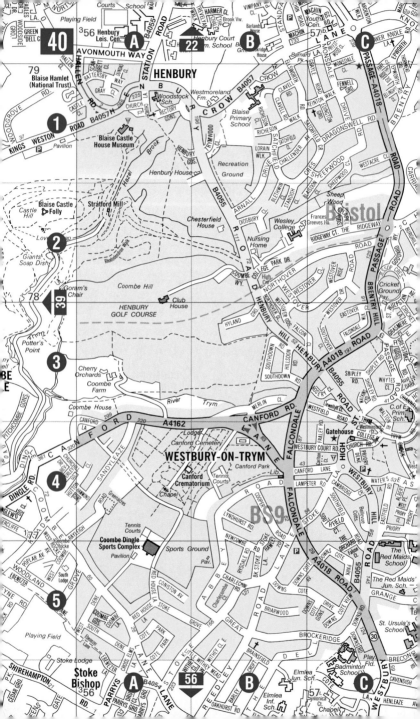

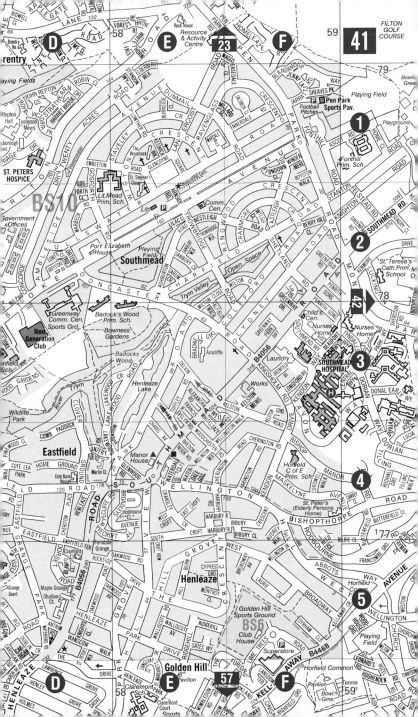

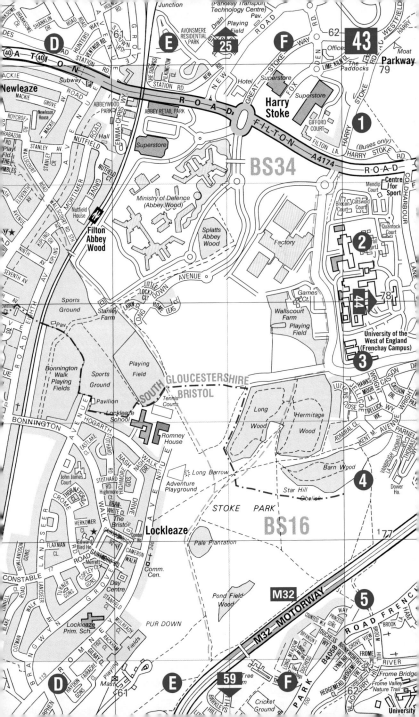

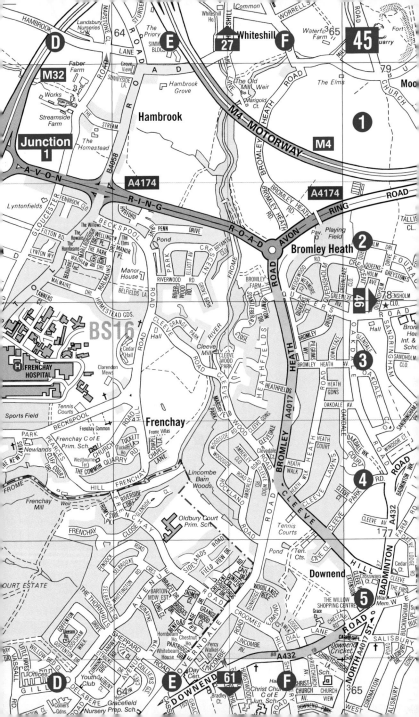

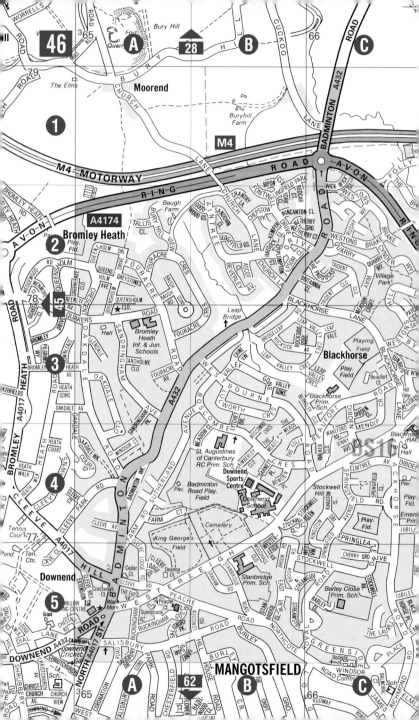

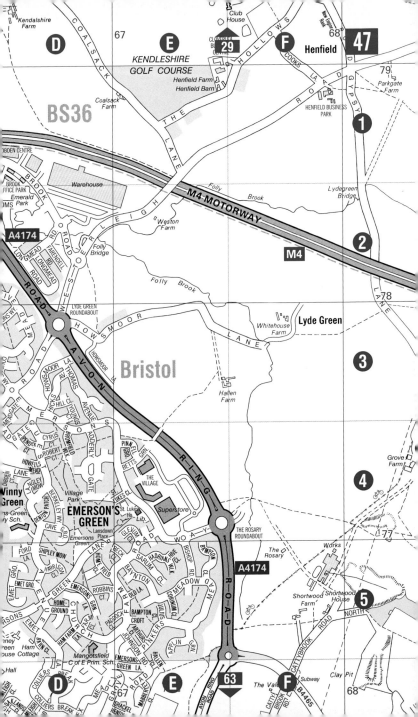

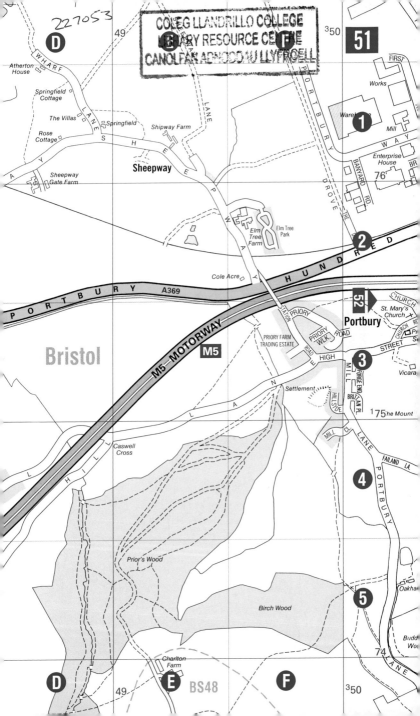

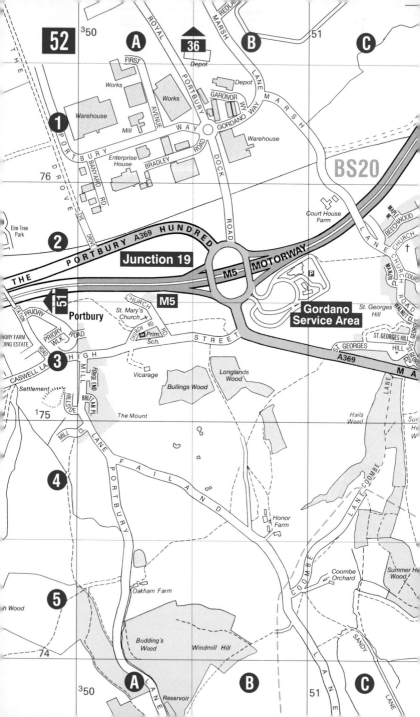

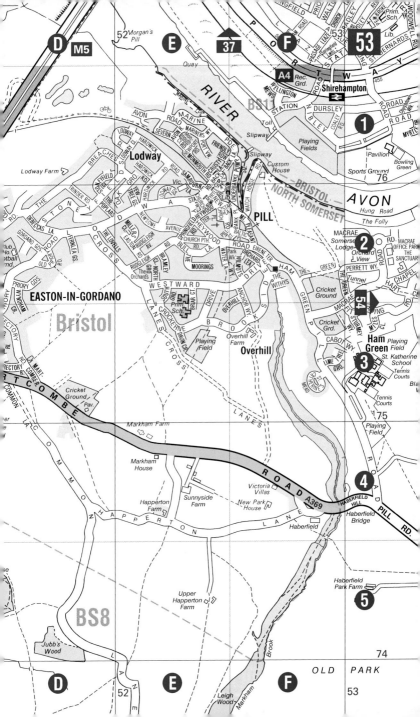

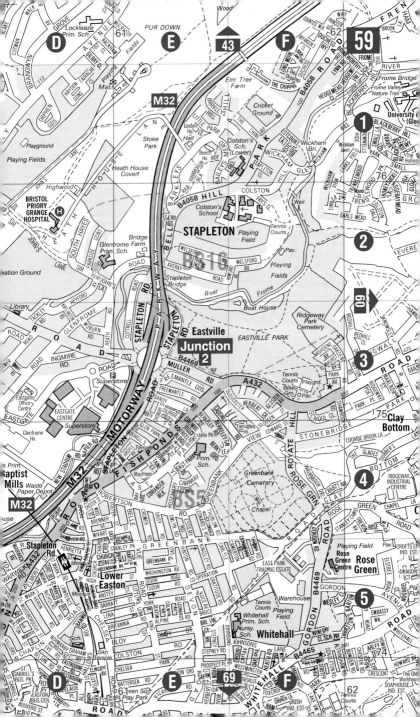

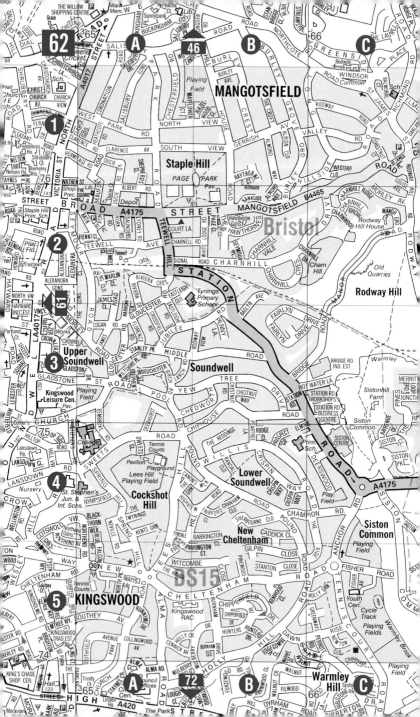

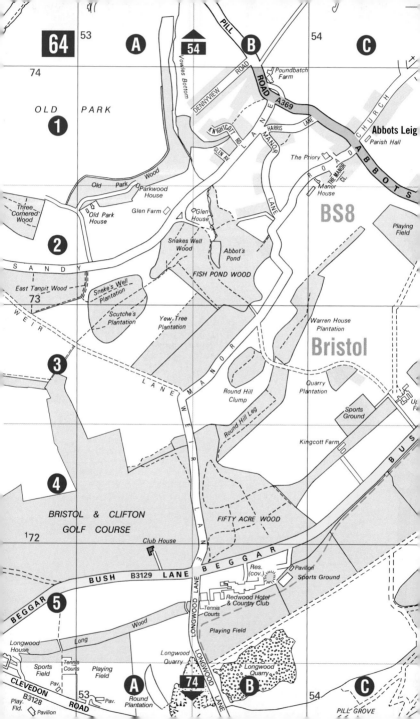

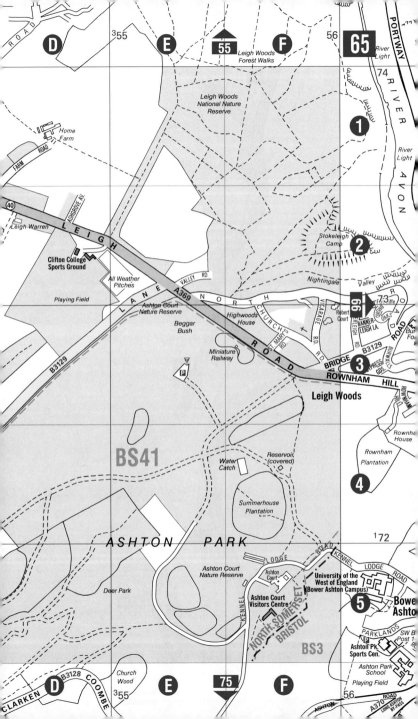

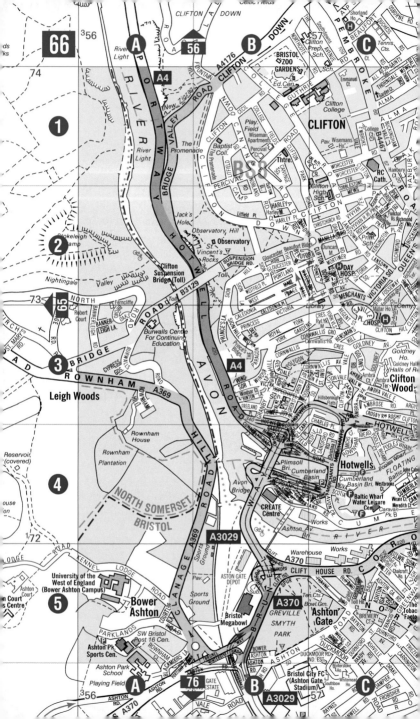

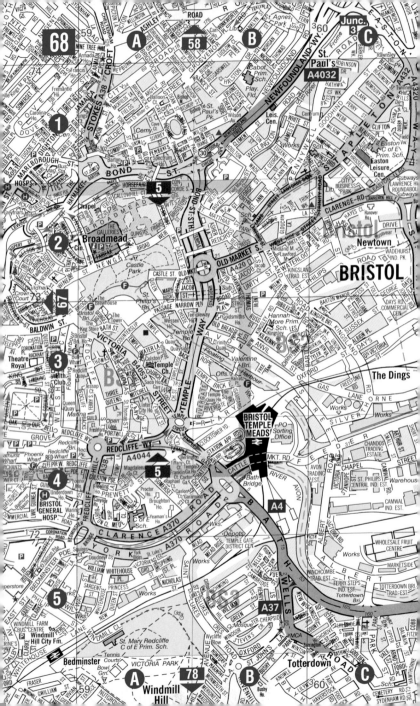

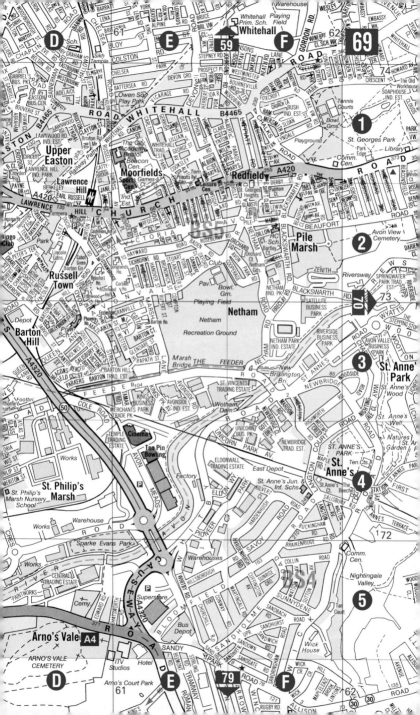

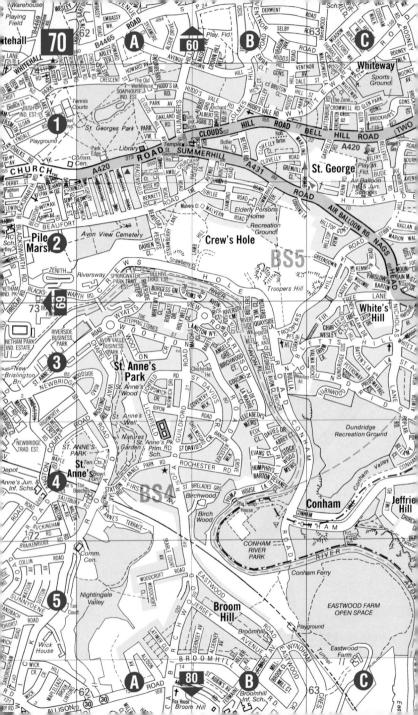

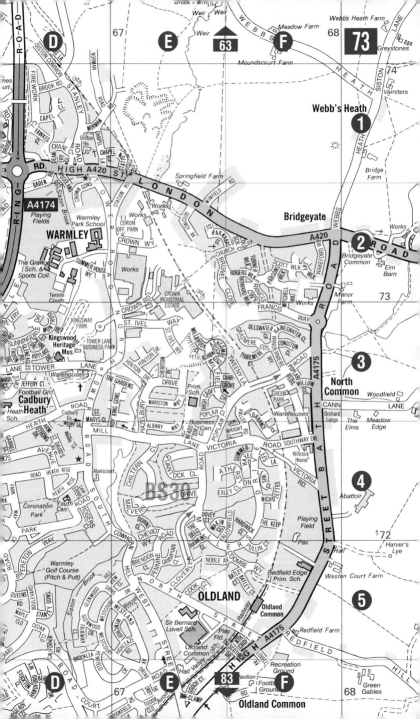

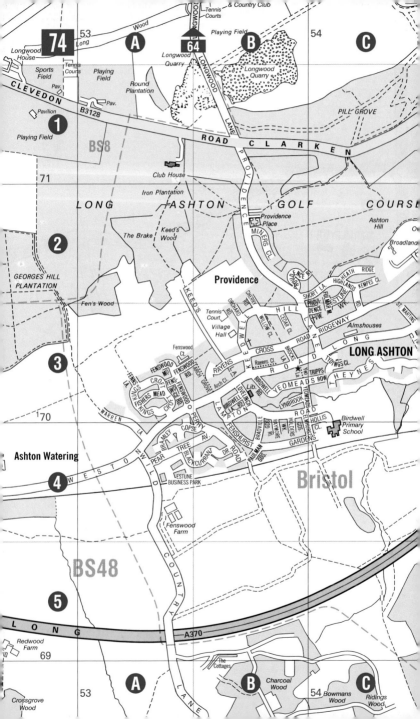

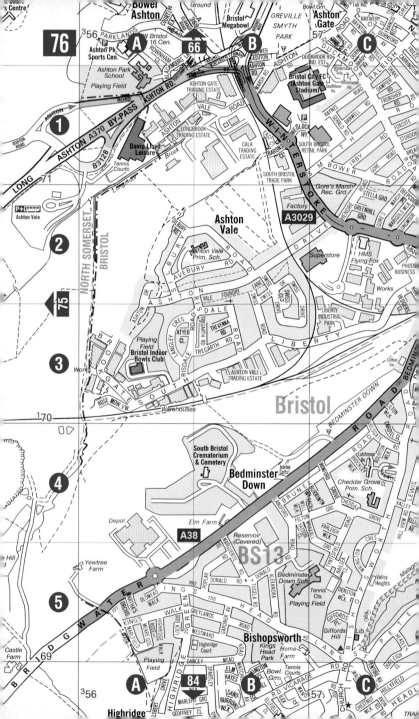

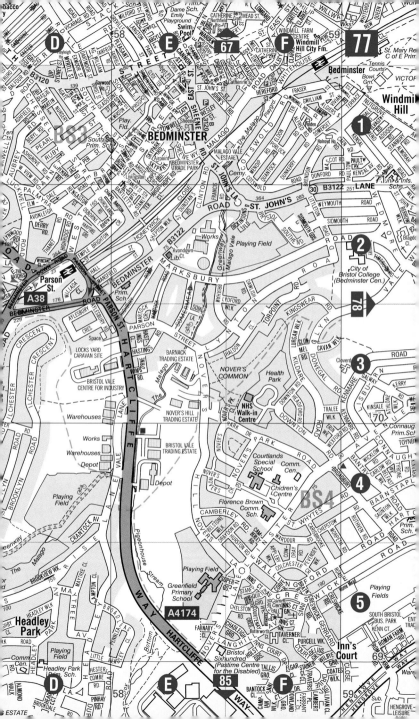

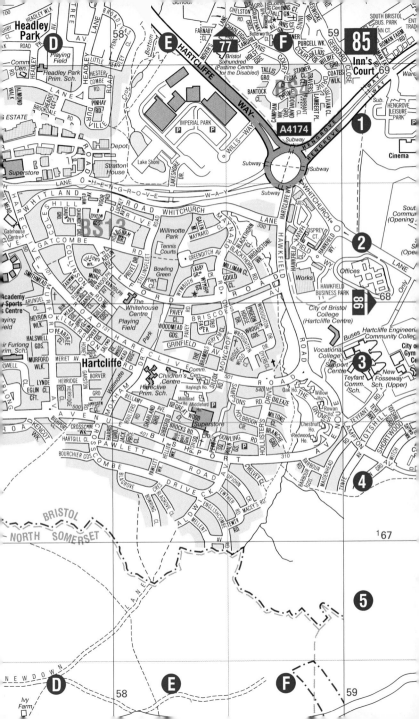

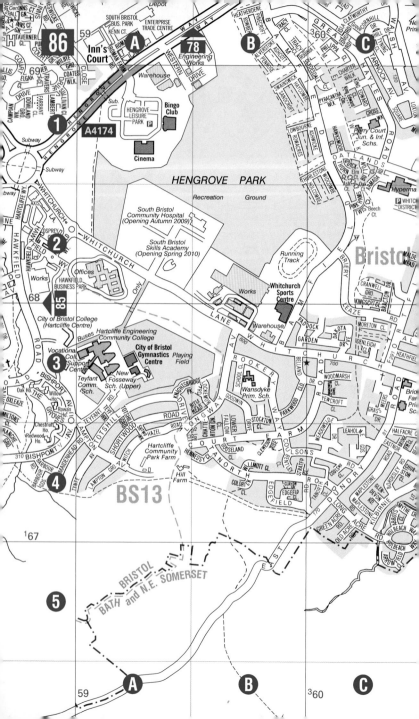

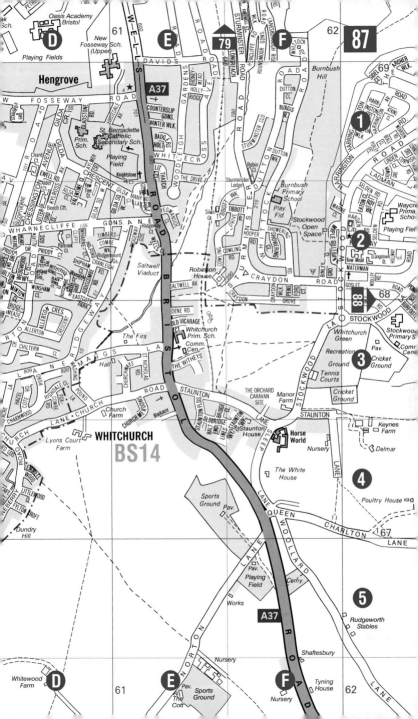

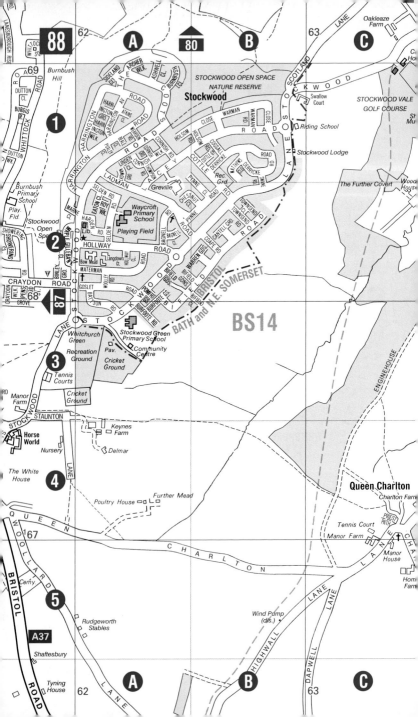

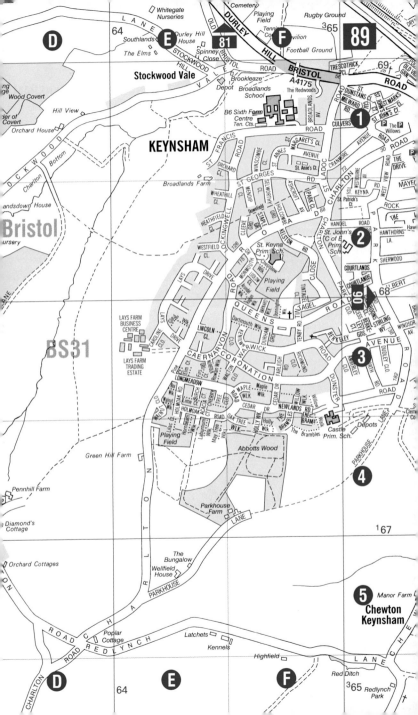

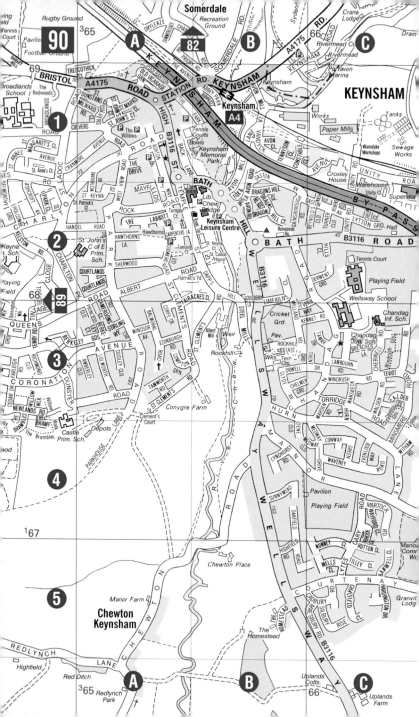

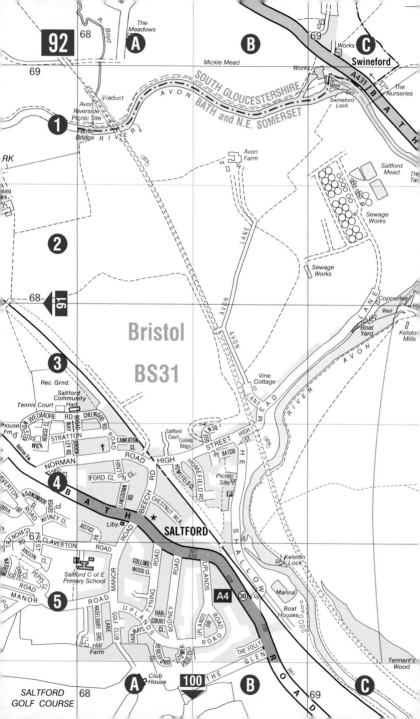

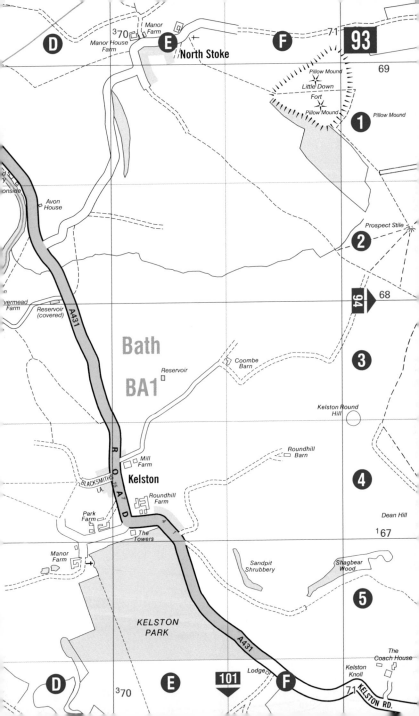

69

Manor
Farm

Manor House
Farm

³70

North Stoke

Pillow Mound

Little Down
Fort

Pillow Mound

1 Pillow Mound

Avon
House

onside

2 Prospect Stile

vermead
Farm

Reservoir
(covered)

94 68

Bath

Coombe
Barn

Reservoir

3

BA1

Kelston Round
Hill

Roundhill
Barn

Mill
Farm

4

BLACKSMITHS
LA.

Kelston

Roundhill
Farm

Dean Hill

Park
Farm

¹67

The
Towers

Manor
Farm

Sandpit
Shrubbery

Shagbear
Wood

5

**KELSTON
PARK**

The
Coach House

Kelston
Knoll

Lodge

A431

KELSTON RD.

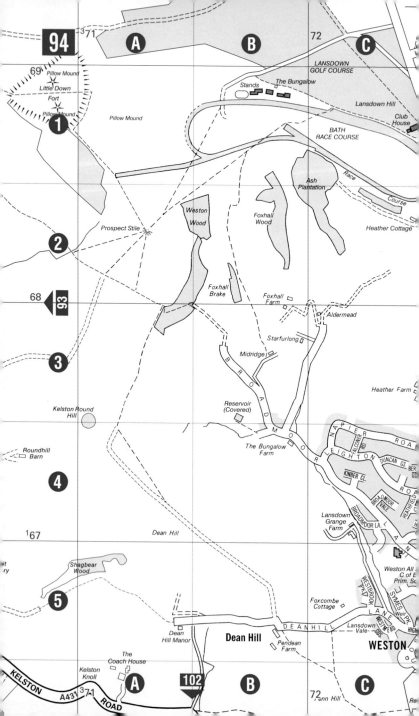

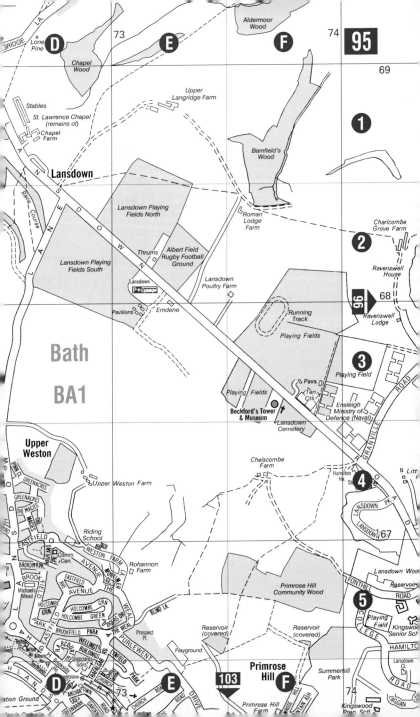

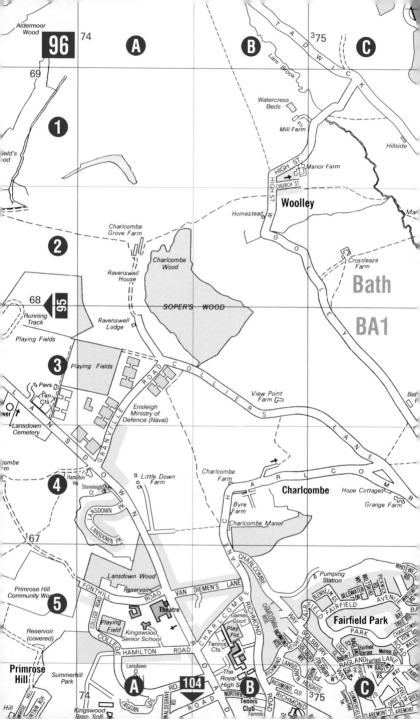

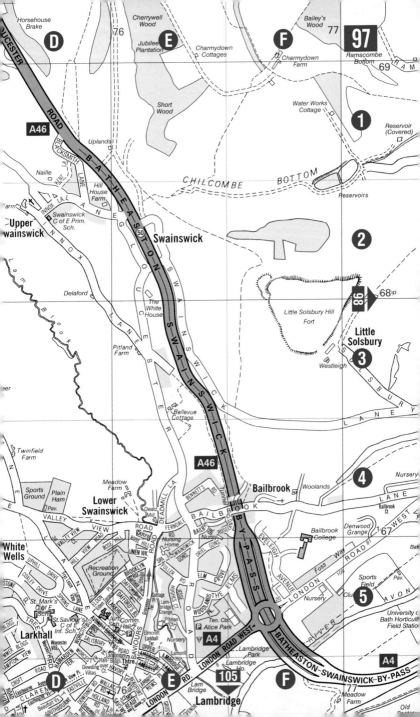

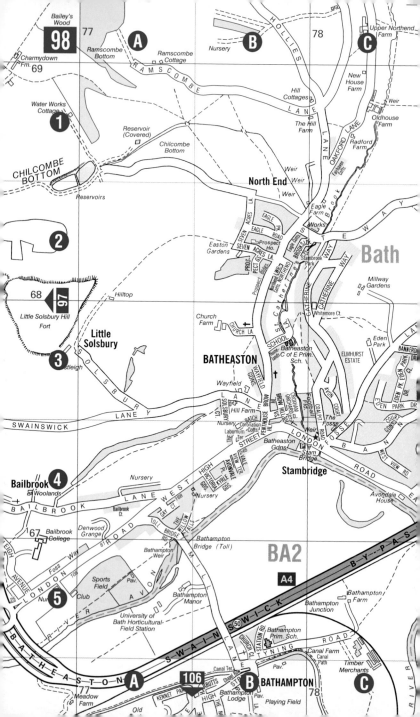

Bannerdown Cottage

Banner Down (Common)

Tennygrove Wood

Reservoir (covered)

Reservoir (covered)

69

Woodleaze Wood

Reservoir (covered)

Upper Shockerwick Farm

Resr. (cov.) **1**

Reservoir (covered)

Lower Shockerwick Farm

Shockerwick

Starfall Farm

BANNERDOWN

Refuse Tip

The Elms

Sheep Sleight

Upper Sleight

LANE

2

Middle Lodge

68

The Mount

HIGH BANNERDOWN

HIGH BANNERDOWN

BA1

The Brow

Bannerdown Gardens

SHOCKERWICK

3   Box Bridge

BANNERDOWN CLO

BRANFIELD WAY

BRANFIELD WAY

LANE

PARK

RECULVER CL.

MEADOW

WEST WOODS

EASTWOODS

Bathford Nurseries

ROAD

A4

By   Brook

ROAD

WILTSHIRE

BATH and N.E. SOMERSET

4   ROAD

167

BRADFORD

B

Mill

X

BATHFORD

Bathford Bridge

Whitehaven

Playing Field

BATHFORD OSTLINGS

Bathford Lodge

Jewson View Farm

Vicarage

BATHFORD HILL STREET

Bathford C of E Prim School

MANOR ROW

DRIVE

DOVERS

DOVERS PK

WOOD

ASHLEY HIGH

GARSTON

New Road

CHAPEL LANE

71

STREET

5

Pleasant Place

Lower House Farm

A363

CHURCH LA.

COURT LA.

CHURCH CL.

MOUNTAIN

MOUNTAIN

DOVERS

WOO

PARK

Mountain Wood

Woodland Place

Prospect PL

FARLEIGH

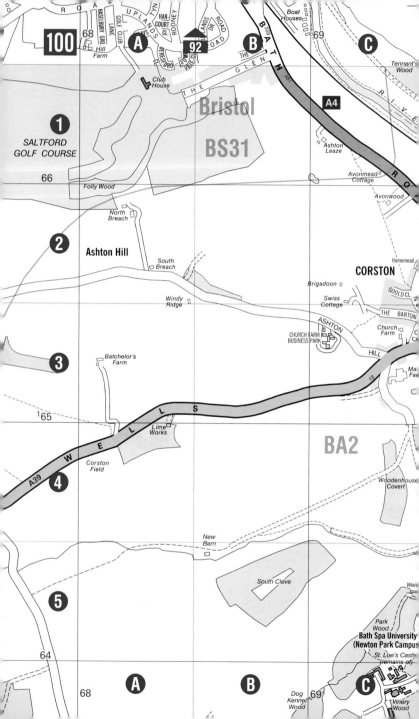

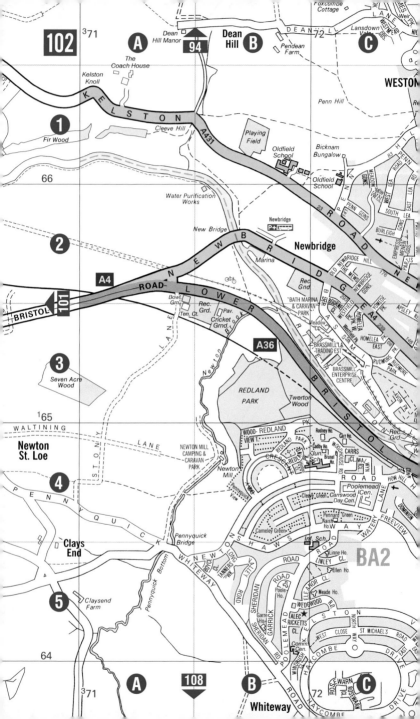

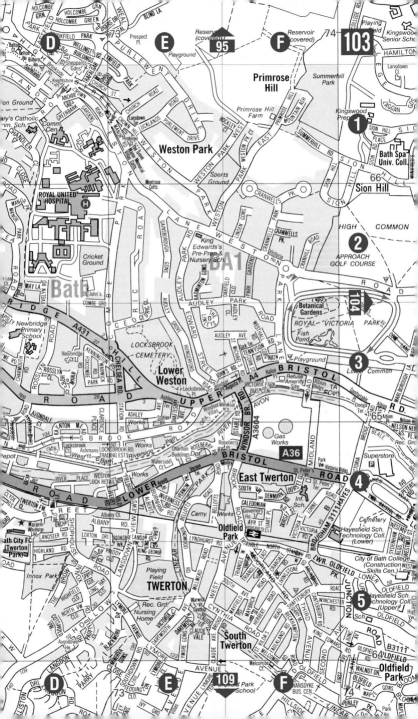

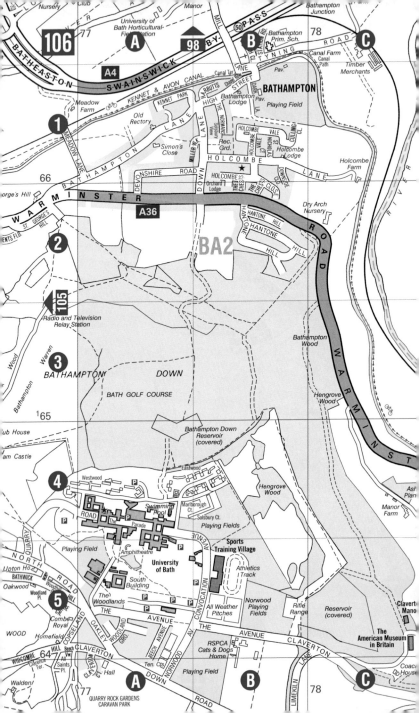

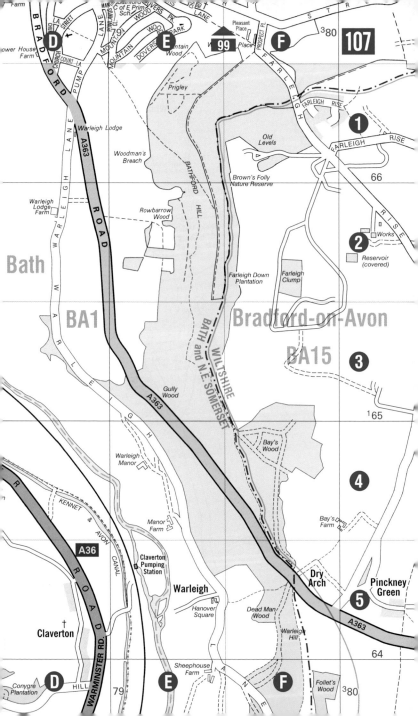

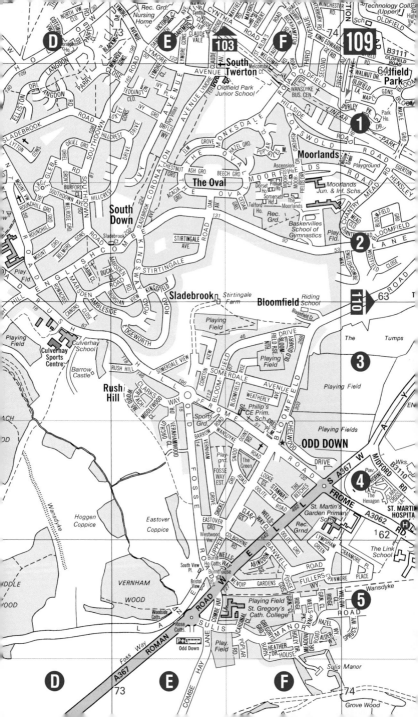

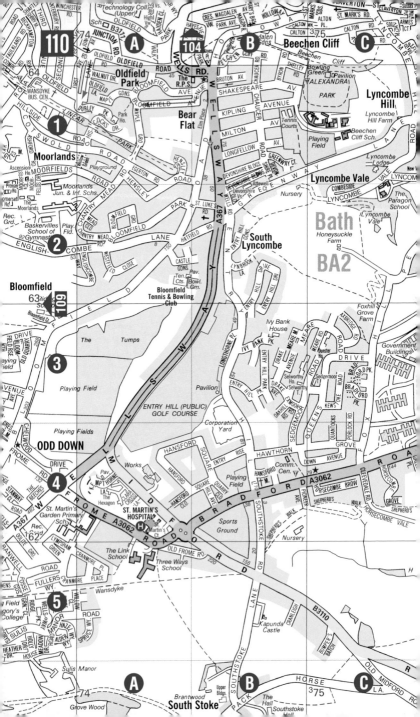

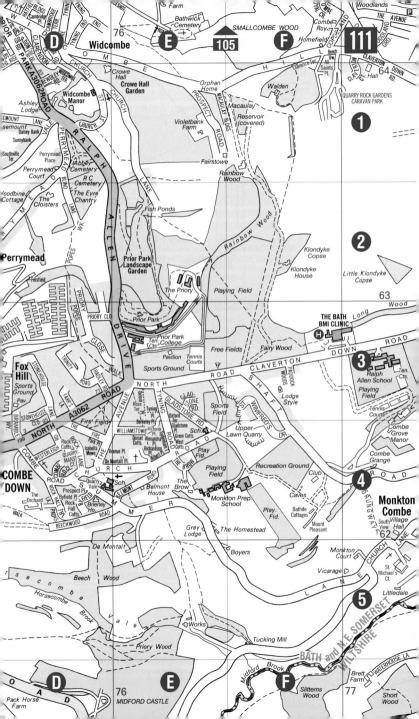

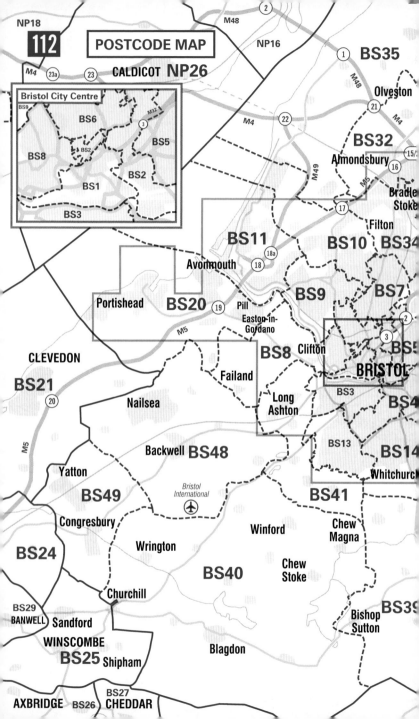

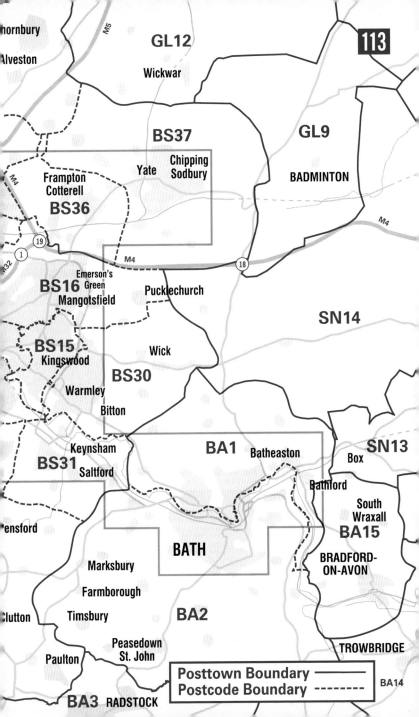

GL12

Thornbury

Alveston

Wickwar

113

BS37

GL9

Chipping
Sodbury

Yate

BADMINTON

Frampton
Cotterell

M5

M4

BS36

M4

19

1

M32

M4

18

Emerson's
Green

BS16

Mangotsfield

Pucklechurch

SN14

BS15

Kingswood

Wick

Warmley

BS30

Bitton

Keynsham

BA1

Batheaston

Box

SN13

BS31

Saltford

Bathford

BS31

Pensford

South
Wraxall

BA15

BATH

BRADFORD-
ON-AVON

Marksbury

Farmborough

BA2

Clutton

Timsbury

Peasedown
St. John

TROWBRIDGE

Paulton

Posttown Boundary ——
Postcode Boundary - - - -

BA14

BA3 RADSTOCK

INDEX

Including Streets, Places & Areas, Industrial Estates,
Selected Flats & Walkways, Service Areas, Stations and Selected Places of Interest.

HOW TO USE THIS INDEX

1. Each street name is followed by its Postcode District, then by its Locality abbreviation(s) and then by its map reference;
   e.g. **Abbey Rd.** BS9: W Trym . . . .5B **40** is in the BS9 Postcode District and the Westbury-on-Trym Locality and is to be found
   in square 5B on page **40**. The page number is shown in bold type.

2. A strict alphabetical order is followed in which Av., Rd., St., etc. (though abbreviated) are read in full and as part of the
   street name; e.g. **Ash Ct.** appears after **Ashcott** but before **Ashcroft Av.**

3. Streets and a selection of flats and walkways too small to be shown on the maps, appear in the index with the thoroughfare
   to which it is connected shown in brackets; e.g. **21 West** BS3: Bedm . . . .1E **77** (off Skypark Rd.)

4. Addresses that are in more than one part are referred to as not continuous.

5. Places and areas are shown in the index in **BLUE TYPE** and the map reference is to the actual map square in which the
   town centre or area is located and not to the place name shown on the map; e.g. **BATHFORD** 5E **99**

6. An example of a selected place of interest is **American Mus. in Britain, The** 5C **106**

7. An example of a station is **Avonmouth Station (Rail)** . . . .2D **37**, also included is **Park & Ride,
   Ashton Vale (Park & Ride)** 2F **75**

8. Service Areas are shown in the index in **BOLD CAPITAL TYPE**; e.g. **GORDANO SERVICE AREA** 2B **52**

9. Map references for entries that appear on the large scale pages **4-7** are shown first, with small scale map references shown
   in brackets; e.g. **Abbeygate St.** BA1: Bath 4C **6** (4C **104**)

GENERAL ABBREVIATIONS

All. : Alley	**Est.** : Estate	**No.** : Number
App. : Approach	**Fld.** : Field	**Pde.** : Parade
Arc. : Arcade	**Flds.** : Fields	**Pk.** : Park
Av. : Avenue	**Gdn.** : Garden	**Pas.** : Passage
Bk. : Back	**Gdns.** : Gardens	**Pl.** : Place
Blvd. : Boulevard	**Ga.** : Gate	**Pct.** : Precinct
Bri. : Bridge	**Gt.** : Great	**Prom.** : Promenade
B'way. : Broadway	**Grn.** : Green	**Res.** : Residential
Bldgs. : Buildings	**Gro.** : Grove	**Ri.** : Rise
Bus. : Business	**Hgts.** : Heights	**Rd.** : Road
Cvn. : Caravan	**Ho.** : House	**Rdbt.** : Roundabout
C'way. : Causeway	**Ho's.** : Houses	**Shop.** : Shopping
Cen. : Centre	**Ind.** : Industrial	**Sth.** : South
Chu. : Church	**Info.** : Information	**Sq.** : Square
Chyd. : Churchyard	**La.** : Lane	**Sta.** : Station
Cir. : Circus	**Lit.** : Little	**St.** : Street
Cl. : Close	**Lwr.** : Lower	**Ter.** : Terrace
Comn. : Common	**Mnr.** : Manor	**Trad.** : Trading
Cnr. : Corner	**Mans.** : Mansions	**Up.** : Upper
Cotts. : Cottages	**Mkt.** : Market	**Va.** : Vale
Ct. : Court	**Mdw.** : Meadow	**Vw.** : View
Cres. : Crescent	**Mdws.** : Meadows	**Vs.** : Villas
Cft. : Croft	**M.** : Mews	**Vis.** : Visitors
Dr. : Drive	**Mt.** : Mount	**Wlk.** : Walk
E. : East	**Mus.** : Museum	**W.** : West
Ent. : Enterprise	**Nth.** : North	**Yd.** : Yard

LOCALITY ABBREVIATIONS

Abb L : **Abbots Leigh**	**B'hll** : **Broomhill**	**Eastv** : **Eastville**
Alm : **Almondsbury**	**C Hth** : **Cadbury Heath**	**Emer G** : **Emersons Green**
Ash G : **Ashton Gate**	**Charl** : **Charlcombe**	**Eng** : **Englishcombe**
Ash V : **Ashton Vale**	**Chip S** : **Chipping Sodbury**	**Fail** : **Failand**
A'mth : **Avonmouth**	**Chit** : **Chittening**	**Fil** : **Filton**
Bar G : **Barrow Gurney**	**Clap G** : **Clapton-in-Gordano**	**Fish** : **Fishponds**
Bar C : **Barrs Court**	**C'ton** : **Claverton**	**Flax B** : **Flax Bourton**
Bar H : **Barton Hill**	**Clav D** : **Claverton Down**	**Fram C** : **Frampton Cotterell**
Bath : **Bath**	**Clif** : **Clifton**	**Fren** : **Frenchay**
B'ptn : **Bathampton**	**Coal H** : **Coalpit Heath**	**Gau E** : **Gaunt's Earthcott**
Bathe : **Batheaston**	**Cod** : **Codrington**	**H'len** : **Hallen**
Bathf : **Bathford**	**C Down** : **Combe Down**	**Ham** : **Hambrook**
Bedm : **Bedminster**	**C Hay** : **Combe Hay**	**Han** : **Hanham**
B'stn : **Bishopston**	**C Din** : **Coombe Dingle**	**Hart** : **Hartcliffe**
Bis : **Bishopsworth**	**Cor** : **Corston**	**Hen** : **Henbury**
Bit : **Bitton**	**Cot** : **Cotham**	**H'fld** : **Henfield**
Bwr A : **Bower Ashton**	**Dod** : **Dodington**	**H'gro** : **Hengrove**
Brad S : **Bradley Stoke**	**Down** : **Downend**	**Henle** : **Henleaze**
Bren : **Brentry**	**Dun** : **Dundry**	**Hor** : **Horfield**
B'yte : **Bridgeyate**	**E Comp** : **Easter Compton**	**Hort** : **Horton**
Brisl : **Brislington**	**E'tn** : **Easton**	**Ing** : **Inglesbatch**
Bris : **Bristol**	**Eas** : **Easton-in-Gordano**	**Iron A** : **Iron Acton**

Kel : **Kelston**
Key : **Keynsham**
K'wd : **Kingswood**
Know : **Knowle**
L'rdge : **Langridge**
L'dwn : **Lansdown**
Law W : **Lawrence Weston**
L Wds : **Leigh Woods**
Lim S : **Limpley Stoke**
Lit S : **Little Stoke**
L'lze : **Lockleaze**
L Ash : **Long Ashton**
L Grn : **Longwell Green**
Mang : **Mangotsfield**
Mon C : **Monkton Combe**
Mon F : **Monkton Farleigh**
New L : **Newton St Loe**
Odd D : **Odd Down**
Old C : **Oldland Common**
Old S : **Old Sodbury**
Pat : **Patchway**
Pill : **Pill**

P'bry : **Portbury**
P'head : **Portishead**
Puck : **Pucklechurch**
Q Char : **Queen Charlton**
Redf : **Redfield**
Redl : **Redland**
St Ap : **St Annes Park**
St G : **St George**
Salt : **Saltford**
Sea M : **Sea Mills**
Shire : **Shirehampton**
Sho : **Shockerwick**
Short : **Shortwood**
Sis : **Siston**
Soun : **Soundwell**
S'mead : **Southmead**
S'ske : **Southstoke**
S'will : **Speedwell**
Stap H : **Staple Hill**
Stap : **Stapleton**
Stoc : **Stockwood**
Stok B : **Stoke Bishop**

Stok G : **Stoke Gifford**
Swa : **Swainswick**
S'frd : **Swineford**
Up Swa : **Upper Swainswick**
Warl : **Warleigh**
Warm : **Warmley**
W Hth : **Webbs Heath**
W Trym : **Westbury-on-Trym**
W'lgh : **Westerleigh**
W'ton : **Weston**
Wes : **Weston-in-Gordano**
Whit : **Whitchurch**
W'hall : **Whitehall**
Will : **Willsbridge**
Wind H : **Windmill Hill**
Wint : **Winterbourne**
Wint D : **Winterbourne Down**
Withy : **Withywood**
W'ly : **Woolley**
Yate : **Yate**

---

21 West BS3: Bedm 1E **77**
(off Skypark Rd.)
100 Steps BS15: Han 4C **70**
5102 BS1: Bris 1A **68**

A

Abbey Chambers BA1: Bath 4C **6**
(off York St.)
Abbey Chu. Ho. BA1: Bath 4B **104**
(off Hetling St.)
Abbey Chyd. BA1: Bath 3C **6**
(off Cheap St.)
Abbey Cl. BS31: Key 1B **90**
Abbey Ct. BA2: Bath 2E **7** (3D **105**)
BS4: St Ap 4B **70**
Abbeydale BS36: Wint 2A **28**
Abbeygate St. BA1: Bath . . .4C **6** (4C **104**)
Abbey Grn. BA1: Bath 4C **6** (4C **104**)
Abbey Ho. BS37: Yate 1F **31**
Abbey Pk. BS31: Key 1B **90**
Abbey Retail Pk. BS34: Fil 1E **43**
Abbey Rd. BS9: W Trym 5B **40**
Abbey St. BA1: Bath 4C **6**
Abbey Vw. BA2: Bath 5F **7** (5D **105**)
Abbey Vw. Gdns.
BA2: Bath 5E **7** (5D **105**)
Abbeywood Dr. BS9: Stok B 1E **55**
Abbeywood Pk. BS34: Fil 1D **43**
Abbots Av. BS15: Han 5E **71**
Abbots Cl. BS14: Whit 4C **86**
Abbotsford Rd. BS6: Cot 5D **57**
ABBOTS LEIGH 1C **64**
Abbots Leigh Rd.
BS8: Abb L, L Wds 1C **64**
Abbots Rd. BS15: Han 1E **83**
Abbots Way BS9: Henle 5F **41**
Abbotswood BS15: K'wd 2F **71**
BS37: Yate 1F **31**
Aberdeen Rd. BS6: Cot 1D **67**
Abi Clay Ct. BS2: Bris 4B **58**
(off Sevier St.)
Abingdon Gdns. BA2: Odd D 5F **109**
Abingdon Rd. BS16: Fish 3C **60**
Ableton La. BS10: H'len 1B **20**
Ableton Wlk. BS9: Sea M 1E **55**
Abona Ct. BS9: Sea M 5E **39**
Abon Ho. BS9: Sea M 2E **55**
Abraham Cl. BS5: Bris 1D **69**
Abraham Fry Ho. BS15: K'wd 2A **72**
Acacia Av. BS16: Stap H 2E **61**
Acacia Cl. BS16: Stap H 3F **61**
Acacia Ct. BS31: Key 3E **89**

Acacia Gro. BA2: Bath 2E **109**
Acacia M. BS16: Stap H 2F **61**
Acacia Rd. BS16: Stap H 2F **61**
Academy, The BA2: Bath . . .5A **6** (5B **104**)
Access 18 West BS11: A'mth 1E **37**
Acer Village BS14: H'gro 5E **79**
Acorn Gro. BS13: Bis 1A **84**
Acraman's Rd. BS3: Bedm 5E **67**
Acresbush Cl. BS13: Bis 2C **84**
Acton Court 1F **13**
Acton Rd. BS16: Fish 3C **60**
Adams Ct. BS8: Clif 3B **66**
(off Cumberland Pl.)
Adams Hay BS4: Brisl 3F **79**
Adams Land BS36: Coal H 1E **29**
Adderly Ga. BS16: Emer G 4D **47**
Addiscombe Rd. BS14: Whit 2D **87**
Addison Rd. BS3: Wind H 1A **78**
Adelaide Pl. BA2: Bath 3F **7** (4D **105**)
BS5: E'tn 1D **69**
BS16: Fish 2B **60**
Adelaide Ter. BS16: Fish 2C **60**
Adelante Cl. BS34: Stok G 4C **26**
Admiral Cl. BS16: Stap 4F **43**
Admirals Wlk. BS20: P'head 1D **49**
Aelfric Mdw. BS20: P'head 2B **50**
Agate St. BS3: Bedm 1D **77**
Aiken St. BS5: Bar H 3D **69**
Ainslie's Belvedere BA1: Bath 1B **6**
(off Caroline Pl.)
Aintree Dr. BS16: Down 2B **46**
Airpoint BS3: Bedm 1E **77**
Air Balloon Rd. BS5: St G 2C **70**
Airport Rd. BS14: H'gro 5B **78**
Akeman Way BS11: Shire 3E **37**
Alanscourt BS30: C Hth 4D **73**
Alard Rd. BS4: Know 5B **78**
Albany Bldgs. BS3: Bedm 5E **67**
Albany Ct. BA2: Bath 4D **103**
Albany Ga. BS34: Stok G 3A **26**
Albany Rd. BA2: Bath 4D **103**
BS6: Bris 5B **58**
Albany St. BS15: K'wd 1E **71**
Albany Way BS30: Old C 4E **73**
Albermarle Row BS8: Clif 3B **66**
Albermarle Ter. BS8: Clif 3B **66**
(off Cumberland Pl.)
Albert Cres. BS2: Bris 4C **68**
Albert Gro. BS5: St G 1B **70**
Albert Gro. Sth. BS5: St G 1B **70**
Albert Mill BS31: Key 3B **90**
Alberton Rd. BS16: B'hll 5B **44**
Albert Pde. BS5: Redf 1F **69**
Albert Pk. BS6: Bris 5B **58**
Albert Pk. Pl. BS6: Bris 5A **58**
Albert Pl. BA2: C Down 4E **111**
BS3: Bedm 1E **77**
BS9: W Trym 4C **40**

Albert Rd. BS2: Bris 5C **68**
BS15: Han 4F **71**
BS20: P'head 1F **49**
BS31: Key 2A **62**
Key 2A **90**
Albert St. BS5: Redf 1E **69**
Albert Ter. BA2: Bath 4E **103**
BS16: Fish 2B **60**
Albion Bldgs. BA1: Bath 3F **103**
Albion Chambers BS1: Bris 2C **4**
Albion Cl. BS16: Mang 1B **62**
Albion Dockside Est. BS1: Bris . . .4D **67**
Albion Pl. BA1: Bath 3A **104**
BS2: Bris 3C **68**
(Kingsland Rd.)
BS2: Bris 1F **5**
(Lawford St.)
Albion Rd. BS5: E'tn 5D **59**
Albion St. BS5: Redf 1E **69**
Albion Ter. BA1: Bath 3A **104**
BS34: Pat 4D **9**
Alcove Rd. BS16: Fish 3A **60**
Aldercombe Rd. BS9: C Din 3E **39**
Alderdown Cl. BS11: Law W 3C **38**
Alder Dr. BS5: W'hall 5A **60**
Alderley Rd. BA2: Bath 1C **108**
Aldermoor Way BS30: L Grn 5A **72**
(not continuous)
Alderney Av. BS4: Brisl 5B **70**
Alders, The BS16: Fren 2D **45**
(off Marlborough Dr.)
Alderton Rd. BS7: Hor 3A **42**
Alder Way BA2: Odd D 5F **109**
Aldwick Av. BS13: Hart 4E **85**
Alec Ricketts Cl. BA2: Bath 5B **102**
Alexander Bldgs. BA1: Bath 1D **105**
Alexandra Cl. BS16: Stap H 2F **61**
Alexandra Gdns. BS16: Stap H 2F **61**
Alexandra Pk. BS6: Redl 4E **57**
BS16: Fish 2B **60**
Alexandra Pl. BA2: C Down 4E **111**
BS16: Stap H 2F **61**
Alexandra Rd. BA2: Bath 5C **104**
BS8: Clif 1D **67**
BS10: W Trym 3E **41**
BS13: Bis 5B **76**
BS15: Han 4F **71**
BS36: Coal H 1F **29**
Alford Rd. BS4: Brisl 2E **79**
Alfred Hill BS2: Bris 1A **4**
Alfred Lovell Gdns. BS30: C Hth . . .5C **72**
Alfred Pde. BS2: Bris 1B **4** (1F **67**)
Alfred Pl. BS1: Bris 5C **4** (4F **67**)
BS2: Bris 1E **67**
Alfred Rd. BS3: Wind H 1F **77**
BS6: Henle 2C **56**

Alfred St. BA1: Bath 1B **6** (3B **104**)
  BS2: Bris 3C **68**
  BS5: Redf 1E **69**
Algars Dr. BS37: Iron A 2A **14**
Algiers St. BS3: Wind H 1F **77**
Allanmead Rd. BS14: H'gro 4D **79**
Allerton Cres. BS14: Whit 3D **87**
Allerton Gdns. BS14: H'gro 2D **87**
Allerton Rd. BS14: Whit 3C **86**
Allfoxton Rd. BS7: Eastv 3C **58**
All Hallows Rd. BS5: E'tn 1D **69**
Allington Dr. BS30: Bar C 5B **72**
Allington Rd. BS3: Bris 4E **67**
Allison Av. BS4: Brisl 1A **80**
Allison Rd. BS4: Brisl 1F **79**
All Saints Cl. BS30: L Grn 1C **82**
All Saints Ct. BS1: Bris 2C **4** (3F **67**)
All Saints Gdns. BS8: Clif 1C **66**
All Saints La. BS1: Bris 2C **4** (2F **67**)
All Saints Pl. BA2: Clav D 5F **105**
All Saints Rd. BA1: Bath 2B **104**
  BS8: Clif 1C **66**
All Saints St. BS1: Bris 2C **4** (2F **67**)
Alma Cl. BS15: K'wd 1A **72**
Alma Ct. BS8: Clif 5D **57**
Alma Rd. BS8: Clif 1C **66**
  BS15: K'wd 5A **62**
Alma Rd. Av. BS8: Clif 1D **67**
Alma Va. Rd. BS8: Clif 1C **66**
Almeda Rd. BS5: St G 3C **70**
ALMONDSBURY 1D **9**
Almondsbury Bus. Cen.
  BS32: Brad S 1F **9**
Almond Wlk. BS13: Bis 1D **85**
Almond Way BS16: Mang 1B **62**
Almorah Rd. BS3: Wind H 1A **78**
Alpha Cen., The BS37: Yate 2E **15**
Alpha Rd. BS3: Bedm 5F **67**
Alpine Gdns. BA1: Bath 2C **104**
Alpine Rd. BS5: E'tn 5E **59**
Alsop Rd. BS15: K'wd 1F **71**
Alton Pl. BA2: Bath 5C **6** (5C **104**)
Alton Rd. BS7: Hor 1B **58**
Altringham Rd. BS5: W'hall 5F **59**
Alverstoke BS14: H'gro 5B **78**
Alveston Wlk. BS9: Sea M 4D **39**
Alwins Ct. BS30: Bar C 5B **72**
Amberley Cl. BS16: Down 4F **45**
  BS31: Key 3A **90**
Amberley Rd. BS16: Down 4F **45**
  BS34: Pat 5D **9**
Amble Cl. BS15: K'wd 2B **72**
Ambleside Av. BS10: S'mead 2D **41**
Ambleside Rd. BA2: Bath 3D **109**
Ambra Ct. BS8: Clif 3C **66**
Ambra Ter. BS8: Clif 3C **66**
Ambra Va. BS8: Clif 3C **66**
Ambra Va. E. BS8: Clif 3C **66**
Ambra Va. Sth. BS8: Clif 3C **66**
Ambra Va. W. BS8: Clif 3C **66**
Ambrose Rd. BS8: Clif 3C **66**
Ambury BA1: Bath 5B **6** (5B **104**)
Amelia Ct. BS1: Bris 3B **4** (3F **67**)
Amercombe Wlk. BS14: Stoc 5F **79**
American Mus. in Britain, The . .5C **106**
Amery La. BA1: Bath 4B **6** (4C **104**)
Amis Wlk. BS7: Hor 3C **42**
Anchorage, The BS20: P'head 5D **35**
Anchor Cl. BS5: St G 3B **70**
Anchor Ho. BS4: Know 2D **79**
Anchor La. BS1: Bris 4A **4** (3E **67**)
Anchor Rd. BA1: W'ton 1D **103**
  BS1: Bris 4A **4** (3D **67**)
  BS15: K'wd 5C **62**
Anchor Sq. BS1: Bris 4A **4** (3E **67**)
Anchor Way BS20: Pill 2F **53**
Andereach Cl. BS14: H'gro 4D **79**
Andover Rd. BS4: Know 2B **78**
Andrew Millman Ct. BS37: Yate . . .4B **16**
Andruss Dr. BS41: Dun 5A **84**
Angels Ground BS4: St Ap 3B **70**

Angers Rd. BS4: Wind H 5B **68**
Anglesea Pl. BS8: Clif 4C **56**
Anglo Office Pk. BS15: K'wd 4D **61**
Anglo Ter. BA1: Bath 2C **104**
  (off London Rd.)
Annie Scott Cl. BS16: Fish 2B **60**
Anson Cl. BS31: Salt 5F **91**
Anstey's Cl. BS15: Han 4D **71**
Anstey's Rd. BS15: Han 4D **71**
Anstey St. BS5: E'tn 5D **59**
Anthea Rd. BS5: S'wll 4A **60**
Antona Ct. BS11: Shire 4F **37**
Antona Dr. BS11: Shire 4F **37**
Antrim Rd. BS9: Henle 5D **41**
Anvil St. BS2: Bris 3F **5** (3B **68**)
Apex Ct. BS32: Brad S 2F **9**
Apollo Apartments BS1: Bris 3C **4**
Apperley Cl. BS37: Yate 5F **15**
Appleby Wlk. BS4: Know 5F **77**
Appledore Cl. BS14: H'gro 4D **79**
Applegate BS10: Bren 5D **23**
Applehayes Ri. BS20: Eas 3D **53**
Applin Grn. BS16: Emer G 5E **47**
Apseleys Mead BS32: Brad S 3E **9**
Apsley Cl. BA1: Bath 3D **103**
Apsley Rd. BA1: Bath 3C **102**
  BS8: Clif 5C **56**
Apsley St. BS5: Eastv 4E **59**
Apsley Vs. BS6: Bris 5F **57**
Arbutus Dr. BS9: C Din 4E **39**
Arbutus Wlk. BS9: C Din 2F **39**
Arcade, The BS1: Bris 1D **5**
Arch Cl. BS41: L Ash 3B **74**
Archer Cl. BS30: L Grn 1B **82**
Archer Wlk. BS14: Stoc 1A **88**
Archfield Rd. BS6: Cot 5E **57**
Arch Gro. BS41: L Ash 3B **74**
Architectural Cen., The BS1: Bris . .5B **4**
  (off Narrow Quay)
Archway St. BA2: Bath 5E **7** (5D **105**)
Ardagh Ct. BS7: Hor 4B **42**
Arden Cl. BS32: Brad S 2A **26**
Ardenton Wlk. BS10: Bren 5C **22**
Ardern Cl. BS9: C Din 3D **39**
Argus Ct. BS3: Bedm 2E **77**
Argus Rd. BS3: Bedm 1E **77**
Argyle Av. BS5: Eastv 4E **59**
Argyle Dr. BS37: Yate 1A **16**
Argyle Pl. BS8: Clif 3C **66**
Argyle Rd. BS2: Bris 1A **68**
  BS16: Fish 4D **61**
Argyle St. BA2: Bath 3D **7** (4C **104**)
  BS3: Bedm 5E **67**
  BS5: Eastv 4E **59**
Argyle Ter. BA2: Bath 4E **103**
Arley Cotts. BS6: Cot 5F **57**
Arley Ct. BS6: Cot 5F **57**
Arley Hill BS6: Cot 5F **57**
Arley Pk. BS6: Cot 5F **57**
Arley Ter. BS5: W'hall 5A **60**
Arlingham Way BS34: Pat 4A **8**
Arlington Rd. BA2: Bath 5F **103**
  BS4: St Ap 3F **69**
Arlington Vs. BS8: Clif 2D **67**
Armada Ho. BS1: Bris 5A **58**
Armadale Av. BS6: Bris 5A **58**
Armada Pl. BS1: Bris 5A **58**
Armada Rd. BS14: Whit 1C **86**
Armes Ct. BA2: Bath 5D **7** (5C **104**)
Armoury Sq. BS5: E'tn 1C **68**
Armstrong Ct. BS37: Yate 2E **15**
Armstrong Dr. BS30: C Hth 4D **73**
Armstrong Way BS37: Yate 2C **14**
Arnall Dr. BS10: Hen 2B **40**
Arncliffe BS10: S'mead 3E **41**
Arnold Ct. BS37: Chip S 4D **17**
Arnold Rd. BS16: Mang, Sis 3D **63**
Arnolfini 5B **4** (4E **67**)
Arno's St. BS4: Wind H 1C **78**
ARNO'S VALE 5D **69**
Arnside Rd. BS10: S'mead 2E **41**

Arrowfield Cl. BS14: Whit 5C **86**
Arthurs Cl. BS16: Emer G 5E **47**
Arthur Skemp Cl. BS5: Bar H 2D **69**
Arthur St. BS2: Bris 4C **68**
  BS5: Redf 1E **69**
Arthurswood Rd. BS13: Withy 3C **84**
Arundel Cl. BS13: Hart 2D **85**
Arundel Ct. BS7: B'stn 3F **57**
Arundel Rd. BA1: Bath 1C **104**
  BS7: B'stn 3F **57**
Arundel Wlk. BS31: Key 2F **89**
Ascension Ho. BA2: Bath 1F **109**
Ascot Cl. BS16: Down 2B **46**
Ascot Rd. BS10: S'mead 1F **41**
Ashbourne Cl. BS30: Old C 3E **73**
Ashburton Rd. BS10: S'mead 2E **41**
Ash Cl. BS16: Fish 3E **61**
  BS34: Lit S 1F **25**
  BS37: Yate 2F **15**
Ashcombe Cres. BS30: Old C 3E **73**
Ashcott BS14: H'gro 5B **78**
Ash Ct. BS14: Whit 1C **86**
Ashcroft Av. BS31: Key 2F **89**
Ashcroft Rd. BS9: Sea M 4E **39**
Ashdene Av. BS5: Eastv 3F **59**
Ashdown Rd. BS20: P'head 1C **48**
Asher La. BS2: Bris 1F **5** (2B **68**)
Ashfield Pl. BS6: Bris 5B **58**
Ashfield Rd. BS3: Bedm 1D **77**
Ashford Rd. BA2: Bath 1F **109**
  BS34: Pat 1C **24**
Ashford Way BS15: K'wd 2C **72**
Ash Gro. BA2: Bath 1E **109**
  BS16: Fish 3E **61**
Ashgrove Av. BS7: B'stn 2B **58**
  BS8: Abb L 2D **65**
Ashgrove Cl. BS7: B'stn 2B **58**
Ashgrove Pl. BS7: B'stn 2B **58**
Ashgrove Rd. BS3: Bedm 1D **77**
  BS6: Redl 5D **57**
  BS7: B'stn 2B **58**
Ashland Rd. BS13: Withy 3C **84**
Ash La. BS32: Alm 2A **8**
Ashley Apartments BS6: Bris 4B **58**
Ashley Av. BA1: Bath 3E **103**
Ashley Cl. BS7: B'stn 2B **58**
Ashley Ct. BS6: Bris 5B **58**
Ashley Ct. Rd. BS7: Bris 4B **58**
ASHLEY DOWN 2B **58**
Ashley Down Rd.
  BS7: B'stn, Bris 3B **58**
  BS7: B'stn, Hor 1A **58**
Ashley Gro. Rd. BS2: Bris 4B **58**
Ashley Hill BS6: Bris 3B **58**
  BS7: Bris 3B **58**
Ashley Pde. BS2: Bris 4B **58**
Ashley Pk. BS6: Bris 3B **58**
Ashley Rd. BA1: Bathf 5E **99**
  BS6: Bris 5A **58**
Ashley St. BS2: Bris 5C **58**
Ashley Ter. BA1: Bath 3E **103**
Ashley Trad. Est. BS2: Bris 4B **58**
Ashman Cl. BS5: E'tn 1C **68**
Ashmans Yd. BA1: Bath 4D **103**
Ashmead Ho. BS5: Bar H 2D **69**
Ashmead Ind. Est. BS31: Key 2D **91**
Ashmead Pk. BS31: Key 2D **91**
Ashmead Rd. BS31: Key 2D **91**
Ashmead Way BS1: Bris 4B **66**
Ash Ridge Rd. BS32: Brad S 2D **9**
Ash Rd. BS7: Hor 1A **58**
Ashton BS16: Fren 2D **45**
  (off Harford Dr.)
Ashton Av. BS1: Bris 4C **66**
Ashton Cl. BS41: L Ash 5F **65**
Ashton Court Nature Reserve 5E **65**
Ashton Court Vis. Cen. 5F **65**
Ashton Dr. BS3: Ash V 3A **76**
ASHTON GATE 5C **66**
Ashton Ga. Rd. BS3: Bris 5C **66**

Ashton Gate Stadium 1B 76
Ashton Ga. Ter. BS3: Bris 5C 66
Ashton Ga. Trad. Est. BS3: Ash V . . .1A 76
Ashton Ga. Underpass
  BS3: Ash V, Bwr A 5B 66
ASHTON HILL 2A 100
Ashton Hill BA2: Cor 3C 100
Ashton Pk. Sports Cen. 5A 66
Ashton Rd. BS3: Ash G 5B 66
  BS3: Ash V 1B 76
  BS41: L Ash 1E 75
ASHTON VALE 2B 76
Ashton Vale (Park & Ride) 2F 75
Ashton Va. Rd. BS3: Ash V 1A 76
Ashton Va. Trad. Est.
  BS3: Ash V 3B 76
ASHTON WATERING 4A 74
Ashton Way BS31: Key 1A 90
Ashville Rd. BS3: Ash G 5C 66
Ash Wlk. BS10: Bren 5D 23
Ashwell Cl. BS14: Stoc 1A 88
Ashwicke BS14: H'gro 1C 86
Aspects Leisure Pk. BS15: K'wd . . .4A 72
Assembly Rooms
  Bath 1B 6
Assembly Rooms La.
  BS1: Bris 4B 4 (3F 67)
Aston Ga. Depot BS3: Ash G 5B 66
Aston Ho. BS1: Bris 3B 68
  (off Burton Cl.)
Astry Cl. BS11: Law W 2C 38
Atchley St. BS5: Bar H 2D 69
Atherston BS30: Old C 4F 73
Athlone Wlk. BS4: Know 3A 78
Atkins Cl. BS14: Stoc 1A 88
Atlantic Rd. BS11: Shire 3E 37
Atlas Cl. BS5: S'wll 4C 60
Atlas Rd. BS3: Wind H 1A 78
Atlas St. BS2: Bris 4D 69
Atrium, The BS2: Bris 3B 68
  (off Anvil St.)
Attewell Ct. BA2: Bath 1B 110
Atwell Cl. BS32: Alm 4D 9
Atwood Dr. BS11: Law W 1D 39
Atyeo Cl. BS3: Ash V 3A 76
Aubrey Rd. BS3: Bedm 1D 77
Auburn Av. BS30: L Grn 1D 83
Auburn Rd. BS6: Redl 4D 57
Auden Mead BS7: Hor 3C 42
Audley Av. BA1: Bath 3E 103
Audley Cl. BA1: Bath 3F 103
Audley Gro. BA1: Bath 3E 103
Audley Pk. Rd. BA1: Bath 2E 103
Audrey Wlk. BS9: Henle 4F 41
Augusta Pl. BA1: Bath 3F 103
Austen Gro. BS7: Hor 3C 42
Austen Ho. BS7: Hor 3C 42
Austen Pl. BS11: Shire 4A 38
Aust La. BS9: W Trym 3C 40
Avalon La. BS5: St G 3D 71
Avalon Rd. BS5: St G 4D 71
Avebury Rd. BS3: Ash V 2A 76
Avening Rd. BS15: K'wd 1C 70
Avenue, The BA2: C Down 4D 111
  BA2: Clav D 5A 106
  (not continuous)
  BS5: St G 2A 70
  BS7: B'stn 3A 58
  BS8: Clif 5B 56
  BS9: Stok B 4F 55
  BS16: Fren 2A 44
  BS31: Key 1A 90
  BS34: Lit S 2E 25
  BS34: Pat 3D 9
  BS37: Yate 4F 15
Avenue Pl. BA2: C Down 4D 111
Averay Rd. BS16: Stap 2E 59
Avonbank Ind. Est. BS11: A'mth . . .4D 37
Avonbridge Trad. Est.
  BS11: Shire 3E 37
Avon Bus. Pk. BS16: Fish 3B 60

Avon Cl. BS5: St G 3B 70
  BS31: Key 1B 90
Avon Ct. BA1: Bathe 3C 98
  BS16: Fish 1D 61
Avon Cres. BS1: Bris 4C 66
Avondale Bldgs. BA1: Bath 5D 97
Avondale Bus. Cen. BS15: K'wd . . .4E 61
Avondale Ct. BA1: Bath 3D 103
  BS9: Stok B 4F 55
  BS30: L Grn 1B 82
Avondale Rd. BA1: Bath 3D 103
Avondale Works BS15: K'wd 4E 61
Avondown Cl. BS10: S'mead 1F 41
Avondown Ho. BA2: Bath 2E 77
Avondown Rd. BS3: Bedm 2E 77
Avon Meads BS2: Bris 4E 69
AVONMOUTH 2D 37
Avonmouth Rd. BS11: A'mth 2D 37
  BS11: Shire 3E 37
Avonmouth Station (Rail) 2D 37
Avonmouth Way BS10: Hen 5A 22
  BS11: A'mth 2D 37
Avonmouth Way W. BS11: A'mth . . .1D 37
Avon Pk. BA1: Bath 3C 102
  BS5: Redf 2F 69
Avon Ring Rd. BS4: Key 4E 81
  BS15: Han 4E 81
  BS15: Warm, Sis 5D 63
  BS16: Down 2F 45
  BS16: Emer G, Mang, Sis 1C 46
  BS16: Ham 1A 44
  BS30: Bar C, Han 4E 81
  BS30: Sis 4D 63
Avon Riverside Est. BS11: A'mth . . .4D 37
Avon Rd. BS13: Bis 1C 84
  BS20: Pill 1E 53
  BS31: Key 2B 90
Avonside Ind. Est. BS2: Bris 3E 69
Avonside Rd. BS2: Bris 3E 69
Avonside Way BS4: St Ap 3B 70
Avonsmere Res. Pk.
  BS34: Stok G 5E 25
Avon St. BA1: Bath 5B 6 (4B 104)
  BS2: Bris 3F 5 (3B 68)
Avon Trad. Est. BS2: Bris 4C 68
Avon Va. BS9: Stok B 2F 55
Avonvale Pl. BA1: Bathe 4B 98
Avonvale Rd. BS5: Bar H, Redf 3D 69
Avon Valley Bus. Pk. BS4: St Ap . . .3A 70
Avon Valley Country Pk. 1E 91
Avon Valley Farm Bus. Pk.
  BS31: Key 2F 91
Avon Valley Pk. 5D 71
Avon Valley Railway
  Bitton Station 3D 83
  Oldland Common Station . . .5F 73
Avon Vw. BS15: Han 1D 81
Avon Way BS9: Stok B 1E 55
  BS10: S'mead 3F 41
  BS20: P'head 1D 49
Avonwood Cl. BS11: Shire 5A 38
Awdelett Cl. BS11: Law W 2D 39
Axbridge Rd. BA2: C Down 3C 110
Axe Cl. BS34: Know 2B 78
Axis BS14: Hart 2F 85
Aylebury Cres. BS3: Bedm 3D 77
Aylesbury Rd. BS3: Bedm 3D 77
Aylmer Cres. BS14: H'gro 1D 87
Aylminton Wlk. BS11: Law W 1D 39
Ayr St. BA2: Bath 4F 103
Azelin Av. BS13: Hart 2D 85
Aztec Cen., The BS32: Alm 3C 8

AZTEC WEST 3C 8
Aztec W. BS32: Alm 3C 8
Azure, The BS6: Bris 5A 58
  (off Bath Bldgs.)

B

Backfields BS2: Bris 1A 68
Backfields La. BS2: Bris 1A 68
  (off Backfields La.)
Backfields La. BS2: Bris 1A 68
Back La. BS20: Pill 1E 53
  (not continuous)
  BS31: Key 1A 90
  BS36: Coal H 2F 29
Bk. of Kingsdown Pde. BS6: Bris . . .1F 67
Back Rd. BS3: Bris 5C 66
Bk. Stoke La. BS9: W Trym 5B 40
Backwell Wlk. BS13: Bis 4B 76
Badenham Gro. BS11: Law W 3B 38
Baden Rd. BS5: Redf 2E 69
  BS15: K'wd 2C 72
Bader Cl. BS37: Yate 2F 15
Badger Cl. BS30: L Grn 1B 82
Badger Ri. BS20: P'head 3A 48
Badgers Cl. BS32: Brad S 2F 9
Badgers Dr. BS10: Bren 4A 24
Badger Sett BS5: St G 2D 71
Badgers Holt BS14: H'gro 1E 87
Badger's La. BS32: Alm 3A 8
Badgers Wlk. BS4: Brisl 2F 79
Badgeworth BS37: Yate 2F 31
Badminton BS16: Fren 2E 45
  (off Penn Dr.)
Badminton Cen. BS37: Yate 3E 15
Badminton Ct. BS37: Yate 3E 15
Badminton Gdns. BA1: Bath 2E 103
Badminton Rd. BS2: Bris 5B 58
  BS16: Down 5A 46
  BS36: Coal H, Wint D 1C 46
  BS36: Fram C 3E 29
  BS37: Chip S 5F 17
  BS37: Yate 3E 29
Badminton Rd. Trad. Est.
  BS37: Yate 4D 15
Badminton Wlk. BS16: Down 4A 46
Badock Hall BS9: Stok B 2A 56
Baglyn Av. BS15: Soun 3B 62
Bagnell Cl. BS14: Stoc 2A 88
Bagnell Rd. BS14: Stoc 2A 88
Bagworth Dr. BS30: L Grn 1B 82
BAILBROOK 4F 97
Bailbrook Ct. BA1: Swa 4A 98
Bailbrook Gro. BA1: Swa 4E 97
Bailbrook La. BA1: Swa 4E 97
Bailey Ct. BS20: P'head 5E 35
Baileys Ct. BS32: Brad S 2B 26
Baileys Ct. Rd. BS32: Brad S 2A 26
Baileys Mead Rd. BS16: Stap 1E 59
Bakersfield BS30: L Grn 1C 82
Bakers Ground BS34: Stok G 3B 26
Balaclava Rd. BS16: Fish 3B 60
Baldwin St. BS1: Bris 3B 4 (3F 67)
Balfour Rd. BS3: Ash G 1D 77
Ballance St. BA1: Bath 1B 6 (2B 104)
Ballast La. BS11: A'mth 1F 37
Balloon Ct. BA1: Bath 1A 68
Balmain St. BS4: Wind H 5C 68
Balmoral Cl. BS34: Stok G 4F 25
Balmoral Ct. BS16: Mang 1C 62
Balmoral Ho. BS1: Bris 5A 4
Balmoral Rd. BS7: Bris 4B 58
  BS30: L Grn 2B 82
  BS31: Key 3A 90
Baltic Pl. BS20: Pill 2F 53
Baltic Wharf Water Leisure Cen.
  . . . . .4C 66
Balustrade BA1: Bath 1D 105
  (off St Saviours Rd.)

Bamfield BS14: H'gro, Whit 5B 78
Bampton Cl. BS13: Bis 5D 77
  BS16: Emer G 5E 47
Bampton Cft. BS16: Emer G 5E 47
Bampton Dr. BS16: Down 3F 45
Banfield Cl. BS11: Law W 3C 38
Bangor Gro. BS4: St Ap 4B 70
Bangrove Wlk. BS11: Law W 3A 38
Banister Gro. BS4: Know 5F 77
Bank Pl. BS20: Pill 2F 53
Bank Rd. BS11: Chit 1F 19
  BS15: K'wd 1F 71
Bankside BS16: Stap H 2B 62
Bankside Rd. BS4: Brisl 1F 79
Bannerdown Cl. BA1: Bathe 3D 99
Bannerdown Dr. BA1: Bathe 3C 98
Bannerdown Rd. BA1: Bathe 4C 98
Bannerleigh La. BS8: L Wds 3A 66
Bannerleigh Rd. BS8: L Wds 3A 66
Bannerman Rd. BS5: E'tn 1D 69
  (not continuous)
Banner Rd. BS6: Bris 5A 58
Bantock Cl. BS4: Know 1F 85
Bantry Rd. BS4: Know 4A 78
Banwell Cl. BS13: Bis 4C 76
  BS31: Key 5C 90
Banwell Rd. BA2: Odd D 5F 109
  BS3: Ash G 1C 76
Banyard Rd. BS20: P'bry 1A 52
BAPTIST MILLS 4C 58
Baptist St. BS5: E'tn 5C 58
Barbour Gdns. BS13: Hart 4F 85
Barbour Rd. BS13: Hart 4F 85
Barcroft Cl. BS15: K'wd 1E 71
Barkers Mead BS37: Yate 1B 16
Barker Wlk. BS5: E'tn 5C 58
Barlands Ho. BS10: Hen 5B 22
Barley Cl. BS16: Mang 5C 46
  BS36: Fram C 5E 13
Barley Cft. BS9: W Trym 1B 56
Barleyfields BS2: Bris 3B 68
Barnabas St. BS2: Bris 5A 58
Barnack Trad. Est. BS3: Bedm ..3E 77
Barnard Wlk. BS31: Key 3F 89
Barn Cl. BS16: Emer G 5D 47
Barnes Ct. BS34: Stok G 4A 26
Barnes St. BS5: St G 1F 69
Barnfield Way BA1: Bathe 3D 99
Barnhill Cl. BS37: Yate 1C 16
Barnhill Rd. BS37: Chip S 4C 16
Barn Owl Way BS34: Stok G 3B 26
Barnstaple Cl. BS4: Know 4A 78
Barnstaple Rd. BS4: Know 4A 78
Barnstaple Wlk. BS4: Know 4B 78
Barnwell Cl. BS10: Bren 4C 22
Barnwood Cl. BS15: K'wd 1B 72
Barnwood Rd. BS37: Yate 1E 31
Baron Cl. BS30: Bit 4F 83
Barons Cl. BS3: Ash V 1B 76
Barossa Pl. BS1: Bris 5C 4 (4F 67)
Barracks La. BS11: Shire 3F 37
Barratt St. BS5: E'tn 5D 59
Barrington Cl. BS15: Soun 4B 62
Barrington Ct. BS4: Wind H 5B 68
  BS15: Soun 5A 62
Barrow Hill Cres. BS11: Shire ..4E 37
Barrow Hill Rd. BS11: Shire 5E 37
Barrowmead Dr. BS11: Law W ..3B 38
Barrow Rd. BA2: Odd D 4E 109
  BS5: Bar H 2D 69
BARRS COURT 4B 72
Barr's Ct. BS1: Bris 1D 5 (1A 68)
Barrs Ct. Av. BS30: Bar C 4C 72
Barrs Ct. Rd. BS30: Bar C 4C 72
Barry Cl. BS30: Bit 3E 83
Barry Rd. BS30: Old C 2E 83
Barstaple Ho. BS2: Bris 2F 5
Barter Cl. BS15: K'wd 1F 71
Bartholomews Sq. BS7: Hor 4B 42
Bartlett's Rd. BS3: Bedm 2E 77

Bartlett St. BA1: Bath 2B 6 (3B 104)
Bartley Ct. BS5: St G 2F 69
Bartley St. BS3: Bedm 5F 67
Barton, The BA2: Cor 3C 100
  BS15: Han 5E 71
Barton Bldgs. BA1: Bath ..2B 6 (3B 104)
Barton Cl. BS4: St Ap 3B 70
  BS36: Wint 3A 28
Barton Ct. BA1: Bath 3C 6
  (off Up. Borough Walls)
Barton Grn. BS5: Bar H 2D 69
BARTON HILL 3D 69
Barton Hill Rd. BS5: Bar H 3D 69
Barton Hill Trad. Est. BS5: Bar H ..3D 69
Barton Ho. BS1: Bris ...1D 5 (1A 68)
  BS5: Redf 3E 69
Bartonia Gro. BS4: Brisl 3F 79
Barton Mnr. BS2: Bris 3C 68
Barton Mdw. Est. BS16: Fish ...5E 45
Barton Rd. BS2: Bris 3B 68
Barton St. BA1: Bath 3B 6 (4B 104)
  BS1: Bris 1F 67
Barton Va. BS2: Bris 3C 68
  (not continuous)
Barwick Ho. BS11: Shire 4A 38
Batch, The BA1: Bathe 4B 98
  BS31: Salt 4B 92
Batches, The BS3: Bedm 2D 77
Bates Cl. BS5: E'tn 1C 68
BATH 3C 6 (4C 104)
Bath Abbey 3C 6 (4C 104)
Bath Abbey Heritage Vaults 3C 6
  (within Bath Abbey)
BATHAMPTON 1B 106
Bathampton La. BA2: B'ptn 1A 106
Bath Aqua Theatre of Glass
  ....1C 6 (3C 104)
Bath Bldgs. BS6: Bris 5A 58
Bath Bus. Cen. BA1: Bath 3C 6
  (off Up. Borough Walls)
Bath City FC 4D 103
Bath County Court 4C 6
BATHEASTON 3B 98
Batheaston Swainswick By-Pass
  BA1: Bath, Swa, Up Swa ...1D 97
  BA2: B'ptn 1D 97
Bath Festival Maze, The
  ....3D 7 (4C 104)
BATHFORD 5E 99
Bathford Hill BA1: Bathf 5D 99
Bath Hill BS31: Key 1B 90
Bathite Cotts. BA2: Mon C 4F 111
Bath Marina & Cvn. Pk.
  BA1: Bath 2B 102
Bath Racecourse 1C 94
Bath Riverside Bus. Pk.
  BA2: Bath 4A 6 (4B 104)
Bath Rd. BA1: Kel, S'frd 1C 92
  BA2: Cor 4A 92
  BS4: Bris, Wind H 4B 68
  BS4: Brisl 3A 80
  (Bonville Rd.)
  BS4: Brisl 2F 79
  (Eagle Rd.)
  BS30: Bit, Will 3D 83
  BS30: B'yte, Old C 4F 73
  BS30: L Grn 5A 72
  BS31: Key, Salt 2B 90
Bath Road (Park & Ride) 4B 80
Bath RUFC 3D 7
Bath Spa Station (Rail) ..5D 7 (5C 104)
Bath Spa University
  Newton Pk. Campus 5C 100
Bath Sports & Leisure Cen.
  ....3D 7 (4C 104)
Bath St. BA1: Bath ...4B 6 (4B 104)
  BS1: Bris 3D 5 (3A 68)
  BS3: Ash G 5C 66
  BS16: Stap H 2A 62
Bathurst Pde. BS1: Bris ...5B 4 (4F 67)

Bathurst Ter. BS1: Bris 4F 67
  (off Commercial Rd.)
Bathwell Rd. BS4: Wind H 1C 78
BATHWICK 1E 7 (3D 105)
Bathwick Hill
  BA2: Bath, Clav D ...2E 7 (4D 105)
Bathwick Ri. BA2: Bath ...1F 7 (2E 105)
Bathwick St. BA2: Bath ...1D 7 (2C 104)
Bathwick Ter. BA2: Bath 3F 7
Batley Cl. BS30: Old C 5F 73
Bat Stall La. BA1: Bath 3C 6
  (off Orange Gro.)
Batstone Cl. BA1: Bath 5D 97
Battenburg Rd. BS5: St G 1C 70
Batten Cl. BS37: Chip S 4E 17
Batten Rd. BS5: St G 2D 71
Batten's La. BS5: E'tn 3C 70
Battersby Way BS10: Hen 1A 40
Battersea Rd. BS5: E'tn 1E 69
Battery La. BS20: P'head 5C 34
Battery Rd. BS20: P'head 5C 34
Battson Rd. BS14: Stoc 2A 88
Baugh Gdns. BS16: Down 2A 46
Baugh Rd. BS16: Down 2A 46
Baxter Cl. BS15: K'wd 1B 72
Bay Gdns. BS5: Eastv 4E 59
Bayham Rd. BS4: Know, Wind H ..1B 78
Bayleys Dr. BS15: K'wd 3E 71
Baynham Ct. BS15: Han 4D 71
  (off Henbury Rd.)
Baynton Ho. BS5: E'tn 2C 68
Baynton Mdw. BS16: Emer G ...5E 47
Baynton Rd. BS3: Ash G 5C 66
Bayswater Av. BS6: Henle 2D 57
Bayswater Rd. BS7: Hor 4B 42
Bay Tree Cl. BS34: Pat 1B 24
Bay Tree Rd. BA1: Bath 5C 96
Bay Willow Dr. BS6: Redl 4D 57
Beachgrove Gdns. BS16: Fish ...2E 61
Beachgrove Rd. BS16: Fish 2D 61
Beach Hill BS20: P'head 5B 34
Beachley Wlk. BS11: Shire 4F 37
Beach Rd. E. BS20: P'head 5C 34
Beach Rd. W. BS20: P'head 5B 34
BEACON HILL 1D 105
Beacon Ho. BS8: Clif 2D 67
  (off Queens Av.)
Beacon La. BS36: Wint 3E 27
Beaconlea BS15: K'wd 3F 71
Beacon Rd. BA1: Bath 1C 104
Beaconsfield Cl. BS5: Bar H 1B 70
Beaconsfield Ct. BS8: Clif 5C 56
  (off Beaconsfield Rd.)
Beaconsfield Rd. BS4: Know 1D 79
  BS5: St G 1A 70
  BS8: Clif 5C 56
Beaconsfield St. BS5: Bar H 3D 69
Beale Cl. BS14: Stoc 1A 88
Beale Wlk. BA2: Bath 4A 104
Beam St. BS5: Redf 2E 69
Bean Acre, The BS11: Shire 3F 37
Bean St. BS5: E'tn 5C 58
Beanwood Pk. BS37: W'lgh 5A 32
Bearbridge Rd. BS13: Withy 3B 84
BEAR FLAT 1A 110
Bear Yd. M. BS8: Clif 3C 66
  (off Charles Pl.)
Beatrix Pl. BS7: Hor 3C 42
Beauchamp Rd. BS7: B'stn 2F 57
Beauford Sq. BA1: Bath ...3B 6 (4B 104)
Beaufort BS16: Fren 2E 45
  (off Harford Dr.)
Beaufort All. BS5: St G 3B 70
Beaufort Av. BS37: Yate 3F 15
Beaufort Bldgs. BS8: Clif 2B 66
Beaufort Cl. BS5: St G 2F 69
Beaufort Ct. BS16: Down 3C 46
Beaufort Cres. BS34: Stok G 4A 26
Beaufort E. BA1: Bath 1E 105
Beaufort Hgts. BS5: St G 2A 70
Beaufort M. BS5: Bar H 2D 69

Beaufort M. BA1: Bath 1E **105**
  BS8: Clif 2B **66**
Beaufort Pk. BS32: Brad S 2F **9**
Beaufort Pl. BA1: Bath 1E **105**
  BS5: E'tn 1C **68**
  BS16: Fren 2D **45**
Beaufort Rd. BS5: St G 2F **69**
  BS7: Hor 5B **42**
  BS8: Clif 5C **56**
  BS15: K'wd 5E **61**
  BS16: Down 4C **46**
  BS16: Stap H 2A **62**
  BS36: Fram C 5C **12**
  BS37: Yate 3F **15**
Beaufort St. BS3: Bedm 2E **77**
  BS5: E'tn 1C **68**
Beaufort Vs. BA1: Bath 1D **105**
Beaufort Way BS10: S'mead 3F **41**
Beaufort W. BA1: Bath 1D **105**
Beauley Rd. BS3: Bris 4D **67**
Beaumont Cl. BS30: L Grn 1C **82**
Beaumont St. BS5: E'tn 1C **68**
Beaumont Ter. BS5: E'tn 1C **68**
Beau St. BA1: Bath 4B **6** (4B **104**)
Beaver Cl. BS36: Wint 1B **28**
Beazer Cl. BS16: Soun 3F **61**
Beck Cl. BS16: Emer G 5E **47**
Beckford Cl. BA2: Bath 1F **7**
  (off Darlington Rd.)
Beckford Gdns.
  BA2: Bath 1F **7** (2D **105**)
  BS14: Whit 4C **86**
Beckford Rd. BA2: Bath . .1E **7** (3D **105**)
Beckford's Tower & Mus. 3F **95**
Beckhampton Rd. BA2: Bath . . .5F **103**
Beck Ho. BS34: Pat 5C **8**
Beckington Rd. BS3: Know 2B **78**
Beckington Wlk. BS3: Know 2B **78**
Beckspool Rd. BS16: Fren 4D **45**
Bedford Cl. BA1: Bath 2C **104**
Bedford Cres. BS7: Hor 1B **58**
Bedford Pl. BS2: Bris 1B **4** (1F **67**)
Bedford St. BA1: Bath 2C **104**
BEDMINSTER 1E **77**
Bedminster Bri. BS1: Bris 4F **67**
  BS3: Bris 4F **67**
BEDMINSTER DOWN 4C **76**
Bedminster Down Rd.
  BS13: Bedm, Bis 3C **76**
Bedminster Pde. BS3: Bedm 5F **67**
Bedminster Pl. BS3: Bedm 5F **67**
Bedminster Rd. BS3: Bedm 3D **77**
Bedminster Station (Rail) 5F **67**
Bedminster Trade Pk.
  BS3: Bedm 1E **77**
Bedwin Cl. BS20: P'head 2B **48**
Beech Av. BA2: Clav D 5A **106**
Beech Cl. BS30: Bar C 4C **72**
Beech Ct. BS14: Whit 2C **86**
Beechcroft BS41: Dun 5A **84**
Beechcroft Wlk. BS7: Hor 3C **42**
BEECHEN CLIFF 5B **104**
Beechen Cliff Rd. BA2: Bath 5B **104**
Beechen Dr. BS16: Fish 4D **61**
Beeches, The BA2: Odd D 4F **109**
  BS4: St Ap 4A **70**
  BS9: Stok B 3F **55**
  BS30: Old C 2E **83**
  BS32: Brad S 5F **9**
Beeches Gro. BS4: Brisl 2F **79**
Beeches Ind. Est. BS37: Yate 3D **15**
Beechfield Cl. BS41: L Ash 2E **75**
Beechfield Gro. BS9: C Din 3E **39**
Beech Gro. BA2: Bath 1E **109**
Beech Ho. BS16: Stap 1E **59**
Beechmount Ct. BS14: H'gro 4D **79**
Beechmount Gro. BS14: H'gro . . .4D **79**
Beech Rd. BS7: Hor 1A **58**
  BS31: Salt 4A **92**
Beech Vw. BA2: Clav D 5F **105**

Beechwood Av. BS15: Han 4F **71**
Beechwood Cl. BS14: Stoc 4E **79**
Beechwood Dr. BS20: P'head 1A **48**
Beechwood Rd. BA2: C Down 4D **111**
  BS16: Fish 2C **60**
  BS20: Eas 2C **52**
  BS20: P'head 1A **48**
Beehive Trad. Est. BS5: St G 2A **70**
Beehive Yd. BA1: Bath . . .2C **6** (3C **104**)
Beesmoor Rd.
  BS36: Coal H, Fram C 1D **29**
Begbrook Dr. BS16: B'hll 5B **44**
Begbrook La. BS16: B'hll 5B **44**
Begbrook Rd. BS16: Fren 3C **44**
Beggar Bush La.
  BS8: Abb L, Fail 5A **64**
Beggarswell Cl. BS2: Bris 1B **68**
Belfast Wlk. BS4: Know 4A **78**
Belfields La. BS16: Fren 2E **45**
Belfry BS30: Warm 3D **73**
Belfry All. BS5: St G 1C **70**
Belfry Av. BS5: St G 1C **70**
Belgrave Cres. BA1: Bath 2C **104**
Belgrave Hill BS8: Clif 4C **56**
Belgrave Pl. BA1: Bath 1C **104**
  BS8: Clif 2C **66**
Belgrave Rd. BA1: Bath 1D **105**
  BS8: Clif 1D **67**
Belgrave Ter. BA1: Bath 1C **104**
Bellamy Av. BS13: Hart 3E **85**
Bellamy Cl. BS15: St G 4C **70**
Belland Dr. BS14: Whit 3B **86**
Bell Av. BS1: Bris 5C **4** (4F **67**)
Bella Vista Rd. BA1: Bath 2B **104**
Bell Barn Rd. BS9: Stok B 5F **39**
Bell Cl. BS10: Hor 4A **42**
Bellevue BS8: Clif 3D **67**
Bellevue Cl. BS15: K'wd 2A **72**
Bellevue Cotts. BS8: Clif 3D **67**
  BS9: W Trym 4C **40**
Bellevue Ct. BS8: Clif 3D **67**
Bellevue Cres. BS8: Clif 3D **67**
Bellevue Pk. BS4: Brisl 2F **79**
Belle Vue Rd. BS5: E'tn 4E **59**
Bellevue Ter. BS4: Brisl 2F **79**
  BS4: Wind H 5B **68**
  BS8: Clif 3D **67**
Bell Hill BS16: Stap 2E **59**
Bell Hill Rd. BS5: St G 1C **70**
Bellhouse Wlk. BS11: Law W 2D **39**
Bell La. BS1: Bris 2B **4** (2F **67**)
  (not continuous)
Bellotts Rd. BA2: Bath 4E **103**
Bell Rd. BS36: Coal H 1E **29**
Belluton Rd. BS4: Know 1E **78**
Belmont BA1: Bath 1B **6** (3B **104**)
Belmont Dr. BS34: Stok G 3A **26**
Belmont Pk. BS7: Fil 2B **42**
Belmont Rd. BA2: C Down 4E **111**
  BS4: Brisl 5E **69**
  BS6: Bris 4A **58**
Belmont St. BS5: E'tn 5D **59**
Belmore Gdns. BA2: Bath 2D **109**
Beloe Rd. BS7: Hor 1A **58**
Belroyal Av. BS4: Brisl 1B **80**
Belsher Dr. BS15: K'wd 3C **72**
Belstone Wlk. BS4: Know 4E **77**
Belton Ct. BA1: W'ton 5D **95**
Belton Ho. BA1: W'ton 5D **95**
Belton Rd. BS5: E'tn 5D **59**
  BS20: P'head 1C **48**
Belvedere Pl. *BA1: Bath 1B 6*
  (off Morford St.)
Belvedere Rd. BS6: Redl 3C **56**
Belvedere Vs. BA1: Bath . . .1B **6** (2B **104**)
Belvoir Rd. BA2: Bath 5F **103**
  BS6: Bris 4A **58**

Bence Ct. *BS15: Han 4D 71*
  (off Memorial Rd.)
Benford Cl. BS16: Fish 5E **45**
Bengough's Almshouses
  BS2: Bris 1A **4** (2E **67**)
Bennett Rd. BS5: St G 2A **70**
Bennetts Ct. BS37: Yate 4B **16**
Bennett's La. BA1: Bath 1C **104**
Bennett's Rd. BA1: Swa 4E **97**
Bennett St. BA1: Bath 1B **6** (3B **104**)
Bennett Way BS8: Clif 4B **66**
Bensaunt Gro. BS10: Bren 4F **23**
Bentley Cl. BS14: Whit 4B **86**
Benville Av. BS9: C Din 3E **39**
Berchel Ho. BS3: Bedm 5E **67**
Berenda Dr. BS30: L Grn 1D **83**
Beresford Cl. BS31: Salt 5A **92**
Beresford Gdns. BA1: W'ton 4C **94**
Berkeley Av. BS7: B'stn 3F **57**
  BS8: Clif 2E **67**
Berkeley Cl. BS16: Down 3B **46**
Berkeley Ct. BA2: Bath 3F **7** (4E **105**)
  BS5: E'tn 2D **69**
  BS7: B'stn 3F **57**
  BS34: Pat 4B **8**
Berkeley Cres. BS8: Clif 2D **67**
Berkeley Gdns. BS31: Key 3F **89**
Berkeley Grn. BS16: Fren 2D **45**
Berkeley Grn. Rd. BS5: Eastv 4E **59**
Berkeley Gro. BS5: Eastv 4E **59**
Berkeley Ho. BA1: Bath 2C **104**
  BS1: Bris 3D **67**
  BS5: Stap H 1F **61**
Berkeley Pl. BA1: Bath 2C **104**
  BA2: C Down 3E **111**
  BS8: Clif 2D **67**
Berkeley Rd. BS6: Henle 2C **56**
  BS7: B'stn 3F **57**
  BS15: K'wd 2A **72**
  BS16: Fish 4C **60**
  BS16: Stap H 2F **61**
Berkeleys Mead BS32: Brad S . . .2B **26**
Berkeley Sq. BS8: Clif 2E **67**
Berkeley St. *BS5: Eastv 4E 59*
  (off Berkeley Grn. Rd.)
  BS5: Eastv 3E **59**
  (Gadshill Rd.)
Berkeley Way BS16: Emer G 4D **47**
Berkshire Rd. BS7: B'stn 3F **57**
Berlington Ct. BS1: Bris . . .5E **5** (4A **68**)
Berners Cl. BS4: Know 5F **77**
Berrow Wlk. BS3: Wind H 2A **78**
Berry Cft. BS3: Bedm 5F **67**
Berry Hill Cl. BS10: S'mead 2F **41**
Berry La. BS7: Hor 5B **42**
BERWICK 2F **21**
Berwick Cl. BS10: H'len 3D **21**
Berwick Dr. BS10: Hen 3A **22**
Berwick La. BS10: H'len 3E **21**
  BS35: E Comp 3E **21**
Berwick Rd. BS5: Eastv 4D **59**
Beryl Gro. BS14: H'gro 4E **79**
Beryl Rd. BS3: Bedm 1D **77**
Besom La. BS37: W'lgh 3E **31**
Bethel Rd. BS5: St G 1B **70**
Betjeman Ct. BS30: Bar C 4C **72**
Betts Grn. BS16: Emer G 4E **47**
Bevan Ct. BS34: Fil 1C **42**
Beverley Av. BS16: Down 2B **46**
Beverley Cl. BS5: St G 3D **71**
Beverley Gdns. BS9: W Trym 4F **39**
Beverley Rd. BS7: Hor 3B **42**
Beverstone BS15: K'wd 1E **71**
Beverston Gdns. BS11: Law W . . .1D **39**
Bevington Cl. BS34: Pat 4A **8**
Bevington Wlk. BS34: Pat 4A **8**
Bewdley Rd. BA2: Bath 1D **111**
Bexley Rd. BS16: Fish 3D **61**
Bibstone BS15: K'wd 1C **72**
Bibury Av. BS34: Pat 5D **9**
Bibury Cl. BS9: Henle 4F **41**

Bibury Cres. BS9: Henle 4F 41
   BS15: Han 4E 71
Bickerton Cl. BS10: Hen 5B 22
Bickford Cl. BS30: Bar C 3C 72
Bickley Cl. BS15: Han 2D 81
Biddestone Rd. BS7: Hor 3A 42
Bideford Cres. BS4: Know 4B 78
Bidwell Cl. BS30: Bren 5D 23
Bifield Cl. BS14: Stoc 2B 88
Bifield Gdns. BS14: Stoc 2A 88
   (not continuous)
Bifield Rd. BS14: Stoc 3A 88
Bigwood La. BS1: Bris 3A 4 (3E 67)
Bilberry Cl. BS9: C Din 3E 39
Bilbie Cl. BS10: Hor 4A 42
Bilbury La. BA1: Bath 4C 6 (4C 104)
Billand Cl. BS13: Withy 4A 84
Bindon Dr. BS10: Bren 4F 23
Binley Gro. BS14: Stoc 2F 87
Binmead Gdns. BS13: Hart 3D 85
Birbeck Rd. BS9: Stok B 1A 56
Birchall Rd. BS6: Redl 2E 57
Birch Cl. BS34: Pat 1A 24
Birch Ct. BS31: Key 3E 89
   BS37: Yate 3F 15
Birch Cft. BS14: Whit 4C 86
Birchdale Rd. BS14: H'gro 4C 78
Birch Gro. BS20: P'head 2E 49
Birchills Trad. Est. BS4: Brisl 3B 80
Birch Rd. BS3: Bris 5D 67
   BS15: Soun 3A 62
   BS37: Yate 3F 15
Birchwood Ct. BS4: St Ap 3B 70
Birchwood Rd. BS4: Brisl, St Ap . .1A 80
Birdale Cl. BS10: Hen 5A 22
Birdwell La. BS41: L Ash 3B 74
Birdwell Rd. BS41: L Ash 3B 74
Birdwood BS15: Han 3F 71
Birkdale BS30: Warm 3C 72
   BS37: Yate 5A 16
Birkin St. BS2: Bris 3C 68
Biscay Dr. BS20: P'head 5E 35
Bishop La. BS7: B'stn 2A 58
Bishop Mnr. Rd. BS10: Hor 4F 41
Bishop M. BS2: Bris 1A 68
Bishop Monk BS16: Fish 1C 60
Bishop Rd. BS7: B'stn 2E 57
   BS16: Emer G 5E 47
Bishops Cl. BS9: Stok B 3A 56
Bishops Ct. BS9: Stok B 3E 55
Bishops Cove BS13: Bis 2B 84
Bishops Knoll BS9: Stok B 3E 55
Bishops Knoll Nature Reserve . . .4F 55
BISHOPSTON 2A 58
Bishop St. BS2: Bris 1A 68
BISHOPSWORTH 2C 84
Bishopsworth Rd. BS13: Bis 5C 76
Bishopsworth Swimming Pool . . .1C 84
Bishopthorpe Rd. BS10: Hor 4F 41
Bishport Av. BS13: Hart, Withy . . .3C 84
Bishport Cl. BS13: Hart 3D 85
Bishport Grn. BS13: Hart 4E 85
Bisley BS37: Yate 1E 31
Bissex Mead BS16: Emer G 1D 63
Bittern Av. BS20: P'head 4E 35
Bitterwell Cl. BS36: H'fld 5F 29
Bittle Mead BS14: Hart 3B 86
BITTON .4F 83
Bitton Station
   Avon Valley Railway 3D 83
Bitton Station Railway Cen. 3D 83
Blackacre BS14: Whit 3E 87
Blackberry Av. BS16: Stap 1A 60
Blackberry Dr. BS36: Fram C 2D 29
Blackberry Hill BS16: Stap 1A 60
Blackberry La. BS20: P'head 4B 48
Black Boy Hill BS8: Clif 4C 56
Blackcurrant Dr. BS41: L Ash 4A 74
Blackdown Cl. BS14: Whit 2D 87

Blackdown Rd. BS20: P'head 1C 48
   (not continuous)
Blackfriars BS1: Bris 1B 4 (2F 67)
BLACKHORSE 3C 46
Blackhorse Cl. BS16: Emer G 3C 46
Blackhorse Ct. BS15: K'wd 1E 71
Blackhorse Hill BS10: Pat 1D 23
Blackhorse La. BS16: Down 2B 46
Blackhorse Pl. BS16: Mang 5C 46
Blackhorse Rd. BS15: K'wd 1F 71
   BS16: Mang 4C 46
Blackmoor Rd. BS8: Abb L 5A 54
Blackmoors La. BS3: Bwr A 1A 76
Blackmore Dr. BA2: Bath 5D 103
Black Nore Point BS20: P'head . . .1B 48
Blacksmith La. BA1: Up Swa 1D 97
Blacksmiths La. BA1: Kel 4D 93
Blackswarth Rd. BS5: St G 2F 69
Blackthorn Cl. BS13: Hart 2F 85
Blackthorn Dr. BS20: P'head 1A 50
   (not continuous)
   BS32: Brad S 1F 25
Blackthorn Rd. BS13: Hart 2F 85
Blackthorn Wlk. BS15: K'wd 4A 62
Bladen Cl. BS20: P'head 2A 50
Bladud Bldgs.
   BA1: Bath 2C 6 (3C 104)
Blagdon Cl. BS3: Wind H 2A 78
Blagdon Pk. BA2: Bath 1C 108
Blagrove Cl. BS13: Hart 4E 85
Blagrove Cres. BS13: Hart 4E 85
Blaisdon BS37: Yate 1A 32
Blaisdon Cl. BS10: Hen 2C 40
Blaise Castle 2F 39
Blaise Castle House Mus. 1A 40
Blaisedell Vw. BS10: Hen 5F 21
BLAISE HAMLET 1E 39
Blaise Hamlet (National Trust) . . .1F 39
Blaise Wlk. BS9: Sea M 4E 39
Blaise Weston Ct. BS11: Law W . . .2C 38
Blakeney Mills BS37: Yate 4F 15
Blakeney Rd. BS7: Hor 5C 42
   BS34: Pat 4A 8
Blake Rd. BS7: L'lze 5D 43
Blanchards BS37: Chip S 5E 17
Blandamour Way BS10: S'mead . .1F 41
Blandford Cl. BS9: W Trym 5D 41
Blenheim Ct. BS1: Bris 1F 67
   (off Dighton St.)
Blenheim Dr. BS34: Fil 4D 25
   BS37: Yate 2E 15
Blenheim Gdns. BA1: Bath 5C 96
Blenheim Rd. BS6: Redl 3D 57
Blenheim St. BS5: E'tn 5C 58
Blenheim Way BS20: P'head 1A 50
Blenman Cl. BS16: B'hll 4C 44
Blethwin Cl. BS10: Hen 2B 40
Blind La. BA1: W'ton 5E 95
   BA2: Bath 1D 111
BLOOMFIELD 3F 109
Bloomfield Av. BA2: Bath 1A 110
Bloomfield Cres. BA2: Bath 3F 109
Bloomfield Dr. BA2: Odd D 3E 109
Bloomfield Gro. BA2: Bath 2A 110
Bloomfield Pk. BA2: Bath 2A 110
Bloomfield Ri. BA2: Odd D 3F 109
Bloomfield Ri. Nth. BA2: Odd D . . .3F 109
Bloomfield Rd.
   BA2: Bath, Odd D 3F 109
   BS4: Brisl 5E 69
   (not continuous)
Bloomfield Tennis & Bowling Club
   . . . . .2A 110
Bloy St. BS5: E'tn 5E 59
   (not continuous)
Bluebell Cl. BS9: Sea M 5D 39
Bluebells, The BS32: Brad S 1A 26
Blue Falcon Rd. BS15: K'wd 4A 62
Boarding Ho. La. BS32: Alm 1A 8
Bodey Cl. BS30: C Hth 3C 72
Bodmin Wlk. BS4: Know 4B 78

Boiling Wells La. BS2: Bris 3C 58
   BS7: Eastv 3C 58
Bolton Rd. BS7: B'stn 3A 58
Bond St. BS1: Bris 1D 5 (1A 68)
   BS2: Bris 1E 5 (1A 68)
Bond St. Sth. BS1: Bris 1F 5 (2B 68)
Bonnington Wlk. BS7: L'lze 3D 43
Bonville Bus. Cen. BS4: Brisl 2B 80
Bonville Rd. BS4: Brisl 3A 80
Bonville Trad. Est. BS4: Brisl 2B 80
Boon Vs. BS11: Law W 4A 38
Booth Rd. BS3: Bedm 5E 67
Boot La. BS3: Bedm 5F 67
Bordesley Rd. BS14: Whit 4C 86
Borleyton Wlk. BS13: Withy 3B 84
Borver Gro. BS13: Hart 3D 85
   (not continuous)
Boscombe Cres. BS16: Down 3B 46
Boston Rd. BS7: Hor 3B 42
Boswell St. BS5: Eastv 4E 59
Botanical Gdns.
   Bath 3F 103
BOTANY BAY 4B 22
Botham Dr. BS4: Brisl 3F 79
Boucher Pl. BS2: Bris 4C 58
Boulters Rd. BS13: Hart 3E 85
Boultons La. BS15: K'wd 1F 71
Boultons Rd. BS15: K'wd 1F 71
Boundary Rd. BS36: Coal H 1F 29
Bourchier Gdns. BS13: Hart 4D 85
Bourne Cl. BS15: K'wd 1D 71
   BS36: Wint 1A 28
Bourne La. BS5: Eastv 4D 59
Bourne Rd. BS15: K'wd 1C 70
Bourneville Rd. BS5: W'hall 1F 69
Boursland Cl. BS32: Brad S 3F 9
Bourton Av. BS34: Pat 5E 9
Bourton Cl. BS34: Pat 5E 9
Bourton Mead BS41: L Ash 3D 75
Bourton Wlk. BS13: Bis 4C 76
Bouverie St. BS5: E'tn 1D 69
Boverton Rd. BS34: Fil 5D 25
Bow Cotts. BS20: Pill 2F 53
   (off Water La.)
Bowden Cl. BS9: C Din 3E 39
Bowden Pl. BS16: Down 4B 46
Bowden Rd. BS5: W'hall 5A 60
BOWER ASHTON 5A 66
Bower Ashton Ter. BS3: Ash G 5B 66
Bowerleaze BS9: Sea M 1E 55
Bower Rd. BS3: Bedm 1C 76
Bower Wlk. BS3: Wind H 1A 78
Bowling Hill BS37: Chip S 4C 16
Bowling Hill Bus. Pk.
   BS37: Chip S 4C 16
Bowling Rd. BS37: Chip S 5D 17
   (not continuous)
Bowlplex
   Kingswood 4A 72
Bow Mead BS14: Stoc 2A 88
Bowood BS16: Fren 2E 45
   (off Avon Ring Rd.)
Bowring Cl. BS13: Hart 4E 85
Bowsland BS32: Brad S 3A 10
Bowsland Way BS32: Brad S 3E 9
Box Hedge La. BS36: H'fld 5A 30
Box Rd. BA1: Bathf 4D 99
Box Wlk. BS31: Key 3E 89
Boyce Cl. BA2: Bath 5B 102
Boyce Dr. BS2: Bris 4C 58
Boyce's Av. BS8: Clif 2C 66
Boyd Rd. BS31: Salt 4F 91
Brabazon Office Pk. BS34: Fil 5B 24
Brabazon Rd. BS34: Fil 1D 43
Bracewell Gdns. BS10: Bren 4E 23
Bracey Dr. BS16: Fish 5E 45
Brackenbury Dr. BS34: Stok G 3B 26
Brackendene BS32: Brad S 4E 9
Brackenwood Gdns.
   BS20: P'head 1B 48
Bracton Dr. BS14: Whit 3C 86

Bradeston Gro. BS16: B'hll 4C 44
Bradford Pk. BA2: C Down 3C 110
   (not continuous)
Bradford Rd. BA1: Bathf, Warl 4D 99
  BA2: C Down 4B 110
Bradhurst St. BS5: Bar H 3D 69
Bradley Av. BS11: Shire 5A 38
  BS36: Wint 3A 28
Bradley Ct. BS16: Down 1E 61
Bradley Cres. BS11: Shire 5A 38
Bradley Ho. BS1: Bris 3F 67
   (off St Stephen's Av.)
Bradley Pavilions BS32: Brad S . . .3E 9
Bradley Rd. BS20: P'bry 1A 52
  BS34: Pat 5B 8
BRADLEY STOKE 3E 9
Bradley Stoke Leisure Cen. 4A 10
Bradley Stoke Way BS32: Brad S . .3D 9
Bradstone Rd. BS36: Wint 3F 27
Bradville Gdns. BS41: L Ash 4B 74
Bradwell Gro. BS10: S'mead 3E 41
Braemar Av. BS7: Fil 2A 42
Braemar Cres. BS7: Fil 2B 42
Bragg's La. BS2: Bris 1F 5 (2B 68)
Braikenridge Rd. BS4: Brisl 5F 69
Brainsfield BS9: W Trym 5B 40
Brake, The BS36: Coal H 3E 29
  BS37: Yate 1A 16
Brake Cl. BS15: K'wd 2B 72
  BS32: Brad S 1A 26
Brakewell Gdns. BS14: Whit 3C 86
Bramble Dr. BS9: Stok B 3E 55
Bramble La. BS9: Stok B 3E 55
Brambles, The BS13: Hart 3E 85
Bramble Way BS31: Key 4F 89
   (not continuous)
Bramble Way BA2: C Down 3D 111
Brambling La. BS20: P'head 5F 35
Brambling Wlk. BS16: B'hll 5B 44
   (not continuous)
Bramley Cl. BS20: Pill 2E 53
Bramley Copse BS41: L Ash 4A 74
Bramley Ct. BS30: Bar C 5B 72
Bramleys, The BS20: P'head 2B 50
Brampton Way BS20: P'head 1F 49
Branche Gro. BS13: Hart 4F 85
Brandash Rd. BS37: Chip S 4E 17
Brandon Hill Nature Pk. 3D 67
Brandon Ho. BS8: Clif 3D 67
Brandon Steep BS1: Bris . . .3A 4 (3E 67)
Brandon Steps BS1: Bris . . .3A 4 (3E 67)
Brandon St. BS1: Bris 4A 4 (3E 67)
Brangwyn Gro. BS7: L'lze 1D 59
Branksome Cres. BS34: Fil 5D 25
Branksome Dr. BS34: Fil 5D 25
  BS36: Wint 2A 28
Branksome Rd. BS6: Redl 3D 57
Branscombe Rd. BS9: Stok B 2E 55
Branscombe Wlk. BS20: P'head . . .3B 48
Branwhite Cl. BS7: L'lze 4D 43
Brassmill Ent. Cen. BA1: Bath . . .3C 102
Brassmill La. BA1: Bath 3C 102
Brassmill La. Trad. Est.
  BA1: Bath 3C 102
Bratton Rd. BS4: Know 5F 77
Braunton Rd. BS3: Bedm 1E 77
Braydon Av. BS34: Lit S 5E 9
Brayne Cl. BS30: L Grn 1B 82
Breaches, The BS20: Eas 2D 53
Breaches Ga. BS32: Brad S 2B 26
Breaches La. BS31: Key 3C 90
Breach Rd. BS3: Bedm 1C 76
Breachwood Vw. BA2: Odd D 3E 109
Brean Down Av. BS9: Henle 1D 57
   (not continuous)
Brean Gdns. BS3: Wind H 2A 78
Brecknock Rd. BS4: Wind H 1C 78
Brecon Cl. BS9: Henle 5D 41
Brecon Ct. BS16: Fren 2F 43
Brecon Rd. BS9: Henle 5C 40
Bredon BS37: Yate 1F 31

Bredon Cl. BS15: K'wd 2B 72
Bredon Nook Rd. BS10: W Trym . . .4E 41
Bredon Cl. BS30: Old C 5E 73
Brendon Rd. BS3: Wind H 1F 77
  BS20: P'head 1C 48
Brenner St. BS5: E'tn 4D 59
Brent Rd. BS7: Hor 1B 58
BRENTRY 5D 23
Brentry Av. BS5: Bar H 2D 69
Brentry Hill BS9: W Trym 2C 40
Brentry Ho. BS10: Bren 5D 23
Brentry La. BS10: Bren 1C 40
Brentry Rd. BS16: Fish 2A 60
Brereton Way BS30: C Hth 5D 73
Brewer Cl. BS30: Bren 5E 23
Brewery Ct. BS3: Ash G 5C 66
Brewhouse, The
  BS1: Bris 3D 5 (3A 68)
Briar Cl. BS20: Pill 3E 53
Briarfield Av. BS15: Han 4D 71
Briars Ct. BA2: Bath 1C 108
Briarside Rd. BS10: Bren 5E 23
Briar Wlk. BS16: Fish 3E 61
Briar Way BS16: Fish 2D 61
Briarwood BS9: W Trym 5B 40
Briary Rd. BS20: P'head 1E 49
Briavels Gro. BS6: Bris 4B 58
Brick St. BS2: Bris 2B 68
Bridewell La.
  BA1: Bath 3B 6 (4B 104)
Bridewell St. BS1: Bris 1C 4 (2F 67)
Bridge Cl. BS14: Whit 3E 87
Bridge Farm Cl. BS14: Whit 4C 86
Bridge Farm Wlk. BS16: Mang 3D 63
Bridgeleap Rd. BS16: Down 3B 46
Bridge Rd. BA2: Bath 5E 103
  BS5: Eastv 3D 59
  BS8: L Wds 3F 65
  BS15: Soun 3B 62
  BS16: Short 2E 63
  BS37: Yate 3C 14
Bridge Rd. Ind. Est. BS15: Soun . . .3C 62
Bridges Ct. BS16: Fish 2D 61
Bridges Dr. BS16: Fish 5E 45
Bridge St. BA2: Bath 3C 6 (4C 104)
  BS1: Bris 3C 4 (3A 68)
  BS5: Eastv 4F 59
Bridge Valley Rd. BS8: Clif 1A 66
Bridge Vw. Cl. BS5: E'tn 5E 59
Bridge Wlk. BS7: Hor 3C 42
Bridge Way BS36: Fram C 5D 13
BRIDGEYATE 2F 73
Bridgman Gro. BS34: Fil 5D 25
Bridgwater Rd. BS13: Bis 5F 75
  BS41: Dun 5F 75
Briercliffe Rd. BS9: Stok B 4F 39
Brierly Furlong BS34: Stok G 5F 25
Brighton Cres. BS3: Bedm 2D 77
Brighton M. BS8: Clif 1D 67
Brighton Pk. BS5: E'tn 1D 69
Brighton Pl. BS15: K'wd 5F 61
Brighton Rd. BS6: Redl 5E 57
  BS34: Pat 5B 8
Brighton St. BS2: Bris 5A 58
Brighton Ter. BS3: Bedm 2D 77
Bright St. BS5: Bar H 2D 69
  BS15: K'wd 1F 71
Brigstocke Rd. BS2: Bris 5A 58
Brigstowe St. BS1: Bris . . .1E 5 (2A 68)
Brimbles, The BS7: Hor 1D 43
Brimsham Pk. Shop. Cen.
  . . . . .1A 16
Brinkworthy Rd. BS16: Stap 5F 43
Brinmead Wlk. BS13: Withy 4B 84
Brins Cl. BS34: Stok G 4B 26
Brinsmead Cres. BS20: Pill 2F 53
   (off Heywood Rd.)
Briscoes Av. BS13: Hart 3E 85
BRISLINGTON 2A 80
Brislington Hill BS4: Brisl 2A 80

Brislington Retail Pk. BS4: Brisl . . .3A 80
Brislington Trad. Est. BS4: Brisl . . .2B 80
   (not continuous)
BRISTOL 2B 4 (2F 67)
Bristol & Anchor Ho.
  BS5: W'hall 1F 69
   (off Park Cres.)
Bristol & Exeter M.
  BS1: Bris 5F 5 (4B 68)
Bristol Bri. Ho. BS1: Bris . . .3C 4 (3A 68)
Bristol Bus. Pk. BS16: Fren 2B 44
Bristol Cathedral 4A 4 (3E 67)
Bristol City FC 1B 76
Bristol Distribution Pk.
  BS32: Brad S 2F 9
Bristol Ga. BS8: Clif 4B 66
Bristol Harbour Railway . . .5A 4 (4E 67)
Bristol Hill BS4: Brisl 2F 79
Bristol Hippodrome 3A 4 (3F 67)
Bristol Ho. BS1: Bris 3D 5
Bristol Ice Rink 2A 4 (2E 67)
Bristol Indoor Bowls Club 3A 76
Bristol Megabowl 5B 66
Bristol Nth Swimming Pool 3A 58
Bristol Parkway Nth.
  BS34: Stok G 3C 26
Bristol Parkway Station (Rail) 4A 26
Bristol Rd. BA2: Cor, New L . . .2D 101
  BS14: Whit 2E 87
  BS16: Fren, Ham 3C 44
  BS16: Ham 5F 27
  BS20: P'head 2F 49
  BS31: Key 1F 89
  BS36: Fram C, Wint 1A 28
  BS37: Iron A 4C 12
Bristol Rovers FC 5B 42
Bristol RUFC 5B 42
Bristol Southend BS3: Wind H 2F 77
Bristol South Swimming Pool 5E 67
Bristol Sports Cen. 1E 69
Bristol Temple Meads Station (Rail)
  . . . . .5F 5 (4B 68)
Bristol Va. Cen. for Industry
  BS3: Bedm 3D 77
Bristol Va. Trad. Est.
  BS3: Bedm 4E 77
Bristol Vw. BA2: Odd D 5E 109
Bristol Zoo 5B 56
Bristow B'way. BS11: A'mth 2E 37
Bristowe Ho. BS16: Fish 1D 61
Britannia Cl. BS16: Down 2C 46
Britannia Cres. BS34: Stok G 3F 25
Britannia Ho. BS34: Fil 1B 42
Britannia Rd. BS5: E'tn 5D 59
  BS15: K'wd 1E 71
  BS34: Pat 1F 23
British, The BS37: Yate 1D 15
British Rd. BS3: Bedm 1D 77
Brittan Pl. BS20: P'bry 3A 52
Britten Cl. BS30: L Grn 5B 72
Britten Gdns. BS15: K'wd 5E 61
Britton Ho. BS15: Warm 1D 73
Brixham Rd. BS3: Wind H 2E 77
Brixton Cl. BS5: E'tn 1D 69
Brixton Rd. M. BS5: E'tn 1D 69
Broadbury Rd. BS4: Know 4F 77
Broad Cft. BS32: Brad S 3E 9
Broadfield Av. BS15: K'wd 1E 71
Broadfield Rd. BS4: Know 4C 78
Broadlands Av. BS31: Key 1F 89
Broadlands Dr. BS11: Law W 3C 38
Broad La. BS36: Coal H 3F 29
  BS37: W'lgh 4C 30
  BS37: Yate 1D 15
   (not continuous)
Broadleas BS13: Bis 5E 77
Broadleaze BS11: Shire 4F 37
Broadleys Av. BS9: Henle 4E 41
BROAD MEAD 4D 25
BROADMEAD 2D 5 (2A 68)
Broadmead BS1: Bris 1D 5 (2A 68)

Broadmead La. BS31: Key 2D 91
Broadmead La. Ind. Est.
BS31: Key 5D 83
Broadmoor La. BA1: W'ton 3B 94
Broadmoor Pk. BA1: W'ton 5D 95
Broadmoor Va. BA1: W'ton 4C 94
Broadoak Hill BS41: Dun 5B 84
Broad Oak Rd. BS13: Withy 3B 84
Broad Oaks BS8: L Wds 3A 66
Broadoak Wlk. BS16: Fish 2D 61
Broad Plain BS2: Bris 3F 5 (2B 68)
Broad Quay BA1: Bath . . .5B 6 (5B 104)
BS1: Bris 3B 4 (3F 67)
Broad Quay Ho. BS1: Bris 4B 4
Broad Rd. BS15: K'wd 5E 61
Broadstone Wlk. BS13: Hart 2F 85
Broad St. BA1: Bath 2C 6 (3C 104)
BS1: Bris 2C 4 (2F 67)
BS16: Stap H 2F 61
BS37: Chip S 4D 17
Broad St. Pl. BA1: Bath . . .2C 6 (3C 104)
Broad Wlk. BS4: Know 2B 78
BS20: P'head 4D 35
Broadwalk Shop. Cen.
BS4: Know 2D 79
Broadway BA2: Bath 4E 7 (4D 105)
BS31: Salt 4F 91
BS37: Yate 3B 16
Broadway Av. BS9: Henle 5F 41
Broadway Cl. BA2: Bath . . .5D 7 (5C 104)
Broadway Rd. BS7: B'stn 3F 57
BS13: Withy 2B 84
Broadways Dr. BS16: B'hll 4B 44
Broad Weir BS1: Bris 2E 5 (2A 68)
Brock End BS20: P'head 3B 48
Brockhurst Gdns. BS15: K'wd 1C 70
Brockhurst Rd. BS15: K'wd 1C 70
Brockley Cl. BS34: Lit S 1E 25
Brockley Rd. BS31: Salt 4F 91
Brockley Wlk. BS13: Bis 4C 76
Brockridge La. BS36: Fram C 1E 29
Brocks La. BS41: L Ash 3B 74
Brocks Rd. BS13: Hart 4E 85
Brock St. BA1: Bath 1A 6 (3B 104)
Brockworth BS37: Yate 2E 31
Brockworth Cres. BS16: B'hll 5B 44
Bromfield Wlk. BS16: Emer G 4D 47
Bromley Dr. BS16: Down 3F 45
Bromley Farm BS16: Down 2F 45
BROMLEY HEATH 3A 46
Bromley Heath Av. BS16: Down . . .3F 45
Bromley Heath Rd. BS16: Down . . .4F 45
BS16: Ham 1F 45
Bromley Rd. BS7: Hor 1B 58
Brompton Cl. BS15: K'wd 1B 72
Brompton Ho. BA2: Bath . . .1D 7 (3C 104)
Broncksea Rd. BS7: Fil 2B 42
Bronte Wlk. BS7: Hor 3C 42
Brook Cl. BS4: L Ash 3D 75
Brookcote Dr. BS34: Lit S 2F 25
Brookdale Rd. BS13: Bis 1D 85
Brookfield Av. BS7: B'stn 3F 57
Brookfield Cl. BS37: Chip S 3E 17
Brookfield La. BS6: Cot 4F 57
Brookfield Pk. BA1: W'ton 5D 95
Brookfield Rd. BS6: Cot 4F 57
BS34: Pat 5D 9
Brookfield Wlk. BS30: Old C 1E 83
Brookgate BS3: Ash V 3A 76
Brook Hill BS6: Bris 5B 58
Brook Ho. BS34: Lit S 5E 9
Brookland Rd. BS6: Henle 1F 57
Brook La. BS6: Bris 5B 58
BS16: B'hll 5A 44
Brooklea BS30: Old C 5D 73
Brookleaze BS9: Sea M 1E 55
Brookleaze Bldgs. BA1: Bath 5D 97
Brook Lintons BS4: Brisl 1F 79
Brooklyn Rd. BA1: Bath 5E 97
BS13: Bis 4D 77
Brook Office Pk. BS16: Emer G . . .1D 47

Brookridge Ho. BS10: Hen 5B 22
Brook Rd. BA2: Bath 4F 103
BS3: Bedm 5F 67
BS5: S'wll 5A 60
BS6: Bris 5B 58
BS15: K'wd, Warm 1C 72
(not continuous)
BS15: Warm 1D 73
BS16: Fish 2C 60
(not continuous)
BS16: Mang 5B 46
Brookside BS20: Pill 3E 53
Brookside Cl. BA1: Bathe 2B 98
Brookside Dr. BS36: Fram C 5D 13
Brookside Ho. BA1: W'ton 1D 103
Brookside Rd. BS4: Brisl 2A 80
Brook St. BS5: Redf 2E 69
BS37: Chip S 4C 16
Brookthorpe BS37: Yate 5F 15
Brookthorpe Av. BS11: Law W . . .2C 38
Brookthorpe Ct. BS37: Yate 5F 15
Brook Vw. BS10: Hen 5B 22
Brookview Wlk. BS13: Bis 5D 77
Brook Way BS32: Brad S 4E 9
BROOM HILL 5B 70
BROOMHILL 5B 44
Broom Hill BS16: B'hll 5A 44
Broomhill Rd. BS4: Brisl 1B 80
Brooms, The BS16: Emer G 1C 46
Brotherswood Ct. BS32: Brad S . . .2F 9
Brougham Hayes BA2: Bath 4D 104
Brougham Pl. BA1: Bath 5E 97
(off St Saviours Rd.)
Broughton Ho. BS1: Bris . . .5E 5 (4A 68)
Brow, The BA2: Bath 5D 103
BA2: C Down 4E 111
Brow Hill BA1: Bathe 3B 98
Brow Hill Vs. BA1: Bathe 3B 98
Browne Cl. BS8: Clif 3B 66
(off Cumberland Pl.)
Browning Ct. BS7: Hor 3D 43
Brown's Folly Nature Reserve . . .1F 107
Broxholme Wlk. BS11: Law W 3B 38
Bruce Av. BS5: E'tn 5E 59
Bruce Rd. BS5: E'tn 5E 59
Brunel Cl. BS30: Warm 2E 73
Brunel Ct. BS20: P'head 5C 34
BS37: Yate 3E 15
Brunel Gro. BS14: H'gro 5C 78
Brunel Ho. BA2: Bath 4C 102
BS1: Bris 3A 4 (3E 67)
Brunel Lock Rd. BS1: Bris 4B 66
Brunel Rd. BS13: Bis 4B 76
Brunel's SS Great Britain 4D 67
Brunel Way BS1: Bris 5B 66
BS3: Ash G, Bwr A 5B 66
Brunswick Ct. BS2: Bris 1A 68
(off Brunswick Sq.)
Brunswick Pl. BA1: Bath 1B 6
BS1: Bris 4B 66
Brunswick Sq. BS2: Bris 1A 68
Brunswick St. BA1: Bath 1D 105
BS2: Bris 1A 68
BS5: Redf 2E 69
Bruton Av. BA2: Bath 1B 110
BS20: P'head 1C 48
Bruton Cl. BS5: St G 1B 70
Bruton Pl. BS8: Clif 2D 67
Bryanson's Cl. BS16: Stap 5F 43
Bryants Cl. BS16: Fren 2E 45
Bryants Hill BS5: St G 3D 71
Brynland Av. BS7: B'stn 2A 58
Buchanans Wharf Nth. BS1: Bris . .4C 4
Buchanans Wharf Sth. BS1: Bris . .4C 4
Buckingham Dr. BS34: Stok G 4F 25
Buckingham Gdns. BS16: Down . . .5A 46
Buckingham Ho. BS34: Fil 1B 42
Buckingham Pl. BS8: Clif 2C 66
BS16: Down 5A 46
Buckingham Rd. BS4: Brisl 4F 69
Buckingham St. BS3: Bedm 2E 77

Buckingham Va. BS8: Clif 1C 66
Bucklewell Cl. BS11: Shire 5B 38
Bude Av. BS5: St G 1C 70
Bude Rd. BS34: Fil 5D 25
Building of Bath Mus. 1B 6 (3C 104)
Bullens Cl. BS32: Brad S 3F 9
Buller Rd. BS4: Know 2E 79
Bull La. BS5: St G 3B 70
BS20: Pill 2E 53
Bull Wharf BS1: Bris 3D 5 (3F 67)
Bumper's Batch BA2: S'ske 5C 110
Burbank Cl. BS30: L Grn 1C 82
Burbarrow La. BS37: Cod, W'lgh . .5F 31
Burchells Av. BS15: K'wd 5D 61
BURCHELLS GREEN 1D 71
Burchells Grn. Cl. BS15: K'wd 5D 61
Burchells Grn. Rd. BS15: K'wd . . .5D 61
Burcombe Cl. BS36: Coal H 1F 29
Burcott Rd. BS11: A'mth 3E 19
Burden Cl. BS32: Brad S 2B 26
Burfoote Gdns. BS14: Stoc 3A 88
Burfoote Rd. BS14: Stoc 3A 88
Burford Av. BS34: Pat 5E 9
Burford Cl. BA2: Bath 2D 109
BS20: P'head 2A 50
Burford Gro. BS11: Shire 1B 54
Burgage Cl. BS37: Chip S 5D 17
Burgess Grn. Cl. BS4: St Ap 2A 70
Burghill Rd. BS10: W Trym 2C 40
Burghley Ct. BS36: Wint 3A 28
Burghley Rd. BS6: Bris 4A 58
Burgis Rd. BS14: Stoc 1F 87
Burleigh Gdns. BA1: Bath 2C 102
Burley Av. BS16: Mang 1B 62
Burley Crest BS16: Mang 5B 46
Burley Gro. BS16: Mang 5B 46
Burlington Ct. BS6: Redl 4D 57
BS20: P'head 5D 35
Burlington Pl. BA1: Bath 1A 6
Burlington Rd. BS6: Redl 4D 57
BS20: P'head 4D 35
Burlington St. BA1: Bath . . .1A 6 (2B 104)
Burnbush Cl. BS14: Stoc 1A 88
Burnell Dr. BS2: Bris 1B 68
Burney Way BS30: L Grn 1C 82
Burnham Cl. BS15: K'wd 5B 62
Burnham Dr. BS15: K'wd 5B 62
Burnham Rd. BA2: Bath 4E 103
BS11: Shire 5F 37
Burnside Cl. BS10: S'mead 1E 41
Burnt Ho. Cotts. BA2: Odd D 5E 109
Burnthouse Ct. BA2: Odd D 5E 109
Burnt Ho. Rd. BA2: Odd D 5F 109
Burrington Wlk. BS13: Bis 4C 76
Burrough Way BS36: Wint 3A 28
Burton Cl. BS1: Bris 4A 68
Burton Ct. BS8: Clif 2D 66
Burton St. BA1: Bath 3C 6 (4C 104)
Burwalls Rd. BS8: L Wds 3A 66
Bury Cl. BS11: Law W 2C 38
Bury Hill BS16: Ham 1A 46
BS36: Wint D 1A 46
Bury Hill Vw. BS16: Down 2A 46
Bush Av. BS34: Lit S 2E 25
Bush Ct. BS4: Wind H 1B 78
Bush Ind. Est. BS5: St G 1F 69
Bush La. BS3: Bris 5D 67
Bushy Ho. BS4: Wind H 1B 78
Bushy Pk. BS4: Wind H 1B 78
Butcombe Wlk. BS14: Whit 2D 87
Butler Ho. BS5: St G 1B 70
Butlers Cl. BS5: St G 3B 70
Butlers Wlk. BS5: St G 3B 70
Buttercliffe Ri. BS41: L Ash 1E 75
Butterfield Cl. BS10: Hor 4A 42
BS36: Fram C 2D 29
Butterfield Rd. BS10: Hor 4A 42
Butterworth Ct. BS4: Know 5F 77
Button Cl. BS14: Whit 1C 86
Buxton Wlk. BS7: Hor 3C 42
Bye Mead BS16: Emer G 3C 46

Byfield BA2: C Down 4D **111**
Byfield Bldgs. *BA2: C Down* *4D 111*
(off Byfield Pl.)
Byfield Pl. BA2: C Down 4D **111**
Byron Pl. BS8: Clif 2D **67**
BS16: Stap H 2A **62**
Byron Rd. BA2: Bath 1B **110**
Byron St. BS2: Bris 5C **58**
BS5: Redf 2E **69**
Byzantine Ct. BS1: Bris 5B **4**

C

Cabot Cl. BS15: K'wd 2E **71**
BS31: Salt 5F **91**
BS37: Yate 4B **16**
Cabot Ct. BS7: Fil 2B **42**
Cabot Grn. BS5: Bar H 2D **69**
Cabot Ri. BS20: P'head 1C **48**
Cabot Tower 3D **67**
Cabot Way BS8: Clif 4B **66**
BS20: Pill 3F **53**
Cabstand BS20: P'head 5C **34**
Cadbury Gdns. BS30: C Hth 3D **73**
Cadbury Halt BS20: Wes 5B **48**
CADBURY HEATH 3D **73**
Cadbury Heath Rd.
BS30: C Hth 4C **72**
Cadbury La. BS20: Wes 5B **48**
Cadbury Rd. BS20: P'head 2F **49**
BS31: Key 5C **90**
Cadby Ho. BA2: Bath 4C **102**
Caddick Cl. BS15: K'wd 4B **62**
Cade Cl. BS15: K'wd 3B **72**
BS34: Stok G 3A **26**
Cadogan Rd. BS14: H'gro 4C **78**
Caen Rd. BS3: Wind H 1F **77**
Caernarvon Rd. BS31: Key 3E **89**
Caern Well Pl. BA1: Bath 1C **6**
Caine Rd. BS7: Hor 4B **42**
Cains Cl. BS15: K'wd 3A **72**
Cairn Gdns. BS36: Wint D 4A **28**
Cairns Ct. BS6: Redl 2E **57**
Cairns Cres. BS2: Bris 5B **58**
Cairns Rd. BS6: Henle, Redl 1D **57**
Cala Trad. Est. BS3: Ash V 1B **76**
Calcott Rd. BS4: Know 2C **78**
Caldbeck Cl. BS10: S'mead 1F **41**
Calder Cl. BS31: Key 3C **90**
Caldicot Cl. BS11: Law W 1E **39**
BS30: Will 2D **83**
Caledonia M. BS8: Clif 3B **66**
Caledonian Rd. BA2: Bath 4F **103**
BS1: Bris 4D **67**
Caledonia Pl. BS8: Clif 3B **66**
California Rd. BS30: L Grn 1C **82**
Callard Ho. BS16: Fish 2B **60**
Callicroft Rd. BS34: Pat 1C **24**
Callington Rd. BS4: Brisl 3D **79**
BS14: H'gro 3D **79**
Callowhill Ct. BS1: Bris 1D **5** (2A **68**)
Calton Gdns. BA2: Bath 5B **104**
Calton Rd. BA2: Bath 5C **6** (5C **104**)
Calton Wlk. BA2: Bath 5B **6** (5B **104**)
Camberley Dr. BS36: Fram C 5B **12**
Camberley Rd. BS4: Know 4E **77**
(not continuous)
Camborne Rd. BS7: Hor 4C **42**
Cambrian Dr. BS37: Yate 2F **15**
Cambridge Cres. BS9: W Trym 4C **40**
Cambridge Pk. BS6: Redl 3D **57**
Cambridge Pl.
BA2: Bath 5E **7** (5D **105**)
Cambridge Rd. BS7: B'stn 2F **57**
Cambridge St. BS3: Wind H 5B **68**
BS5: Redf 2E **69**
Cambridge Ter.
BA2: Bath 5E **7** (5D **105**)
Camden Ct. BA1: Bath 2B **104**
Camden Cres. BA1: Bath 2B **104**

Camden Rd. BA1: Bath 2C **104**
BS3: Bris 4D **67**
Camden Row BA1: Bath 2B **104**
(not continuous)
Camden Ter. *BA1: Bath* *2C 104*
(off Camden Rd.)
BS8: Clif 3C **66**
Cameley Grn. BA2: Bath 4B **102**
Camelford Rd. BS5: E'tn 5F **59**
Cameron Wlk. BS7: L'lze 5E **43**
Cameroons Cl. BS31: Key 3A **90**
Camerton Cl. BS31: Salt 4A **92**
Camerton Rd. BS5: E'tn 5F **59**
Camomile Wlk. BS20: P'head 1B **50**
Campbells Farm Dr.
BS11: Law W 2B **38**
Campbell St. BS2: Bris 5A **58**
Campian Wlk. BS4: Know 1F **85**
Campion Dr. BS32: Brad S 3F **9**
Camp Rd. BS8: Clif 2B **66**
Camp Vw. BS36: Wint D 4A **28**
Camwal Ind. Est. BS2: Bris 4C **68**
Camwal Rd. BS2: Bris 4C **68**
Canada Way BS1: Bris 4C **66**
Canal Path BA2: B'ptn 5C **98**
Canal Ter. BA2: B'ptn 1B **106**
Canberra Gro. BS34: Fil 4D **25**
Canford Crematorium
BS9: W Trym 4A **40**
Canford La. BS9: W Trym 4F **39**
Canford Rd. BS9: W Trym 3B **40**
Cannans Cl. BS36: Wint 1A **28**
Cann La. BS30: B'yte, Old C 3F **73**
Cannon St. BS1: Bris 1C **4** (1F **67**)
BS3: Bedm 5E **67**
Canons Cl. BA2: Bath 3D **109**
Canons Rd. BS1: Bris 5A **4** (4E **67**)
CANON'S MARSH 4A **4** (3E **67**)
Canon's Rd. BS1: Bris 4A **4** (3E **67**)
(Anchor Sq., not continuous)
BS1: Bris 4D **67**
(Lime Kiln Rd.)
Canon St. BS5: Redf 1E **69**
Canon's Wlk. BS15: Soun 4A **62**
Canons Way BS1: Bris 4A **4** (3E **67**)
Canowie Rd. BS6: Redl 3D **57**
Cantell Gro. BS14: Stoc 2B **88**
Canterbury Cl. BS37: Yate 2A **16**
Canterbury Rd. BA2: Bath 5F **103**
Canterbury St. BS5: Bar H 3D **69**
Cantock's Cl. BS8: Clif 2A **4** (2E **67**)
Canton Pl. BA1: Bath 2C **104**
Canvey Cl. BS10: Hor 4A **42**
Canynge Ho. BS1: Bris 5D **5** (4A **68**)
Canynge Rd. BS8: Clif 1B **66**
Canynge Sq. BS8: Clif 1B **66**
Canynge St. BS1: Bris 4D **5** (3A **68**)
Capel Cl. BS15: Warm 1D **73**
Capel Rd. BS11: Law W 2D **39**
Capenor Cl. BS20: P'head 2E **49**
Capgrave Cl. BS4: Brisl 1C **80**
Capgrave Cres. BS4: Brisl 1C **80**
Capital Edge BS8: Clif 4D **67**
Capricorn Quay BS8: Clif 3D **67**
Caraway Gdns. BS5: Eastv 4E **59**
Cardigan La. BS9: Henle 5D **41**
Cardigan M. BS9: Henle 1D **57**
Cardigan Rd. BS9: Henle 5D **41**
Cardill Cl. BS13: Bis 4C **76**
Cardinal Cl. BA2: Odd D 5F **109**
Carfax Rd. BS6: Redl 3C **56**
Carisbrooke Rd. BS4: Know 4F **77**
Carlow Rd. BS4: Know 4A **78**
Carlton Ct. BS9: W Trym 4C **40**
Carlton Pk. BS5: Redf 1E **69**
Carlyle Rd. BS5: E'tn 5E **59**
Carmarthen Cl. BS37: Yate 1B **16**
Carmarthen Gro. BS30: Will 3D **83**
Carmarthen Rd. BS6: Henle 5C **40**
Carnarvon Rd. BS6: Redl 4E **57**
Carolina Ho. BS2: Bris 1F **67**

Caroline Bldgs. BA2: Bath 5E **7**
Caroline Cl. BS31: Key 3E **89**
BS37: Chip S 3D **17**
Caroline Pl. BA1: Bath 1B **6** (2B **104**)
Carpenters La. BS31: Key 2A **90**
Carpenters Pl. *BS4: Know* *3A 78*
(off Leinster Av.)
Carpenters Shop La.
BS16: Down 5A **46**
Carr Ho. BA2: Bath 4C **102**
BS2: Bris 5B **58**
Carriage Ct. BA1: Bath 1A **6**
Carriage Dr. BS10: Bren 1D **41**
Carrick Ho. *BS8: Clif* *3B 66*
(off Hotwell Rd.)
Carrington Rd. BS3: Ash G 5C **66**
Carroll Ct. BS16: Fren 2A **44**
Carrs Cl. BA2: Bath 4C **102**
Carsons Rd. BS16: Mang, Sis 3D **63**
Carter Wlk. BS32: Brad S 5F **9**
Cart La. BS1: Bris 4E **5** (3A **68**)
Cartledge Rd. BS5: E'tn 5E **59**
Cashmore Ho. BS5: Bar H 2D **69**
Caslon Ct. BS1: Bris 5E **5** (4A **68**)
Cassell Rd. BS16: Down, Fish 1E **61**
Cassey Bottom La. BS5: St G 2C **70**
Casson Dr. BS16: Stap 3A **44**
Castle Cl. BS10: Hen 1F **39**
Castle Ct. BS34: Stok G 4C **26**
Castle Farm Rd. BS15: Han 2D **81**
Castle Gdns. BA2: Bath 2A **110**
Castlegate Ho. BS4: Brisl 2A **80**
Castle Rd. BS15: K'wd 4F **61**
BS30: Old C 1E **83**
Castle St. BS1: Bris 2E **5** (2A **68**)
Caswell Hill BS20: Clap G 5C **50**
Caswell La. BS20: Clap G, P'bry . . .5B **50**
CATBRAIN 2D **23**
Catbrain Hill BS10: Pat 2D **23**
Catbrain La. BS10: Pat 2D **23**
Cater Rd. BS13: Bis 1C **84**
Catharine Pl. BA1: Bath . . .1A **6** (3B **104**)
Cathay BS1: Bris 5D **5**
Cathcart Ho. BA1: Bath 1C **104**
Cathedral, The BS8: Clif 2D **67**
Cathedral Sq. BS1: Bris 4A **4** (3E **67**)
Cathedral Wlk. BS1: Bris . . .5A **4** (4E **67**)
Catherine Ct. *BS6: Bris* *5A 58*
(off Backfields La.)
Catherine Mead St. BS3: Bedm . . .5E **67**
Catherine St. BS11: A'mth 3E **37**
Catherine Way BA1: Bathe 3B **98**
Catley Gro. BS41: L Ash 3D **75**
Cato St. BS5: E'tn 4D **59**
Catsley Pl. BA1: Swa 4E **97**
Cattistock Dr. BS5: St G 3C **70**
Cattle Mkt. Rd. BS1: Bris . . .5F **5** (4B **68**)
Cattybrook Rd. BS16: Short 1F **63**
Cattybrook Rd. Nth. BS16: Short . . .1F **63**
Cattybrook St. BS5: E'tn 1D **69**
Causeway, The BS20: Clap G 5A **50**
BS36: Coal H 1E **29**
Causley Dr. BS30: Bar C 4B **72**
Cavan Wlk. BS4: Know 3F **77**
Cave Cl. BS16: Down 5F **45**
Cave Ct. BS16: Down 1A **68**
Cave Dr. BS16: Fish 5F **45**
Cave Gro. BS16: Emer G 4D **47**
Cavendish Cl. BS31: Salt 5F **91**
Cavendish Cres. BA1: Bath 2A **104**
Cavendish Gdns. BS9: Stok B 2E **55**
Cavendish Lodge BA1: Bath 2A **104**
Cavendish Pl. BA1: Bath 2A **104**
Cavendish Rd.
BA1: Bath 1A **6** (2A **104**)
BS9: Henle 1C **56**
BS34: Pat 5B **8**
Cave St. BS2: Bris 1A **68**
Caxton Ct. BA2: Bath 2C **6** (3C **104**)
Caxton Ga. BS1: Bris 5E **5** (4A **68**)
Cecil Av. BS5: S'wll 5B **60**

Cecil Rd. BS8: Clif 1B 66
BS15: K'wd 1F 71
Cedar Cl. BS30: Old C 5D 73
BS34: Pat 1B 24
BS41: L Ash 3B 74
Cedar Ct. BS9: Stok B 2E 55
BS16: Down 5A 46
Cedar Dr. BS31: Key 3F 89
Cedar Gro. BA2: Bath 2F 109
BS9: Stok B 1F 55
Cedar Hall BS16: Fren 3E 45
Cedar Hill Ct. BS16: Stap H 2F 61
Cedarhurst Rd. BS20: P'head 3A 48
Cedar Pk. BS9: Stok B 1F 55
Cedar Row BS11: Shire 5B 38
Cedars, The BS9: Stok B 3F 55
Cedars Way BS36: Wint 3F 27
Cedar Vs. BA2: Bath 5A 6 (5A 104)
Cedar Wlk. BA2: Bath 5A 104
(not continuous)
Cedar Way BA2: Bath 5A 6 (5A 104)
BS20: P'head 2E 49
Cedric Cl. BA1: Bath 3E 103
Cedric Rd. BA1: Bath 3E 103
Celestine Rd. BS37: Yate 2E 15
Celia Ter. BS4: St Ap 3B 70
Cemetery Rd. BS4: Wind H 1C 78
Cennick Av. BS15: K'wd 5A 62
Centaurus Rd. BS34: Pat 1E 23
Central Av. BS15: Han 4E 71
Central Pk. BS14: H'gro 4D 79
Central Trad. Est. BS4: Bris 5D 69
Central Way BS10: S'mead 3A 42
Centre, The BS31: Key 2A 90
Centre for Sport 1A 44
Centre for Sport, Exercise and Health
. . . . .1A 4 (1E 67)
Centre Quay BS20: P'head 4D 35
Centro BS1: Bris 1F 67
(off Charles St.)
Centrum BS5: E'tn 1B 68
Ceres Cl. BS30: L Grn 2B 82
Cerimon Ga. BS34: Stok G 3A 26
Cerney La. BS11: Shire 1A 54
Cesson Cl. BS37: Chip S 5E 17
Chadleigh Gro. BS4: Know 5F 77
Chakeshill Cl. BS10: Bren 5E 23
Chakeshill Dr. BS10: Bren 5E 23
Chalcombe Cl. BS34: Lit S 5E 9
Chalcroft Ho. BS3: Bris 5C 66
Chalcroft Wlk. BS13: Withy 3A 84
Chalet, The BS10: Hen 5B 22
Chalfield Cl. BS31: Key 5C 90
Chalford Cl. BS37: Yate 5F 15
Chalks Rd. BS5: St G 1F 69
Challender Av. BS10: Hen 1B 40
Challoner Ct. BS1: Bris 5B 4 (4F 67)
Champion Rd. BS15: K'wd 4B 62
Champneys Av. BS10: Hen 5B 22
Champs Sur Marne
BS32: Brad S 5A 10
Chancel Cl. BS9: Stok B 3F 55
Chancery St. BS5: Bar H 2D 69
Chandag Rd. BS31: Key 3B 90
Chandler Cl. BA1: Bath 1D 103
Chandos BS6: Redl 4E 57
Chandos Bldgs. BA1: Bath 4B 6
(off Westgate Bldgs.)
Chandos Rd. BS6: Redl 5D 57
BS31: Key 5A 82
Chandos Trad. Est. BS2: Bris 4C 68
Channells Hill BS9: W Trym 3C 40
Channel Vw. Cres. BS20: P'head . . .1D 49
Channel Vw. Rd. BS20: P'head 1D 49
Channon's Hill BS16: Fish 2B 60
Chantry Cl. BS11: Law W 1E 39
Chantry Ct. BS1: Bris 3A 4
(off Denmark St.)
Chantry La. BS16: Down 2B 46
Chantry Mead Rd. BA2: Bath 2A 110
Chantry Rd. BS8: Clif 5D 57

Chapel Barton BS3: Bedm 2D 77
Chapel Cl. BS15: Warm 1D 73
Chapel Ct. BA1: Bath 4B 6
(off Westgate Bldgs.)
BS4: Brisl 2F 79
Chapel Gdns. BS10: W Trym 2C 40
Chapel Grn. La. BS6: Redl 4D 57
Chapel Ho. BS1: Bris 2B 4
Chapel La. BS5: S'wll 4A 60
BS11: Law W 1D 39
BS15: Warm 1D 73
BS16: Fren 4E 45
Chapel Orchard BS37: Yate 3D 15
Chapel Pill La. BS20: Pill 2A 54
Chapel Rd. BS5: E'tn 5D 59
BS13: Bis 1C 84
BS15: Bis 3A 48
Chapel Row BA1: Bath . . .3A 6 (4B 104)
BA1: Bathf 5E 99
BA2: B'ptn 1B 106
BS20: P'head 2E 53
Chapel St. BS2: Bris 4C 68
Chapel Way BS4: St Ap 3A 70
Chaplains Wood BS20: P'head 1A 48
Chaplin Rd. BS5: E'tn 5D 59
Chapter St. BS2: Bris 1A 68
Chapter Wlk. BS6: Redl 3D 57
Charbon Ga. BS34: Stok G 3B 26
Charborough Ct. BS34: Fil 1B 42
Charborough Rd. BS34: Fil 1B 42
Charbury Wlk. BS11: Shire 1A 54
Chard Ct. BS14: H'gro 1D 87
Chardstock Av. BS9: C Din 3E 39
Charfield BS15: K'wd 1C 72
Charfield Rd. BS10: S'mead 2E 41
Chargrove BS30: Old C 3F 73
BS37: Yate 1F 31
Charis Av. BS10: W Trym 4E 41
CHARLCOMBE 4B 96
Charlcombe La. BA1: Bath, Charl . . .5B 96
Charlcombe Pk. BS20: P'head 3A 48
Charlcombe Ri. BA1: Bath 5B 96
BS20: P'head 3A 48
Charlcombe Vw. Rd. BA1: Bath 5C 96
Charlcombe Way BA1: Bath 5B 96
Charlecombe Ct. BS9: W Trym 5B 40
Charlecombe Rd. BS9: W Trym 5B 40
Charles Av. BS34: Stok G 4A 26
Charles Ct. BS8: Clif 3C 66
(off Charles Pl.)
Charles England Ho. BS34: Pat 1B 24
Charles Pl. BS8: Clif 3C 66
Charles Rd. BS34: Fil 5D 25
Charles St. BA1: Bath 3A 6 (4B 104)
BS1: Bris 1F 67
Charles Wesley Ct. BS5: St G 3C 70
Charleton Ho. BS2: Bris 1F 5
(off Gt. Ann St.)
Charlotte St. BA1: Bath . . .3A 6 (4B 104)
BS1: Bris 2A 4 (2E 67)
Charlotte St. Sth. BS1: Bris 3E 67
Charlton Av. BS34: Fil 1B 42
Charlton Bldgs. BA2: Bath 4E 103
Charlton Comn. BS10: Bren 4F 23
Charlton Ct. BS34: Pat 4B 8
Charlton Gdns. BS10: Bren 4F 23
Charlton La. BS10: Bren 5C 22
Charlton Leaze BS10: Pat 2C 22
Charlton Mead Ct. BS10: Bren 4F 23
Charlton Mead Dr. BS10: Bren 4F 23
Charlton Pk. BS31: Key 2F 89
Charlton Pl. BS10: Bren 4F 23
Charlton Rd. BS10: Bren 2C 40
BS15: K'wd 5D 61
BS31: Q Char, Key 5D 89
Charlton St. BS5: Bar H 2D 69
Charlton Vw. BS20: P'head 1E 49
Charminster Rd. BS16: Fish 3D 61
Charmouth Rd. BA1: Bath 3D 103
Charnell Rd. BS16: Stap H 2A 62
Charnhill Brow BS16: Mang 2C 62

Charnhill Cres. BS16: Mang 2B 62
Charnhill Dr. BS16: Mang 2B 62
Charnhill Ridge BS16: Mang 2C 62
Charnhill Va. BS16: Mang 2B 62
Charnwood BS16: Mang 2C 62
Charnwood Rd. BS14: Whit 3D 87
Charter Ho. BS1: Bris 3D 67
(off St George's Rd.)
Charterhouse Rd. BS5: St G 1F 69
Charter Wlk. BS14: H'gro 1C 86
Chase, The BS16: Fish 3E 61
Chasefield La. BS16: Fish 2D 61
Chase Rd. BS15: K'wd 4F 61
Chatcombe BS37: Yate 1A 32
Chatham Pk. BA2: Bath 4E 105
Chatham Row BA1: Bath 1C 6 (3C 104)
Chatsworth Rd. BS4: Bris 5E 69
BS16: Fish 3D 61
Chattenden Ho. BS9: Stok B 3A 56
Chatterton Grn. BS14: Whit 4B 86
Chatterton Ho. BS1: Bris 4A 68
(off Ship La.)
Chatterton Rd. BS37: Yate 4F 15
Chatterton Sq. BS1: Bris 5F 5 (4B 68)
Chatterton St. BS1: Bris 4B 68
Chaucer Rd. BA2: Bath 1B 110
Chaundey Gro. BS13: Hart 2D 85
Chavenage BS15: K'wd 5C 62
Cheapside BS2: Bris 1B 68
Cheapside St. BS3: Wind H 5B 68
Cheap St. BA1: Bath 3C 6 (4C 104)
Cheddar Gro. BS13: Bis 4C 76
Chedworth BS15: Soun 3A 62
BS37: Yate 1D 31
Chedworth Rd. BS7: Hor 5C 42
Cheese La. BS2: Bris 3E 5 (3A 68)
Chelford Gro. BS34: Pat 5D 9
Chelmer Gro. BS31: Key 3B 90
Chelmsford Wlk. BS4: St Ap 4B 70
Chelscombe BA1: W'ton 1D 103
Chelsea Cl. BS31: Key 2C 90
Chelsea Ho. BA1: Bath 2C 104
(off London Rd.)
Chelsea Pk. BS5: E'tn 1E 69
Chelsea Rd. BA1: Bath 3E 103
BS5: E'tn 5D 59
Chelston Rd. BS4: Know 5F 77
Cheltenham La. BS6: Bris 4F 57
Cheltenham Rd. BS6: Bris 4F 57
Cheltenham St.
BA2: Bath 5A 6 (5A 104)
Chelvey Cl. BS13: Hart 4F 85
Chelwood Dr. BA2: Odd D 4F 109
Chelwood Rd. BS11: Shire 4F 37
BS31: Salt 3A 92
Chepstow Pk. BS16: Down 2B 46
Chepstow Rd. BS4: Know 4A 77
Chepstow Wlk. BS31: Key 2F 89
Chequers Cl. BS30: Old C 1E 83
Chequers Ct. BS32: Brad S 1C 26
Cherington BS15: Han 4D 71
BS37: Yate 2F 31
Cherington Rd. BS10: W Trym 4E 41
Cheriton Pl. BS9: W Trym 4D 41
BS30: Old C 3E 73
Cherry Ct. BS1: Bris 1A 68
(off Barton St.)
Cherry Gdn. La. BS30: Bit, Old C . . .1D 83
Cherry Gdn. Rd. BS30: Bit 3D 83
Cherry Gdns. BS30: Bit 3E 83
Cherry Gro. BS16: Mang 5C 46
Cherry La. BS1: Bris 1A 68
Cherry Orchard La. BS5: St G 1B 70
Cherry Rd. BS37: Chip S 4C 16
BS41: L Ash 2B 74
Cherry Tree Cl. BS31: Key 3E 89
Cherrytree Cl. BS16: Fish 4E 61
Cherrytree Cres. BS16: Fish 4E 61
Cherrytree Rd. BS16: Fish 4E 61
Cherry Wood BS30: Old C 2D 83
Chertsey Rd. BS6: Redl 5D 57

Cherwell Rd. BS31: Key 3C **90**
Chesham Way BS15: K'wd 5F **61**
Cheshire Cl. BS37: Yate 2A **16**
Chesle Cl. BS20: P'head 3A **48**
Cheslefield BS20: P'head 3A **48**
Chesle Way BS20: P'head 3A **48**
Chessel Cl. BS32: Brad S 3E **9**
Chessel M. BS3: Bedm *1E 77*
      (off West St.)
Chessel St. BS3: Bedm 1D **77**
Chessington Av. BS14: H'gro 2D **87**
Chesterfield Av. BS6: Bris 4A **58**
Chesterfield Rd. BS6: Bris 4A **58**
  BS16: Down 1A **62**
CHESTER PARK 4E **61**
Chester Pk. BS5: W'hall 1A **70**
Chester Pk. Rd. BS16: Fish 4D **61**
      (not continuous)
Chester Rd. BS5: W'hall 5A **60**
Chesters BS30: C Hth 5C **72**
Chester St. BS5: E'tn 4D **59**
Chestertons, The BA2: B'ptn 2B **106**
      (not continuous)
Chestnut Cl. BS14: Stoc 2A **88**
Chestnut Ct. BS16: Mang 1C **62**
Chestnut Dr. BS37: Chip S 4C **16**
Chestnut Gro. BA2: Bath 1E **109**
Chestnut Ho. BS13: Hart 4F **85**
  BS16: Fish 5E **45**
Chestnut Rd. BS15: Soun 3B **62**
  BS16: Down 5F **45**
  BS41: L Ash 2D **75**
Chestnut Wlk. BS13: Bis 1C **84**
  BS31: Salt 4A **92**
Chestnut Way BS15: Soun 3B **62**
Chetwode Cl. BS10: Bren 5F **23**
Chevening Cl. BS34: Stok G 4F **25**
Cheviot Way BS30: Old C 4E **73**
Chewton Cl. BS16: Fish 3D **61**
CHEWTON KEYNSHAM 5A **90**
Chewton Rd. BS31: Key 5A **90**
Cheyne Rd. BS9: Stok B 5F **39**
Chichester Ho. BS4: St Ap 3B **70**
Chichester Way BS37: Yate 2F **15**
Childrens Av. BA1: Bath 2A **104**
  BS30: Old C 4E **73**
Chilton Rd. BA1: Bath 1D **105**
  BS4: Know 4C **78**
Chilwood Cl. BS37: Iron A 2A **14**
Chimney Steps BS2: Bris 3B **68**
Chine, The BS16: Stap 1F **59**
Chine Vw. BS16: Down 3B **46**
Chiphouse Rd. BS15: Soun 4B **62**
Chipperfield Dr. BS15: K'wd 5B **62**
Chipping Edge Ind. Est.
  BS37: Chip S 4D **17**
Chippings, The BS16: Stap 1F **59**
CHIPPING SODBURY 4D **17**
Chisbury St. BS5: Eastv 3E **59**
Chittening Ind. Est.
  BS11: Chit 1F **19**
Chittening Rd. BS11: Chit 1A **20**
Chock La. BS9: W Trym 4C **40**
Christchurch Av. BS16: Down 1F **61**
Christ Chu. Cotts. *BA1: Bath 1B 6*
      (off Julian Rd.)
Christchurch Hall BA1: Bath 1B **6**
Christchurch La. BS16: Down 5F **45**
Christchurch Rd. BS8: Clif 2C **66**
Christina Ter. BS8: Clif 4C **66**
Christmas Steps
  BS1: Bris 2B **4** (2F **67**)
Christmas St. BS1: Bris . . .2B **4** (2F **67**)
Chubb Cl. BS30: Bar C 4B **72**
Church Av. BS5: E'tn 5D **59**
  BS9: Stok B 2A **56**
  BS30: Warm 2E **73**
Church Cl. BA1: Bathf 5D **99**
  BA2: B'ptn 5B **98**
  BS10: Hen 1A **40**

Church Cl. BS20: P'head 1F **49**
  BS36: Fram C 5D **13**
Churchdown Wlk. BS11: Shire . . .1A **54**
Church Dr. BS5: St G 1A **70**
Church Farm Bus. Pk. BA2: Cor . . .3C **100**
Churchfarm Cl. BS37: Yate 2B **16**
Church Farm Paddock BS30: Bit . . .5F **83**
Church Farm Rd. BS16: Emer G . . .5D **47**
Church Hill BS4: Brisl 2F **79**
Churchill Cl. BS30: Bar C 4C **72**
Churchill Dr. BS9: W Trym 4F **39**
Churchill Hall BS9: Stok B 3B **56**
Churchill Rd. BS4: Brisl 5E **69**
Churchlands Rd. BS3: Bedm 2D **77**
Church La. BA1: Bathe 3B **98**
  BA2: Bath 1E **111**
  BA2: Mon C 5F **111**
  BS1: Bris 4E **5** (3A **68**)
  BS3: Bedm 5F **67**
      (not continuous)
  BS5: St G 1F **69**
  BS8: Clif 3D **67**
  BS10: Hen 1A **40**
  BS14: Whit 4D **87**
  BS16: Down, Ham 1A **46**
      (not continuous)
  BS30: Bit 5F **83**
  BS36: Coal H 2E **29**
  BS36: Wint 2E **27**
  BS41: L Ash 1E **75**
Church Leaze BS11: Shire 5F **37**
Church Mdws. BS14: Whit 4E **87**
Church Pde. BS4: Brisl 2A **80**
Church Path BS2: Bris 4B **58**
  BS3: Bedm 1E **77**
  BS7: Bris 4B **58**
Church Path Rd. BS20: Pill 2E **53**
Church Path Steps BS8: Clif 4C **66**
Church Pl. BS20: Pill 2E **53**
Church Rd. BA1: W'ton 1E **103**
  BA2: C Down 4D **111**
  BS3: Bedm 5E **67**
  BS5: Redf, St G 2E **69**
  BS7: Hor 5A **42**
  BS8: Abb L 1C **64**
  BS8: L Wds 3F **65**
  BS9: Stok B 3F **55**
  BS9: W Trym 4C **40**
  BS13: Bis 2B **84**
  BS14: Whit 3D **87**
  BS15: Han 4D **71**
  BS15: K'wd 1A **72**
  BS16: Fren 4D **45**
  BS16: Soun 3F **61**
  BS20: Eas 2C **52**
  BS20: P'bry 2A **52**
  BS30: Bit 4F **83**
  BS32: Alm 1C **8**
  BS34: Fil 5C **24**
  BS34: Stok G 4A **26**
  BS36: Fram C 4C **12**
  BS36: Wint D 4A **28**
  BS37: Yate 2A **16**
      (not continuous)
  BS41: Dun 5A **84**
Church Rd. Nth. BS20: P'head 1F **49**
Church Rd. Sth. BS20: P'head 2F **49**
Church St. *BA1: Bath 4C 6*
      (off York St.)
  BA1: Bathf 5D **99**
  BA1: W'ly 1B **96**
  BA1: W'ton 1D **103**
  BA2: Bath 1D **111**
  BS1: Bris 4E **5** (3A **68**)
  BS5: Bar H 3D **69**
  BS5: E'tn 5D **59**
Church Vw. *BS15: K'wd 1A 72*
      (off High St.)
  BS16: Down 1F **61**
  BS32: Alm 1B **8**
  BS34: Fil 5C **24**

Church Wlk. BS20: Pill 2E **53**
Churchward Cl. BS15: Han 4C **70**
Churchward Rd. BS37: Yate 2D **15**
Churchways BS14: Whit 3E **87**
Churchways Av. BS7: Hor 5A **42**
Churchways Cres. BS7: Hor 5A **42**
Churston Cl. BS14: Whit 4C **86**
Cineworld Cinema
  Whitchurch 1A **86**
Circle, The BA2: Bath 2D **109**
Circuit 32 BS5: E'tn 1D **69**
Circular Rd. BS9: Stok B 4F **55**
Circus, The BA1: Bath 1B **6** (3B **104**)
Circus M. BA1: Bath 1A **6** (3B **104**)
Circus Pl. BA1: Bath 1A **6** (3B **104**)
      (not continuous)
City Academy, The *1E 69*
      (within Bristol Sports Cen.)
City Bus. Pk. BS5: E'tn 2C **68**
City Mus. & Art Gallery . . .1A **4** (2E **67**)
City of Bristol Gymnastics Cen. . . .3A **86**
City Rd. BS2: Bris 1A **68**
City Vw. *BA1: Bath 2C 104*
      (off Camden Rd.)
City Vw. Apartments *BS5: Bar H . . .2D 69*
      (off Chancery St.)
Clamp, The BS30: Old C 1E **83**
Clanage Rd. BS3: Bwr A 5A **66**
Clan Ho. BA2: Bath 1F **7** (3D **105**)
Clapton Drove BS20: Clap G 5E **49**
CLAPTON IN GORDANO 5A **50**
Clapton La.
  BS20: Clap G, P'head 3F **49**
Clapton Wlk. BS9: Sea M 1E **55**
Clara Cross La. BA2: Odd D 4A **110**
Clare Av. BS7: B'stn 3E **57**
Clare Gdns. BA2: Odd D 4F **109**
Claremont Av. BS7: B'stn 3E **57**
Claremont Bldgs. *BA1: Bath 1C 104*
Claremont Ct. BS9: Henle 1C **55**
Claremont Rd. BA1: Bath 1D **105**
  BS7: B'stn 3F **57**
Claremont St. BS5: E'tn 5C **58**
Claremont Ter. *BA1: Bath 1D 105*
      (off Camden Rd.)
  BS5: St G 2F **69**
Claremont Vs. *BA1: Bath 1C 104*
      (off Camden Rd.)
Clarence Av. BS16: Stap H 1A **62**
Clarence Ct. *BS15: K'wd 5D 61*
      (off Clarence Rd.)
Clarence Gdns. BS16: Stap H 1A **62**
Clarence Ho. *BS15: K'wd 5D 61*
      (off Clarence Rd.)
Clarence Pl. BA1: Bath 3D **103**
  BS2: Bris 1E **67**
Clarence Rd. BS1: Bris 5F **5** (4A **68**)
  BS2: Bris 2C **68**
  BS15: K'wd 5D **61**
  BS16: Down 1F **61**
Clarence St. BA1: Bath 2C **104**
Clarence Ter. BA2: Clav D 1F **111**
Clarendon M. BS16: Fren 3D **45**
Clarendon Rd. BA2: Bath 5D **105**
  BS6: Redl 4E **57**
Clarendon Vs. BA2: Bath 5D **105**
Clare Rd. BS5: Eastv 4D **59**
  BS6: Cot 5F **57**
  BS15: K'wd 2C **61**
Clare St. BS1: Bris 3B **4** (3F **67**)
  BS5: Redf 1E **69**
Clarke Dr. BS16: B'hll 4B **44**
Clarken Coombe BS41: L Ash 1B **74**
Clarke St. BS3: Bedm 5F **67**
Clark St. BS5: E'tn 1C **68**
Clatworthy Dr. BS14: H'gro 5C **78**
Claude Av. BA2: Bath 5E **103**
Claude Ter. BA2: Bath 5E **103**

Claude Va. BA2: Bath 5E **103**
Clavell Rd. BS10: Hen 1B **40**
Claverham Rd. BS16: Fish 1C **60**
CLAVERTON 5D **107**
Claverton Bldgs. BA2: Bath 5D **7**
Claverton Ct. BA2: Clav D 1F **111**
Claverton Down Rd.
   BA2: Clav D, C Down
      . . . . .5A **106** & 3F **111**
Claverton Hill
   BA2: C'ton, Clav D 5B **106**
Claverton Manor 5C **106**
Claverton Pumping Station 5E **107**
Claverton Rd. BS31: Salt 4F **91**
Claverton Rd. W. BS31: Salt 4F **91**
Claverton St. BA2: Bath . . .5C **6** (5C **104**)
CLAY BOTTOM 4F **59**
Clay Bottom BS5: Eastv 4F **59**
Claydon Grn. BS14: Whit 4B **86**
Clayfield BS37: Yate 1A **16**
Clayfield Rd. BS4: Brisl 1A **80**
CLAY HILL 4A **60**
Clay Hill BS5: S'wll 4A **60**
Clay La. BS30: Bit 4F **83**
   BS34: Lit S 1D **25**
Claymore Cres. BS15: K'wd 5D **61**
Claypiece Rd. BS13: Withy 3B **84**
Claypit Hill BS37: Chip S 1D **33**
Clay Pit Rd. BS6: Henle 3C **56**
Claypool Rd. BS15: K'wd 2F **71**
CLAYS END 5F **101**
Clayton Cl. BS20: P'head 2A **50**
Clayton St. BS5: E'tn 1D **69**
   BS11: A'mth 2C **36**
Cleave St. BS2: Bris 4C **58**
Cleeve Av. BS16: Down 4A **46**
Cleeve Ct. BS16: Down 4F **45**
Cleevedale Rd.
   BA2: C Down 4C **110**
Cleeve Gdns. BS16: Down 4F **45**
Cleeve Grn. BA2: Bath 4B **102**
Cleeve Gro. BS31: Key 2F **89**
Cleeve Hill BS16: Down 4F **45**
Cleeve Hill Extension
   BS16: Down 5A **46**
Cleeve Lawns BS16: Down 4F **45**
Cleeve Lodge Cl. BS16: Down . . .5A **46**
Cleeve Lodge Rd. BS16: Down . .4A **46**
Cleeve Pk. Rd. BS16: Down 4F **45**
Cleeve Rd. BS4: Know 1D **79**
   BS16: Down 5A **46**
   BS16: Fren 3E **45**
   BS37: Yate 4A **16**
Cleeves Ct. BS30: L Grn 2B **82**
Cleeve Wood Pk. BS16: Down . . .3E **45**
Cleeve Wood Rd. BS16: Down . . .3E **45**
      (not continuous)
Clement St. BS2: Bris 1B **68**
Clermont Cl. BS34: Pat 5B **8**
Cleve Ct. *BS8: Clif* *3B 66*
      (off Cumberland Pl.)
   BS34: Fil 4D **25**
Clevedale BS16: Down 4F **45**
Clevedale Cl. BS16: Down 4F **45**
Clevedon La. BS20: Clap G 5A **50**
Clevedon Rd. BS7: B'stn 2F **57**
   BS8: Fail 1A **74**
   BS20: P'head 4E **49**
   BS41: L Ash 1A **74**
Clevedon Ter. BS6: Bris 1F **67**
Cleveland Cotts. BA1: Bath 2C **104**
Cleveland Ct. BA2: Bath 4E **105**
Cleveland Pl. BA1: Bath 2C **104**
Cleveland Pl. E. *BA1: Bath* *2C 104*
      (off Cleveland Pl.)
Cleveland Pl. W. *BA1: Bath* *2C 104*
      (off Cleveland Pl.)
Cleveland Reach BA1: Bath 2C **104**
Cleveland Row BA2: Bath 2D **105**
Cleveland Ter. *BA1: Bath* *2C 104*
      (off London Rd.)

Cleveland Wlk.
   BA2: Bath 4F **7** (4E **105**)
Cleve Rd. BS34: Fil 4C **24**
Cleweson Ri. BS14: Whit 4B **86**
Cliff Ct. Dr. BS16: Fren 4D **45**
Clifford Gdns. BS11: Shire 5A **38**
Clifford Rd. BS16: Fish 2E **61**
Clift Ho. Rd. BS3: Ash G 5B **66**
Clift Ho. Spur BS3: Ash G 5B **66**
CLIFTON 1C **66**
Clifton Arc. *BS8: Clif* *2C 66*
      (off Boyce's Av.)
Clifton Cl. BS8: Clif 2B **66**
Clifton College Sports Ground . .2D **65**
Clifton Down BS8: Clif 1B **66**
Clifton Down Rd. BS8: Clif 2B **66**
Clifton Down Shop. Cen.
   BS8: Clif 5D **57**
Clifton Down Station (Rail) 5D **57**
Clifton Hgts. BS8: Clif 2D **67**
Clifton High Gro. BS9: Stok B . . .1A **56**
Clifton Hill BS8: Clif 3C **66**
Clifton Hill Ho. BS8: Clif 3D **67**
Clifton Observatory and Camera Obscura
      . . . . .2B **66**
Clifton Pk. BS8: Clif 2C **66**
Clifton Pk. Rd. BS8: Clif 1B **66**
Clifton Pl. BS5: E'tn 1C **68**
Clifton Rd. BS8: Clif 2C **66**
Clifton Roman Catholic Cathedral
      . . . . .1C **66**
Clifton St. BS3: Bedm 1E **77**
   BS20: P'head 4E **49**
Clifton Suspension Bridge 2A **66**
Clifton Suspension Bridge (Toll)
      . . . . .2A **66**
Clifton Suspension Bridge Vis. Cen.
      . . . . .2B **66**
Clifton Va. BS8: Clif 3C **66**
Clifton V. Cl. BS8: Clif 3C **66**
Clifton Vw. BS3: Wind H 5B **68**
   BS13: Bis 3C **76**
CLIFTON WOOD 3C **66**
Clifton Wood Ct. BS8: Clif 3D **67**
Clifton Wood Cres. BS8: Clif 3D **67**
Clifton Wood Rd. BS8: Clif 3D **67**
Cliftonwood Ter. BS8: Clif 3C **66**
Clift Pl. BS1: Bris 5C **4** (4F **67**)
Clift Rd. BS3: Ash G 5C **66**
Clinton Rd. BS3: Bedm 2E **77**
Clive Rd. BS14: H'gro 4E **79**
Clockhouse M. BS20: P'head 5C **34**
Clocktower Yd. BS1: Bris . . .5F **5** (4B **68**)
Cloisters Ct. BS36: Wint 2A **28**
Cloisters Rd. BS36: Wint 2B **28**
Clonmel Rd. BS4: Know 3F **77**
Close, The BS10: Hen 3B **22**
   BS16: Fren 2B **44**
   BS16: Soun 3F **61**
   BS20: Wes 5B **48**
   BS34: Lit S 2E **25**
   BS34: Pat 4E **9**
   BS36: Coal H 2E **29**
Clothier Rd. BS4: Brisl 2B **80**
Clouds Hill Av. BS5: St G 1A **70**
Clouds Hill Rd. BS5: St G 1B **70**
Clovelly Cl. BS5: St G 1B **70**
Clovelly Rd. BS5: St G 1B **70**
Cloverdale Dr. BS30: L Grn 1C **82**
Cloverdown BS4: Know 3A **78**
Clover Ground BS9: W Trym 3D **41**
Cloverlea Bus. Cen. BS36: H'fld . .5E **29**
Cloverlea Rd. BS30: Old C 5E **73**
Clover Leaze BS32: Brad S 2F **25**
Clyde Av. BS31: Key 3B **90**
Clyde Gdns. BA2: Bath 4D **103**
   BS5: St G 3D **71**
Clyde Gro. BS34: Fil 1B **42**
Clyde La. BS6: Redl 4D **57**
Clyde M. BS6: Redl 4E **57**
Clyde Pk. BS6: Redl 4D **57**

Clyde Rd. BS4: Know 1C **78**
   BS6: Redl 4D **57**
   BS36: Fram C 5D **13**
Clydesdale Cl. BS14: H'gro 1C **86**
Clyde Ter. BS3: Bedm 1E **77**
   BS4: Know 1C **78**
Coach Ho. La. *BS5: St G* *1A 70*
      (off Beaconsfield Rd.)
Coaley Rd. BS11: Shire 1F **53**
COALPIT HEATH 2E **29**
Coalpit Rd. BA1: Bathe 3C **98**
Coalsack La. BS36: H'fld 5D **29**
Coalville Rd. BS36: Coal H 1F **29**
Coape Rd. BS14: Stoc 2B **88**
Coates Wlk. BS4: Know 1F **85**
Cobblestone M. BS8: Clif 2C **66**
Cob Ct. BS34: Stok G 5E **25**
Cobden Cen., The BS16: Emer G . .1C **46**
Cobden St. BS5: Redf 2D **69**
Coberley BS15: K'wd 3E **71**
Cobhorn Dr. BS13: Withy 3B **84**
Cobourg Rd. BS6: Bris 5B **58**
Coburg Vs. BA1: Bath 1C **104**
Cock Rd. BS15: K'wd 3A **72**
COCKSHOT HILL 4A **62**
CODRINGTON 5D **33**
Codrington Pl. BS8: Clif 2C **66**
Codrington Rd. BS7: B'stn 3F **57**
   BS37: W'lgh 5F **31**
Cody Ct. BS15: Han 4D **71**
Cogan Rd. BS16: Soun 3A **62**
Cogmill La. BS36: Fram C 1B **12**
   BS37: Iron A 1B **12**
Cogsall Rd. BS14: Stoc 1B **88**
Colbourne Rd. BA2: Odd D 4F **109**
Colchester Cres. BS4: Know 5F **77**
Coldharbour La.
   BS16: Fren, Stap 2A **44**
Coldharbour Rd. BS6: Redl 3D **57**
Coldpark Gdns. BS13: Withy 2A **84**
Coldpark Rd. BS13: Withy 2A **84**
Coldrick Cl. BS14: Whit 4B **86**
Colebrook Rd. BS15: K'wd 1E **71**
Coleford Rd. BS10: S'mead 3F **41**
Cole Mead BS13: Bis 2D **85**
Coleridge Rd. BS5: Eastv 3E **59**
Cole Rd. BS2: Bris 3D **69**
Colesborne Cl. BS37: Yate 5F **15**
Coleshill Dr. BS13: Hart 2D **85**
College Av. BS16: Fish 1C **60**
College Ct. BS8: Clif 1C **66**
   BS16: Fish 1C **60**
College Flds. BS8: Clif 1B **66**
College Grn. BS1: Bris 3A **4** (3E **67**)
College Ho. *BS1: Bris* *3A 4*
      (off Orchard St.)
College La. BS1: Bris 3A **4**
College Pk. Dr. BS10: Hen 2B **40**
College Rd. BA1: L'dwn, Bath . . .5A **96**
   BS8: Clif 1B **66**
   BS9: W Trym 4C **40**
   BS16: Fish 1C **60**
College Sq. BS1: Bris 4A **4** (3E **67**)
College St. BS1: Bris 4A **4** (3E **67**)
College Vw. BA1: Bath 1C **104**
College Way BS34: Fil 4C **24**
Collett Cl. BS15: Han 4D **71**
Collett Way BS37: Yate 2E **15**
Colliers Break BS16: Emer G 1D **63**
Colliers Gdns. BS16: Fish 1E **61**
      (Halbrow Cres.)
   BS16: Fish 1D **61**
      (Sherston Cl.)
Collier's La. BA1: Charl 3A **96**
Collier's Pl. BS16: Soun 4F **61**
Collingwood Av. BS15: K'wd 5A **62**
Collingwood Cl. BS31: Salt 5A **92**
Collingwood Rd. BS6: Redl 5D **57**
Collin Rd. BS4: Brisl 5F **69**
Collins Av. BS34: Lit S 2E **25**
Collins Bldgs. BS31: Salt 4A **92**

Collinson Rd. BS13: Hart 2D **85**
Collins St. BS11: A'mth 3D **37**
Colliter Cres. BS3: Bedm 2C **76**
Colne Grn. BS31: Key 3C **90**
Colonnades, The BA1: Bath 4B **6**
Colston Av. BS1: Bris 3B **4** (3F **67**)
Colston Cen. BS1: Bris 2B **4**
                      (off Colston St.)
Colston Cl. BS16: Soun 3F **61**
    BS36: Wint D 4A **28**
Colston Ct. BS7: B'stn 3F **57**
Colston Dale BS16: Stap 2A **60**
Colston Fort BS6: Bris 1F **67**
                 (off Montague Pl.)
Colston Hall 2B **4** (2F **67**)
Colston Hill BS16: Stap 2F **59**
Colston M. BS6: Bris 5A **58**
Colston Pde. BS1: Bris 5D **5** (4A **68**)
Colston Pl. BS1: Bris 4E **5** (3A **68**)
Colston Rd. BS5: E'tn 5E **59**
Colston's Almshouses BS2: Bris . . .1A **4**
Colston St. BS1: Bris 2B **4** (2F **67**)
    BS16: Soun 3F **61**
Colston Yd. BS2: Bris 1B **4**
                 (off Colston St.)
Colthurst Dr. BS15: Han 4A **72**
COLT'S GREEN 5F **17**
Colwyn Rd. BS5: E'tn 5E **59**
Combe Av. BS20: P'head 5B **34**
COMBE DOWN 4D **111**
Combe Flds. BS20: P'head 5B **34**
Combe Gro. BA1: Bath 2D **103**
Combe Hay La.
    BA2: C Hay, Odd D 5E **109**
Combe Pk. BA1: Bath 3E **103**
Combe Rd. BA2: C Down 4D **111**
    BS20: P'head 1F **49**
Combe Rd. Cl. BA2: C Down 4D **111**
Combe Royal Cres. BA2: Clav D . .5F **105**
Combeside BA2: Bath 2C **110**
Comb Paddock BS9: W Trym 4D **41**
Comfortable Pl. BA1: Bath 3A **104**
Commercial Rd. BS1: Bris 4F **67**
Common, The BS16: Fren 4D **45**
    BS34: Pat 4D **9**
Common E., The BS34: Brad S . . .4E **9**
Commonfield Rd. BS11: Law W . . .2D **39**
Common La. BS8: Fail 3D **53**
    BS20: Eas 3D **53**
Common Mead La. BS16: Ham . . .2C **44**
Common Rd. BS15: Han 1D **81**
    BS36: Wint 1B **28**
Como Ct. BS20: P'head 1A **48**
                 (off Kilkenny Pl.)
Compass Ct. BA1: Bath 1A **6**
Compton Dr. BS9: Sea M 4E **39**
Compton Grn. BS31: Key 3A **90**
Compton Lodge BS6: Redl 5D **57**
             (off Hampton Rd.)
Compton St. BS5: Redf 2E **69**
Comyn Wlk. BS16: Fish 1C **60**
Concorde Dr. BS10: S'mead 2D **41**
Concorde Ho. BS34: Fil 1B **42**
Concorde Rd. BS34: Pat 1A **24**
Concorde St. BS1: Bris 1E **5** (2A **68**)
Concourse, The BS4: Brisl 2A **80**
Condor Ho. BS7: L'lze 4E **43**
Condover Rd. BS4: Brisl 1B **80**
Conduit Pl. BS2: Bris 5C **58**
Conduit Rd. BS2: Bris 5C **58**
Coneygree BS13: Bis 2B **84**
Conference Av. BS20: P'head 1A **50**
Conference Cl. BS20: P'head 2B **50**
Congleton Rd. BS5: W'hall 5F **59**
CONHAM .4B **70**
Conham Hill BS15: Han 4C **70**
Conham Rd. BS5: St G 4B **70**
    BS15: St G 4B **70**
Conham Va. BS15: St G 4B **70**
             (not continuous)

Conifer Cl. BS16: Fish 5F **45**
    BS36: Fram C 4C **12**
Coniston Av. BS9: W Trym 5A **40**
Coniston Cl. BS30: Old C 3F **73**
Coniston Rd. BS34: Pat 5A **8**
Connaught Rd. BS4: Know 4A **78**
Connection Rd. BA2: Bath 4C **102**
Constable Cl. BS31: Key 1B **90**
Constable Rd. BS7: L'lze 5D **43**
Constantine Av. BS34: Stok G 3A **26**
Constitution Hill BS8: Clif 3C **66**
Contempóris BS8: Clif 2C **66**
             (off Merchants Rd.)
Convent Cl. BS10: Hen 5F **21**
Convocation Av. BA2: Clav D 5B **106**
Conway Grn. BS31: Key 4C **90**
Conway Rd. BS4: Brisl 5E **69**
Conygre Grn. BS34: Fil 4D **25**
Conygre Rd. BS34: Fil 5C **24**
Cook Cl. BS30: Old C 5E **73**
Cooks Cl. BS32: Brad S 2E **9**
Cooks Folly Rd. BS9: Stok B 3F **55**
Cooks La. BS36: H'fld 5F **29**
Cooksley Rd. BS5: Redf 1E **69**
Cook St. BS11: A'mth 3D **37**
Cookworthy Cl. BS5: Bar H 3D **69**
Coombe Bri. Av. BS9: Stok B 5F **39**
Coombe Brook Cl. BS15: K'wd . . .5D **61**
Coombe Brook La. BS5: Eastv 4A **60**
Coombe Cl. BS10: Hen 5F **21**
    BS20: P'head 1F **49**
Coombe Dale BS9: Sea M 5E **39**
COOMBE DINGLE 4F **39**
Coombe Dingle Sports Complex
    . . . . .4A **40**
Coombe Gdns. BS9: Stok B 5A **40**
Coombe La. BS8: Fail 5B **52**
    BS9: Stok B, W Trym 4F **39**
    BS20: Eas 4C **52**
Coombe Rd. BS5: Eastv 4E **59**
Coombe Rocke BS9: Stok B 4F **39**
Coombes Way BS30: Old C 5F **73**
Coombe Way BS10: Hen 2B **40**
Cooperage La. BS3: Bris 4D **67**
Cooperage Rd. BS5: Redf 2F **69**
Co-operation Rd. BS5: E'tn 5E **59**
Cooper Rd. BS9: W Trym 4B **40**
Coopers Dr. BS37: Yate 1B **16**
Coots, The BS14: Stoc 1A **88**
Copeland Dr. BS14: Whit 2D **87**
Copford La. BS41: L Ash 3D **75**
Copley Ct. BS15: Han 4A **72**
Copley Gdns. BS7: L'lze 5D **43**
Coppice, The BS13: Withy 3A **84**
    BS32: Brad S 1A **26**
Copseland BA2: Clav D 5F **105**
Copse Rd. BS4: Know 1D **79**
    BS31: Salt 3E **91**
Copthorne Cl. BS14: H'gro 2D **87**
Corbet Cl. BS11: Law W 1D **39**
Corbett Cl. BS37: Yate 1B **16**
Corbett Ho. BS5: Bar H 2E **69**
Cordwell Wlk. BS10: Hor 4F **41**
Corey Cl. BS2: Bris 5B **58**
Corfe Cres. BS31: Key 3A **90**
Corfe Pl. BS30: Will 3D **83**
Corfe Rd. BS4: Know 5F **77**
Coriander Dr. BS32: Brad S 2C **26**
Coriander Wlk. BS5: Eastv 4E **59**
Corinthian Ct. BS1: Bris 5E **5**
Corinium Cl. BS16: Emer G 5E **47**
Corkers Hill BS5: St G 3B **70**
Cork Pl. BA1: Bath 3F **103**
                 (off Cork St.)
Cork St. BA1: Bath 3F **103**
Cork Ter. BA1: Bath 3F **103**
Cornfield Cl. BS32: Brad S 4E **9**
Cornhill Dr. BS14: H'gro 5C **78**
Cornish Gro. BS14: Stoc 1A **88**
Cornish Rd. BS14: Stoc 1A **88**
Cornish Wlk. BS14: Stoc 1A **88**

Cornleaze BS13: Bis 2C **84**
Corn St. BA1: Bath 4B **6** (4B **104**)
    BS1: Bris 3C **4** (3F **67**)
Cornwall Cres. BS37: Yate 2B **16**
Cornwallis Av. BS8: Clif 3C **66**
Cornwallis Cres. BS8: Clif 3B **66**
Cornwallis Gro. BS8: Clif 3B **66**
Cornwallis Ho. BS8: Clif 3C **66**
Cornwall Rd. BS7: B'stn 2F **57**
Coromandel Hgts. BA1: Bath 2B **104**
           (off John Slessor Ct.)
Coronation Av. BA2: Bath 2E **109**
    BS16: Fish 2C **60**
    BS31: Key 3F **89**
Coronation Cl. BS30: C Hth 4C **72**
Coronation Cotts. BA1: Bathe 4B **98**
Coronation Pl. BS1: Bris 3C **4** (3F **67**)
Coronation Rd. BA1: Bath 3F **103**
    BS3: Ash G, Bris 5C **66**
    BS15: K'wd 2B **72**
    BS16: Down 1A **62**
    BS30: C Hth 4C **72**
Corridor, The
    BA1: Bath 3C **6** (4C **104**)
Corsley Wlk. BS4: Know 4B **78**
CORSTON 3D **101**
Corston Dr. BA2: New L 4D **101**
Corston La. BA2: Cor 3C **100**
Corston Vw. BA2: Odd D 3E **109**
Corum Office Pk. BS30: Warm 2E **73**
Cossham Rd. BS5: St G 1F **69**
Cossham St. BS16: Mang 1C **62**
Cossham Wlk. BS5: St G 5C **60**
Cossington Rd. BS4: Know 3B **78**
Cossins Rd. BS6: Redl 3D **57**
Costiland Dr. BS13: Bis 1B **84**
Cote Bank Ho. BS9: W Trym 4D **41**
Cote Dr. BS9: W Trym 2C **56**
Cote Ho. La. BS9: W Trym 1C **56**
Cote La. BS9: W Trym 1C **56**
Cote Lea Pk. BS9: W Trym 4C **40**
Cote Paddock BS9: W Trym 2B **56**
Cote Pk. BS9: W Trym 5A **40**
Cote Rd. BS9: W Trym 1C **56**
COTHAM .5E **57**
Cotham Brow BS6: Cot 5F **57**
Cotham Gdns. BS6: Cot 5D **57**
Cotham Gro. BS6: Cot 5F **57**
Cotham Hill BS6: Cot 5D **57**
Cotham Lawn Apartments
    BS6: Cot 1E **67**
            (off Cotham Lawn Rd.)
Cotham Lawn Rd. BS6: Cot 1E **67**
Cotham Pk. BS6: Cot 5E **57**
Cotham Pk. Nth. BS6: Cot 5E **57**
Cotham Pl. BS6: Cot 5E **57**
Cotham Rd. BS6: Cot 1E **67**
Cotham Rd. Sth. BS6: Cot 1F **67**
Cotham Side BS6: Cot 5F **57**
Cotham Va. BS6: Cot 5E **57**
Cotman Wlk. BS7: L'lze 5D **43**
Cotrith Gro. BS10: Hen 5A **22**
Cotswold Cl. BS20: P'head 2A **50**
Cotswold Ct. BS16: Fren 2A **44**
    BS37: Chip S 4D **17**
Cotswold Rd. BA2: Bath 1F **109**
    BS3: Wind H 1F **77**
    BS37: Chip S 5D **17**
Cotswold Vw. BA2: Bath 5D **103**
    BS15: K'wd 4F **61**
    BS34: Fil 5C **24**
Cottage Gdns. BS5: St G 2C **70**
Cottage Pl. BA1: Bath 5E **97**
    BS2: Bris 1F **67**
Cottages, The BS48: Bar G 5B **74**
Cottington Ct. BS15: Han 4A **72**
Cottisford Rd. BS5: Eastv 2D **59**
Cottle Gdns. BS14: Stoc 1B **88**
Cottle Rd. BS14: Stoc 1B **88**
Cotton Mead BA2: Cor 3D **101**

Cotton Mill La. BS5: Bar H 3E 69
Cottonwood Dr. BS30: L Grn 1C 82
Cottrell Av. BS15: K'wd 4D 61
Cottrell Rd. BS5: Eastv 3E 59
Coulson Ho. BS7: B'stn 2B 58
Coulsons Cl. BS14: Whit 4C 86
Coulson's Rd. BS14: Whit 4B 86
Coulson Wlk. BS15: K'wd 4E 61
Counterpool Rd. BS15: K'wd 2E 71
Counterslip BS1: Bris 3D 5 (3A 68)
Counterslip Gdns. BS14: H'gro 1E 87
Countess Wlk. BS16: Stap 5F 43
County St. BS4: Wind H 5C 68
County Way BS34: Stok G 4C 26
Court Av. BS34: Stok G 3B 26
Court Cl. BS7: Hor 4A 42
   BS20: P'head 2F 49
Courtenay Cres. BS4: Know 5F 77
Courtenay Rd. BS31: Key, Salt 5C 90
Court Farm Rd. BS14: Whit 4B 86
   BS30: L Grn 3F 81
Courtfield Gro. BS16: Fish 2C 60
Court Hay BS20: Eas 2C 52
Courtlands BS31: Key 2A 90
   BS32: Brad S 4E 9
Courtlands La. BS3: Bwr A 5A 66
Court La. BA1: Bathf 5D 99
   BS16: Stap H 2A 62
Courtney Rd. BS15: K'wd 2A 72
Courtney Way BS15: K'wd 2B 72
Court Rd. BS7: Hor 4B 42
   BS15: K'wd 2F 71
   BS30: Old C 1D 83
   BS36: Fram C 5B 12
Courtside BS15: K'wd 2B 72
Courtside M. BS6: Cot 5E 57
Courtyard, The BS32: Brad S 2F 9
Cousins Cl. BS10: Hen 5F 21
Cousins La. BS5: St G 2B 70
Cousins M. BS4: St Ap 3B 70
Cousins Way BS16: Emer G 3D 47
Couzens Cl. BS37: Chip S 3D 17
Couzens Pl. BS34: Stok G 3B 26
Coventry Wlk. BS4: St Ap 3B 70
Cowdray Rd. BS4: Know 5F 77
Cowhorn Hill BS30: Old C 4E 73
Cow La. BA1: Bath 3A 104
Cowler Wlk. BS13: Withy 3B 84
Cowling Dr. BS14: Stoc 2E 87
Cowling Rd. BS14: Stoc 2F 87
Cowmead Wlk. BS2: Bris 5C 58
Cowper Rd. BS6: Redl 5E 57
Cowper St. BS5: Redf 2E 69
Cox Ct. BS30: Bar C 5B 72
Coxley Dr. BA1: Bath 5D 97
Crabtree La. BS41: Dun 5A 84
Craddock Cl. BS5: Eastv 4F 59
Cranberry Wlk. BS9: C Din 3E 39
Cranbourne Rd. BS34: Pat 1B 24
Cranbrook Rd. BS6: Redl 2E 57
Crandale Rd. BA2: Bath 5F 103
Crandell Cl. BS10: Hen 4B 22
Crane Cl. BS15: Warm 1D 73
Cranford Ct. BS9: Henle 5D 41
Cranham BS37: Yate 1E 31
Cranham Cl. BS15: Soun 4B 62
Cranham Dr. BS34: Pat 4E 9
Cranham Rd. BS10: W Trym 3E 41
Cranhill Rd. BA1: W'ton 2F 103
Cranleigh BA2: S'ske 5B 110
Cranleigh Ct. Rd. BS37: Yate 3F 15
Cranleigh Gdns. BS9: Stok B 2A 56
Cranleigh Rd. BS14: Whit 2D 87
Cranmore Av. BS31: Key 1F 89
Cranmore Cres. BS10: S'mead 2F 41
Cranmore Pl. BA2: Odd D 5F 109
Cranside Av. BS6: Redl 2E 57
Cransley Cres. BS9: Henle 4E 41
Crantock Av. BS13: Bis 4D 77

Crantock Dr. BS32: Alm 1D 9
Crantock Rd. BS37: Yate 4F 15
Cranwell Gro. BS14: Whit 2C 86
Cranwells Pk. BA1: W'ton 2F 103
Crapnell Cl. BS15: K'wd 1A 72
Craven Cl. BS30: Bar C 4B 72
Craven Way BS30: Bar C, C Hth . . .4B 72
Craydon Gro. BS14: Stoc 2F 87
Craydon Rd. BS14: Stoc 2F 87
Craydon Wlk. BS14: Stoc 2F 87
Create Environment Cen. 4B 66
Crediton Cres. BS4: Know 3B 78
Crescent, The BS1: Bris 4E 67
   BS9: Henle 5E 41
   BS9: Sea M 5E 39
   BS16: Fren 2B 44
   BS16: Soun 3F 61
Crescent Cen., The BS1: Bris 3E 5
Crescent Gdns.
   BA1: Bath 2A 6 (3A 104)
Crescent La. BA1: Bath 1A 6 (2A 104)
Crescent Pl. M. BA2: Odd D 4F 109
Crescent Rd. BS16: Fish 5E 45
Crescent Vw. BA2: Bath 5A 6 (5B 104)
Crest, The BS4: Brisl 2E 79
Creswicke Av. BS15: Han 4E 71
Creswicke Rd. BS4: Know 5F 77
CREW'S HOLE 2B 70
Crews Hole Rd. BS5: St G 2A 70
CRIBBS CAUSEWAY 3C 22
Cribbs C'way. BS10: Hen, Pat 4B 22
   BS10: Pat 1D 23
Cribbs C'way. Cen. BS10: Hen 3C 22
Cribbs C'way. Regional Shop. Cen.
   BS34: Pat 2F 23
Cribbs C'way. Retail Pk.
   BS34: Pat 2E 23
Cricket La. BS10: W Trym 3C 40
Cricklade Rd. BS7: B'stn 2A 58
Cripps Rd. BS3: Bedm 1E 77
Crispin Way BS15: Soun 4B 62
Crockerne Dr. BS20: Pill 3E 53
Crockerne Ho. BS20: Pill 2E 53
   (off Underbanks)
Croft, The BS16: Mang 1B 62
   BS30: Old C 1E 83
Croft Av. BS16: Stap 2E 59
Croft Cl. BS30: Bit 4F 83
Crofters Wlk. BS32: Brad S 5F 9
Crofton Av. BS7: Hor 5B 42
Crofton Flds. BS36: Wint 2A 28
Crofton M. BS15: K'wd 2A 72
Croft Rd. BA1: Bath 1D 105
CROFTS END 5A 60
Crofts End Ind. Est. BS5: S'wll 5A 60
Crofts End Rd. BS5: S'wll 5A 60
Croft Vw. BS9: Henle 5E 41
Crokeswood Wlk. BS11: Law W . . .2C 38
Crome Rd. BS7: L'lze 4D 43
Cromer Rd. BS5: E'tn 4E 59
Cromwell Cl. BS15: Han 4A 72
Cromwell Rd. BS5: St G 1C 70
   BS6: Bris 4F 57
Cromwells Hide BS16: Stap 1A 60
Cromwell St. BS3: Bedm 1E 77
Crookes Hill BS16: Down 5F 45
Cropthorne Rd. BS7: Hor 2C 42
Cropthorne Rd. Sth. BS7: Hor 3C 42
Crosby Row BS8: Clif 3C 66
Crosscombe Dr. BS13: Hart 4D 85
Crosscombe Wlk. BS13: Hart 4D 85
Cross Elms La. BS9: Stok B 1A 56
Crossfield Rd. BS16: Soun 3A 62
Cross Lanes BS20: Pill 2D 53
Crossleys BS15: Han 1E 81
Crossley Cl. BS36: Wint 1B 28
Crossley Farm Bus. Cen.
   BS36: Wint 1A 28
Crossman Av. BS36: Wint 3A 28
Cross St. BS15: K'wd 5E 61
   BS31: Key 5B 82

Cross Tree Gro. BS32: Brad S 5F 9
Cross Wlk. BS14: H'gro 1C 86
Crossways Ct. BS16: Down 5A 46
Crossways Rd. BS4: Know 3C 78
Crowe Hall Garden 1E 111
Crow La. BS1: Bris 3C 4 (3F 67)
   BS10: Hen 1B 40
Crowley Way BS11: A'mth 1D 37
Crowndale Rd. BS4: Know 1C 78
Crown Gdns. BS30: Warm 2D 73
Crown Hill BA1: W'ton 1E 103
   BS5: S'wll 1B 70
Crown Hill Wlk. BS5: S'wll 5B 60
Crown Ind. Est. BS30: Warm 2E 73
Crown La. BS16: Soun 3F 61
Crownleaze BS16: Soun 3F 61
Crown Rd. BA1: W'ton 1D 103
   BS15: K'wd 4F 61
   BS30: Warm 3E 73
Crown Way BS30: Warm 2E 73
Crows Gro. BS32: Brad S 2F 9
Crowther Pk. BS7: L'lze 2C 58
Crowther Rd. BS7: L'lze 2C 58
Crowthers Av. BS37: Yate 2A 16
Crowther St. BS3: Bedm 1D 77
Croxham Orchard BA1: Bathe 3B 98
Croydon Ho. BS5: E'tn 1D 69
Croydon St. BS5: E'tn 1D 69
Crunnis, The BS32: Brad S 2A 26
Crusader Ho. BS1: Bris 2B 4
Crusty La. BS20: Pill 1E 53
Crystal Way BS32: Brad S 5A 10
Cube, The 1F 67
   (off Princess Row)
Cuckoo La. BS36: Wint D 5B 28
Cuffington Av. BS4: Brisl 5F 69
Culverhay Sports Cen. 3D 109
Culverhill Rd. BS37: Chip S 4C 16
Culvers Cl. BS31: Key 1A 90
Culvers Rd. BS31: Key 1A 90
Culver St. BS1: Bris 3A 4 (3E 67)
Culvert, The BS32: Brad S 5F 9
Culvert Av. BS37: Yate 4D 15
Culverwell Rd. BS13: Withy 3C 84
Cumberland Basin Rd. BS8: Clif . . .4B 66
Cumberland Cl. BS1: Bris 4C 66
Cumberland Ct. BS1: Bris 4D 67
Cumberland Gro. BS6: Bris 4B 58
Cumberland Ho. BA1: Bath 3A 6
Cumberland Pl. BS8: Clif 3B 66
Cumberland Rd. BS1: Bris 4B 66
Cumberland Row
   BA1: Bath 3A 6 (4B 104)
Cumberland St. BS2: Bris 1A 68
Cunningham Gdns. BS16: Fish 1D 61
Cunnington Cl. BS30: Will 3C 82
Curland Gro. BS14: Whit 2D 87
Curlew Cl. BS16: B'hll 5B 44
Curlew Pl. BS20: P'bry, P'head 5E 35
Curtis La. BS34: Stok G 5C 26
Custom Cl. BS14: H'gro 5C 78
Custom Ho., The BS1: Bris 5C 4
Cutler Rd. BS13: Bis 1B 84
Cutters Row BS3: Bedm 5A 68
   (off York Rd.)
Cynder Way BS16: Emer G 2C 46
Cynthia Rd. BA2: Bath 5E 103
Cynthia Vs. BA2: Bath 5E 103
Cypress Cl. BS9: Stok B 3F 55
Cypress Gdns. BS8: L Wds 3A 66
Cypress Gro. BS9: Henle 5E 41
Cyrus Ct. BS16: Emer G 4D 47

D

Dafford's Bldgs. BA1: Bath 5E 97
Dafford's Pl. BA1: Bath 5E 97
   (off Dafford St.)
Dafford St. BA1: Bath 5E 97
Dahlia Gdns. BA2: Bath . . .1F 7 (3D 105)

Daisey Bank BA2: Bath 1D 111
Daisy Rd. BS5: E'tn 4E 59
Dakin Cl. BS4: Know 3A 78
Dakota Dr. BS14: Whit 3C 86
Dalby Av. BS3: Bedm 5F 67
Dale St. BS5: St G 1B 70
Dalkeith Av. BS15: K'wd 5E 61
Dalrymple Rd. BS2: Bris 5A 58
Dalston Rd. BS3: Bris 5D 67
Dalton Sq. BS2: Bris 1A 68
Dampier Rd. BS3: Ash G 1C 76
Danbury Cres. BS10: S'mead 2E 41
Danbury Wlk. BS10: S'mead 2E 41
Danby Ho. BS7: L'lze 1C 58
Dancey Mead BS13: Bis 5B 76
Dandy's Mdw. BS20: P'head 1A 50
Dangerfield Av. BS13: Bis 1B 84
Daniel M. BA2: Bath 1E 7 (3D 105)
Daniel St. BA2: Bath 1E 7 (3D 105)
Dapp's Hill BS31: Key 2B 90
Dapwell La. BS31: Q Char 5C 88
Dark La. BA2: B'ptn 1B 106
BS9: W Trym 3C 40
Darley Cl. BS10: Hen 5F 21
Darlington M. BA2: Bath . .2E 7 (3D 105)
Darlington Pl. BA2: Bath . .4F 7 (4D 105)
Darlington Rd.
  BA2: Bath 1F 7 (3D 105)
Darlington St. BA2: Bath . .2E 7 (3D 105)
Darlington Wharf
  BA2: Bath 1F 7 (2D 105)
Darnley Av. BS7: Hor 5B 42
Dartmoor St. BS3: Bedm 5D 67
Dartmouth Av. BA2: Bath 5E 103
Dartmouth Wlk. BS31: Key 3F 89
Daubeny Cl. BS16: Fish 1D 61
Davenport Cl. BS30: L Grn 2C 82
Daventry Rd. BS4: Know 3A 78
Davey St. BS2: Bris 5B 58
David Lloyd Leisure
  Bristol 1A 76
David's Rd. BS14: H'gro 5E 79
David St. BS2: Bris 2F 5 (2B 68)
David Thomas Ho. BS6: Bris 4A 58
Davies Dr. BS4: St Ap 4B 70
Davin Cres. BS20: Pill 3E 53
Davis Cl. BS30: Bar C 4B 72
Davis St. BS11: A'mth 3D 37
Dawes Ct. BS8: Clif 3B 66
  (off Cumberland Pl.)
Dawley Cl. BS36: Wint 1A 28
Dawlish Rd. BS3: Wind H 2F 77
Dawn Ri. BS15: K'wd 5B 62
Daws Ct. BS16: Fish 2D 61
Day Cres. BA2: Bath 4B 102
Days La. BS2: Bris 2C 68
Day's Rd. BS2: Bris 3C 68
  BS5: Bar H 3C 68
Days Rd. Commercial Cen.
  BS2: Bris 3C 68
Deacon Cl. BS36: Wint 3A 28
Deadmill La. BA1: Swa 4E 97
Dean Cl. BS15: Han 4C 70
Dean Ct. BS37: Yate 2D 15
Dean Cres. BS3: Bedm 5E 67
  (not continuous)
Deanery Rd. BS1: Bris 4A 4 (3E 67)
  BS15: Warm 1C 72
DEAN HILL 5B 94
Deanhill La. BA1: W'ton 5B 94
Dean La. BS3: Bedm 5E 67
Deanna Ct. BS16: Down 5A 46
Dean Rd. BS11: A'mth 3E 19
  BS37: Yate 2E 15
Deans, The BS20: P'head 2D 49
Dean's Ct. BS1: Bris 3A 4 (3E 67)
Deans Dr. BS5: S'wll 4C 60
Deans Mead BS11: Law W 3C 38
Dean St. BS2: Bris 1A 68
  BS3: Bedm 5E 67
Debeccas La. BS20: Eas 2D 53

De Clifford Rd. BS11: Law W 1E 39
Deep Coombe Rd. BS3: Bedm . . .2C 76
Deep Pit Rd. BS5: S'wll 5A 60
Deep St. BS1: Bris 1C 4 (2F 67)
Deerhurst BS15: K'wd 4A 62
  BS37: Yate 5E 15
Deering Cl. BS11: Law W 2D 39
Deerswood BS15: Soun 4C 62
Delabere Av. BS16: Fish 1D 61
De La Warre Ct. BS4: St Ap 3B 70
Delius Gro. BS4: Know 5F 77
Dell, The BS9: W Trym 1B 56
  BS30: Old C 4E 73
  BS32: Brad S 1A 26
Delvin Rd. BS10: W Trym 3E 41
De Montalt Pl. BA2: C Down 4D 111
Denbigh St. BS2: Bris 5B 58
Dene Cl. BS31: Key 4B 90
Dene Ct. BS14: Whit 3E 87
Denleigh Cl. BS14: Whit 3C 86
Denmark Av. BS1: Bris 3A 4 (3E 67)
Denmark Pl. BS7: B'stn 3A 58
Denmark Rd. BA2: Bath 4F 103
Denmark St. BS1: Bris 3A 4 (3E 67)
Dennor Pk. BS14: H'gro 5D 79
Denny Cl. BS20: P'head 1C 48
Denny Vw. BS20: P'head 1B 48
Dennyview Rd. BS8: Abb L 1B 64
Denston Dr. BS20: P'head 2A 50
Denston Wlk. BS13: Bis 5C 76
Denton Patch BS16: Emer G 4D 47
Dentwood Gro. BS9: C Din 4D 39
Derby Rd. BS7: B'stn 3A 58
Derby St. BS5: St G 1F 69
Derham Rd. BS13: Bis 2C 84
Dermot St. BS2: Bris 5B 58
Derricke Rd. BS14: Stoc 1B 88
Derrick Rd. BS15: K'wd 1F 71
Derry Rd. BS3: Bedm 2D 77
Derwent Cl. BS34: Pat 5D 9
Derwent Gro. BS31: Key 2C 90
Derwent Rd. BS5: S'wll 5B 60
Devaney Cl. BS4: St Ap 4B 70
Deveron Gro. BS31: Key 3C 90
Devercote St. BS15: Han 5A 72
Devon Gro. BS5: E'tn 1E 69
Devon Rd. BS5: E'tn 5E 59
Devonshire Bldgs. BA2: Bath 1B 110
  (not continuous)
Devonshire Dr. BS20: P'head 1B 48
Devonshire M. BA1: Bath 4C 104
  (off St James's Pde.)
  BA2: Bath 2B 110
  (off Devonshire Bldgs.)
Devonshire Pl. BA2: Bath 1B 110
Devonshire Rd. BA2: B'ptn 1A 106
  BS6: Henle 2D 57
Devonshire Vs. BA2: Bath 2B 110
Dewfalls Dr. BS32: Brad S 4F 9
Dial La. BS16: Down 5F 45
Diamond Rd. BS5: St G 2B 70
Diamond St. BS3: Bedm 1E 77
Diana Gdns. BS32: Brad S 5A 10
Dibden Cl. BS16: Down 3C 46
Dibden Ct. BS16: Emer G 4D 47
Dibden La. BS16: Emer G 4C 46
Dibden Rd. BS16: Down 3C 46
Dickens Cl. BS7: Hor 3C 42
Dickinsons Fld. BS3: Wind H 2F 77
Didsbury Cl. BS10: Hen 2B 40
Dighton Ct. BS2: Bris 1F 67
  (off Princess Rd.)
Dighton Ga. BS34: Stok G 3A 26
Dighton St. BS2: Bris 1F 67
Dillon Ct. BS5: St G 2F 69
Dingle, The BS9: C Din 4F 39
  BS36: Wint D 4A 28
  BS37: Yate 1B 16
Dingle Cl. BS9: Sea M 5E 39
Dingle Rd. BS9: C Din 4F 39
Dingle Vw. BS9: Sea M 4E 39

Dinglewood Cl. BS9: C Din 4F 39
DINGS, THE 4C 68
Dings Wlk. BS2: Bris 3C 68
Dirac Rd. BS7: B'stn 2B 58
District Cen. Rdbt. BS32: Brad S . .5A 10
Dixon Gdns. BA1: Bath 1B 104
Dixon Rd. BS4: Brisl 2B 80
Dock Ga. La. BS8: Clif 4C 66
Doctor White's Cl.
  BS1: Bris 5D 5 (4A 68)
Dodington La. BS37: Dod 2D 33
Dodington Rd. BS37: Chip S 1D 33
Dodisham Wlk. BS16: Fish 5D 45
Dodmore Crossing BS37: W'lgh . .4D 31
Dog La. BS10: H'len 4E 21
Dogwood Rd. BS32: Alm 1F 9
Dolman Cl. BS10: Hen 5A 22
Dominion Rd. BA2: Bath 4C 102
  BS16: Fish 3B 60
Donald Rd. BS13: Bis 5B 76
Donal Early Way BS7: Hor 3A 42
Doncaster Rd. BS10: S'mead 2D 41
Donegal Rd. BS4: Know 3F 77
Dongola Av. BS7: B'stn 2A 58
Dongola Rd. BS7: B'stn 2A 58
Donnington Wlk. BS31: Key 3F 89
Doone Rd. BS7: Hor 3B 42
Dorcas Av. BS34: Stok G 3B 26
Dorchester Rd. BS7: Hor 4C 42
Dorchester St.
  BA1: Bath 5C 6 (5C 104)
Dorester Cl. BS10: Bren 4E 23
Dorian Cl. BS7: Hor 4A 42
Dorian Rd. BS7: Hor 4A 42
Dorian Way BS7: Hor 3A 42
Dormer Cl. BS36: Coal H 2F 29
Dormer Rd. BS5: Eastv 3D 59
Dorset Cl. BA2: Bath 4F 103
Dorset Cotts. BA2: C Down 4E 111
Dorset Gro. BS2: Bris 4C 58
Dorset Ho. BA2: Bath 2F 109
Dorset Rd. BS9: W Trym 5D 41
  BS15: K'wd 5F 61
Dorset St. BA2: Bath 4F 103
  BS3: Bedm 1D 77
Dorset Way BS37: Yate 2C 16
Doudney Cl. BS3: Bedm 5A 68
Douglas Rd. BS7: Hor 4B 42
  BS15: K'wd 2F 71
Douglas Rd. Ind. Pk.
  BS15: K'wd 2F 71
Doulton Way BS14: Whit 2D 87
Dovecote BS37: Yate 5A 16
Dove La. BS2: Bris 1B 68
  BS5: Redf 2E 69
Dovercourt Rd. BS7: Hor 1C 58
Dover Ho. BA1: Bath 2C 104
Dover Pl. BA1: Bath 2C 104
  BS8: Clif 2D 67
Dover Pl. Cotts. BS8: Clif 2D 67
Dovers La. BA1: Bathf 5E 99
Dovers Pk. BA1: Bathf 5E 99
Dover Ter. BA1: Bath 2D 105
  (off London Rd.)
Dove St. BS2: Bris 1F 67
Dove St. Sth. BS2: Bris 1F 67
Doveswell Gro. BS13: Withy 3C 84
Dovey Ct. BS30: Old C 4E 73
Dowdeswell Cl. BS10: Hen 5B 22
Dowding Cl. BS37: Chip S 3E 17
Dowding Rd. BA1: Bath 1D 105
Dowding Vs. BA1: Bath 1D 105
Dower Ho. BS16: Stap 4A 44
  (not continuous)
Dowland Gro. BS4: Know 1F 85
Dowling Rd. BS13: Hart 4E 85
Down Av. BA2: C Down 4C 110
Down Cl. BS20: P'head 1B 48
DOWNEND 5A 46
Downend Pk. BS7: Hor 1B 58
Downend Pk. Rd. BS16: Down 1F 61

Downend Rd. BS7: Hor 1B 58
  BS15: K'wd 5F 61
  BS16: Down 1D 61
  BS16: Fish 1D 61
Downend Sports Cen. 4B 46
Down Farm Ho. BS36: Wint 2F 27
Downfield BS9: Sea M 4E 39
  BS31: Key 2F 89
Downfield Dr.
  BS36: Fram C 5D 13
Downfield Lodge BS8: Clif 5C 56
Downfield Rd. BS8: Clif 5C 56
Down La. BA2: B'ptn 1B 106
Downleaze BS9: Stok B 3B 56
  BS16: Down 3F 45
  BS20: P'head 1C 48
Downleaze Dr. BS37: Chip S 5C 16
Downman Rd. BS7: L'lze 1C 58
Down Rd. BS20: P'head 3A 48
  BS36: Wint D 4A 28
Downs, The BS20: P'head 2D 49
Downs Cote Av. BS9: W Trym 5B 40
Downs Cote Dr. BS9: W Trym 5B 40
Downs Cote Gdns.
  BS9: W Trym 5C 40
Downs Cote Pk. BS9: W Trym 5C 40
Downs Cote Vw. BS9: W Trym . . .5C 40
Downside BS20: P'head 1E 49
Downside Cl. BA2: B'ptn 1B 106
  BS30: Bar C 4B 72
Downside Ct. *BS8: Clif* *5C 56*
(off Downside Rd.)
Downside Rd. BS8: Clif 5C 56
Downs Pk. E. BS6: Henle 1C 56
Downs Pk. W. BS6: Henle 1C 56
Downs Rd. BS9: W Trym 5C 40
(not continuous)
Downton Rd. BS4: Know 3F 77
Down Vw. BS7: B'stn 3B 58
Dowry Pl. BS8: Clif 4B 66
Dowry Rd. BS8: Clif 3C 66
Dowry Sq. BS8: Clif 3B 66
Dragon Ct. BS5: S'wll 5A 60
Dragonfly Cl. BS15: K'wd 2F 71
Dragon Rd. BS36: Wint 3F 27
Dragons Hill Cl. BS31: Key 2B 90
Dragons Hill Ct. BS31: Key 2B 90
Dragons Hill Gdns.
  BS31: Key 2B 90
Dragonswell Rd. BS10: Hen 1C 40
Dragon Wlk. BS5: St G 5B 60
Drake Av. BA2: C Down 3B 110
Drake Cl. BS31: Salt 5F 91
Drake Ho. *BS1: Bris* *2C 4*
(off Rupert St.)
Drake Rd. BS3: Ash G 1C 76
Drakes Way BS20: P'head 1C 48
Dram La. BS5: St G 3C 70
Dramway Footpath, The
  BS36: Coal H 4F 29
Dransfield Way BA2: Bath 1E 109
Draycot Pl. BS1: Bris 5B 4 (4F 67)
Draycott Ct. BA2: Bath 1D 7 (3C 104)
Draycott Rd. BS7: Hor 1B 58
Draydon Rd. BS4: Know 4E 77
Drayton Cl. BS14: H'gro 4D 79
Drayton Rd. BS9: C Din 3E 39
Drill Hall, The BS2: Bris 2F 5
Drive, The BS9: Henle 5D 41
  BS14: H'gro 1E 87
  BS31: Key 1A 90
Drove, The BS20: P'bry 1F 51
Druett's Cl. BS10: Hor 4A 42
Druid Cl. BS9: Stok B 1A 56
Druid Hill BS9: Stok B 1A 56
Druid Rd. BS9: Stok B 2F 55
Druid Stoke Av. BS9: Stok B 1E 55
Druid Woods BS9: Stok B 1E 55
Drummond Ct. BS30: L Grn 5B 72
Drummond Rd. BS2: Bris 5A 58
  BS16: Fish 3B 60

Drungway BA2: Mon C 4F 111
DRY ARCH 5F 107
Dryleaze BS31: Key 5A 82
  BS37: Yate 1A 16
(off Leechpool Way)
Dryleaze Rd. BS16: B'hll 5B 44
Dubber's La. BS5: Eastv 4A 60
Dublin Cres. BS9: Henle 5D 41
Duchess Rd. BS8: Clif 5C 56
Duchess Way BS16: Stap 1F 59
Ducie Rd. BS5: Bar H 2D 69
  BS16: Stap H 1A 62
Ducie Rd. Bus. Pk.
  BS5: Bar H 2D 69
Duckmoor Rd. BS3: Ash G 5C 66
Duckmoor Rd. Ind. Est.
  BS3: Ash G 5B 66
Dudley Cl. BS31: Key 3A 90
Dudley Ct. BS30: Bar C 5B 72
Dudley Gro. BS7: Hor 3C 42
Dugar Wlk. BS6: Redl 3E 57
Duicie Ct. BS16: Stap H 2A 62
Duke St. BA2: Bath 4D 7 (4C 104)
Dulverton Rd. BS7: B'stn 2F 57
Dumaine Av. BS34: Stok G 3A 26
Duncan Gdns. BA1: W'ton 4C 94
Duncan M. BS8: Clif 2C 66
Duncombe La. BS15: K'wd 4C 60
Duncombe Rd. BS15: K'wd 5D 61
Dundas Cl. BS10: Hen 1A 40
Dundee Dr. BS16: Fish 1E 61
Dundonald Rd. BS6: Redl 3D 57
Dundridge Gdns. BS5: St G 3C 70
Dundridge La. BS5: St G 3C 70
DUNDRY .5A 84
Dundry Cl. BS15: K'wd 3F 71
Dundry La. BS41: Dun 5A 84
Dundry Vw. BS4: Know 3C 78
Dunford Rd. BS3: Wind H 1F 77
Dunkeld Av. BS34: Fil 1B 42
Dunkerry Rd. BS3: Wind H 1F 77
Dunkirk Rd. BS16: Fish 3B 60
Dunlin Dr. BS20: P'bry, P'head . . .5E 35
Dunmail Rd. BS10: S'mead 1E 41
Dunmore St. BS4: Wind H 5B 68
Dunsford Pl. BA2: Bath 3F 7 (4D 105)
Dunster Gdns. BS30: Will 2D 83
Dunster Ho. BA2: C Down 3C 110
Dunster Rd. BS4: Know 4B 78
  BS31: Key 3F 89
Durban Rd. BS34: Pat 5B 8
Durbin Wlk. BS5: E'tn 1C 68
Durdham Cl. BS6: Redl 3C 56
Durdham Hall BS9: Stok B 2B 56
Durdham Pk. BS6: Redl 3C 56
Durham Gro. BS31: Key 3F 89
Durham Rd. BS2: Bris 4C 58
Durleigh Cl. BS13: Bis 1C 84
Durley Hill BS31: Key 4D 81
Durley La. BS31: Key 5E 81
Durley Pk. BA2: Bath 1A 110
  BS31: Key 5E 81
Durnford Av. BS3: Ash G 5C 66
Durnford St. BS3: Ash G 5C 66
Dursley Cl. BS37: Yate 4A 16
Dursley Rd. BS11: Shire 1F 53
Durville Rd. BS13: Bis 1D 85
Durweston Wlk. BS14: Stoc 4E 79
Dutton Cl. BS14: Stoc 1F 87
Dutton Rd. BS14: Stoc 1F 87
Dutton Wlk. BS14: Stoc 1F 87
Dyers Cl. BS13: Hart 3F 85
Dyer's La. BS37: Iron A 1C 14
Dylan Thomas Ct.
  BS30: Bar C 4C 72
Dyrham *BS16: Fren* *2E 45*
(off Harford Dr.)
Dyrham Cl. BS9: Henle 5F 41
  BS15: K'wd 1B 72
Dyrham Pde. BS34: Pat 5E 9
Dyrham Rd. BS15: K'wd 1B 72

E

Eagle Cotts. BA1: Bathe 2B 98
Eagle Dr. BS34: Pat 5A 8
Eagle Pk. BA1: Bathe 2B 98
Eagle Rd. BA1: Bathe 2B 98
  BS4: Brisl 2F 79
Eagles Wood Bus. Pk.
  BS32: Brad S 2E 9
Earl Russell Way BS5: E'tn 2D 69
Earls Mead BS16: Stap 2A 60
Earlstone Cl. BS30: C Hth 5C 72
Earlstone Cres. BS30: C Hth 5C 72
Earl St. BS1: Bris 1C 4 (1F 67)
Easedale Cl. BS10: S'mead 1F 41
Eastbourne Av. BA1: Bath 1D 105
Eastbourne Rd. BS5: E'tn 1D 69
Eastbourne Vs. BA1: Bath 1D 105
Eastbury Rd. BS16: Fish 2C 60
Eastcliff BS20: P'head 4D 35
East Cl. BA2: Bath 5C 102
Eastcote Pk. BS14: Whit 2D 87
East Ct. BS3: Ash V 1B 76
East St. BS1: Bris 1C 4 (1F 67)
Eastfield BS9: W Trym 4E 41
Eastfield Rd. BS9: W Trym 4D 41
Eastfield Av. BA1: W'ton 4D 95
Eastfield Dr. BS37: Yate 1A 16
Eastfield Rd. BS6: Cot 4F 57
  BS9: W Trym 4C 40
Eastfield Ter. BS9: Henle 5D 41
Eastgate Cen. BS5: Eastv 3D 59
Eastgate Office Cen. BS5: Eastv . .3D 59
Eastgate Rd. BS5: Eastv 3D 59
East Gro. BS6: Bris 5B 58
Eastlake Cl. BS7: L'lze 4D 43
E. Lea Rd. BA1: Bath 2C 102
Eastleigh Cl. BS16: Soun 2A 62
Eastleigh Rd. BS10: S'mead 2F 41
  BS16: Soun 3A 62
Eastlyn Rd. BS13: Bis 4D 77
Eastmead Ct. BS9: Stok B 2A 56
Eastmead La. BS9: Stok B 2A 56
Eastnor Rd. BS14: Whit 4C 86
Easton Bus. Cen. BS5: E'tn 1D 69
Easton Ho. BA1: Bath 1E 105
EASTON-IN-GORDANO 2C 52
Easton Leisure Cen. 1C 68
Easton Rd. BS2: Bris 2C 68
  BS5: E'tn 2C 68
  BS20: Pill 2E 53
Easton Way BS5: E'tn 1D 69
Eastover Cl. BS9: W Trym 3C 40
Eastover Gro. BA2: Odd D 4E 109
East Pde. BS9: Sea M 5E 39
East Pk. BS5: Eastv 4E 59
East Pk. Dr. BS5: Eastv 4E 59
East Pk. Trad. Est.
  BS5: E'tn, W'hall 5F 59
E. Priory Cl. BS9: W Trym 4C 40
Eastridge Dr. BS13: Bis 2B 84
East Shrubbery BS6: Redl 4D 57
East St. BS3: Bedm 1E 77
  BS11: A'mth 2C 36
East St. M. *BS3: Bedm* *5F 67*
(off East St.)
EAST TWERTON 4F 103
East Vw. BS16: Mang 5B 46
EASTVILLE 3E 59
Eastville BA1: Bath 1D 105
East Wlk. BS37: Yate 4A 16
East Way BA2: Bath 5C 102
Eastwood BA2: B'ptn 4A 106
Eastwood Cres. BS4: Brisl 5B 70
Eastwood Pl. BS20: P'head 4C 34
Eastwood Rd. BS4: Brisl 5B 70

Eastwoods BA1: Bathf 4D 99
Eaton Cl. BS14: Stoc 2A 88
  BS16: Fish 2D 61
Eaton Cres. BS8: Clif 1C 66
Eaton St. BS3: Bedm 1E 77
Ebenezer La. BS9: Stok B 5F 39
  (not continuous)
Ebenezer St. BS5: St G 2F 69
Ebenezer Ter. BA2: Bath 5D 7
Eccleston Ho. BS5: Bar H 3D 69
Eclipse Office Pk.
  BS16: Stap H 2E 61
Eden Gro. BS7: Hor 2B 42
Eden Pk. Cl BA1: Bathe 3C 98
Eden Pk. Dr. BA1: Bathe 3C 98
Eden Ter. BA1: Bath 5D 97
Eden Vs. BA1: Bath 5E 97
  (off Dafford's Bldgs.)
Edgar Bldgs. BA1: Bath 2B 6
Edgecombe Cl. BS15: K'wd 5B 62
Edgecumbe Rd. BS6: Redl 4F 57
Edgefield Cl. BS14: Whit 4B 86
Edgefield Rd. BS14: Whit 4B 86
Edgeware Rd. BS3: Bris 5E 67
  BS16: Stap H 2F 61
Edgewood Cl. BS14: H'gro 4D 79
  BS30: L Grn 1C 82
Edgeworth BS37: Yate 2E 31
Edgeworth Rd. BA2: Bath 3E 109
Edinburgh Rd. BS31: Key 3A 90
Edington Gro. BS10: Hen 1C 40
Edmund Cl. BS16: Down 5F 45
Edmund Rd. BS14: H'gro 5C 78
Edna Av. BS4: Brisl 1A 80
Edward Bird Ho. BS7: L'lze 4D 43
Edward Rd. BS4: Bris 5D 69
  BS15: K'wd 1A 72
Edward St. BA1: Bath 3E 103
  BA2: Bath 2E 7 (3D 105)
  BS5: Eastv 4F 59
  BS5: Redf 1E 69
Edwin Short Cl. BS30: Bit 4F 83
Effingham Rd. BS6: Bris 4A 58
Egerton Brow BS7: B'stn 2F 57
Egerton Ct. BS7: B'stn 2A 58
  (off Gloucester Rd.)
Egerton La. BS7: B'stn 2F 57
Egerton Rd. BA2: Bath 1A 110
  BS7: B'stn 2F 57
Eggshill La. BS37: Yate 4F 15
Egg Theatre, The 3B 6
Eglin Cft. BS13: Withy 3D 85
Eighth Av. BS7: Hor 3D 43
  BS14: H'gro 5C 78
Eirene Ter. BS20: Pill 2F 53
Elberton BS15: K'wd 1C 72
Elberton Rd. BS9: Sea M 4D 39
Elbridge Ho. BS2: Bris 1F 5
Elbury Av. BS15: K'wd 4E 61
Elderberry Wlk. BS10: S'mead 1E 41
Elderwood Dr. BS30: L Grn 1C 82
Elderwood Rd. BS14: H'gro 5D 79
Eldon Pl. BA1: Bath 5D 97
Eldon Ter. BS3: Wind H 1F 77
Eldonwall Trad. Est. BS4: Brisl . . .4E 69
Eldon Way BS4: Brisl 4E 69
Eldred Cl. BS9: Stok B 1F 55
Eleanor Cl. BA2: Bath 5B 102
Eleventh Av. BS7: Hor 2D 43
Elfin Rd. BS16: Fish 1C 60
Elgar Cl. BS4: Know 1F 85
Elgin Av. BS7: Fil 2B 42
Elgin Pk. BS6: Redl 4D 57
Elgin Rd. BS16: Fish 4D 61
Eliot Cl. BS7: Hor 2C 42
Elizabeth Ct. BS13: Withy 3B 84
Elizabeth Cres. BS34: Stok G 4A 26
Elizabeth's M. BS4: St Ap 3B 70
Elizabeth Way BS16: Mang 3D 63
Elkstone Wlk. BS30: Bit 2E 83
Ella Cl. BS16: Fish 5E 45

Ellacombe Rd. BS30: L Grn 2A 82
Ellan Hay Rd. BS32: Brad S 2C 26
Ellbridge Cl. BS9: Stok B 1F 55
Ellenborough Ho. BS8: Clif 3C 66
  (off Argyle Pl.)
Ellen Ho. BA2: Bath 5C 102
Ellesmere Rd. BS4: Brisl 4F 79
  BS15: K'wd 1F 71
Ellfield Cl. BS13: Bis 1B 84
Ellicks Cl. BS32: Brad S 3A 10
Ellicott Rd. BS7: Hor 5B 42
Ellinghurst Cl. BS10: Bren 1C 40
Elliott Av. BS16: Fren 2E 45
Ellis Av. BS13: Bis 4C 76
Elliston Dr. BA2: Bath 1D 109
Elliston La. BS6: Redl 4E 57
Elliston Rd. BS6: Redl 4E 57
Elm Cl. BS11: Law W 2B 38
  BS34: Lit S 1F 25
  BS37: Chip S 4C 16
Elm Ct. BS6: Redl 4D 57
  BS14: Whit 1C 86
  BS31: Key 3E 89
Elmcroft BA1: Bath 5E 97
Elmcroft Cres. BS7: L'lze 2C 58
Elmdale Gdns. BS16: Fish 2C 60
Elmdale Rd. BS3: Bedm 2D 77
  BS8: Clif 1D 67
Elmfield BS15: K'wd 3A 72
Elmfield Cl. BS15: K'wd 3A 72
Elmfield Rd. BS9: S'mead 3C 40
Elm Gro. BA1: Swa 5E 97
  BA2: Bath 1E 109
Elmgrove Av. BS5: E'tn 1D 69
Elmgrove Dr. BS37: Yate 3B 16
Elmgrove Pk. BS6: Cot 5F 57
Elmgrove Rd. BS6: Cot 5F 57
  BS16: Fish 3A 60
Elm Hayes BS13: Bis 1B 84
Elmhirst Gdns. BS37: Yate 3C 16
Elmhurst Av. BS5: Eastv 3F 59
Elmhurst Est. BA1: Bathe 3C 98
Elmhurst Gdns. BS41: L Ash 3B 74
Elming Down Cl. BS32: Brad S . . .2F 25
Elm La. BS6: Redl 4D 57
Elmlea Av. BS9: W Trym 1B 56
Elmleigh Av. BS16: Mang 1D 63
Elmleigh Cl. BS16: Mang 1D 63
Elmleigh Rd. BS16: Mang 1C 62
Elmore BS15: Soun 4B 62
  BS37: Yate 5F 15
Elmore Rd. BS7: Hor 5C 42
  BS34: Pat 4B 8
Elm Pk. BS34: Fil 1C 42
Elm Pl. BA2: Bath 1B 110
Elm Rd. BS7: Hor 1A 58
  BS15: K'wd 3A 72
Elms, The BA1: Bath 5E 97
  BS16: Fren 2E 45
  BS16: Stap H 3F 61
Elms Gro. BS34: Pat 4D 9
Elmtree Av. BS16: Mang 4C 46
Elmtree Cl. BS15: K'wd 5F 61
Elmtree Dr. BS13: Withy 3B 84
Elm Tree Pk. BS20: P'bry 2F 51
Elmtree Way BS15: K'wd 5F 61
Elm Wlk. BS20: P'head 2E 49
Elmwood BS37: Yate 5A 16
Elsa Nunn BS16: Fish 1C 60
Elsbert Dr. BS13: Bis 1A 84
Elstree Rd. BS5: W'hall 5A 60
Elton Ho. BS2: Bris 1F 5
Elton La. BS7: B'stn 4F 57
Elton Mans. BS7: B'stn 3F 57
Elton Rd. BS7: B'stn 3F 57
  BS8: Clif 1A 4 (2D 67)
  BS15: K'wd 5D 61
Elton St. BS2: Bris 1B 68
Elvard Cl. BS13: Withy 3C 84

Elvard Rd. BS13: Withy 2C 84
Elvaston Rd. BS3: Wind H 1A 78
Ely Gro. BS9: Sea M 4D 39
Embassy Rd. BS5: W'hall 5A 60
Embassy Wlk. BS5: W'hall 5A 60
Embleton Rd. BS10: S'mead 1D 41
EMERSON'S GREEN 5D 47
Emersons Grn. La.
  BS16: Emer G 5C 46
  (Blackhorse La.)
  BS16: Emer G 5E 47
  (Johnson Rd.)
Emerson Sq. BS7: Hor 3C 42
Emerson Way BS16: Emer G 3D 47
Emery Rd. BS4: Brisl 2B 80
Emet Gro. BS16: Emer G 5D 47
Emet La. BS16: Emer G 5D 47
Eminence BS1: Bris 5D 5
Emlyn Rd. BS5: E'tn 4E 59
Emma Chris Way BS34: Fil 1E 43
Emmanuel Ct. BS8: Clif 1C 66
Emmett Wood BS14: Whit 4D 87
Empire Cres. BS15: Han 5A 72
Empress Menen Gdns.
  BA1: Bath 2C 102
Emra Cl. BS5: St G 5B 60
Enfield Rd. BS16: Fish 3C 60
Engine Comn. La. BS37: Yate 1E 15
Enginehouse La.
  BS31: Q Char 3C 88
England's Cres. BS36: Wint 1A 28
ENGLISHCOMBE 3B 108
Englishcombe La. BA2: Bath 2D 109
Englishcombe Ri. BA2: Bath 2C 108
Englishcombe Rd. BA2: Eng 3B 108
  BS13: Hart 4E 85
Englishcombe Way BA2: Bath . . .2A 110
Ennerdale Rd. BS10: S'mead 1F 41
Enterprise Trade Cen.
  BS4: Know 5A 78
Entry Hill BA2: Bath, C Down . . .2B 110
Entry Hill Dr. BA2: Bath 2B 110
Entry Hill Gdns. BA2: Bath 2B 110
Entry Hill Pk. BA2: C Down 3B 110
Entry Ri. BA2: C Down 4B 110
Epney Cl. BS34: Pat 4B 8
Epsom Cl. BS16: Down 2B 46
Epworth Rd. BS10: Bren 5C 22
Equinox BS32: Brad S 2E 9
Erin Wlk. BS4: Know 4F 77
Ermine Way BS11: Shire 4E 37
Ermleet Rd. BS6: Redl 4E 57
Ernest Barker Cl. BS5: Bar H 2D 69
Ernestville Rd. BS16: Fish 3B 60
Ervine Ter. BS2: Bris 1B 68
Esplanade Rd. BS20: P'head 5B 34
Esporta Health & Fitness Club
  Stoke Gifford 4B 26
Essence BS6: Bris 5A 58
Essery Rd. BS5: E'tn 4E 59
Esson Rd. BS15: K'wd 5D 61
Estcourt Gdns. BS16: Stap 1F 59
Estcourt La. BS16: Stap 1F 59
Estelle Pk. BS5: Eastv 4E 59
Estoril BS37: Yate 4B 16
Estuary Ho. BS20: P'head 4D 35
Estune Bus. Pk. BS41: L Ash 4A 74
Estune Wlk. BS41: L Ash 2C 74
Etloe Rd. BS6: Henle 2C 56
Eton Rd. BS4: Brisl 1F 79
Ettricke Dr. BS16: Fish 5D 45
Eugene Flats BS2: Bris 1F 67
  (off Eugene St.)
Eugene St. BS2: Bris 1F 67
  BS5: E'tn 1B 68
Evans Cl. BS4: St Ap 4B 70
Evans Rd. BS6: Redl 4D 57
Eveleigh Av. BA1: Swa 5F 97
Eveleigh Ho. BA2: Bath 2C 6
  (off Grove St.)
Evelyn La. BS11: A'mth 2D 37

Evelyn Rd. BA1: Bath 2D **103**
   BS10: W Trym 3E **41**
Evelyn Ter. BA1: Bath 1C **104**
Evenlode Gdns. BS11: Shire 1B **54**
Evenlode Way BS31: Key 4C **90**
Evercreech Rd. BS14: Whit 3C **86**
Everest Av. BS16: Fish 2A **60**
Everest Rd. BS16: Fish 2A **60**
Eve Rd. BS5: E'tn 5D **59**
Ewell Rd. BS14: H'gro 1D **87**
Excelsior St. BA2: Bath 5D **7** (5D **105**)
Exchange Av. BS1: Bris 3C **4** (3F **67**)
Exeter Bldgs. BS6: Redl 4D **57**
Exeter Rd. BS3: Bris 5D **67**
   BS20: P'head 2A **50**
Exley Cl. BS30: Old C 4E **73**
Exmoor Rd. BA2: C Down 3B **110**
Exmoor St. BS3: Bedm 5D **67**
Exmouth Rd. BS4: Know 3B **78**
Explore-at-Bristol 4A **4** (3E **67**)
Explore La. BS1: Bris 4A **4** (3E **67**)
Exton Cl. BS14: Whit 3C **86**
Eyer's La. BS2: Bris 1F **5** (2B **68**)

F

Faber Gro. BS13: Hart 3E **85**
Fabian Dr. BS34: Stok G 3A **26**
Factory Rd. BS36: Wint 1B **28**
Failand Cres. BS9: Sea M 1E **55**
Failand La. BS8: Fail 4A **52**
   BS20: P'bry 4A **52**
Failand Wlk. BS9: Sea M 5E **39**
Fairacre Cl. BS7: L'lze 1D **59**
Fairacres Cl. BS31: Key 3A **90**
Fairfax St. BS1: Bris 2C **4** (2F **67**)
Fairfield Av. BA1: Bath 5C **96**
FAIRFIELD PARK 5C **96**
Fairfield Pk. Rd. BA1: Bath 5B **96**
Fairfield Pl. BS3: Bedm 5D **67**
Fairfield Rd. BA1: Bath 1C **104**
   BS3: Bedm 5E **67**
   BS6: Bris 4B **58**
Fairfield Ter. BA1: Bath 5C **96**
Fairfield Vw. BA1: Bath 5C **96**
Fairfoot Rd. BS4: Wind H 1C **78**
Fairford Cl. BS15: Soun 4B **62**
Fairford Cres. BS34: Pat 5E **9**
Fairford Rd. BS11: Shire 4F **37**
Fair Furlong BS13: Withy 3C **84**
Fairhaven BS37: Yate 4B **16**
Fairhaven Cotts. BA1: Bathe 1C **98**
Fairhaven Rd. BS6: B'stn 2E **57**
Fair Lawn BS30: Old C 5C **72**
Fairlawn BS16: Stap H 2F **61**
Fairlawn Av. BS34: Fil 5C **24**
Fairlawn Rd. BS6: Bris 4B **58**
Fairlyn Dr. BS15: Soun 3B **62**
Fairoaks BS30: L Grn 1C **82**
Fairview Ct. BS15: K'wd 3F **71**
Fair Vw. Dr. BS6: Redl 4E **57**
Fairview Rd. BS15: K'wd 1B **72**
Fairview Ter. BS37: Iron A 1F **13**
Fairway BS4: Brisl 3F **79**
Fairway Cl. BS30: Old C 5D **73**
Fairway Ind. Cen. BS34: Fil 5B **24**
Fairways BS31: Salt 5A **92**
Falcon Cl. BS9: W Trym 3B **40**
   BS20: P'head 2F **49**
   BS34: Pat 5A **8**
Falcon Ct. BS9: W Trym 5C **40**
Falcondale Rd. BS9: W Trym 4B **40**
Falcondale Wlk. BS9: W Trym . . .3C **40**
Falcon Dr. BS34: Pat 5A **8**
Falconer Rd. BA1: W'ton 4C **94**
Falcon Wlk. BS34: Pat 4A **8**
Falfield Rd. BS4: Brisl 1E **79**
Falfield Wlk. BS10: S'mead 3E **41**
Falkland Rd. BS6: Bris 4B **58**
Fallodon Ct. BS9: Henle 1D **57**

Fallodon Way BS9: Henle 1D **57**
Fallowfield BS30: Old C 4E **73**
Falmouth Rd. BS7: B'stn 2F **57**
Fane Cl. BS10: Bren 1C **40**
Fanshawe Rd. BS14: H'gro 5C **78**
Faraday Rd. BS8: Clif 4B **66**
Farendell Rd. BS16: Emer G 2D **47**
Far Handstones BS30: C Hth 5C **72**
Farington Rd. BS10: W Trym 4F **41**
Farleigh Ri. BA1: Bathf 1F **107**
   BA15: Mon F 1F **107**
     (not continuous)
Farleigh Rd. BS31: Key 3F **89**
Farleigh Vw. BA1: Bath 1C **104**
     (off Beacon Rd.)
Farleigh Wlk. BS13: Bis 4C **76**
Farley Cl. BS34: Lit S 5E **9**
Farm Cl. BS16: Emer G 5D **47**
Farm Ct. BS16: Down 4A **46**
Farmer Rd. BS13: Withy 3A **84**
Farm Rd. BS16: Down 4A **46**
Farmwell Cl. BS13: Hart 2D **85**
Farnaby Cl. BS4: Know 5E **77**
Farndale Rd. BS5: St G 3C **70**
Farne Cl. BS9: Henle 1D **57**
Farrant Cl. BS4: Know 1F **85**
Farringford Ho. BS5: Eastv 4F **59**
Farrs La. BA2: C Down 3D **111**
   BS1: Bris 4B **4** (3F **67**)
Farr St. BS11: A'mth 3D **37**
Faulkland Rd. BA2: Bath 5F **103**
Favell Ho. BS1: Bris 3C **4**
Fawkes Cl. BS15: Warm 1D **73**
Featherstone Rd. BS16: Fish 2B **60**
Fedden Village BS20: P'head 1B **48**
Feeder Rd. BS2: Bris 4B **68**
Felix Ct. BS15: K'wd 1F **71**
     (off Downend Rd.)
Felix Rd. BS5: E'tn 1D **69**
Felstead Rd. BS10: S'mead 2A **42**
Feltham Ct. BS34: Fil 1B **42**
Felton Gro. BS13: Bis 4B **76**
Fenbrook Cl. BS16: Ham 2D **45**
Fennel Dr. BS32: Brad S 1C **26**
Fennell Gro. BS10: Hen 1C **40**
Fennel Rd. BS20: P'head 5E **35**
Fenns La. BS41: L Ash 3A **74**
Fenshurst Gdns. BS41: L Ash . . .4B **74**
Fenswood Cl. BS41: L Ash 3A **74**
Fenswood Ct. BS41: L Ash 3A **74**
Fenswood Mead BS41: L Ash . . .3A **74**
Fenswood Rd. BS41: L Ash 3A **74**
Fenton Cl. BS31: Salt 4F **91**
Fenton Rd. BS7: B'stn 2F **57**
Fermaine Av. BS4: Brisl 1B **80**
Fernbank Rd. BS6: Redl 4E **57**
Ferncliffe BS8: L Wds 2A **66**
Fern Cl. BS10: Bren 5D **23**
Ferndale Av. BS30: L Grn 1B **82**
Ferndale Grange BS9: Henle 5D **41**
Ferndale Rd. BA1: Swa 4E **97**
   BS7: Hor 1C **42**
   BS20: P'head 5C **34**
Ferndene BS32: Brad S 3E **9**
Ferndown BS37: Yate 4A **16**
Ferndown Cl. BS11: Law W 4C **38**
Fern Gro. BS32: Brad S 5F **9**
Fernhill La. BS11: Law W 2D **39**
Fernhurst Rd. BS5: S'wll 5B **60**
Fernlea Gdns. BS20: Eas 2D **53**
Fernleaze BS36: Coal H 2E **29**
Fernleigh Ct. BS6: Redl 3D **57**
Fern Rd. BS16: Down 1F **61**
Fernsteed Rd. BS13: Bis 1B **84**
Fern St. BS2: Bris 5B **58**
Ferry La. BA2: Bath 4D **7** (4C **104**)
Ferryman's Ct. BS2: Bris 2E **5**
Ferry Rd. BS15: Han 3F **81**
Ferry Steps Ind. Est.
   BS2: Bris 5C **68**
Ferry St. BS1: Bris 4D **5** (3A **68**)

Fersfield BA2: Bath 2D **111**
Fiddes Rd. BS6: Redl 2E **57**
Fiddlers Wood La.
   BS32: Brad S 5A **10**
Fieldfare Av. BS20: P'head 5F **35**
Field Farm Cl. BS34: Stok G 4B **26**
Fieldgrove La. BS30: Bit 4E **83**
Fieldings Rd. BA2: Bath 4E **103**
Field La. BS30: L Grn 1A **82**
Field Marshal Slim Ct.
   BS2: Bris 1F **5** (2B **68**)
Field Rd. BS15: K'wd 5E **61**
Field Vw. BS5: E'tn 1C **68**
Field Vw. Dr. BS16: Fish 5E **45**
Fiennes Cl. BS16: Stap H 2A **62**
Fifth Av. BS7: Hor 2C **42**
   BS14: H'gro 5D **79**
Fifth Way BS11: A'mth 1A **38**
Filby Dr. BS34: Lit S 5E **9**
FILTON .5C **24**
Filton Abbey Wood Station (Rail)
   . . . . .2D **43**
FILTON AIRFIELD 3B **24**
Filton Av. BS7: Hor 5A **42**
   BS34: Fil 4C **24**
Filton Gro. BS7: Hor 5B **42**
Filton Hill BS34: Fil 4C **24**
Filton La. BS34: Stok G 1F **43**
Filton Recreation Cen. 1C **42**
Filton Rd. BS7: Hor 4B **42**
   BS16: Fren 2D **45**
   BS16: Ham 1A **44**
   BS34: Stok G 1F **43**
Filwood B'way. BS4: Know 4A **78**
Filwood Ct. BS16: Fish 3D **61**
Filwood Dr. BS15: K'wd 1B **72**
Filwood Ho. BS16: Fish 3D **61**
FILWOOD PARK 3A **78**
Filwood Pool 4A **78**
Filwood Rd. BS16: Fish 2C **60**
Finches, The BS20: P'head 5E **35**
Finch Rd. BS37: Chip S 5B **16**
Finisterre Pk. BS20: P'head 5E **35**
Fircliff Pk. BS20: P'head 4C **34**
Fireclay Rd. BS5: St G 3F **69**
Fire Engine La. BS36: Coal H 1F **29**
Firework Cl. BS15: Warm 1D **73**
Firfield St. BS4: Wind H 5C **68**
Firgrove Cres. BS37: Yate 3B **16**
Firs, The BA2: C Down 4D **111**
   BS16: Down 5A **46**
Firs Ct. BS31: Key 3E **89**
First Av. BA2: Bath 1F **109**
   BS4: St Ap 4A **70**
   BS14: H'gro 5C **78**
   BS20: P'bry 5A **36**
First Way BS11: A'mth 1A **38**
Fir Tree Cl. BS34: Pat 1A **24**
Fir Tree La. BS5: St G 3C **70**
Fisher Av. BS15: K'wd 5C **62**
Fisher Rd. BS15: K'wd 5C **62**
Fishers Mead BS41: L Ash 3A **74**
FISHPONDS 2C **60**
Fishponds Rd. BS5: Eastv 4E **59**
   BS16: Fish 4E **59**
Fishponds Trad. Est. BS5: S'wll . .4A **60**
     (not continuous)
Fishpool Hill BS10: Bren 4D **23**
Fitchett Wlk. BS10: Hen 5B **22**
Fitness First
   Cribbs Causeway 2E **23**
   Kingswood 3A **72**
Fitzgerald Rd. BS3: Wind H 1B **78**
Fitzharding Rd. BS20: Pill 3A **54**
Fitzroy Cir. BS20: P'head 5E **35**
Fitzroy Rd. BS16: Fish 1D **61**
Fitzroy St. BS4: Wind H 5C **68**
Fitzroy Ter. BS6: Redl 4D **57**
Five Acre Dr. BS16: B'hll 4B **44**
Flaxman Cl. BS7: L'lze 5D **43**
FLAXPITS 3A **28**

Flaxpits La. BS36: Wint 2F **27**
Florence Pk. BS6: Henle 2D **57**
  BS32: Alm 1E **9**
Florence Rd. BS16: Soun 3A **62**
Flowers Hill BS4: Brisl 4A **80**
Flowers Hill Cl. BS4: Brisl 3A **80**
Flowers Ind. Est. BS4: Brisl 3B **80**
Flowerwell Rd. BS13: Hart 2D **85**
Folleigh Cl. BS41: L Ash 2D **75**
Folleigh Dr. BS41: L Ash 2D **75**
Folleigh La. BS41: L Ash 2D **75**
Folliot Cl. BS16: B'hll 4C **44**
Folly, The BS16: Down 4B **46**
  BS31: Salt 5B **92**
Folly Bri. Cl. BS37: Yate 3F **15**
Folly Brook Rd. BS16: Emer G . . .1C **46**
Folly La. BS2: Bris 2C **68**
Folly Rd. BS37: Iron A 1B **12**
Fontana Cl. BS30: L Grn 1D **83**
Fonthill Rd. BA1: L'dwn 5A **96**
  BS10: S'mead 1F **41**
Fonthill Way BS30: Bit 2D **83**
Fontmell Ct. BS14: Stoc 5F **79**
Fontwell Dr. BS30: Down 2B **46**
Footes La. BS36: Fram C 1D **29**
Footshill Cl. BS15: K'wd 3E **71**
Footshill Dr. BS15: K'wd 2E **71**
Footshill Gdns. BS15: K'wd 3E **71**
Footshill Rd. BS15: K'wd 3E **71**
Forde Cl. BS30: Bar C 4B **72**
Fordell Pl. BS4: Wind H 1C **78**
Ford La. BS16: Emer G 5D **47**
Ford St. BS5: Bar H 3E **69**
Forefield Pl. BA2: Bath 5C **104**
Forefield Ri. BA2: Bath 1C **110**
Forefield Ter. BA2: Bath 5D **105**
Forest Av. BS16: Fish 3D **61**
Forest Dr. BS10: Bren 5E **23**
Forest Edge BS15: Han 5E **71**
Forester Av. BA2: Bath 1E 7 (2C **104**)
Forester Ct. BA2: Bath 2C **104**
Forester La. BA2: Bath 1F 7 (2D **105**)
Forester Rd. BA2: Bath 1E 7 (3D **105**)
  BS20: P'head 2F **49**
Forest Rd. BS15: K'wd 2F **71**
  BS16: Fish 3D **61**
Forest Wlk. BS15: K'wd 2E **71**
  BS16: Fish 3D **61**
Forge End BS20: P'bry 3A **52**
Fortfield Rd. BS14: H'gro, Whit . . .3C **86**
Forth Av. BS20: P'head 5E **35**
Forum Bldgs. BA1: Bath 5C **6**
  (off St James's Pde.)
Fossedale Av. BS14: H'gro 1E **87**
Fosse Gdns. BA2: Odd D 5F **109**
Fosse La. BA2: Bathe 4C **98**
Fosseway, The BS8: Clif 2C **66**
Fosseway Ct. BS8: Clif 2C **66**
Fosse Way Est. BA2: Odd D 4E **109**
Foster St. BS5: E'tn 4D **59**
Foundry La. BS5: S'wll 4B **60**
Fountain Bldgs.
  BA1: Bath 2C **6** (3C **104**)
Fountain Ct. BS32: Brad S 2E **9**
  BS37: Yate *1F **31***
  (off Abbotswood)
Fountaine Ct. BS5: Eastv 4E **59**
Fountain Hill BS9: Stok B 1B **56**
Fountains Dr. BS30: Bar C 3B **72**
Fouracre Av. BS16: Down 3A **46**
Fouracre Cres. BS16: Down 2A **46**
Fouracre Rd. BS16: Down 2A **46**
Four Acres BS13: Withy 3A **84**
Four Acres Cl. BS13: Withy 3B **84**
Fourth Av. BS7: Hor 1C **42**
  BS14: H'gro 5D **79**
Fourth Way BS11: A'mth 2F **37**
Fox & Hounds La. BS31: Key 5B **90**
Fox Av. BS37: Yate 3F **15**
Foxborough Gdns. BS32: Brad S . . .3F **9**
Fox Cl. BS4: St Ap 4B **70**

Foxcombe Rd. BA1: Bath 3D **103**
  BS14: Whit 3D **87**
Foxcote BS15: K'wd 2B **72**
Foxcote Rd. BS3: Bedm 1C **76**
Fox Ct. BS30: L grn 1B **82**
Foxcroft Cl. BS32: Brad S 1B **26**
Foxcroft Rd. BS5: St G 1F **69**
Fox Den Rd. BS34: Stok G 1F **43**
Foxe Rd. BS36: Fram C 5C **12**
Foxfield Av. BS32: Brad S 3F **9**
Foxglove Cl. BS16: Stap 2A **60**
FOX HILL 3D **111**
Fox Hill BA2: C Down 4C **110**
Fox Ho. BS4: Brisl 1A **80**
Fox Rd. BS5: E'tn 5D **59**
Fraley Rd. BS9: W Trym 4C **40**
FRAMPTON COTTERELL 5C **12**
Frampton Ct. BS30: L Grn 5B **72**
Frampton Cres. BS16: Fish 2E **61**
FRAMPTON END 5E **13**
Frampton End Rd. BS36: Fram C . .5E **13**
  BS37: Iron A 3F **13**
Frances Greeves Ho. BS10: Hen . .2C **40**
Francis Ct. BS15: Han 1F **67**
Francis Pl. BS30: L Grn 5B **72**
Francis Rd. BS3: Bedm 2E **77**
  BS10: W Trym 3E **41**
Francis Way BS30: B'yte 2F **73**
Francombe Gro. BS10: Hor 5A **42**
Francombe Ho. *BS1: Bris* *4F **67***
  (off Commercial Rd.)
Frankcom Ho. BA2: Bath . .1E **7** (3D **105**)
Frankland Cl. BA1: Bath 1C **102**
Frankley Bldgs. BA1: Bath 1D **105**
Frankley Ter. *BA1: Bath* *1D **105***
  (off Snow Hill)
Franklin Ct. BS1: Bris 5E **5** (4A **68**)
Franklyn La. BS2: Bris 5B **58**
Franklyn St. BS2: Bris 5B **58**
Fraser St. BS3: Wind H 1F **77**
Frayne Rd. BS3: Ash G 5C **66**
Frederick Cl. BS31: Salt 2D **67**
Frederick St. BS4: Wind H 5C **68**
Freeland Bldgs. BS5: Eastv 4E **59**
Freeland Pl. BS8: Clif 3B **66**
Freeling Ho. BS1: Bris 5D **5** (4A **68**)
Freemantle Gdns. BS5: Eastv 3E **59**
Freemantle Rd. BS5: Eastv 3E **59**
Freestone Rd. BS2: Bris 3C **68**
Free Tank BS2: Bris 4F **5** (3B **68**)
Freeview Rd. BA2: Bath 4C **102**
Fremantle Ho. BS2: Bris 1F **67**
Fremantle La. BS6: Cot 5F **57**
Fremantle Rd. BS6: Bris, Cot 5F **57**
Fremantle Sq. BS6: Bris 5F **57**
FRENCHAY 4D **45**
Frenchay Cl. BS16: Fish 4D **45**
Frenchay Comn. BS16: Fren 4D **45**
Frenchay Hill BS16: Fren 4E **45**
Frenchay Pk. Rd. BS16: B'hll 5A **44**
Frenchay Rd. BS16: Fish 4E **45**
Frenchay Village Mus. 3C **44**
Freshford Ho. BS1: Bris 5D **5** (4A **68**)
Freshland Way BS15: K'wd 1D **71**
Friars Ho. BS37: Yate 1F **31**
Friary BS1: Bris 5F **5** (4B **68**)
Friary Grange Pk. BS36: Wint 2A **28**
Friary Rd. BS7: B'stn 2F **57**
  BS20: P'head 1D **49**
Friendly Row BS20: Pill 1E **53**
Friendship Rd. BS4: Know 2B **78**
Friezewood Rd. BS3: Ash G 5C **66**
Frobisher Av. BS20: P'head 1C **48**
Frobisher Cl. BS20: P'head 1C **48**
Frobisher Rd. BS3: Ash G 1C **76**
FROGLAND CROSS 1F **13**
Frog La. BS1: Bris 3A **4** (3E **67**)
  BS36: Coal H 5A **14**
Frogmore St. BS1: Bris 3A **4** (3E **67**)
Frome Bank Gdns. BS36: Wint D . . .5A **28**

Frome Glen BS36: Wint D 4A **28**
Frome Pl. BS16: Stap 5A **44**
Frome Rd. BA2: Odd D 3E **109**
  BS37: Chip S 4E **17**
Fromeside Pk. BS16: Fish 4D **45**
Frome Ter. BS16: Stap 1A **60**
Frome Valley Nature Trail 1A **60**
Frome Valley Rd. BS16: B'hll 5B **44**
Frome Valley Walkway
  BS37: Chip S *4C **16***
  (off Brook St.)
Frome Vw. BS36: Fram C 1D **29**
Frome Vs. BS16: Fren 4E **45**
Frome Way BS36: Wint 3A **28**
Froomshaw Rd. BS16: B'hll 4C **44**
Fry Ct. BS3: Bris 5E **67**
Fry's Cl. BS16: Stap 2F **59**
Fry's Hill BS4: Brisl 2F **79**
  BS15: Soun 5A **62**
  (not continuous)
Frys Leaze BA1: Bath 5D **97**
Fulford Rd. BS13: Hart 2D **85**
Fulford Wlk. BS13: Hart 2D **85**
Fuller Rd. BA1: Bath 5E **97**
Fullers Way BA2: Odd D 5F **109**
Funchal Vs. BS8: Clif 2C **66**
Furber Ct. BS5: St G 3D **71**
Furber Ridge BS5: St G 3D **71**
Furber Rd. BS5: St G 2D **71**
Furber Va. BS5: St G 3D **71**
Furlong, The BS6: Henle 1E **57**
Furnwood BS5: St G 3C **70**
Furze Rd. BS16: Fish 3E **61**
Furzewood Rd. BS15: K'wd 1B **72**
Fussell Ct. BS15: K'wd 1B **72**
Fylton Cft. BS14: Whit 4D **87**

G

Gable Rd. BS5: E'tn 5C **58**
Gabriel Cl. BS30: C Hth 4D **73**
Gadshill Dr. BS34: Stok G 3A **26**
Gadshill Rd. BS5: Eastv 3E **59**
Gages Cl. BS15: K'wd 2B **72**
Gages Rd. BS15: K'wd 2A **72**
Gainsborough Gdns. BA1: Bath . . .2E **103**
Gainsborough M. BS10: Bren 1D **41**
Gainsborough Rd. BS31: Key 2B **90**
Gainsborough Sq. BS7: L'lze 4D **43**
Gala Bingo
  Whitchurch 1A **86**
Galingale Way BS20: P'head 1B **50**
Gallagher Shop. Pk.
  BS30: L Grn 4A **72**
Galleries, The BS1: Bris . . .2D **5** (2A **68**)
Gallivan Cl. BS34: Lit S 5D **9**
Galway Rd. BS4: Know 3A **78**
Gander Cl. BS13: Hart 2D **85**
Garamond Ct. BS1: Bris 5E **5** (4A **68**)
Garden Cl. BS9: Sea M 1E **55**
Garden Ct. BS8: Clif 1C **66**
Gardeners Wlk. BS41: L Ash 3D **75**
Gardens, The BS16: Fren 2A **44**
  BS16: Stap H 3A **62**
  BS30: C Hth 3E **73**
Gardner Av. BS13: Bis 5B **76**
Gardner Rd. BS20: P'head 5C **34**
Garfield Rd. BS5: St G 1C **70**
Garfield Ter. BA1: Bath 5E **97**
Garnet St. BS3: Bedm 1D **77**
Garnett Pl. BS16: Down 4B **46**
Garonne Way BS20: P'bry 1B **52**
Garre Ho. BA2: Bath 5B **102**
Garrett Dr. BS32: Brad S 1F **25**
Garrick Rd. BA2: Bath 5B **102**
Garstons BA1: Bathf 5F **99**
Garstons, The BS20: P'head 2E **49**
Garth Rd. BS13: Bis 4C **76**
Gasferry Rd. BS1: Bris 4D **67**
  (not continuous)

Gaskins, The BS7: L'lze 1C 58
Gas La. BS2: Bris 3C 68
Gaston Av. BS31: Key 1B 90
Gastons BS11: Law W 3C 38
Gastons, The BS11: Law W 3C 38
Gasworks La. BS1: Bris 3D 67
Gatcombe Dr. BS34: Stok G 4A 26
Gatcombe Rd. BS13: Hart 2D 85
Gatehouse Av. BS13: Withy 2C 84
Gatehouse Cen. BS13: Withy 2D 85
Gatehouse Cl. BS13: Withy 2C 84
Gatehouse Ct. BS13: Withy 2C 84
Gatehouse Way BS13: Withy 2C 84
Gatesby Mead BS34: Stok G 3A 26
Gateway Ter. BS20: P'head 5D 35
Gathorne Cres. BS37: Yate 3F 15
Gathorne Rd. BS3: Bris 5D 67
Gatton Rd. BS2: Bris 5C 58
Gaunts Cl. BS20: P'head 2B 48
GAUNT'S EARTHCOTT 1D 11
Gaunt's Earthcott La.
  BS32: Gau E 1D 11
Gaunts La. BS1: Bris 3A 4 (3E 67)
Gaunts Rd. BS37: Chip S 5D 17
Gay Ct. BA1: Bathe 4A 98
Gay Elms Rd. BS13: Withy 3C 84
Gayner Rd. BS7: Fil 2C 42
Gay's Hill BA1: Bath 2C 104
Gay's Rd. BS15: Han 5D 71
Gay St. BA1: Bath 2B 6 (3B 104)
Gaywood Ho. BS3: Bedm 1D 77
Gazzard Cl. BS36: Wint 1A 28
Gazzard Rd. BS36: Wint 1A 28
Gee Moors BS15: K'wd 2B 72
Gefle Cl. BS1: Bris 4D 67
Geoffrey Cl. BS13: Bis 1A 84
George & Dragon La. BS5: St G . . .1F 69
                              (off Church Rd.)
  BS5: St G 2F 69
                           (off Claremont Ter.)
George Ct. BS6: Redl 5D 57
                          (off Hampton Pk.)
George Jones Rd. BS2: Bris 2C 68
George's Bldgs.
  BA1: Bath 1C 6 (2C 104)
George's Pl. BA2: Bath 3F 7
                          (off Bathwick Hill)
George's Rd. BA1: Bath 1C 104
Georges Sq. BS1: Bris 3D 5 (3A 68)
George St. BA1: Bath 2B 6 (3B 104)
  BA2: Bath 3F 7 (4D 105)
  BS5: Redf 1E 69
  BS20: P'head 4E 49
George White St.
  BS1: Bris 1E 5 (2A 68)
Georgian Garden 2A 6 (3B 104)
Georgian House 3A 4 (3E 67)
Georgian Vw. BA2: Bath 2E 109
Gerald Rd. BS3: Ash G 1C 76
Gerrard Bldgs.
  BA2: Bath 2E 7 (3C 104)
Gerrard Cl. BS4: Know 5F 77
Gerrish Av. BS5: Redf 1E 69
  BS16: Mang 1B 62
Gibbsfold Rd. BS13: Hart 4E 85
Gibson Rd. BS6: Cot 5F 57
Giffard Ho. BS34: Lit S 2F 25
Gifford Cl. BS34: Stok G 1F 43
Gifford Cres. BS34: Lit S 2E 25
Gifford Rd. BS10: Hen 4B 22
Giffords Pl. BS13: Bis 5C 76
Gilbert Rd. BS5: Redf 1E 69
  BS15: K'wd 5F 61
Gilda Cl. BS14: H'gro 2E 87
Gilda Cres. BS14: H'gro 1D 87
Gilda Pde. BS14: H'gro 2E 87
Gilda Sq. W. BS14: H'gro 2D 87
                            (not continuous)
Gillard Cl. BS15: K'wd 1D 71
Gillard Rd. BS15: K'wd 1D 71
Gill Av. BS16: Fish 1D 61

Gillebank Cl. BS14: Stoc 2F 87
Gillingham Hill BS5: St G 4D 71
Gillingham Ter. BA1: Bath 1D 105
Gilpin Cl. BS15: K'wd 5B 62
Gilray Cl. BS7: L'lze 5D 43
Gilroy Cl. BS30: L Grn 1D 83
Gilslake Av. BS10: Bren 5D 23
Gilton Ho. BS4: Brisl 2A 80
Gingell's Grn. BS5: St G 1C 70
Gipsy Patch La. BS34: Lit S 2D 25
Glades, The BS5: Eastv 4A 60
Gladstone Dr. BS16: Soun 3F 61
Gladstone La. BS6: Fram C 1E 29
Gladstone Pl. BA2: C Down 4E 111
Gladstone Rd. BA2: C Down 3E 111
  BS14: H'gro 1D 87
  BS15: K'wd 5F 61
Gladstone St. BS3: Bedm 1D 77
  BS5: Redf 2F 69
  BS16: Soun 3F 61
Glaisdale Rd. BS16: Fish 1C 60
Glanville Gdns. BS15: K'wd 2A 72
Glasscutter BS14: H'gro 4D 79
                          (off Petherton Rd.)
Glass Ho. La. BS2: Bris 4D 69
Glastonbury Cl. BS30: Bar C 4B 72
Glaze BS5: St G 2C 70
Glebe Av. BS20: P'head 2A 50
Glebe Cl. BS41: L Ash 2D 75
Glebe Fld. BS32: Alm 1C 8
Glebelands Rd. BS34: Fil 5C 24
Glebe Rd. BA2: Bath 1D 109
  BS5: St G 1A 70
  BS20: P'head 2A 50
  BS41: L Ash 3E 75
Glebe Wlk. BS31: Key 3E 89
Gledemoor Dr. BS36: Coal H 1F 29
Gleeson Ho. BS16: Fish 5D 45
Glen, The BS6: Redl 3D 57
  BS15: Han 5D 71
  BS31: Salt 1B 100
  BS37: Yate 3A 16
Glena Av. BS4: Know 2D 79
Glenarm Rd. BS4: Brisl 2A 80
Glenarm Wlk. BS4: Brisl 2A 80
Glen Av. BS8: Abb L 1B 64
Glenavon Ct. BS9: Stok B 2E 55
Glenavon Pk. BS9: Stok B 2E 55
Glenburn Rd. BS15: K'wd 5D 61
Glencairn Ct. BA2: Bath . . .3E 7 (4D 105)
Glencoyne Sq. BS10: S'mead 1E 41
Glendale BS8: Clif 3B 66
  BS16: Down 3A 46
  BS16: Fish 3E 61
Glendare St. BS5: Bar H 3E 69
Glendevon Rd. BS14: Whit 4C 86
Glen Dr. BS9: Stok B 2F 55
Gleneagles BS37: Yate 4A 16
Gleneagles Dr. BS10: Hen 5F 21
Gleneagles Rd. BS30: Warm 3D 73
Glenfall BS37: Yate 1F 31
Glenfrome Ho. BS5: Eastv 4D 59
Glenfrome Rd. BS2: Bris 4C 58
  BS5: Eastv 3D 59
Glen La. BS4: Brisl 2F 79
Glen Pk. BS5: Eastv 4E 59
  BS5: St G 1C 70
Glen Pk. Gdns. BS5: St G 1C 70
Glenroy Av. BS15: K'wd 5D 61
Glenside Cl. BS16: Fish 1E 45
Glenside Hospital Mus. 1A 60
Glenside Pk. BS16: Stap 1A 60
Glentworth Rd. BS6: Redl 4E 57
  BS8: Clif 3D 67
Glenview Rd. BS4: Brisl 2F 79
Glenwood BS16: Fish 3E 61
Glenwood Dr. BS30: Old C 5D 73
Glenwood Ri. BS20: P'head 1B 48
Glenwood Rd. BS10: W Trym 4E 41
Glevum Cl. BS16: Emer G 4E 47
Gloster Av. BS5: Eastv 3F 59

Gloster Vs. BA1: Bath 2C 104
Gloucester Cl. BS34: Stok G 3F 25
Gloucester Ho. BS2: Bris 2B 68
                          (off Lawfords Ga.)
Gloucester La. BS2: Bris . . .1F 5 (2B 68)
Gloucester Mans. BS7: B'stn 4F 57
Gloucester Pl. BS2: Bris 1B 4
                          (off Horfield Rd.)
Gloucester Rd. BA1: Bath, Swa . . .2E 97
  BA1: Up Swa 1D 97
  BS7: B'stn, Hor 4F 57
  BS11: A'mth 2C 36
  BS16: Soun 3A 62
  BS32: Alm, Brad S 1D 9
  BS34: Pat 1C 24
Gloucester Rd. Nth. BS7: Fil 2B 42
  BS34: Fil 5C 24
Gloucester Row BS8: Clif 2B 66
Gloucestershire County Cricket Club
  . . . . .2A 58
Gloucester St.
  BA1: Bath 1A 6 (3B 104)
  BS1: Bris 1E 5 (1A 68)
  BS2: Bris 1E 5 (1A 68)
  BS5: Eastv 3F 59
  BS8: Clif 2B 66
Glyn Va. BS3: Know 3F 77
Goddard Way BS10: W Trym 2C 40
Godfrey Ct. BS30: L Grn 5B 72
Goffenton Dr. BS16: Fish 5D 45
Goldcrest Rd. BS37: Chip S 1B 32
Goldcrest Way BS20: P'head 5F 35
GOLDEN HILL 1E 57
Golden Hill BS6: B'stn 1F 57
Golden Lion Ct. BS1: Bris 4D 5
Golden Valley La. BS30: Bit 4F 83
Goldney Av. BS8: Clif 3C 66
  BS30: Warm 2E 73
Goldney Hall BS8: Clif 3C 66
Goldney La. BS8: Clif 3C 66
Goldney Rd. BS8: Clif 3C 66
Goldsbury Wlk. BS11: Law W 2C 38
Goldsmiths Ho. BS2: Bris . . .3F 5 (3B 68)
Golf Club La. BS31: Salt 5A 92
Golf Course La. BS34: Fil 5B 24
Golf Course Rd. BA2: Bath 4E 105
Gooch Ct. BS30: Old C 1E 83
Goodeve Pk. BS9: Stok B 3F 55
                           (not continuous)
Goodeve Rd. BS9: Stok B 3F 55
Goodhind St. BS5: E'tn 1C 68
Goodneston Rd. BS16: Fish 3C 60
Goodrich Cl. BS37: Yate 4C 14
Goodring Hill BS11: Law W 2C 38
Good Shepherd Cl.
  BS7: B'stn 2E 57
Goodwin Dr. BS14: Whit 3B 86
Goodwood Gdns. BS16: Down 2B 46
Goold Cl. BA2: Cor 2C 100
Goolden St. BS4: Wind H 1C 78
Goose Acre BS32: Brad S 2B 26
Gooseberry La. BS31: Key 2B 90
GOOSE GREEN
  BS30 . . . . .5E 63
  BS37 . . . . .1A 16
Goose Grn. BS30: Sis 5E 63
  BS36: Fram C 5E 13
  BS37: Yate 1A 16
Goose Grn. Way BS37: Yate 1E 15
Gooseland Cl. BS14: Whit 4B 86
Gordano Cl. BS20: P'head 1A 50
Gordano Gdns. BS20: Eas 2D 53
Gordano Gate Bus. Pk.
  BS20: P'head 1A 50
Gordano Rd. BS20: P'bry 4A 36
GORDANO SERVICE AREA 2B 52
Gordano Sports Cen. 3E 49
Gordano Vw. BS20: P'head 1E 49
Gordano Way BS20: P'bry 1B 52
Gordon Av. BS5: W'hall 5F 59
Gordon Cl. BS5: W'hall 5A 60

Gordon Rd. BA2: Bath 5D 105
  BS2: Bris 5B 58
  BS5: W'hall 5F 59
  BS8: Clif 2D 67
Gore Rd. BS3: Bedm 1C 76
Gore's Marsh Rd. BS3: Bedm 2C 76
Gorham Cl. BS11: Law W 1E 39
Gorlands Rd. BS37: Chip S 4E 17
Gorlangton Cl. BS14: H'gro 5C 78
Gorse Covert Local Nature Reserve
. . . . .5A 8
Gorse Hill BS16: Fish, Stap H . . .3D 61
Gorse La. BS8: Clif 3D 67
Gosforth Cl. BS10: S'mead 2D 41
Gosforth Rd. BS10: S'mead 1D 41
Goshawk Dr. BS20: P'head 4E 35
Goslet Rd. BS14: Stoc 2A 88
Gotley Rd. BS4: Brisl 2F 79
Gott Dr. BS4: St Ap 4F 69
Gould Cl. BS13: Hart 2F 85
Goulston Rd. BS13: Bis 2C 84
Goulston Wlk. BS13: Bis 1C 84
Goulter St. BS5: Bar H 3D 69
Gourney Cl. BS11: Law W 1D 39
Governors Ho. BA2: Bath 4F 103
Gover Rd. BS15: Han 1E 81
Grace Cl. BS37: Chip S 4E 17
Grace Ct. BS16: Down 5F 45
Grace Dr. BS15: K'wd 5B 62
Grace Pk. Rd. BS4: Brisl 3F 79
Grace Rd. BS16: Down 1E 61
Graeme Cl. BS16: Fish 2C 60
Graham Rd. BS3: Bedm 1E 77
  BS5: E'tn 5D 59
  BS16: Down 5B 46
Grainger Ct. BS11: Shire 4A 38
Grampian Cl. BS30: Old C 5E 73
Granby Ct. BS8: Clif 3B 66
Granby Hill BS8: Clif 3B 66
Grand Pde. BA2: Bath 3C 6 (4C 104)
Grange, The BS9: C Din 4F 39
Grange Av. BS15: Han 4E 71
  BS34: Lit S 2E 25
Grange Cl. BS32: Brad S 3E 9
  BS34: Stok G 4C 26
Grange Cl. Nth. BS9: W Trym 5D 41
Grange Ct. BS9: Henle 5D 41
  BS15: Han 4F 71
Grange Ct. Rd. BS9: Henle 5C 40
Grange Dr. BS16: Fish 5E 45
Grange La. BS13: Withy 3B 84
Grange Pk. BS9: W Trym 5D 41
  BS16: Fren 3E 45
Grange Rd. BS8: Clif 2C 66
  BS13: Bis 2C 84
  BS31: Salt 5E 91
Grangeville Cl. BS30: L Grn 1D 83
Grangewood Cl. BS16: Fish 5E 45
Granny's La. BS15: Han 3A 72
Grantham Apartments
  BS15: K'wd 1E 71
                (off Two Mile Hill Rd.)
Grantham La. BS15: K'wd 1E 71
Grantham Rd. BS15: K'wd 1E 71
Grantson Cl. BS4: Brisl 2A 80
Granville Cl. BS15: Han 1D 81
Granville Rd. BA1: L'dwn 4A 96
Granville St. BS5: Bar H 3E 69
Grasmere Cl. BS10: S'mead 3C 40
Grasmere Gdns. BS30: Old C 3F 73
Grassington Dr. BS37: Chip S 5C 16
Grass Meers Dr. BS14: Whit 3C 86
Gratitude Rd. BS5: E'tn 5E 59
Gravel Hill Rd. BS37: Yate 1B 16
                (not continuous)
Gravel Wlk. BA1: Bath 1A 6 (3A 104)
Graveney Cl. BS4: Brisl 3F 79
Gray Cl. BS10: Hen 1A 40
Grayle Rd. BS10: Hen 1C 40
Gt. Ann St. BS2: Bris 1F 5 (2B 68)
Gt. Bedford St. BA1: Bath 2B 104

Great Brockeridge BS9: W Trym . . .5B 40
Great Dowles BS30: C Hth 5C 72
Gt. George St. BS1: Bris . . .3A 4 (3E 67)
  BS2: Bris 1F 5 (2B 68)
Gt. Hayles Rd. BS14: H'gro 5B 78
Great Leaze BS30: C Hth 5C 72
Gt. Mdw. Rd. BS32: Brad S 1B 26
Great Pk. Rd. BS32: Brad S 2E 9
Gt. Pulteney St.
  BA2: Bath 2D 7 (3C 104)
Gt. Stanhope St.
  BA1: Bath 3A 6 (4A 104)
GREAT STOKE 3B 26
Gt. Stoke Way BS34: Stok G 1F 43
                        (Filton Rd.)
  BS34: Stok G 3C 26
                (Winterbourne Rd.)
Gt. Swanmoor Cl. BS34: Stok G . .5E 25
Gt. Western Bus. Pk.
  BS37: Yate 2D 15
                (not continuous)
Gt. Western Ct. BS34: Stok G 4B 26
Gt. Western La. BS5: Bar H 3E 69
Gt. Wood Cl. BS13: Hart 3E 85
Green, The BA2: Odd D 4F 109
  BS11: Shire 5A 38
  BS15: Soun 4A 62
  BS20: Pill 2F 53
                (not continuous)
  BS34: Stok G 4A 26
Green Acre Rd. BS14: Whit 4C 86
Greenacres BA1: W'ton 4D 95
  BS9: W Trym 4A 40
Greenacres Pk. BS36: Coal H 3F 29
Greenbank Av. E. BS5: E'tn 5E 59
Greenbank Av. W. BS5: E'tn 5D 59
Greenbank Gdns. BA1: W'ton 1D 103
Greenbank Rd. BS3: Bris 4C 66
  BS5: E'tn 5E 59
  BS15: Han 5F 71
Greenbank Vw. BS5: Eastv 4E 59
                . . . . .2A 72
Green Cl. BS7: Hor 3C 42
Green Cotts. BA2: C Down 4E 111
Green Cft. BS5: S'wll 5C 60
Greendale Rd. BS3: Wind H 1A 78
  BS6: Redl 2D 57
Green Dell Cl. BS10: Hen 5F 21
Greenditch Av. BS13: Hart 2E 85
Greendown BS5: St G 2C 70
Greendown Pl. BA2: C Down 4C 110
Green Dragon Rd. BS36: Wint 3F 27
Greenfield Av. BS10: S'mead 3F 41
Greenfield Pk. BS20: P'head 3E 49
Greenfield Rd. BS10: S'mead 2F 41
Greenfinch Lodge BS16: B'hll 5B 44
Green Hayes BS37: Chip S 5E 17
Greenhill Gro. BS3: Bedm 2C 76
Greenhill La. BS11: Law W 2E 39
Greenlands Rd. BS10: Hen 4A 22
Greenlands Way BS10: Hen 5A 22
Green La. BS11: A'mth 3D 37
  BS36: Wint 2E 27
Greenleaze BS4: Know 3D 79
Greenleaze Av. BS16: Down 2F 45
Greenleaze Cl. BS16: Down 2F 45
Greenmore Rd. BS4: Know 2D 79
Greenpark Rd. BS15: K'wd 2E 71
Green Pk. BA1: Bath 4A 6 (4A 104)
  BS30: Old C 3F 73
Green Pk. Ho. BA1: Bath 4A 6
Green Pk. M. BA1: Bath . . .4A 6 (4A 104)
Green Pk. Rd. BA1: Bath . . .4A 6 (4B 104)
Greenpark Rd. BS10: S'mead 2A 42
Green Pk. Sta.
  BA1: Bath 3A 6 (4A 104)
Greenridge Cl. BS13: Withy 3A 84
Greens Hill BS16: Fish 3A 60
Greenside BS16: Mang 5C 46
Greenside Cl. BS10: Hen 5F 21
Greensplott Rd. BS11: Chit 1A 20

Green St. BA1: Bath 3B 6 (4B 104)
  BS3: Wind H 5B 68
Green Wlk. BS4: Know 3C 78
Greenway, The BS16: Fish 3E 61
Greenway Bush La. BS3: Bris 5C 66
Greenway Ct. BA2: Bath 1B 110
Greenway Dr. BS10: S'mead 2F 41
Greenway La. BA2: Bath 2B 110
  BS10: S'mead 2F 41
Greenway Rd. BS10: S'mead 3F 41
Greenway Rd. BS6: Redl 4D 57
Greenways BS15: K'wd 5C 62
Greenways Rd. BS37: Yate 2F 15
Greenwood Cl. BS7: Hor 4A 42
Greenwood Rd. BS4: Know 2C 78
  BS13: Bis 3C 72
Gregory Cl. BS30: C Hth 4D 72
Gregorys Gro. BA2: Odd D 5F 109
Grenville Cl. BS5: St G 1B 70
Grenville Pl. BS1: Bris 4B 66
                (off Brunel Lock Rd.)
Grenville Rd. BS6: Bris 3A 58
Greve Ct. BS30: Bar C 5B 72
Greville M. BS3: Bris 5D 67
Greville Rd. BS3: Bris 5D 67
Greville St. BS3: Bedm 5D 67
Greyfriars BS1: Bris 1B 4 (2F 67)
Greylands Rd. BS13: Bis 5B 76
Greystoke BS10: W Trym 2C 40
Greystoke Av. BS10: S'mead 3C 40
Greystoke Gdns. BS10: S'mead . .3D 41
                (not continuous)
Greystones BS16: Down 2A 46
Griffin Ct. BA1: Bath 4A 6
Griggfield Wlk. BS14: H'gro 5B 78
Grimsbury Rd. BS15: K'wd 1C 72
Grindell Rd. BS5: St G 2F 69
Grinfield Av. BS13: Hart 3E 85
Grittleton Rd. BS7: Hor 3A 42
Grosvenor Bri. Rd. BA1: Bath 1E 105
Grosvenor Pk. BA1: Bath 1E 105
Grosvenor Pl. BA1: Bath 1E 105
Grosvenor Rd. BS2: Bris 5B 58
Grosvenor Ter. BA1: Bath 5E 97
Grosvenor Vs. BA1: Bath 1D 105
Grove, The BA1: W'ton 1E 103
  BS1: Bris 5B 4 (4F 67)
  BS30: C Hth 5C 72
  BS34: Pat 1D 25
Grove Av. BS1: Bris 5C 4 (4F 67)
  BS9: C Din 4E 39
  BS16: Fish 2B 60
Grove Bank BS16: Fren 2E 45
Grove Ho. BS8: Clif 3C 66
                (off Cornwallis Gro.)
Grove Ind. Est., The BS34: Pat 5D 9
Grove Leaze BS11: Shire 5E 37
Grove M., The BS36: Wint 1A 28
Grove Pk. BS4: Brisl 2F 79
  BS6: Redl 4E 57
Grove Pk. Av. BS4: Brisl 2F 79
Grove Pk. Ct. BS4: Brisl 2F 79
Grove Pk. Rd. BS4: Brisl 2F 79
Grove Pk. Ter. BS16: Fish 2B 60
Grove Rd. BS6: Redl 4C 56
  BS9: C Din 3E 39
  BS16: Fish, Stap 2A 60
Groves, The BS13: Hart 3E 85
Grove St. BA2: Bath 2C 6 (3C 104)
Grove Vw. BS16: Ham 5E 27
Guernsey Av. BS4: Brisl 5B 70
Guest Av. BS16: Emer G 4D 47
Guild Ct. BS1: Bris 5D 5 (3A 68)
Guildford Rd. BS4: St Ap 4A 70
Guildhall Market 3C 6
                (off High St.)
Guillemot Rd. BS20: P'head 5E 35
Guinea La. BA1: Bath 1B 6 (3B 104)
  BS16: Fish 1C 60
                (not continuous)

Guinea St. BS1: Bris 5C **4** (4F **67**)
Gullimore Gdns. BS13: Hart 3D **85**
Gullivers Pl. BS37: Chip S 5C **16**
Gullons Cl. BS13: Bis 1C **84**
Gullon Wlk. BS13: Withy 2B **84**
Gully, The BS36: Wint 1B **28**
Gullybrook La. BS5: Bar H 3D **69**
Gunning Cl. BS15: K'wd 3F **71**
Gunter's Hill BS5: St G 3C **70**
Guthrie Rd. BS8: Clif 1B **66**
Gwilliam St. BS3: Wind H 1F **77**
Gwyn St. BS2: Bris 5A **58**
Gypsy La. BS16: Puck 1F **47**
　　BS36: H'fld 1F **47**

H

Haberfield Hill BS8: Abb L 4A **54**
Haberfield Ho. *BS8: Clif* *3B 66*
　　(off Hotwell Rd.)
Hadley Ct. BS30: C Hth 3D **73**
Hadley Rd. BA2: C Down 3D **111**
Hadrian Cl. BS9: Stok B 2E **55**
Hadrians Wlk. BS16: Emer G 5E **47**
Haig Cl. BS9: Sea M 4D **39**
Halbrow Cres. BS16: Fish 1E **61**
Haldon Cl. BS3: Wind H 3F **77**
Hale Cl. BS15: Han 5F **71**
Hales Horn Cl. BS32: Brad S 2F **25**
Halfacre Cl. BS14: Whit 4C **86**
Halfacre La. BS14: Whit 4D **87**
Halifax Rd. BS37: Yate 1F **15**
Hallards Cl. BS11: Law W 3B **38**
HALLEN 4E **21**
Hallen Cl. BS10: Hen 5F **21**
　　BS16: Emer G 5E **47**
Hallen Dr. BS9: Sea M 4E **39**
Hallen Ind. Est. BS10: H'len 1C **20**
Hallen Rd. BS10: H'len, Hen 4E **21**
Halletts Way BS20: P'head 1F **49**
Halliwell Rd. BS20: P'head 2A **48**
Halls Gdn. BS34: Stok G 4C **26**
Halls Rd. BS15: K'wd 1F **71**
Hall St. BS3: Bedm 2D **77**
Halsbury Rd. BS6: Henle, Redl . . .2D **57**
Halstock Av. BS16: Fish 3B **60**
Halston Dr. BS2: Bris 1B **68**
Halswell Gdns. BS13: Hart 3D **85**
Halt End BS14: Whit 4E **87**
Halwyn Cl. BS9: Stok B 1F **55**
HAMBROOK 1E **45**
Hambrook La. BS16: Ham 5B **26**
　　BS34: Stok G 5B **26**
Ham Farm La. BS16: Emer G 5D **47**
Ham Gdns. BA1: Bath 4C **6** (4C **104**)
HAM GREEN 3F **53**
Ham Grn. BS20: Pill 2F **53**
Hamilton Ct. *BS1: Bris* *1F 67*
　　(off Montague St.)
Hamilton Ho. BA1: L'dwn 4F **95**
Hamilton Rd. BA1: Bath 5A **96**
　　BS3: Bris 5D **67**
　　BS5: E'tn 1D **69**
Ham La. BS16: B'hll 5A **44**
　　(not continuous)
　　BS41: Dun 4A **84**
Hamlet's Yd. BS31: Key 2A **90**
Hammersmith Rd. BS5: St G 1F **69**
Hammond Cl. BS4: Brisl 3F **79**
Hammond Gdns. BS9: W Trym . . .4A **40**
Hampden Cl. BS37: Yate 1F **15**
Hampden Rd. BS4: Know 1D **79**
Hampshire Way BS37: Yate 1B **16**
Hampstead Rd. BS4: Brisl 1E **79**
Hampton Cl. BS30: C Hth 4C **72**
Hampton Cnr. BS11: Shire 5A **38**
Hampton Ct. BS6: Redl 5D **57**
Hampton Ho. *BA1: Bath* 1E **105**
Hampton La. BS6: Cot 5D **57**
Hampton Pk. BS6: Redl 5D **57**

Hampton Rd. BS6: Cot, Redl 4D **57**
Hampton Row BA2: Bath 2D **105**
Hampton St. BS15: K'wd 5F **61**
Hampton Vw. BA1: Bath 1D **105**
Hanbury Cl. BS15: Han 4F **71**
Hanbury Ct. BS8: Clif 1C **66**
Hanbury Rd. BS8: Clif 1C **66**
Handel Av. BS5: St G 2F **69**
Handel Cossham Ct.
　　BS15: K'wd 5E **61**
Handel Rd. BS31: Key 2F **89**
Handford Way BS30: L Grn 1D **83**
Hanford Ct. BS14: Stoc 5F **79**
HANHAM 4E **71**
Hanham Bus. Pk. BS15: Han 5D **71**
HANHAM GREEN 1D **81**
Hanham Mt. BS15: K'wd 3F **71**
Hanham Rd. BS15: K'wd 3F **71**
Hanna Cl. BA2: Bath 4C **102**
Hanover Cl. BA1: Bath 1D **105**
　　BS1: Bris 1E **5** (1A **68**)
　　BS34: Fil 5C **24**
Hanover Ho. BS2: Bris 2C **68**
Hanover Pl. *BA1: Bath* *2D 105*
　　(off London Rd.)
　　BS1: Bris 4D **67**
Hanover Quay *BS1: Bris* *4E 67*
　　(off Canons Way)
Hanover St. BA1: Bath 1D **105**
　　BS1: Bris 3B **4**
　　BS5: Redf 2E **69**
Hanover Ter. *BA1: Bath* 1D **105**
　　(off Gillingham Ter.)
Hansford Cl. BA2: C Down 4A **110**
Hansford M. BA2: C Down 4B **110**
Hansford Sq. BA2: C Down 4A **110**
Hantone Hill BA2: B'ptn 2B **106**
Hapgood St. BS5: Bar H 2D **69**
Hapgood St. Sth. BS5: Bar H 2D **69**
Happerton La. BS20: Eas 4E **53**
Happy La. BS7: B'stn, Bris 3B **58**
Harbour Cres. BS20: P'head 1A **50**
Harbour Ho. *BS8: Clif* *4C 66*
　　(off Hotwell Rd.)
Harbour Rd. BS20: P'head 5C **34**
Harbour Rd. Trad. Est.
　　BS20: P'head 1A **50**
Harbourside Wlk. *BS1: Bris* *4E 67*
　　(off Canon's Rd.)
Harbour Wlk. *BS1: Bris* *4E 67*
　　(off Cumberland Rd.)
Harbour Wall BS9: Sea M 1A **54**
Harbour Way BS1: Bris 5A **4** (4E **67**)
Harbury Rd. BS9: Henle 4E **41**
Harbutts BA2: B'ptn 1B **106**
Harcombe Hill BS36: Wint D 4A **28**
Harcombe Rd. BS36: Wint 3F **27**
Harcourt Av. BS5: St G 3C **70**
Harcourt Cl. BS31: Salt 5A **92**
Harcourt Gdns. BA1: W'ton 5D **95**
Harcourt Hill BS6: Redl 3E **57**
Harcourt Rd. BS6: Redl 2D **57**
Hardenhuish Rd. BS4: Brisl 4F **69**
Harden Rd. BS14: Stoc 2A **88**
Harding Pl. BS31: Key 2D **91**
Hardings Ter. *BS5: St G* *1B 70*
　　(off Clovelly Rd.)
Hardington Dr. BS31: Key 5C **90**
Hardwick Cl. BS4: Brisl 1A **80**
　　BS30: Old C 4F **73**
Hardwick Rd. BS20: Pill 1E **53**
Hardy Av. BS3: Ash G 5C **66**
Hardy Ct. BS30: Bar C 4B **72**
Hardy Rd. BS3: Bedm 2D **77**
Hareclive Rd. BS13: Hart 2D **85**
Harefield Cl. BS15: Han 2E **81**
Harescombe BS37: Yate 1A **32**
Harewood Rd. BS5: S'wll 5C **60**
Harford Cl. BS9: C Din 4E **39**
Harford Dr. BS16: Fren 2E **45**

Harington Ct. BA2: New L 5D **101**
Harington Pl. BA1: Bath . . .3B **6** (4B **104**)
Harlech Way BS30: Will 2D **83**
Harleston St. BS5: E'tn 1C **68**
Harley Ct. BS8: Clif 2B **66**
Harley M. BS8: Clif 2B **66**
Harley Pl. BS8: Clif 2B **66**
Harley St. BA1: Bath 1A **6** (2B **104**)
Harmer Cl. BS10: Hen 5B **22**
Harmony Dr. BS20: P'head 2B **48**
Harnhill Cl. BS13: Hart 3D **85**
Harolds Way BS15: K'wd 3E **71**
Harptree Cl. BS30: Bar C 5C **72**
Harptree Gro. BS3: Bedm 2D **77**
Harratz Pl. BS1: Bris 4F **5** (3B **68**)
Harriet Brook BS10: Bren 1D **41**
Harrington Av. BS14: Stoc 1A **88**
Harrington Cl. BS30: Bit 4F **83**
Harrington Gro. BS14: Stoc 1A **88**
Harrington Rd. BS14: Stoc 2F **87**
Harrington Wlk. BS14: Stoc 1A **88**
Harris Barton BS36: Fram C 1D **29**
Harris Ct. BS30: L Grn 5B **72**
Harris Gro. BS13: Hart 4D **85**
Harris La. BS8: Abb L 1B **64**
Harrison Cl. BS16: Emer G 5D **47**
Harrowdene Rd. BS4: Know 1D **79**
Harrow Rd. BS4: Brisl 1F **79**
HARRY STOKE 1A **44**
Harry Stoke Rd. BS34: Stok G 1A **44**
HARTCLIFFE 3E **85**
Hartcliffe Rd. BS4: Know 4A **78**
Hartcliffe Wlk. BS4: Know 4B **78**
Hartcliffe Way BS3: Bedm 3E **77**
　　BS13: Bis 3E **77**
　　BS13: Hart 2F **85**
Hart Cl. BS20: Pill 2A **54**
Hatfield Av. BS6: Cot 5E **57**
Hartgill Cl. BS13: Hart 4D **85**
Hartington Pk. BS6: Redl 4D **57**
Hartley Cl. BS37: Chip S 4E **17**
Harts Cft. BS37: Yate 1B **16**
Harvest Cl. BS32: Brad S 4F **9**
Harvey's La. BS5: St G 1B **70**
Harwood Ho. BS5: Bar H 2D **69**
Harwood Sq. BS7: Hor 1A **58**
Haselbury Gro. BS31: Salt 5A **92**
Haskins Ct. BS30: Bar C 5C **72**
Haslemere Ind. Est.
　　BS11: A'mth 1E **37**
Hassell Dr. BS2: Bris 2C **68**
Hastings Cl. BS3: Bedm 3E **77**
Hastings Rd. BS3: Bedm 3E **77**
Hatchet La. BS34: Stok G 4A **26**
Hatchet Rd. BS34: Stok G 3F **25**
Hatfield Bldgs.
　　BA2: Bath 5E **7** (5D **105**)
Hatfield Rd. BA2: Bath 2A **110**
Hathaway Ho. *BS2: Bris* *1F 67*
　　(off Dove St. Sth.)
Hatherley BS37: Yate 1A **32**
Hatherley Rd. BS7: B'stn 2A **58**
Hathway Wlk. BS5: E'tn 1C **68**
Hatters Cl. BS36: Wint 1A **28**
Hatters La. BS37: Chip S 4D **17**
Haven, The BS15: K'wd 5A **62**
Haverstock Rd. BS4: Wind H 1C **78**
Haviland Gro. BA1: W'ton 4C **94**
Haviland Ho. BS2: Bris 1F **5**
Haviland Pk. BA1: W'ton 5D **95**
Havory BA1: Bath 1E **105**
Hawarden Ter. BA1: Bath 1D **105**
Hawburn Cl. BS4: Brisl 2F **79**
Haweswater BS10: S'mead 1D **41**
Haweswater Cl. BS30: Old C 3F **73**
Hawkesbury Rd. BS16: Fish 3A **60**
Hawkesley Dr. BS34: Lit S 2F **25**
　　(not continuous)
Hawkesworth Rd. BS37: Yate 2E **15**
Hawkfield Bus. Pk. BS14: Hart . . .2F **85**
Hawkfield Cl. BS14: Hart 2F **85**

Hawkfield Rd. BS13: Hart 2F **85**
Hawkfield Way BS14: Hart 2F **85**
Hawkins Cl. BS30: Old C 5E **73**
Hawkins Cres. BS32: Brad S 5F **9**
Hawkins St. BS2: Bris 2F **5** (2B **68**)
Hawkley Dr. BS32: Brad S 2F **9**
Hawksmoor Cl. BS14: H'gro 1C **86**
Hawksmoor La. BS16: Stap 3A **44**
Hawksworth Dr. BS15: Han 4D **71**
Hawthorn Av. BS15: Han 4D **71**
Hawthorn Cl. BS20: P'head 1B **48**
BS34: Pat 5A **8**
Hawthorne Gdns.
BS16: Stap H 2B **62**
Hawthorne Ri. BS10: Bren 5E **23**
Hawthornes, The BS16: Stap H . . .2B **62**
Hawthorne St. BS4: Wind H 1C **78**
Hawthorn Gro. BA2: C Down 4B **110**
Hawthorns BS31: Key 2A **90**
Hawthorns, The BS8: Clif 1E **67**
Hawthorns La. BS31: Key 2A **90**
Hawthorn Way BS34: Stok G 3A **26**
Haycombe BS14: H'gro 1B **86**
Haycombe Crematorium
BA2: Bath 1B **108**
Haycombe Dr. BA2: Bath 5C **102**
Haycombe La. BA2: Eng 2B **108**
Haycroft Rd. BS34: Fil 5B **24**
Hayden Cl. BA2: Bath 5A **6** (5A **104**)
Haydock Cl. BS16: Down 2B **46**
Haydon Gdns. BS7: L'lze 1D **59**
Hayeley Dr. BS32: Brad S 2A **26**
Hayes Cl. BS2: Bris 2C **68**
Hayes Ct. BS34: Pat 1D **25**
Hayesfield Pk.
BA2: Bath 5A **6** (5B **104**)
Hayes Pl. BA2: Bath 5B **104**
Haygarth Ct. *BA1: Bath 2B **104**
(off Lansdown Gro.)
Hay Hill BA1: Bath 1B **6** (3B **104**)
Hay Leaze BS37: Yate 1F **15**
Hayleigh Ho. BS3: Bedm 5D **67**
BS13: Hart 3E **85**
Haymans Ct. *BS15: K'wd 4E **61**
(off Cherrytree Cres.)
Haymarket, The BS1: Bris . . .1C **4** (2F **67**)
Haymarket Wlk. BS1: Bris 1C **4**
Haynes La. BS16: Stap H 1F **61**
Haythorne Ct. BS16: Stap H 1B **62**
Haytor Pk. BS9: Stok B 5F **39**
Hayward Ind. Est. BS16: Soun . . .3F **61**
Hayward Rd. BS5: Redf 2E **69**
BS16: Stap H 2F **61**
Hazel Av. BS6: Redl 4D **57**
Hazelbury Dr. BS30: Old C 4E **73**
Hazelbury Rd. BS14: H'gro 4E **79**
Hazel Cote Rd. BS14: Whit 3D **87**
Hazeldene Rd. BS34: Pat 1C **24**
Hazel Gro. BA2: Bath 1F **109**
BS7: Hor 3C **42**
Hazelgrove BS36: Wint 3F **27**
Hazelton Rd. BS7: B'stn 3F **57**
Hazel Way BA2: Odd D 5F **109**
Hazelwood Cl. BS16: Stap H 1B **62**
Hazelwood Ct. BS9: Stok B 3F **55**
Hazelwood Rd. BS9: Stok B 3F **55**
Headford Av. BS5: St G 2D **71**
Headford Rd. BS4: Know 3F **77**
Headington Cl. BS15: Han 5F **71**
Headley Cl. BS13: Bis 1D **85**
Headley La. BS13: Bis 1C **84**
HEADLEY PARK 5D **77**
Headley Pk. Av. BS13: Bis 1D **85**
Headley Pk. Rd. BS13: Bis 5C **76**
Headley Rd. BS13: Bis 1C **84**
Headley Wlk. BS13: Bis 5D **77**
Heart Meers BS14: H'gro 2D **87**
Heath Cl. BS36: Wint 2A **28**
Heathcote Dr. BS36: Coal H 1F **29**
Heathcote La. *BS36: Coal H 1F **29**
(off Boundary Rd.)

Heathcote Rd. BS16: Fish 4D **61**
BS16: Stap H 1A **62**
Heathcote Wlk. BS16: Fish 4E **61**
Heath Ct. BS16: Down 4F **45**
Heather Av. BS36: Fram C 2D **29**
Heather Cl. BS15: K'wd 1D **71**
Heatherdene BS14: H'gro 5B **78**
Heather Dr. BA2: Odd D 5F **109**
Heathfield Cl. BA1: W'ton 4C **94**
BS31: Key 2E **89**
Heathfield Cres. BS14: Whit 3C **86**
Heathfields BS16: Down 3F **45**
Heath Gdns. BS16: Down 3F **45**
BS36: Coal H 2E **29**
Heath Ho. La. BS16: Stap 2D **59**
Heath Ridge BS41: L Ash 2C **74**
Heath Ri. BS30: C Hth 4D **73**
Heath Rd. BS5: Eastv 3D **59**
BS15: Han 5D **71**
BS16: Down 4F **45**
Heath St. BS5: Eastv 3E **59**
Heath Wlk. BS16: Down 4F **45**
Heber St. BS5: Redf 2E **69**
Hebron Rd. BS3: Bedm 1E **77**
Hedgemead Cl. BS16: Stap 1F **59**
Hedgemead Ct. *BA1: Bath 2C **104**
(off Margaret's Hill)
Hedgemead Vw. BS16: Stap 1A **60**
Hedgerows, The BS32: Brad S 4F **9**
Hedgers Cl. BS3: Bedm 2C **76**
Hedwick Av. BS5: St G 2A **70**
Hedwick St. BS5: St G 2A **70**
Heggard Cl. BS13: Bis 2C **84**
Hellier Wlk. BS13: Hart 4E **85**
Hemmings Pde. BS5: Bar H 2D **69**
Hemplow Cl. BS14: Stoc 5F **79**
Hempton La. BS32: Alm 3C **8**
Henacre Rd. BS11: Law W 3B **38**
HENBURY 1A **40**
Henbury Ct. BS10: Hen 5A **22**
Henbury Gdns. BS10: Hen 1A **40**
Henbury Hill BS9: W Trym 3B **40**
Henbury Leisure Cen. 5A **22**
Henbury Rd. BS9: W Trym 3B **40**
BS10: Hen 1A **40**
BS15: Han 4D **71**
Hencliffe Rd. BS14: Stoc 5F **79**
Hencliffe Way BS15: Han 1D **81**
Hencliffe Wood 2D **81**
Henderson Rd. BS15: Han 4D **71**
Hendre Rd. BS3: Bedm 2C **76**
HENFIELD 5F **29**
Henfield Bus. Pk.
BS36: H'fld 1F **47**
Henfield Cres. BS30: Old C 5D **73**
Henfield Rd. BS36: Coal H 4E **29**
Hengaston St. BS3: Bedm 2D **77**
HENGROVE 1D **87**
Hengrove Av. BS14: H'gro 4D **79**
Hengrove La. BS14: H'gro 4C **78**
Hengrove Leisure Pk.
BS14: H'gro 1A **86**
Hengrove Rd. BS4: Know 2C **78**
Hengrove Way BS13: Bis 1D **85**
BS14: H'gro 1F **85**
HENLEAZE 5D **41**
Henleaze Av. BS9: Henle 1C **56**
Henleaze Gdns. BS9: Henle 1C **56**
Henleaze Pk. BS9: Henle 1E **57**
Henleaze Pk. Dr. BS9: Henle 5D **41**
Henleaze Rd. BS9: Henle 1C **56**
Henleaze Ter. BS9: Henle 4D **41**
Henley Gro. BS9: Henle 1D **57**
Hennessy Cl. BS14: Whit 4B **86**
Henrietta Ct. BA2: Bath . . .1D **7** (2C **104**)
Henrietta Gdns.
BA2: Bath 1D **7** (3C **104**)
Henrietta M. BA2: Bath . . .2D **7** (3C **104**)
Henrietta Pl. BA2: Bath . . .2C **6** (3C **104**)
Henrietta Rd.
BA2: Bath 1D **7** (3C **104**)

Henrietta St. BA2: Bath . . .2D **7** (3C **104**)
BS2: Bris 1E **67**
BS5: E'tn 5D **59**
Henrietta Vs.
BA2: Bath 1D **7** (3C **104**)
Henry Ho. BS13: Withy 3B **84**
Henry St. BA1: Bath 4C **6** (4C **104**)
BS3: Wind H 5B **68**
Henry Williamson Ct.
BS30: Bar C 4B **72**
Henshaw Cl. BS15: K'wd 4E **61**
Henshaw Rd. BS15: K'wd 4E **61**
Henshaw Wlk. BS15: K'wd 4E **61**
Hensley Gdns. BA2: Bath 1A **110**
Hensley Rd. BA2: Bath 1A **110**
Hensman's Hill BS8: Clif 3C **66**
Hepburn Rd. BS2: Bris 1A **68**
Herald Cl. BS9: Stok B 1F **55**
Herapath St. BS5: Bar H 3E **69**
Herbert Cres. BS5: Eastv 3F **59**
Herbert Rd. BA2: Bath 5F **103**
Herbert St. BS3: Bedm 5E **67**
(not continuous)
BS5: W'hall 1E **69**
Hercules Cl. BS34: Lit S 2F **25**
Hereford Rd. BS2: Bris 4C **58**
Hereford St. BS3: Bedm 1F **77**
Herkomer Cl. BS7: L'lze 4D **43**
Hermes Cl. BS31: Salt 5F **91**
Hermitage Cl. BS11: Shire 4A **38**
Hermitage Rd. BA1: Bath 1A **104**
BS16: Stap H 1F **61**
Heron Gdns. BS20: P'head 2A **50**
Heron Rd. BS5: E'tn 5D **59**
Heron Way BS37: Chip S 1B **32**
Herridge Cl. BS13: Hart 3D **85**
Herridge Rd. BS13: Hart 3D **85**
Herschel Mus. of Astronomy, The
. . . . .3A **6** (4B **104**)
Herschel Pl. BA2: Bath . . .1E **7** (3C **104**)
Hersey Gdns. BS13: Withy 4A **84**
Hesding Cl. BS15: Han 1E **81**
Hestercombe Rd. BS13: Bis 1D **85**
Hester Wood BS37: Yate 1B **16**
Hetling Ct. BA1: Bath 4B **6** (4B **104**)
Hewlands Ct. BS11: Law W 1E **39**
Hexagon, The BA2: Odd D 4A **110**
Heyford Av. BS5: Eastv 2D **59**
Heyron Wlk. BS13: Hart 3D **85**
Heywood Rd. BS20: Pill 2E **53**
Heywood Ter. BS20: Pill 2E **53**
Hiatt Baker Hall BS9: Stok B 2B **56**
Hicking Ct. BS15: K'wd 5F **61**
Hicks Av. BS16: Emer G 3D **47**
Hick's Barton BS5: St G 1B **70**
HICKS COMMON 2B **28**
Hicks Comn. Rd. BS36: Wint 4A **28**
Hicks Ct. BS5: St G 1B **70**
BS30: L Grn 5B **72**
HICKS GATE 4D **81**
Hicks Ga. Ho. BS31: Key 4D **81**
Hide Mkt. BS2: Bris 2B **68**
Higham St. BS4: Wind H 5B **68**
High Bannerdown BA1: Bathe 3D **99**
Highbury Pl. BA1: Bath 1C **104**
Highbury Rd. BS3: Bedm 3E **77**
BS7: Hor 4B **42**
Highbury Ter. BA1: Bath 1C **104**
Highbury Vs. *BA1: Bath 1C **104**
(off Highbury Pl.)
BS2: Bris 1E **67**
High Cnr. BS10: Hen 2B **40**
High Cft. BS30: Old C 3E **73**
Highdale Cl. BS14: Whit 3D **87**
High Elm BS15: K'wd 3A **72**
Highett Dr. BS5: E'tn 5C **58**
Highfield Av. BS15: Han 4F **71**
Highfield Cl. BA2: Bath 5D **103**
Highfield Dr. BS20: P'head 3A **48**
Highfield Gdns. BS30: Bit 2E **83**
Highfield Gro. BS7: Hor 1F **57**

Highfield Rd. BS31: Key 5B 90
  BS37: Chip S 4C 16
Highfields Cl. BS34: Stok G . . .5B 26
High Gro. BS9: Sea M 5D 39
Highgrove St. BS4: Wind H 5C 68
High Kingsdown BS2: Bris 1E 67
Highland Cres. BS8: Clif 4C 56
Highland Pl. BS8: Clif 4C 56
Highland Rd. BA2: Bath 5D 103
Highland Sq. BS8: Clif 4C 56
Highlands Rd. BS20: P'head 1D 49
  BS41: L Ash 2C 74
Highland Ter. BA2: Bath 4F 103
High La. BS36: Wint 5E 11
             (not continuous)
Highleaze Rd. BS30: Old C 5E 73
Highmead Gdns. BS13: Withy . . .3A 84
Highmore Ct. BS7: L'lze 4D 43
Highmore Gdns. BS7: L'lze 4E 43
Highnam Cl. BS34: Pat 4D 9
High Pk. BS14: H'gro 3D 79
Highpoint Ho. BS15: K'wd 5E 61
             (off Lodge Rd.)
HIGHRIDGE
  BS13 . . . . .1C 84
  BS41 . . . . .3A 84
Highridge Ct. BS13: Bis 5B 76
Highridge Cres. BS13: Bis 2B 84
Highridge Grn. BS13: Bis 5A 76
Highridge Pk. BS13: Bis 1B 84
Highridge Rd. BS3: Bedm 2D 77
  BS13: Bis, Withy 3A 84
Highridge Wlk. BS13: Bis 5A 76
High St. BA1: Bath 3C 6 (4C 104)
  BA1: Bathe 4B 98
  BA1: Bathf 5E 99
  BA1: W'ly 1B 96
  BA1: W'ton 5C 94
  BA2: Bath 4C 102
  BA2: B'ptn 1B 106
  BS1: Bris 2C 4 (2F 67)
  BS5: E'tn 5D 59
  BS8: Clif 4C 56
  BS9: W Trym 4C 40
  BS11: Shire 4F 37
  BS15: Han 4E 71
  BS15: K'wd 1A 72
  BS15: Warm 1D 73
  BS16: Stap H 2E 61
  BS20: P'bry 3F 51
  BS20: P'head 2F 49
  BS30: Bit 4F 83
  BS30: Old C 1E 83
  BS31: Key 1A 90
  BS31: Salt 4A 92
  BS36: Wint 2F 27
  BS37: Chip S 4D 17
  BS37: Iron A 1F 13
High Vw. BA2: Bath 5A 104
  BS20: P'head 2C 48
Highview Rd. BS15: Soun 4A 62
Highwall La. BS31: Q Char 5B 88
Highway BS37: Yate 3B 16
Highwood La. BS34: Pat 1D 23
Highwood Pk. BS34: Pat 2A 24
Highwood Rd. BS34: Pat 2A 24
Highworth Cres. BS37: Yate 5F 15
Highworth Rd. BS4: St Ap 4F 69
Hill, The BS32: Alm 1D 9
Hill Av. BA2: C Down 4B 110
  BS3: Wind H 1A 78
Hill Burn BS9: Henle 5E 41
Hillburn Rd. BS5: St G 2C 70
Hill Cl. BS16: Emer G 3D 47
Hill Crest BS4: Know 3F 79
Hillcrest Dr. BA2: Bath 1D 109
Hillcrest Rd. BS20: P'head 2A 48
Hillcroft Cl. BS15: Han 5A 72
Hill End Dr. BS10: Hen 5F 21
HILLFIELDS 3D 61
Hillfields Av. BS16: Fish 4E 61

Hill Gay Cl. BS20: P'head 2B 48
Hill Gro. BS9: Henle 5E 41
Hillgrove St. BS2: Bris 1A 68
Hillgrove St. Nth. BS2: Bris 1F 67
Hillhouse BS9: Sea M 5E 39
  BS16: Stap H 2B 62
Hill Ho. Rd. BS16: Stap H 5B 46
Hill La. BS20: Wes 5B 48
Hill Lawn BS4: Brisl 1F 79
Hill Rd. BA41: Dun 5A 84
Hills Barton BS3: Bis 3C 76
Hillsborough Flats BS8: Clif 3C 66
Hillsborough Rd. BS4: Brisl 5E 69
Hills Cl. BS31: Key 2C 90
Hillsdon Rd. BS9: W Trym 3B 40
Hillside BS6: Cot 1E 67
  BS8: Clif 3D 67
  BS16: Mang 1B 62
  BS20: P'bry 3F 51
Hillside Av. BS15: K'wd 1E 71
Hillside Cl. BS36: Fram C 1E 29
Hillside Ct. BS5: St G 2D 71
Hillside La. BS36: Fram C 1E 29
Hillside Rd. BA2: Bath 1F 109
  BS5: St G 2C 70
  BS20: P'head 2A 48
  BS41: L Ash 2D 75
Hillside St. BS4: Wind H 5C 68
Hill St. BS1: Bris 2A 4 (2E 67)
  BS3: Wind H 5B 68
  BS5: St G 1B 70
  BS15: K'wd 1B 72
Hilltop BS20: P'head 2C 48
Hilltop Gdns. BS5: St G 2C 70
  BS16: Soun 4F 61
            (not continuous)
Hilltop Rd. BS16: Soun 4F 61
Hilltop Vw. BS5: St G 2C 70
Hill Vw. BS8: Clif 3D 67
  BS9: Henle 5E 41
  BS16: Emer G 3C 46
  BS16: Soun 4F 61
  BS34: Fil 5C 24
Hill Vw. Cl. BS30: Old C 5E 73
Hill Vw. Ho. BS15: K'wd 5E 61
             (off Lodge Rd.)
Hill Vw. Rd. BA1: Bath 5D 97
  BS13: Bis 4C 76
Hillyfield Rd. BS13: Bis 1C 84
Hilton Ct. BS5: E'tn 1D 69
Hinton Cl. BA2: Bath 4B 102
  BS31: Salt 4A 92
Hinton Dr. BS30: Old C 3E 73
Hinton La. BS8: Clif 3B 66
Hinton Rd. BS5: E'tn 5E 59
  BS16: Fish 2C 60
Hiscocks Ct. BA2: New L 4D 101
Hiscocks Dr. BA2: Bath 1A 110
Hither Bath Bri. BS4: Brisl 4E 79
Hither Mead BS36: Fram C 2D 29
Hi-Ways Cvn. Pk. BS10: H'len . . .4D 21
HMP Bristol BS7: B'stn 2F 57
Hobbs La. BS1: Bris 3A 4 (3E 67)
  BS30: Sis 5D 63
Hobhouse Cl. BS9: Henle 4E 41
Hobwell La. BS41: L Ash 2E 75
Hockey's La. BS16: Fish 2C 60
Hockley Ct. BA1: W'ton 1F 103
Hogarth Wlk. BS7: L'lze 3D 43
Hogues Wlk. BS13: Hart 3D 85
Holbeach Way BS14: Whit 4C 86
Holbrook Cres. BS13: Hart 3F 85
Holburne Mus. of Art 1E 7 (3D 105)
Holcombe BS14: H'gro 2C 86
Holcombe Cl. BA2: B'ptn 1B 106
Holcombe Grn. BA1: W'ton 5D 95
             (not continuous)
Holcombe Gro. BS31: Key 2F 89
Holcombe La. BA2: B'ptn 1B 106
Holcombe Va. BA2: B'ptn 1B 106
Holdenhurst Rd. BS15: K'wd 5E 61

Holders Wlk. BS41: L Ash 4B 74
Holford Ct. BS14: Whit 2D 87
Holland Rd. BA1: Bath 1D 105
Hollidge Gdns. BS3: Bedm 5F 67
Hollies, The BS15: K'wd 3A 72
  BS16: Stap 1A 60
Hollies Av. BS20: P'head 3E 49
Hollis Cl. BS41: L Ash 3C 74
Hollis Cres. BS20: P'head 3E 49
Hollister's Dr. BS13: Hart 4F 85
Hollow, The BA2: Bath 1C 108
Holloway Cl. BA2: Bath 5B 6 (5B 104)
Hollow Rd. BS15: K'wd 1A 72
  BS32: Alm 1C 8
Hollows, The BS36: H'fld 1E 47
Hollway Cl. BS14: Stoc 2A 88
Hollway Rd. BS14: Stoc 2A 88
Hollybrook Pk. BS15: K'wd 4D 61
Hollybush La. BS9: Stok B 1A 56
            (not continuous)
Holly Cl. BS5: S'wll 4C 60
Holly Ct. BS2: Bris 1E 67
Holly Cres. BS15: K'wd 5A 62
Holly Dr. BA2: Odd D 5F 109
Holly Grn. BS15: K'wd 5C 62
Holly Gro. BS16: Fish 3E 61
Hollyguest Rd. BS15: Han 3F 71
Holly Hill BS37: Iron A 2A 14
Holly Hill Rd. BS15: K'wd 1A 72
Hollyleigh Av. BS34: Fil 1B 42
Holly Lodge Cl. BS5: S'wll 4B 60
Holly Lodge Rd. BS5: S'wll 4B 60
Hollymead La. BS9: Stok B 2A 56
Holly Ridge BS20: P'head 1C 48
Hollyridge BS14: H'gro 1E 87
Holly Wlk. BS31: Key 4F 89
Hollywood Bowl
  Bristol 4E 69
  Cribbs Causeway 2E 23
Hollywood La. BS10: Pat 1C 22
  BS35: E Comp, Pat 1C 22
Hollywood Rd. BS4: Brisl 1F 79
Holmdale Rd. BS34: Fil 5D 25
Holmes, The BS9: Stok B 2B 56
Holmesdale Rd. BS3: Wind H 1A 78
Holmes Gro. BS9: Henle 1D 57
Holmes Hill Rd. BS5: St G 1C 70
Holmes St. BS5: Bar H 3D 69
Holmlea BS20: P'head 1B 50
Holm-Mead La. BS30: Bit 5E 83
Holmoak Rd. BS31: Key 3E 89
Holmwood BS15: Han 4E 71
Holmwood Cl. BS36: Wint 2F 27
Holmwood Gdns. BS9: W Trym . . .3C 40
Holroyd Ho. BS3: Wind H 1F 77
Holsom Cl. BS14: Stoc 1A 88
Holsom Rd. BS14: Stoc 1B 88
Holst Gdns. BS4: Know 5F 77
Holton Rd. BS7: Hor 5C 42
Holyrood Cl. BS34: Stok G 4F 25
Holy Well Cl. BS4: St Ap 3A 70
Homeavon Ho. BS31: Key 2B 90
Home Cl. BS10: S'mead 1A 42
Home Farm Rd. BS8: Abb L 1D 65
Homefield BS37: Yate 2A 16
Home Fld. Cl. BS16: Emer G 5D 47
Homefield Cl. BS31: Salt 4A 92
Homefield Dr. BS16: Fish 1C 60
Homefield Rd. BS31: Salt 4B 92
Home Gdns. BS8: Clif 4C 56
Home Ground BS9: W Trym 4D 41
  BS11: Shire 4F 37
Homeground BS16: Emer G 5D 47
Homelands BA1: Bathe 3B 98
Homelea Pk. E. BA1: Bath 3C 102
Homelea Pk. W. BA1: Bath 3C 102
Home Leas Cl. BS34: L'lze 3E 43
Homeleaze Rd. BS10: S'mead 5F 23
Home Mead BS4: Know 5A 78

Homemead BA2: Cor 2C **100**
  BS30: C Hth 5C **72**
Homemead Dr. BS4: Brisl 3F **79**
Home Orchard BS37: Yate 3F **15**
Homestead BS20: P'head 3A **48**
Homestead, The BS31: Key 5B **90**
Homestead Cl. BS36: Fram C . . .1F **29**
Homestead Gdns. BS16: Fren . . .3D **45**
Homestead Rd. BS34: Fil 5B **24**
Honey Garston Cl. BS13: Hart . . .3D **85**
Honey Garston Rd. BS13: Hart . . .3D **85**
Honey Hill Rd. BS15: K'wd 1B **72**
Honeylands BS20: P'head 3E **49**
Honeymead BS14: H'gro 1E **87**
Honeysuckle Cl. BS32: Brad S . . .3A **10**
Honeysuckle La. BS16: Stap 2A **60**
Honey Way BS15: K'wd 1B **72**
Honeywick Cl. BS3: Bedm 2E **77**
Honiton Rd. BS16: Fish 3C **60**
Hooper Rd. BS14: Stoc 2F **87**
Hopechapel Hill BS8: Clif 3B **66**
Hope Ct. BS1: Bris 4D **67**
Hope Ho. *BS20: Pill 1E* **53**
                          (off Underbanks)
Hope Rd. BS3: Bedm 1E **77**
  BS37: Yate 3C **14**
Hope Sq. BS8: Clif 3B **66**
Hopetoun Rd. BS2: Bris 3B **58**
Hopewell Gdns. BS11: Law W . . .4B **38**
Hopkins Ct. BS6: Redl 5D **57**
Hopland Cl. BS30: L Grn 1D **83**
Hopp's Rd. BS15: K'wd 2F **71**
Horatio Ho. BS20: P'head 5C **34**
Horesham Gro. BS13: Hart 2E **85**
HORFIELD 4B **42**
Horfield Leisure Cen. 4B **42**
Horfield Rd. BS2: Bris 1B **4** (2F **67**)
Horley Rd. BS2: Bris 4C **58**
Hornbeam Cl. BS32: Brad S 5F **9**
Hornbeam Ho. BS16: Fish 5E **45**
Hornbeams, The BS16: Fren 2D **45**
Hornbeam Wlk. BS31: Key 4E **89**
Hornhill Cl. BS13: Hart 3D **85**
Horsecombe Brow
  BA2: C Down 4C **110**
Horsecombe Gro. BA2: C Down . .4C **110**
Horsecombe Va. BA2: C Down . . .4C **110**
Horsecroft Gdns. BS30: Bar C . . .3C **72**
Horsefair, The BS1: Bris . . .1C **4** (2A **68**)
Horsepool Rd. BS13: Withy 3A **84**
Horse Shoe Dr. BS9: Stok B 2E **55**
Horseshoe La. BS37: Chip S 4D **17**
Horseshoe Rd.
  BA2: Bath 5F **7** (5E **105**)
Horseshoe Wlk.
  BA2: Bath 5F **7** (5D **105**)
Horse St. BS37: Chip S 4D **17**
                          (not continuous)
Horse World 4F **87**
Horstmann Cl. BA1: Bath 3D **103**
Horton Ho. BA2: Bath 2C **104**
Horton Rd. BS37: Chip S, Hort . . .3E **17**
                          (not continuous)
Horton St. BS2: Bris 2F **5** (2B **68**)
Horwood Ct. BS30: Bar C 5C **72**
Hosey Wlk. BS13: Withy 2C **84**
Host St. BS1: Bris 2B **4** (2F **67**)
Hotbath Gallery **4B 6**
                          (off Hot Bath St.)
Hot Bath St. BA1: Bath 4B **6** (4B **104**)
Hottom Gdns. BS7: Hor 4C **42**
Hot Water La. BS15: Soun 3B **62**
Hotwell Rd. BS8: Clif 2A **66**
HOTWELLS 4C **66**
Hotwells Ho. *BS8: Clif 3C* **66**
                          (off Hotwell Rd.)
Houlton St. BS2: Bris . . .1F **5** (1B **68**)
Hounds Cl. BS37: Chip S 4D **17**
Hounds Rd. BS37: Chip S 4D **17**
Hover's La. BS36: Fram C 2E **13**
  BS37: Iron A 2E **13**

Howard Av. BS5: W'hall 1A **70**
Howard Cl. BS31: Salt 4F **91**
Howard Rd. BS3: Bris 5D **67**
  BS6: Henle 2D **57**
  BS16: Stap H 2F **61**
Howard St. BS5: W'hall 5A **60**
Howard Wlk. BS30: B'yte 2F **73**
Howecroft Ct. BS9: Stok B 2A **56**
Howecroft Gdns. BS9: Stok B . . .2A **56**
Howells Mead BS16: Emer G 4D **47**
Howes Cl. BS30: Bar C 3C **72**
Howett Rd. BS5: Redf 2E **69**
How Hill BA2: Bath 4C **102**
Howsmoor La. BS16: Emer G 3D **47**
                          (not continuous)
Hoylake BS37: Yate 5A **16**
Hoylake Dr. BS30: Warm 3D **73**
Huckford La. BS36: Wint 4C **28**
Huckford Quarry Local Nature Reserve
                          . . . . .4B **28**
Huckford Rd. BS36: Wint 3A **28**
Huckley Way BS32: Brad S 2B **26**
Hudd's Hill Gdns. BS5: St G 5B **60**
Hudd's Hill Rd. BS5: St G 1B **70**
Hudd's Va. Rd. BS5: St G 1A **70**
                          (not continuous)
Hudson Cl. BS37: Yate 5B **16**
Hughenden Rd. BS7: Hor 1A **58**
  BS8: Clif 4C **56**
Hughes Gdns. BS7: Hor 3C **42**
Hulbert Cl. BS4: Brisl 2C **80**
Hulse Rd. BS4: Brisl 3F **79**
Humberstan Wlk. BS11: Law W . .3A **38**
Humber Way BS11: A'mth 3F **19**
Humphrey Davy Way BS8: Clif . . .4B **66**
Humphrys Barton BS4: St Ap 4B **70**
Hungerford Cl. BS4: Brisl 4A **80**
Hungerford Ct. BA2: New L 5D **101**
Hungerford Cres. BS4: Brisl 3A **80**
Hungerford Gdns. BS4: Brisl 4A **80**
Hungerford Rd. BA1: Bath 3E **103**
  BS4: Brisl 3A **80**
Hungerford Wlk. BS4: Brisl 3A **80**
Hung Rd. BS11: Shire 5A **38**
Hunters Cl. BS15: Han 4E **71**
Hunters Dr. BS15: K'wd 5B **62**
Hunter's Rd. BS15: Han 4E **71**
Hunters Way BS34: Fil 5D **25**
Huntingham Rd. BS13: Withy 3A **84**
Hunts Ground Rd. BS34: Stok G . .4B **26**
Hunts La. BS7: Hor 5A **42**
Hurle Cres. BS8: Clif 5C **56**
Hurle Rd. BS8: Clif 5D **57**
Hurlingham Rd. BS7: Bris 4B **58**
Hurn La. BS31: Key 3B **90**
Hurston Rd. BS4: Know 4F **77**
Hurst Rd. BS4: Know 4B **78**
Hurst Wlk. BS4: Know 4B **78**
Hurstwood Rd. BS16: Down 1F **61**
Hutton Cl. BS9: W Trym 4F **39**
  BS31: Key 5C **90**
Huyton Rd. BS5: Eastv 3A **60**
Hyland Gro. BS9: W Trym 3B **40**

Imperial Wlk. BS14: H'gro 3D **79**
Ingleside Rd. BS15: K'wd 5D **61**
Ingmire Rd. BS5: Eastv 3D **59**
Inkerman Cl. BS7: Hor 4A **42**
Inman Ho. BA1: Bath 1C **104**
Innox Gdns. BS13: Withy 2C **84**
Innox Gro. BA2: Eng 3B **108**
Innox La. BA1: Up Swa 2D **97**
Innox Rd. BA1: Swa, Up Swa 2D **97**
  BA2: Bath 5D **103**
INN'S COURT 5F **77**
Inns Ct. Av. BS4: Know 5F **77**
Inns Ct. Dr. BS4: Know 5F **77**
Inn's Ct. Grn. BS4: Know 5F **77**
                          (not continuous)
Instow Rd. BS4: Know 4A **78**
Instow Wlk. BS4: Know 4A **78**
Inter City Ho. BS1: Bris 4E **5** (3A **68**)
International Trad. Est.
  BS11: A'mth 1D **37**
Interplex BS32: Brad S 2E **9**
Inverness Rd. BA2: Bath 4E **103**
IO Centre BS11: A'mth 3B **20**
Ipswich Dr. BS4: St Ap 3A **70**
Irby Rd. BS3: Bedm 1C **76**
Irena Rd. BS16: Fish 3B **60**
Ireton Rd. BS3: Bedm 1D **77**
IRON ACTON 1F **13**
Iron Acton Way BS37: Yate 2C **14**
Ironchurch Rd. BS11: A'mth 4D **19**
Ironmould La. BS4: Brisl 2C **80**
Irving Cl. BS16: Stap H 2A **62**
Irving Ho. BS1: Bris 2A **4**
Isabella Cotts. *BA2: C Down 4D* **111**
                          (off Rock La.)
Isabella M. BA2: C Down 4D **111**
Isabella Rd. BS14: H'gro 5C **78**
Isambard Wlk. BS1: Bris . . .4F **5** (3B **68**)
Island Gdns. BS16: Stap 2E **59**
Island Trade Pk. BS11: A'mth 2E **37**
Isleys Ct. BS30: L Grn 1B **82**
Islington Rd. BS3: Bris 5D **67**
Ison Hill BS10: Hen 5F **21**
Ison Hill Rd. BS10: Hen 5F **21**
Ivo Peters Rd. BA2: Bath 4A **104**
Ivor Rd. BS5: W'hall 1E **69**
IVORY HILL 4C **28**
Ivy Av. BA2: Bath 1E **109**
Ivy Bank Pk. BA2: C Down 3B **110**
Ivy Ct. BS20: P'head 1B **48**
Ivy Gro. BA2: Bath 1E **109**
Ivy La. BS16: Fish 3C **60**
Ivy Pl. BA2: Bath 1E **109**
Ivy Ter. BS37: W'lgh 4D **31**
Ivy Vs. BA2: Bath 1E **109**
Ivywell Rd. BS9: Stok B 3A **56**

I

Ida Rd. BS5: W'hall 1E **69**
Iddesleigh Rd. BS6: Redl 3D **57**
Idstone Rd. BS16: Fish 2D **61**
Iford Cl. BS31: Salt 4A **92**
Ilchester Cres. BS13: Bis 3D **77**
Ilchester Rd. BS13: Bis 3C **76**
Iles Cl. BS15: Han 5F **71**
Ilex Cl. BS13: Bis 1B **84**
Ilminster Av. BS4: Know 3A **78**
Ilsyn Gro. BS14: Stoc 5F **79**
Imbercourt Cl. BS14: H'gro 4D **79**
Imperial Pk. BS13: Bis 1E **85**
Imperial Rd. BS6: Redl 5D **57**
  BS14: H'gro 4E **79**

J

Jack Knight Ho. BS7: Hor 1B **58**
Jack Price Cl. BS13: Hart 4E **85**
Jacob Bldg., The BS8: Clif 2D **67**
Jacob Ct. BS2: Bris 2F **5** (2B **68**)
Jacobs Ct. *BS1: Bris 3E* **67**
                          (off Queen's Pde.)
Jacob's Mdw. BS20: P'head 2B **50**
Jacob St. BS2: Bris 2F **5** (2B **68**)
                          (Hawkins St.)
  BS2: Bris 2E **5** (2A **68**)
                          (Tower Hill)
Jacob's Wells Rd. BS8: Clif 3D **67**
Jamaica St. BS2: Bris 1A **68**
James Cl. BS16: Soun 2A **62**
James Rd. BS16: Soun 3A **62**
James St. BS2: Bris 4C **58**
  BS5: E'tn 1B **68**
James St. W. BA1: Bath . . .3A **6** (4B **104**)
Jane Austen Cen. 2B **6**
Jane St. BS5: E'tn 2D **69**
Jarratts Rd. BS10: S'mead 1F **41**

Jarvis St. BS5: Bar H 3D 69
Jasmine Gro. BS11: Law W 1E 39
Jasper St. BS3: Bedm 1D 77
Jays Cl. BS15: K'wd 3F 71
Jean Rd. BS4: Brisl 2A 80
Jeffery Ct. BS30: C Hth 3D 73
JEFFRIES HILL 4D 71
Jeffries Hill Bottom BS15: St G . .4D 71
Jekyll Cl. BS16: Stap 3A 44
Jellicoe Av. BS16: Stap 3A 44
Jena St. BS31: Salt 4F 91
Jenner Cl. BS37: Chip S 5F 17
Jennings Ct. BS3: Bris 5C 66
    (off Lwr. Sidney St.)
Jenny La. BS10: S'mead 1F 41
Jersey Av. BS4: Brisl 5B 70
Jesse Hughes Ct. BA1: Bath 5E 97
Jessop Cl. BS1: Bris 4D 5 (3A 68)
Jessop Cres. BS10: W Trym 2C 40
Jessop Underpass BS3: Ash G . . .5B 66
Jew's La. BA2: Bath 4E 103
Jim O'Neil Ho. BS11: Shire 4F 37
Jinty La. BS16: Sis 4D 63
Jobbins Cl. BS37: Chip S 5C 16
Jocelyn Rd. BS7: Hor 4B 42
Jockey La. BS5: St G 2C 70
John Cabot Ct. BS1: Bris 4C 66
John Carr's Ter. BS8: Clif 3D 67
John Cozens Ho. BS2: Bris 1F 5
John James Ct. BS7: L'lze 4D 43
Johnny Ball La. BS2: Bris . .1B 4 (2F 67)
John Repton Gdns.
    BS10: Bren 1D 41
John Slessor Ct. BA1: Bath 2B 104
Johnson Dr. BS30: Bar C 4B 72
Johnson Rd. BS16: Emer G 5E 47
Johnsons La. BS5: W'hall 5F 59
Johnsons Rd. BS5: W'hall 5F 59
Johnstone St. BA2: Bath . .3D 7 (4C 104)
John St. BA1: Bath 2B 6 (3B 104)
    BS1: Bris 2C 4 (2F 67)
    BS2: Bris 4C 58
    BS15: K'wd 1E 71
John Wesley Rd. BS5: St G 3D 71
    BS15: St G 4D 71
John Wesley's Chapel 1D 5 (2A 68)
Jordan Wlk. BS32: Brad S 5F 9
Jorrocks Ind. Est.
    BS37: W'lgh 4E 31
Joyce Cl. BS7: Hor 3C 42
Joy Hill BS8: Clif 3B 66
Jubilee Cotts. BS13: Bis 4B 76
Jubilee Cres. BS16: Mang 4C 46
Jubilee Gdns. BS37: Yate 3C 16
Jubilee Ho. BS34: Lit S 5E 9
Jubilee Pl. BS1: Bris 5C 4 (4F 67)
    BS15: K'wd 2C 72
Jubilee Rd. BS2: Bris 5C 58
    BS4: Know 2E 79
    BS5: St G 2B 70
    BS15: Soun 3A 62
Jubilee Row BS2: Bris 5C 58
    (off Ashley St.)
Jubilee St. BS2: Bris 3F 5 (3B 68)
Jubilee Swimming Pool 2D 79
Jubilee Way BS11: A'mth 1D 37
Julian Cl. BS9: Stok B 3A 56
Julian Ct. BS9: Stok B 3A 56
Julian Rd. BA1: Bath 1A 6 (2B 104)
    BS9: Stok B 3A 56
Julier Ho. BA1: Bath 2C 104
    (off Pera Rd.)
Julius Cl. BS16: Emer G 5E 47
Julius Rd. BS7: B'stn 3F 57
Junction Av. BA2: Bath 5A 104
Junction Rd. BA2: Bath 5A 104
Junction Way BS16: Soun 3C 62
Juniper Cl. BS5: Eastv 4E 59
Juniper Way BS32: Brad S 1B 26
Jupiter Rd. BS34: Pat 1F 23
Justice Av. BS31: Salt 4A 92

Justice Rd. BS16: Fish 3B 60
Jutland Rd. BS11: A'mth 2D 37

K

Kathdene Gdns. BS7: Bris 3B 58
Kaynton Mead BA1: Bath 4D 103
Keats Cl. BS7: Hor 3C 42
Keble Av. BS13: Withy 3B 84
Keed's La. BS41: L Ash 2A 74
Keedwell Hill BS41: L Ash 3B 74
Keel Cl. BS5: St G 3B 70
Keep, The BS30: Old C 4F 73
Keepers La. BS7: Bris 3B 58
Keg Store, The BS1: Bris . .3D 5 (3A 68)
Keinton Wlk. BS10: Hen 1C 40
Kelbra Cres. BS36: Fram C 2D 29
Kellaway Av. BS6: B'stn, Hor 1E 57
    BS7: Hor 1E 57
Kellaway Cres. BS9: Henle 5F 41
Kelso Pl. BA1: Bath 3F 103
KELSTON 4E 93
Kelston Cl. BS31: Salt 4F 91
    BS37: Yate 1F 31
Kelston Gdns. BS10: W Trym 3F 41
Kelston Gro. BS15: Han 3A 72
Kelston M. BS10: W Trym 3F 41
Kelston Rd. BA1: Bath 1A 102
    BS10: W Trym 3F 41
    BS31: Key 2F 89
Kelston Vw. BA2: Bath 5B 102
    BS31: Salt 4F 91
Kelston Wlk. BS16: Fish 2E 61
Kelwith Cl. BS15: K'wd 3A 72
Kemble Gdns. BS11: Shire 1A 54
Kemperleye Way BS32: Brad S 1F 25
Kempes Cl. BS41: L Ash 2C 74
Kempthorne La. BA2: Odd D 4A 110
Kempton Cl. BS16: Down 2B 46
Kencot Wlk. BS13: Withy 4D 85
Kendall Cl. BS37: Yate 4D 15
Kendall Gdns. BS16: Stap H 2F 61
Kendall Rd. BS16: Stap H 2F 61
Kendal Rd. BS7: Hor 4C 42
KENDLESHIRE 5C 28
Kendon Dr. BS10: Hor 4F 41
Kendon Way BS10: S'mead 3F 41
Kenilworth BS37: Yate 5B 16
Kenilworth Cl. BS31: Key 3F 89
Kenilworth Ct. BA1: Bath 2D 105
    (off Longacre Ho.)
Kenilworth Dr. BS30: Will 2F 73
Kenilworth Rd. BS6: Cot 5E 57
Kenmare Rd. BS4: Know 3A 78
Kenmore Cres. BS7: Hor 2A 42
Kenmore Dr. BS7: Hor 2A 42
Kenmore Gro. BS7: Hor 2A 42
Kennard Cl. BS15: K'wd 2E 71
Kennard Ri. BS15: K'wd 1E 71
Kennard Rd. BS15: K'wd 1E 71
Kenn Ct. BS4: Know 5A 78
Kennedy Ho. BS37: Yate 4B 16
Kennedy Way
    BS37: Chip S, Yate 4A 16
Kennel Lodge Rd. BS3: Bwr A 5A 66
    BS41: L Ash 5F 65
Kenneth Rd. BS4: Brisl 2F 79
Kennet Pk. BA2: B'ptn 1A 106
Kennet Rd. BS31: Key 3C 90
Kennington Av. BS7: B'stn 2A 58
    BS15: K'wd 5F 61
Kennington Rd. BA1: Bath 3D 103
Kennion Rd. BS5: St G 2C 70
Kennmoor Cl. BS30: C Hth 3C 72
Kenn Rd. BS5: St G 2C 70
Kensal Av. BS3: Wind H 1A 78
Kensal Rd. BS3: Wind H 1A 78
Kensington Cl. BA1: Bath 1D 105
    BS8: Clif 2C 66
Kensington Gdns. BA1: Bath 1D 105

KENSINGTON HILL 2F 79
KENSINGTON PARK 1E 79
Kensington Pk. BS5: E'tn 5C 58
Kensington Pk. Rd. BS4: Brisl 2E 79
Kensington Pl. BA1: Bath 2D 105
    BS8: Clif 2C 66
Kensington Rd. BS5: St G 1C 70
    BS6: Redl 5E 57
    BS16: Stap H 2F 61
Kent Av. BS37: Yate 2B 16
Kent Cl. BS34: Stok G 4F 25
Kent La. BA1: Up Swa 1D 97
Kent M. BS16: Stap 4A 44
Kenton M. BS9: Henle 1E 57
Kent Rd. BS7: B'stn 3A 58
Kents Grn. BS15: K'wd 4A 62
Kent St. BS3: Bedm 1E 77
Kenwood Cl. BS15: K'wd 5B 62
Keppel Cl. BS31: Salt 5F 91
Kerry Rd. BS4: Know 3A 78
Kersteman Rd. BS6: Redl 4E 57
Kestrel Cl. BS34: Pat 5A 8
    BS37: Chip S 5B 16
Kestrel Ct. BS20: P'head 5D 35
Keswick Wlk. BS10: S'mead 1E 41
Ketch Rd. BS3: Wind H 1B 78
Kewstoke Rd. BA2: C Down 3C 110
    BS9: Stok B 2A 56
Kew Wlk. BS4: Brisl 4D 79
KEYNSHAM 1A 90
Keynsham By-Pass
    BS31: Key 4E 81
Keynsham Leisure Cen. 2B 90
Keynsham Rd. BS30: Will 1B 90
    BS31: Key 1B 90
Keynsham Station (Rail) 1B 90
Key Point BS32: Brad S 1F 9
Keys Av. BS7: Hor 4B 42
Kilbirnie Rd. BS14: Whit 4C 86
Kilburn St. BS5: E'tn 1D 69
Kildare Rd. BS4: Know 3F 77
Kilkenny La. BA2: Eng, Ing 5A 108
Kilkenny Pl. BS20: P'head 5B 34
Kilkenny St. BS2: Bris 3F 5 (3B 68)
Kilmersdon Rd. BS13: Hart 3D 85
Kilminster Cl. BS34: Lit S 2F 25
Kilminster Rd. BS11: Shire 4F 37
Kiln Cl. BS15: K'wd 4D 61
Kilnhurst Cl. BS30: L Grn 2B 82
Kilvert Cl. BS4: Brisl 4F 69
Kimberley Av. BS16: Fish 1E 61
Kimberley Cl. BS16: Down 4B 46
Kimberley Cres. BS16: Fish 1E 61
Kimberley Rd. BS15: K'wd 5F 61
    BS16: Fish 1E 61
    (not continuous)
Kinber Cl. BA1: W'ton 4C 94
Kinema Ho. BS4: Brisl 5E 69
    (off Belmont Rd.)
King Dick's La. BS5: St G 1B 70
King Edward Cl. BS14: H'gro 1C 86
    (not continuous)
King Edward Rd. BA2: Bath 5F 103
Kingfisher Cl. BS10: Bren 4D 23
    BS32: Brad S 3A 10
Kingfisher Dr. BS16: B'hll 5A 44
Kingfisher Rd.
    BS20: P'bry, P'head 4E 35
    BS37: Chip S 5C 16
King George V Pl.
    BS1: Bris 4B 4 (3F 67)
King Georges Rd. BA2: Bath 5E 103
    BS13: Bis 2C 84
King John's Rd. BS15: K'wd 4D 61
King Rd. BS4: Know 3E 79
King Rd. Av. BS11: A'mth 1C 36
Kingrove Cres. BS37: Chip S 5E 17
Kingrove La. BS37: Chip S 1E 33
Kings Av. BS7: B'stn 2E 57
    BS15: Han 5D 71
Kings Bus. Pk. BS2: Bris 3E 69

King's Chase Shop. Cen.
BS15: K'wd 1F **71**
Kingscote BS37: Yate 2F **31**
Kingscote Pk. BS5: St G 3D **71**
Kings Ct. BS2: Bris 1A **68**
BS3: Withy 3B **84**
BS34: Lit S 2E **25**
Kingscourt Cl. BS14: Whit 2C **86**
Kings Cft. BS41: L Ash 3A **74**
KINGSDOWN 1A **4** (1E **67**)
Kingsdown Pde. BS6: Bris 1F **67**
Kingsdown Sports Cen. 1E **67**
Kingsdown Vw. BA1: Bath 1C **104**
Kings Dr. BS7: B'stn 1E **57**
BS15: Han 5D **71**
BS34: Stok G 4C **26**
Kingsfield BA2: Bath 2E **109**
Kingsfield La. BS15: Han 4A **72**
(not continuous)
BS30: L Grn 5A **72**
Kings Head La. BS13: Bis 5A **76**
Kingshill Rd. BS4: Know 3D **79**
Kingsholme Rd. BS15: K'wd 5F **61**
Kingsholm Rd. BS10: S'mead 3F **41**
Kingsland Cl. BS2: Bris 3C **68**
Kingsland Rd. BS2: Bris 3C **68**
Kingsland Rd. Bri. BS2: Bris 3C **68**
Kingsland Trad. Est. BS2: Bris . . .2B **68**
Kingsleigh Ct. BS15: K'wd 2B **72**
Kingsleigh Gdns. BS15: K'wd 2B **72**
Kingsleigh Pk. BS15: K'wd 2B **72**
Kingsley Ho. BS2: Bris 3F **5** (3B **68**)
Kingsley Pl. BS3: Bris 5D **67**
(off Beauley Rd.)
Kingsley Rd. BS5: E'tn 5E **59**
BS6: Cot 4F **57**
Kingsmarsh Ho. BS5: E'tn 2D **69**
Kingsmead Ct. BA1: Bath 4A **6**
(off Kingsmead Nth.)
Kingsmead E. BA1: Bath 4A **6** (4B **104**)
Kingsmead Ho. BA1: Bath 3A **6**
Kingsmead Nth.
BA1: Bath 4A **6** (4B **104**)
Kingsmead Rd. BS5: S'wll 5C **60**
Kingsmead Sq.
BA1: Bath 4B **6** (4B **104**)
Kingsmead St.
BA1: Bath 3B **6** (4B **104**)
Kingsmead Ter. BA1: Bath 4B **6**
Kingsmead Wlk. BS5: S'wll 5C **60**
Kingsmead W.
BA1: Bath 4A **6** (4B **104**)
Kings M. BS6: Bris 1F **67**
Kingsmill BS9: Stok B 1F **55**
Kings Pde. Av. BS8: Clif 5D **57**
Kings Pde. M. BS8: Clif 5C **56**
Kings Pk. Av. BS2: Bris 3E **69**
King Sq. BS2: Bris 1F **67**
(not continuous)
King Sq. Av. BS2: Bris 1F **67**
Kings Quarter Apartments
BS1: Bris 1F **67**
(off Charles St.)
King's Rd. BS4: Brisl 1E **79**
BS8: Clif 2C **66**
BS20: P'head 2B **48**
Kings Sq. BS30: Bit 4F **83**
Kingston Av. BS31: Salt 5E **91**
Kingston Bldgs. BA1: Bath 4C **6**
(off York St.)
Kingston Cl. BS16: Mang 4C **46**
Kingston Dr. BS16: Mang 4C **46**
Kingston Pde. BA1: Bath 4C **6**
(off York St.)
Kingston Rd. BA1: Bath . . .4C **6** (4C **104**)
BS3: Bedm 5E **67**
Kingstree St. BS4: Wind H 5C **68**
King St. BS1: Bris 4B **4** (3F **67**)
BS5: E'tn 5E **59**
BS11: A'mth 2C **36**
BS15: K'wd 1D **71**

King's Wlk. BS13: Bis 5A **76**
Kingsway BA2: Bath 2E **109**
BS5: St G 2D **71**
BS15: K'wd 2D **71**
BS20: P'head 2B **48**
BS34: Lit S 2E **25**
Kingsway Av. BS5: St G 1D **71**
BS15: K'wd 1D **71**
Kingsway Cvn. Pk.
BS20: P'head 5C **34**
Kingsway Cres. BS15: K'wd 1E **71**
Kingsway Pk. BS30: Warm 3D **73**
Kingsway Shop. Pct.
BS5: St G 3D **71**
Kingswear Rd. BS3: Know 3F **77**
Kings Weston Av. BS11: Shire 4F **37**
Kingsweston Down Nature Reserve
. . . . .2E **39**
Kings Weston La.
BS11: A'mth, Law W 4E **19**
Kings Weston Rd. BS10: Hen 2E **39**
BS11: Law W 4C **38**
KINGSWOOD 1F **71**
Kingswood Douglas Est.
BS15: K'wd 2F **71**
Kingswood Fountain Est.
BS15: K'wd 1E **71**
Kingswood Hgts. BS15: K'wd 5F **61**
Kingswood Heritage Mus. 3D **73**
Kingswood Ind. Est.
BS30: L Grn 5B **72**
Kingswood Leisure Cen. 3F **61**
Kingswood Theatre 5A **46**
Kingswood Trad. Est.
BS15: K'wd 5F **61**
King William Av.
BS1: Bris 4C **4** (3F **67**)
King William St. BS3: Bedm 5D **67**
Kinsale Rd. BS14: H'gro 5E **79**
Kinsale Wlk. BS4: Know 3A **78**
Kinvara Rd. BS4: Know 4A **78**
Kipling Av. BA2: Bath 1B **110**
Kipling Rd. BS7: Hor 2D **43**
Kirkby Rd. BS11: Law W 2C **38**
Kirkstone Gdns.
BS10: S'mead 1E **41**
Kirtlington Rd. BS5: Eastv 3D **59**
Kite Hay Cl. BS16: Stap 1A **60**
Kites Cl. BS32: Brad S 3E **9**
Knapp, The BS37: Yate 1B **16**
Knapps La. BS5: S'wll 4A **60**
Kneller Cl. BS11: Law W 3C **38**
Knightcott Rd. BS8: Abb L 1B **64**
Knighton Rd. BS10: S'mead 2A **42**
Knightsbridge Pk.
BS13: Hart 3A **86**
Knights Cl. BS9: Henle 5D **41**
Knightstone Ho. BS2: Bris 1F **67**
(off Portland St.)
Knightstone Lodge BS6: Cot 5F **57**
(off Archfield Rd.)
Knightstone Mt. BS5: St G 3C **70**
(off Nicholas La.)
Knightstone Pl. BA1: W'ton 1D **103**
BS15: Han 1D **81**
Knightstone Ri. BS5: St G 1B **70**
(off Summerhill Rd.)
Knightstone Sq. BS14: H'gro 1E **87**
Knightwood Rd. BS34: Stok G 3B **26**
Knole Cl. BS32: Alm 1B **8**
Knole La. BS10: Bren 5C **22**
Knole Pk. BS32: Alm 2B **8**
Knoll, The BS20: P'head 4C **34**
Knoll Ct. BS9: Stok B 3F **55**
Knoll Hill BS9: Stok B 3F **55**
Knovill Cl. BS11: Law W 1D **39**
KNOWLE 2D **79**
KNOWLE PARK 3D **79**
Knowle Rd. BS4: Wind H 1B **78**
Knowsley Rd. BS16: Fish 3A **60**
Kyght Cl. BS15: Warm 1C **73**

Kylross Av. BS14: H'gro 2D **87**
Kynges Mill Cl. BS16: B'hll 4C **44**
Kyrle Gdns. BA1: Bathe 4B **98**

L

Labbott, The BS31: Key 2A **90**
Laburnum Gro. BS16: Fish 2D **61**
Laburnum Rd. BS15: Han 4E **71**
Laburnum Ter. BA1: Bathe 4B **98**
Laburnum Wlk. BS31: Key 4E **89**
Lacey Rd. BS14: Stoc 1A **88**
Lacock Dr. BS30: Bar C 4B **72**
Ladd Cl. BS15: K'wd 2B **72**
Laddon Mead BS37: Yate 1F **15**
Ladies Mile BS9: Stok B 5B **56**
Ladman Gro. BS14: Stoc 1A **88**
Ladman Rd. BS14: Stoc 1A **88**
Ladymead BS20: P'head 1B **50**
Ladysmith Rd. BS6: Henle 2D **57**
Laggan Gdns. BA1: Bath 1A **104**
Lakemead Gdns. BS13: Withy 3B **84**
Lakemead Gro. BS13: Bis 1B **84**
Lake Rd. BS10: W Trym 4E **41**
BS20: P'head 5B **34**
Lake Shore BS13: Bis 1E **85**
Lakeshore Dr. BS13: Bis 1E **85**
Lakeside BS16: Fish 3A **60**
Lake Vw. BS16: Fish 3B **60**
Lake Vw. Rd. BS5: St G 1F **69**
Lakewood Cres. BS10: W Trym . . .3D **41**
Lakewood Rd. BS10: W Trym 3D **41**
Lambert Pl. BS4: Know 1F **85**
Lamb Hill BS5: St G 2B **70**
Lambley Rd. BS5: St G 1A **70**
Lambourn Cl. BS3: Wind H 1F **77**
Lambourne Way BS20: P'head 2B **50**
Lambourn Rd. BS31: Key 3C **90**
LAMBRIDGE 1E **105**
Lambridge Bldgs. BA1: Bath 5D **97**
Lambridge Bldgs. M.
BA1: Bath 1E **105**
(off St Saviours Rd.)
Lambridge Grange BA1: Bath 5E **97**
Lambridge M. BA1: Bath 1E **105**
Lambridge Pl. BA1: Bath 1E **105**
Lambridge St. BA1: Bath 5E **97**
(not continuous)
Lambrook Rd. BS16: Fish 2C **60**
Lamb St. BS2: Bris 1F **5** (2B **68**)
Lamington Cl. BS13: Bis 1B **84**
Lamont Ho. BA1: Bath 5E **97**
Lamord Ga. BS34: Stok G 3A **26**
Lampards Bldgs.
BA1: Bath 1B **6** (2B **104**)
Lampeter Rd. BS9: W Trym 4B **40**
Lampton Av. BS13: Hart 4A **86**
Lampton Gro. BS13: Hart 4A **86**
Lampton Rd. BS41: L Ash 3B **74**
Lanaway Rd. BS16: Fish 5D **45**
Lancashire Rd. BS7: B'stn 3A **58**
Lancaster Cl. BS34: Stok G 4F **25**
Lancaster Rd. BS2: Bris 4C **58**
BS37: Yate 2A **16**
Lancaster St. BS5: Redf 2E **69**
Lancelot Rd. BS16: Stap 3A **44**
Landmark Ct. BS1: Bris 5A **4**
Landrail Wlk. BS16: B'hll 5B **44**
Landseer Av. BS7: L'lze 5D **43**
Landseer Rd. BA2: Bath 4D **103**
Lanercost Rd. BS10: S'mead 1E **41**
Lanesborough Ri. BS14: Stoc 5F **79**
Lanes End BS4: Brisl 3E **79**
Langdale Ct. BS34: Pat 5C **8**
Langdale Rd. BS16: Fish 2B **60**
Langdon Rd. BA2: Bath 1D **109**
Langdown Ct. BS14: Stoc 2A **88**
Langfield Cl. BS10: Hen 5A **22**
Langford Rd. BS13: Bis 4B **76**

Langford Way. BS15: K'wd 2A 72
Langham Rd. BS4: Know 2E 79
Langhill Av. BS4: Know 5E 77
Langley Cres. BS3: Ash V 3A 76
Langley Mow BS16: Emer G 4D 47
Langridge La.
    BA1: L'rdge, L'dwn 1C 94
Langthorn Cl. BS36: Fram C 1E 29
Langton Ct. BA2: New L 5D 101
Langton Ct. Rd. BS4: St Ap 4F 69
Langton Ho. BS2: Bris 1F 5
Langton Pk. BS3: Bedm 5E 67
Langton Rd. BS4: St Ap 4F 69
Langton Way BS4: St Ap 3B 70
LANSDOWN 1D 95
Lansdown BS37: Yate 5A 16
Lansdown Cl. BA1: Bath 1A 104
    BS15: K'wd 4F 61
Lansdown Cres. BA1: Bath 1B 104
Lansdowne BS16: Fren 2E 45
    (off Avon Ring Rd.)
Lansdowne Ct. BS5: E'tn 1C 68
Lansdown Gro.
    BA1: Bath 1B 6 (2B 104)
Lansdown Gro. Ct. BA1: Bath . . .2B 104
    (off Lansdown Gro.)
Lansdown Hgts. BA1: Bath 5B 96
Lansdown Ho. BS16: Soun 4F 61
Lansdown La.
    BA1: L'dwn, W'ton 5D 95
Lansdown Lawn Tennis &
    Squash Racquets Club 1B 104
Lansdown M. BA1: Bath . . .2B 6 (3B 104)
Lansdown Pk. BA1: L'dwn 4A 96
Lansdown (Park & Ride) 2E 95
Lansdown Pl. BS8: Clif 2C 66
    BS16: Emer G 4D 47
Lansdown Pl. E. BA1: Bath 2B 104
Lansdown Pl. W. BA1: Bath 1B 104
Lansdown Rd. BA1: Bath 2B 104
    BA1: L'dwn 1D 95
    BS5: E'tn 5C 58
    BS6: Redl 5E 57
    BS8: Clif 2C 66
    BS15: K'wd 4F 61
    BS31: Salt 4A 92
Lansdown Ter. BA1: Bath 2B 104
    (off Lansdown Rd.)
    BA1: W'ton 1E 103
    BS6: Henle 1F 57
Lansdown Vw. BA2: Bath 4E 103
    BS15: K'wd 1A 72
Laphams Ct. BS30: L Grn 5B 72
Lapwing Cl. BS20: P'bry, P'head . . .5E 35
    BS32: Brad S 3F 9
Lapwing Gdns. BS16: B'hll 5B 44
Larch Rd. BS15: Soun 3A 62
Larch Way BS34: Pat 1A 24
Larkfield BS36: Coal H 1F 29
LARKHALL 5D 97
Larkhall Bldgs. BA1: Bath 5E 97
    (off Larkhall Ter.)
Larkhall Ter. BA1: Bath 5E 97
Larkhill Pl. BA1: Bath 5E 97
Larkin Pl. BS7: Hor 2C 42
Lark Pl. BA1: Bath 3F 103
    (off Up. Bristol Rd.)
Lark Ri. BS37: Yate 1A 16
Larks Fld. BS16: Stap 1A 60
Larksleaze Rd. BS30: L Grn 2A 82
Lasbury Gro. BS13: Hart 2E 85
Latchmoor Ho. BS13: Bis 4C 76
Latimer Cl. BS4: Brisl 5A 70
Latteridge Rd. BS37: Iron A 1F 13
Latton Rd. BS7: Hor 3B 42
Launceston Av. BS15: Han 4D 71
Launceston Rd. BS15: K'wd 5D 61
Laura Pl. BA2: Bath 2D 7 (3C 104)
Laurels, The BS10: Hen 2C 22
    BS16: Mang 5C 46
Laurel St. BS15: K'wd 1F 71

Laurie Cres. BS9: Henle 5F 41
Laurie Lee Ct. BS30: Bar C 4C 72
Lavender Cl. BS5: S'wll 5B 60
Lavender Way BS32: Brad S 1B 26
Lavenham Rd. BS37: Yate 3D 15
Lavers Cl. BS15: K'wd 3A 72
Lavington Rd. BS5: St G 3D 71
Lawford Av. BS34: Lit S 2E 25
Lawford M. BS2: Bris 2F 5 (2B 68)
Lawfords Ga. BS5: E'tn 2B 68
Lawfords Ga. Ho. BS2: Bris 2F 5
    (off Lawford St.)
Lawford St. BS2: Bris 1F 5 (2B 68)
Lawn Av. BS16: Fish 1D 61
Lawn Cl. BS34: L'lze 3E 43
Lawn Rd. BS16: Fish 1D 61
Lawns, The BS11: Shire 4A 38
Lawns Rd. BS37: Yate 3A 16
Lawnwood Rd. BS5: E'tn 1D 69
Lawnwood Rd. Ind. Est.
    BS5: E'tn 1D 69
Lawrence Av. BS5: E'tn 5D 59
Lawrence Cl. BS15: Soun 4C 62
Lawrence Dr. BS37: Yate 3D 15
Lawrence Gro. BS9: Henle 1D 57
Lawrence Hill BS2: Bris 2C 68
    BS5: E'tn 2D 69
Lawrence Hill Ind. Pk. BS5: E'tn . .1D 69
Lawrence Hill Rdbt. BS5: E'tn 2C 68
Lawrence Hill Station (Rail) 2D 69
LAWRENCE WESTON 2C 38
Lawrence Weston Meadows
    Nature Reserve 5D 21
Lawrence Weston Rd.
    BS11: A'mth, Law W 3A 20
    (not continuous)
    BS11: Law W 1D 39
Lawson Cl. BS31: Salt 5E 91
Laxey Rd. BS7: Hor 4B 42
Lays Dr. BS31: Key 2E 89
Lays Farm Bus. Cen. BS31: Key . . .3E 89
Lays Farm Trad. Est. BS31: Key . . .3E 89
Lea Cft. BS13: Withy 2C 84
Leaholme Gdns. BS14: Whit 4C 86
Leaman Cl. BS37: Chip S 4C 16
Leap Va. BS16: Down 3C 46
Leap Valley Cres. BS16: Down 3B 46
Lear Cl. BS30: C Hth 4D 73
Leaze, The BS37: Yate 3F 15
Leda Av. BS14: H'gro 5C 78
Ledbury Rd. BS16: Fish 2E 61
Leechpool Way BS37: Yate 1A 16
Lee Cl. BS34: Pat 5B 8
Leeming Way BS11: Shire 3E 37
Lees Hill BS15: Soun 5A 62
Leeside BS20: P'head 1E 49
Lees La. BS30: Old C 4F 73
Leicester Sq. BS16: Soun 3F 61
Leicester St. BS3: Bedm 5F 67
Leicester Wlk. BS4: St Ap 4B 70
Leigh Cl. BA1: Bath 5C 96
Leigh Ct. Bus. Cen. BS8: Abb L . . .4C 54
Leigh Rd. BS8: Clif 1D 67
Leigh St. BS3: Bris 5C 66
Leighton Rd. BA1: W'ton 4C 94
    BS3: Bris 5D 67
    BS4: Know 2D 79
Leigh Vw. Rd. BS20: P'head 4C 34
LEIGH WOODS 3F 65
Leigh Woods Forest Walks 5F 55
Leigh Woods National Nature Reserve
    . . . . .1E 65
Leinster Av. BS4: Know 5F 77
Leisure Box, The 5C 60
Leisure Rd. BS15: K'wd 4A 72
Lemon La. BS2: Bris 1B 68
Lena Av. BS5: E'tn 5E 59
Lena St. BS5: E'tn 5D 59
Lenover Gdns. BS13: Hart 3D 85
Leonard La. BS1: Bris 2B 4
Leonard Rd. BS5: Redf 2E 69

Leonard's Av. BS5: E'tn 5E 59
Leopold Bldgs. BA1: Bath 2C 104
    (off Up. Hedgemead Rd.)
Leopold Rd. BS6: Bris 4A 58
Les Brown Ct. BS2: Bris 3B 68
Lescren Way BS11: A'mth 2F 37
Lewington Rd. BS16: Fish 2E 61
Lewins Mead BS1: Bris 2B 4 (2F 67)
Lewin St. BS5: St G 2F 69
Lewis Cl. BS16: Emer G 1E 63
    BS30: Old C 4F 73
Lewis Rd. BS13: Bis 4C 76
Lewis St. BS2: Bris 4D 69
Lewton La. BS36: Wint 1A 28
Leyland Wlk. BS13: Withy 3B 84
Leyton Vs. BS6: Redl 4D 57
Liberty Gdns. BS1: Bris 4E 67
Liberty Ind. Pk. BS3: Ash V 3C 76
Lichfield Rd. BS4: St Ap 3A 70
Lilac Cl. BS10: S'mead 2E 41
Lilac Ct. BS31: Key 4E 89
Lillian St. BS5: Redf 1E 69
LILLIPUT .5C 16
Lilliput Av. BS37: Chip S 5C 16
Lilliput Ct. BA1: Bath 4C 6
    (off Nth. Parade Pas.)
    BS37: Chip S 5C 16
Lilstock Av. BS7: B'stn 2B 58
Lilton Wlk. BS13: Bis 3C 76
Lilymead Av. BS4: Wind H 1B 78
Lime Cl. BS10: Bren 5D 23
Lime Ct. BS31: Key 3E 89
Lime Cft. BS37: Yate 1C 16
Lime Gro. BA2: Bath 4E 7 (4D 105)
Lime Gro. Gdns.
    BA2: Bath 4E 7 (4D 105)
Lime Kiln Cl. BS34: Stok G 1F 43
Lime Kiln Gdns. BS32: Brad S 2F 9
Limekiln La. BA2: Clav D 5B 106
Lime Kiln Rd. BS1: Bris 3D 67
Lime Kilns Cl. BS31: Key 2B 90
Limerick Rd. BS6: Redl 4E 57
Lime Rd. BS3: Bris 5D 67
    BS15: Han 4C 70
Limes, The BS16: Fren 2D 45
    (off Wellington Pl.)
Lime Tree Gro. BS20: Pill 3F 53
Lime Trees Rd. BS6: Henle 5F 41
Lincoln Cl. BS31: Key 3E 89
Lincoln Gdns. BS5: Bar H 2D 69
Lincoln St. BS5: Bar H 2D 69
Lincombe Av. BS16: Down 5F 45
Lincombe Rd. BS16: Down 1E 61
Linden Cl. BS34: Stoc 1A 88
    BS16: Fish 4C 60
    BS36: Wint 2A 28
Linden Ct. BS15: K'wd 5D 61
Linden Dr. BS32: Brad S 5A 10
Linden Gdns. BA1: W'ton 2F 103
Linden Grange BS6: Redl 3E 57
Linden Ho. BS15: K'wd 1A 72
Linden Rd. BS6: Henle, Redl 2D 57
Linder Quarter BS3: Bedm 1E 77
    (off Cromwell St.)
Lindon Ho. BS4: Brisl 1A 80
Lindrea St. BS3: Bedm 1D 77
Lindsay Rd. BS7: L'lze 2C 58
Lindsey Cl. BS20: P'head 2B 48
Linen Wlk. BA1: Swa 5E 97
Lines Way BS14: Whit 4E 87
Lingfield Pk. BS16: Down 2B 46
Link Rd. BS20: P'head 1E 49
    BS34: Fil 5B 24
    (New Rd.)
    BS34: Fil 1C 42
    (Springfields)
    BS37: Yate 4B 16
Link Rd. W. BS10: Pat 2D 23
Linley Cl. BA2: Bath 5C 102
Linleys, The BA1: Bath 3E 103

Linne Ho. BA2: Bath 5C **102**
Linnell Cl. BS7: L'lze 5D **43**
Linnet Cl. BS34: Pat 5A **8**
Linnet Gdns. BS20: P'head 5E **35**
Linnet Way BS14: Stoc 5F **79**
Lintern Cres. BS30: C Hth 3D **73**
Lintham Dr. BS15: K'wd 3B **72**
Linton's Wlk. BS14: H'gro 5C **78**
Lipgate Pl. BS20: P'head 3F **49**
Lisburn Rd. BS4: Know 3A **78**
Litfield Pl. BS8: Clif 2B **66**
Litfield Rd. BS8: Clif 1B **66**
Lit. Ann St. BS2: Bris 1F **5** (2B **68**)
Lit. Birch Cft. BS14: Whit 4C **86**
Lit. Bishop St. BS2: Bris 1A **68**
Lit. Caroline Pl. BS8: Clif 4B **66**
Littlecross Ho. BS3: Bris 5D **67**
Littledean BS37: Yate 1A **32**
Little Dowles BS30: C Hth 5C **72**
Lit. George St. BS2: Bris . . .1F **5** (1B **68**)
Little Green BS32: Brad S 4F **9**
Little Halt BS20: P'head 2A **48**
Little Hayes BS16: Fish 5D **45**
Lit. Headley Cl. BS13: Bis 5D **77**
Little Hill BA2: Bath 4C **102**
Lit. John St. BS1: Bris 2C **4** (2F **67**)
Lit. King St. BS1: Bris 4C **4** (3F **67**)
Little Locky Cl. BS34: L'lze 2E **43**
Little Mead BS11: Law W 2D **39**
Little Mdw. BS32: Brad S 2C **26**
Little Paradise BS3: Bedm 5F **67**
Lit. Parr Cl. BS16: Stap 1E **59**
Lit. Paul St. BS2: Bris 1E **67**
LITTLE SOLSBURY 3A **98**
Little Solsbury Hill Fort 3F **97**
Lit. Stanhope St.
  BA1: Bath 3A **6** (4A **104**)
LITTLE STOKE 2F **25**
Lit. Stoke La. BS34: Lit S 5E **9**
Lit. Stoke Rd. BS9: Stok B 2A **56**
Lit. Thatch Cl. BS14: H'gro 1E **87**
Little Theatre Cinema 4B **6**
Littleton Cl. BS34: Pat 4A **8**
Littleton Rd. BS3: Wind H 2F **77**
Littleton St. BS5: E'tn 1E **69**
Lit. Withey Mead BS9: W Trym 5A **40**
Littlewood Cl. BS14: Whit 4D **87**
Livingstone Rd. BA2: Bath 5F **103**
Livingstone Ter. BA2: Bath 5A **104**
  (off Junction Rd.)
Livingston M. BS3: Bedm 1E **77**
LivingWell Bristol Premier 5F **57**
Llewellyn Ct. BS9: W Trym 3C **40**
Lockemor Rd. BS13: Hart 3B **86**
Lock Gdns. BS13: Bis 5A **76**
Lockingwell Rd. BS31: Key 2E **89**
LOCKLEAZE 4D **43**
Lockleaze Rd. BS7: Hor 5C **42**
Locksbrook Ct. BA1: Bath 4D **103**
Locksbrook Pl. BA1: Bath 3E **103**
Locksbrook Rd. BA1: Bath 4D **103**
Locksbrook Rd. Trad. Est.
  BA1: Bath 4D **103**
Lockside BS20: P'head 4D **35**
Lockside Sq. BS20: P'head 4D **35**
Lock's La. BS37: Iron A 5A **14**
Locks Yd. Cvn. Site BS3: Bedm . . .3D **77**
Lodge C'way. BS16: Fish 3B **60**
Lodge C'way. Trad. Cen.
  BS16: Fish 3B **60**
Lodge Ct. BS9: Stok B 2A **56**
Lodge Dr. BS30: Old C 2E **83**
  BS41: L Ash 2D **75**
Lodge Gdns. BA2: Odd D 4F **109**
Lodge Hill BS15: K'wd 4E **61**
Lodge Pl. BS1: Bris 2A **4** (2F **67**)
Lodge Rd. BS15: K'wd 4E **61**
  BS37: Yate 2D **15**
  (North Rd.)
  BS37: Yate 2C **14**
  (Yate Rd.)

Lodgeside Av. BS15: K'wd 5E **61**
Lodgeside Gdns. BS15: K'wd 5E **61**
Lodge St. BS1: Bris 2A **4** (2E **67**)
Lodge Wlk. BS16: Down 5F **45**
Lodore Rd. BS16: Fish 3B **60**
LODWAY 1E **53**
Lodway BS20: Eas, Pill 2D **53**
Lodway Cl. BS20: Pill 1E **53**
Lodway Ct. BS20: Pill 2E **53**
Lodway Gdns. BS20: Pill 2E **53**
Lodway Rd. BS4: Brisl 2E **79**
Logan Rd. BS7: B'stn 3F **57**
Logus Ct. BS30: L Grn 5B **72**
Lombard St. BS3: Bedm 5F **67**
Lomond Rd. BS7: Fil 2B **42**
London Rd. BA1: Bath 2C **104**
  BS2: Bris 5B **58**
  BS30: B'yte, Warm 2E **73**
London Rd. E. BA1: Bathe, Bathf . .4B **98**
London Rd. W.
  BA1: Bath, Bathe 1E **105**
London Sq. BS20: P'head 4D **35**
London St. BA1: Bath 1C **6** (2C **104**)
  BS15: K'wd 1F **71**
Long Acre BA1: Bath 2C **104**
Long Acre Ho. BA1: Bath 2C **104**
Long Acre Rd. BS14: Whit 4C **86**
Long Acres Cl. BS9: C Din 4F **39**
LONG ASHTON 3B **74**
Long Ashton Bus. Pk.
  BS41: L Ash 3D **75**
Long Ashton By-Pass
  BS41: L Ash 5A **74**
  BS48: Flax B, L Ash 5A **74**
Long Ashton Rd. BS41: L Ash 3C **74**
Long Beach Rd. BS30: L Grn 1C **82**
Longbrook Trad. Est. BS3: Ash V . .1A **76**
Long Cl. BS16: Fish 5E **45**
  BS32: Brad S 2A **26**
Long Cft. BS37: Yate 1F **15**
Long Cross BS11: Law W 3A **38**
Longden Rd. BS16: Down 5B **46**
Long Down Av. BS34: L'lze 3E **43**
Long Eaton Dr. BS14: H'gro 4D **79**
Longfellow Av. BA2: Bath 1B **110**
Longfield Rd. BS7: B'stn 3A **58**
Longford BS37: Yate 5E **15**
Longford Av. BS10: S'mead 3F **41**
Long Fow Mnr. BS4: Brisl 3C **80**
Long Handstones BS30: C Hth 5C **72**
Long Hay Cl. BA2: Bath 5D **103**
Longhills Hostel BS5: S'wll 4C **60**
Longlands Ho. BS5: Bar H 2E **69**
Longleat Cl. BS9: Henle 1E **57**
Long Mead BS37: Yate 1A **16**
Longmead Av. BS7: Hor 1F **57**
Longmead Cft. BS13: Withy 3B **84**
Long Meadow BS16: Stap 1F **59**
Longmeadow Rd. BS31: Key 3E **89**
Longmoor Ct. BS3: Bedm 2D **47**
Longmoor Rd. BS3: Bedm 2C **76**
Longney Pl. BS34: Pat 4B **8**
Longreach BS31: Salt 3E **91**
Longreach Gro. BS14: Stoc 5F **79**
Long Rd. BS16: Mang 1C **62**
Long Row BS1: Bris 4D **5** (3A **68**)
Longs Dr. BS37: Yate 3E **15**
Longthorne Pl. BA2: C Down 3B **110**
Long Valley Rd. BA2: Bath 5B **102**
Longway Av. BS14: Whit 3B **86**
LONGWELL GREEN 1B **82**
Longwell Grn. Trad. Pk.
  BS30: L Grn 5A **72**
Longwell Ho. BS30: L Grn 1B **82**
Longwood BS4: Brisl 2C **80**
Longwood La. BS8: Fail 5B **64**
Lonsdale Bus. Cen.
  BS15: K'wd 4E **61**
Loop Rd. BA1: Bath 2C **6** (3C **104**)
  BS16: Soun 3C **62**
Lorain Wlk. BS10: Hen 1B **40**

Lorne Rd. BA2: Bath 4F **103**
Lorton Cl. BS10: S'mead 2D **41**
Lorton Rd. BS10: S'mead 2D **41**
Loughman Cl. BS15: K'wd 1A **72**
Louisa St. BS2: Bris 3B **68**
Louise Av. BS16: Mang 1C **62**
Love La. BS37: Chip S 5C **16**
  BS37: Yate 1C **16**
Lovelinch Gdns. BS41: L Ash 3B **74**
Lovell Av. BS30: Old C 5F **73**
Lovells, The BS20: Eas 2D **53**
Lovells Hill BS15: Han 4D **71**
Loveridge Ct. BS36: Fram C 1D **29**
Loverings Cl. BS10: Hen 4B **22**
Lovers' Wlk. BS6: Cot, Redl 4E **57**
  (not continuous)
Lowbourne BS14: H'gro 1B **86**
LOWER ALMONDSBURY 1C **8**
Lower App. Rd.
  BS1: Bris 5F **5** (4B **68**)
Lwr. Ashley Rd. BS2: Bris 5B **58**
  BS5: E'tn 5C **58**
Lwr. Borough Walls
  BA1: Bath 4B **6** (4B **104**)
Lwr. Bristol Rd.
  BA2: Bath 4A **6** (2B **102**)
Lwr. Burlington Rd.
  BS20: P'head 5D **35**
Lwr. Camden Pl. BA1: Bath 2C **104**
Lwr. Castle St.
  BS1: Bris 1E **5** (2A **68**)
Lwr. Chapel La. BS36: Fram C 2E **29**
Lwr. Chapel Rd. BS5: Han 4E **71**
Lwr. Cheltenham Pl. BS6: Bris 5B **58**
Lwr. Church La. BS2: Bris . . .2A **4** (2F **67**)
Lwr. Clifton Hill BS8: Clif 3C **66**
Lwr. Cock Rd. BS15: K'wd 2B **72**
Lwr. College St. BS1: Bris 3E **67**
Lwr. Down Rd. BS20: P'head 1E **49**
Lwr. East Hayes BA1: Bath 2D **105**
LOWER EASTON 5D **59**
Lwr. Fallow Cl. BS14: Whit 3B **86**
Lwr. Farm La. BA2: Cor 3D **101**
Lwr. Gay St. BS2: Bris 1F **67**
Lwr. Gro. Rd. BS16: Fish 2A **60**
Lwr. Guinea St. BS1: Bris . . .5C **4** (4F **67**)
Lwr. Hanham Rd. BS15: Han 4E **71**
Lwr. Hedgemead Rd.
  BA1: Bath 2C **104**
Lwr. High St. BS11: Shire 3F **37**
Lower Ho. BS34: Fil 5D **25**
Lwr. Ho. Cres. BS34: Fil 4D **25**
Lwr. Knole La. BS10: Bren 5C **22**
LOWER KNOWLE 2A **78**
Lwr. Lamb St. BS1: Bris 4A **4** (3E **67**)
Lwr. Maudlin St.
  BS1: Bris 1C **4** (2F **67**)
Lwr. Moor Rd. BS37: Yate 1A **16**
Lwr. Myrtle Hill BS20: Pill 1F **53**
  (off Pump Sq.)
Lower Northend BA1: Bathe 2B **98**
Lwr. Oldfield Pk.
  BA2: Bath 5A **6** (5F **103**)
Lwr. Park Row BS1: Bris . . .2B **4** (2F **67**)
Lwr. Redland M. BS6: Redl 4D **57**
Lwr. Redland Rd. BS6: Redl 4D **57**
Lwr. Sidney St. BS3: Bris 5C **66**
LOWER SOUNDWELL 4B **62**
Lwr. Station Rd. BS16: Fish 2C **60**
  BS16: Stap H 2E **61**
Lwr. Stone Cl. BS36: Fram C 5E **13**
LOWER SWAINSWICK 5E **97**
Lwr. Thirlmere Rd. BS34: Pat 5C **8**
LOWER WESTON 3E **103**
Lowlis Cl. BS10: Hen 5B **22**
Lowther Rd. BS10: S'mead 1E **41**
Loxley Gdns. BA2: Bath 1E **109**
Loxton Dr. BA2: Bath 4D **103**
Loxton Sq. BS14: H'gro 1C **86**
Lucas Cl. BS4: Brisl 3F **79**
Luccombe Hill BS6: Redl 4D **57**

Luckington Rd. BS7: Hor 2A 42
Lucklands Rd. BA1: W'ton 1E 103
Luckley Av. BS13: Hart 2E 85
Luckwell Rd. BS3: Bedm 1D 77
Lucky La. BS3: Bedm 5F 67
Ludlow Cl. BS2: Bris 5B 58
  BS30: Will 2D 83
  BS31: Key 2F 89
Ludlow Ct. BS30: Will 3D 83
Ludlow Rd. BS7: Hor 4C 42
Ludwell Cl. BS36: Wint 3F 27
Lullington Rd. BS4: Know 2D 79
Lulsgate Rd. BS13: Bis 4C 76
Lulworth Cres. BS16: Down 3B 46
Lulworth Rd. BS31: Key 3A 90
Lundy Ga. BS20: P'head 5E 35
Lurgan Wlk. BS4: Know 3F 77
Lutyens Cl. BS16: Stap 3F 43
Lux Furlong BS9: Sea M 4D 39
Luxton St. BS5: E'tn 1D 69
Lydbrook Cl. BS37: Yate 5F 15
Lyddington Rd. BS7: Hor 2A 42
LYDE GREEN 3F 47
Lyde Grn. Rdbt. BS16: Emer G . . .3D 47
Lydford Wlk. BS3: Wind H 2F 77
Lydia Ct. BS7: B'stn 2B 58
Lydiard Cft. BS15: Han 5E 71
Lydney Rd. BS10: S'mead 3F 41
  BS16: Stap H 2A 62
Lydstep Ter. BS3: Bedm 5E 67
Lyme Gdns. BA1: Bath 3D 103
Lyme Rd. BA1: Bath 3D 103
Lymore Av. BA2: Bath 5E 103
Lymore Cl. BA2: Bath 1E 109
Lymore Gdns. BA2: Bath 5E 103
Lymore Ter. BA2: Bath 1E 109
Lympsham Grn. BA2: Odd D 4F 109
Lynbrook BS41: L Ash 3B 74
Lynbrook La. BA2: Bath 2B 110
Lynch Cl. BS30: L Grn 5B 72
LYNCOMBE HILL 1C 110
Lyncombe Hill
  BA2: Bath 5D 7 (5C 104)
LYNCOMBE VALE 2C 110
Lyncombe Va. BA2: Bath 1C 110
Lyncombe Va. Rd. BA2: Bath . . .2C 110
Lyncombe Wlk. BS16: Fish 4D 61
Lyndale Av. BS9: Stok B 1F 55
Lyndale Rd. BS5: St G 1F 69
  BS37: Yate 4F 15
Lynde Cl. BS13: Hart 3D 85
Lyndhurst Pl. BA1: Bath 2C 104
Lyndhurst Rd. BA2: Bath 4E 103
  BS9: W Trym 4B 40
  BS31: Key 4B 90
Lyndhurst Ter. BA1: Bath 2C 104
Lynfield Pk. BA1: W'ton 5E 95
Lynmouth Rd. BS2: Bris 4B 58
Lynn Rd. BS16: Stap 1F 59
Lynton BS15: K'wd 1C 72
Lynton Cl. BS20: P'head 2A 50
Lynton Pl. BS5: Redf 1E 69
Lynton Rd. BS3: Wind H 3E 77
Lynton Way BS16: Fren 2D 45
Lynwood Rd. BS3: Bedm 2D 77
Lyons Ct. Rd. BS14: Stoc 5F 79
Lyppiatt Rd. BS5: Redf 1F 69
Lyppincourt Rd.
  BS10: Bren 5C 22
Lysander Rd. BS10: Pat 2D 23
  BS34: Pat 2D 23
Lysander Wlk. BS34: Stok G 3A 26
Lytchet Dr. BS16: Down 3B 46
Lytes Cary Rd. BS31: Key 5C 90
Lytham Ho. BS4: Brisl 3F 79
Lytton Av. BS7: Hor 3C 42
Lytton Gdns. BA2: Bath 1D 109
Lytton Gro. BS7: Hor 3C 42
  BS31: Key 2C 90
Lyveden Gdns. BS13: Hart 2D 85
Lyvedon Way BS41: L Ash 3D 75

M

Mabberley Cl. BS16: Emer G 1E 63
McAdam Way BS1: Bris 4B 66
Macaulay Bldgs. BA2: Bath 1E 111
Macauley Rd. BS7: Hor 3C 42
Macdonald Wlk. BS15: K'wd 1F 71
Macey's Rd. BS13: Hart 4F 85
Machin Cl. BS10: Hen 5B 22
Machin Gdns. BS10: Hen 5C 22
Machin Rd. BS10: Hen 5B 22
Macies, The BA1: W'ton 4D 95
Mackie Av. BS34: Fil 1D 43
Mackie Gro. BS34: Fil 1D 43
Mackie Rd. BS34: Fil 1D 43
McLaren Rd. BS11: A'mth 2D 37
Macrae Ct. BS15: K'wd 1A 72
Macrae Office Pk. BS20: Pill 2A 54
Macrae Rd. BS20: Pill 2A 54
Madeline Rd. BS16: Fish 4B 60
Madison Cl. BS37: Yate 3F 15
Maesbury BS15: K'wd 3A 72
Maesbury Rd. BS31: Key 5C 90
Maeskroll Rd. BS4: Know 1C 78
Magdalena Ct. BS1: Bris . . .5D 5 (4A 68)
Magdalene Av. BA2: Bath . . .5A 6 (5B 104)
Magdalene Pl. BS2: Bris 5B 58
Magdalen Rd. BA2: Bath . . .5A 6 (5B 104)
Maggs Cl. BS10: S'mead 5F 23
Maggs La. BS5: S'will 4A 60
  BS14: Whit 3D 87
Magpie Bottom La. BS5: St G 3D 71
  BS15: K'wd 3E 71
MAIDEN HEAD 5B 84
Maidenhead Rd. BS13: Hart 4F 85
Maiden Way BS11: Shire 4E 37
Maidstone St. BS3: Wind H 1B 78
Main Rd. BS16: Short 1E 63
Main Vw. BS36: Coal H 1F 29
Maisemore BS37: Yate 2F 31
Maisemore Av. BS34: Pat 4D 9
Makin Cl. BS30: Old C 4E 73
Malago Greenway BS13: Bis 5C 76
Malago Rd. BS3: Bedm 1E 77
Malago Va. Est. BS3: Bedm 1E 77
Malago Wlk. BS13: Withy 3A 84
Malden Mead BS14: Whit 2C 86
Maldowers La. BS5: St G 5C 60
Malin Pde. BS20: P'head 5E 35
Mall, The BS8: Clif 2B 66
Mallard Cl. BS5: S'will 5B 60
  BS32: Brad S 3F 9
  BS37: Chip S 5C 16
Malmains Dr. BS16: Fren 2D 45
Malmesbury Cl. BS6: Redl 2E 57
  BS30: Bar C 4B 72
Malthouse, The BS6: Bris 4B 58
Maltings, The BS6: Bris 4B 58
  (off Fairlawn Rd.)
Maltings Ind. Est., The
  BA1: Bath 3C 102
Malvern Bldgs. BA1: Bath 5C 96
Malvern Ct. BS5: St G 2A 70
Malvern Dr. BS30: Old C 4E 73
Malvern Rd. BA1: Bath 1F 79
  BS5: St G 2B 70
Malvern Ter. BA1: Bath 1C 104
  (off Camden Rd.)
Malvern Vs. BA1: Bath 1C 104
  (off Camden Rd.)
Mancroft Av. BS11: Law W 4A 38
MANGOTSFIELD 1C 62
Mangotsfield Rd.
  BS16: Mang, Stap H 2B 62
Manilla Rd. BS8: Clif 2C 66
Manor Cl. BS20: Eas 2C 52
  BS20: P'head 1C 48
  BS36: Coal H 2E 29
Manor Cl., The BS8: Abb L 1C 64
Manor Ct. BS16: Stap 2A 60
Manor Ct. Dr. BS7: Hor 4A 42

Manor Dr. BA1: Bathf 5E 99
Mnr. Farm Cotts. BS32: Brad S . . .4E 9
Mnr. Farm Cres. BS32: Brad S . . .5F 9
Mnr. Farm Rdbt. BS32: Brad S . . .5F 9
Manor Gdns. Ho. BS16: Fish 1B 60
Manor Gro. BS16: Mang 2C 62
  BS34: Pat 3D 9
Manor Hall BS8: Clif 2D 67
Manor Ho. La. BS14: H'gro 2E 87
Manor La. BS8: Abb L 1B 64
  BS36: Wint 1B 28
Manor Pk. BA1: Bath 2D 103
  BS6: Redl 3D 57
Manor Pl. BS16: Fren 2E 45
  BS34: Stok G 4C 26
Manor Rd. BA1: W'ton 1E 103
  BS7: B'stn 2A 58
  BS8: Abb L 3B 64
  BS13: Bis 1B 84
  BS16: Fish 1B 60
  BS16: Mang 2C 62
  BS31: Key, Salt 4B 90
Manor Vs. BA1: W'ton 1E 103
Manor Way BS37: Chip S 4E 17
Mansel Cl. BS31: Salt 4E 91
Mansfield St. BS3: Bedm 2D 77
Manston Cl. BS14: Stoc 5E 79
Manvers St. BA1: Bath 4D 7 (4C 104)
Manworthy Rd. BS4: Brisl 1F 79
Manx Rd. BS7: Hor 4B 42
Maple Av. BS16: Fish 3E 61
Maple Cl. BS14: Stoc 2F 87
  BS30: Old C 5D 73
  BS34: Lit S 1E 25
Maple Ct. BS15: K'wd 5F 61
Maple Gdns. BA2: Bath 1A 110
Maple Grange BS9: W Trym 5D 41
Maple Gro. BA2: Bath 1A 110
Maple Ho. BS2: Bris 1F 67
  (off Dove St. Sth.)
Maple Leaf Ct. BS8: Clif 1F 79
Mapleleaze BS4: Brisl 1F 79
Maplemeade BS7: B'stn 2E 57
Maple Rd. BS4: St Ap 4F 69
  BS7: Hor 1F 57
Maplestone Rd. BS14: Whit 4C 86
Maple Wlk. BS31: Key 3F 89
Mapstone Cl. BS16: Ham 5D 27
Marbeck Rd. BS10: S'mead 2D 41
Marconi Rd. BS20: P'head 1B 48
Mardale Cl. BS10: S'mead 1E 41
Marden Rd. BS31: Key 3C 90
Mardon Rd. BS4: St Ap 3F 69
Mardyke Ferry Rd. BS1: Bris 4D 67
Margaret Rd. BS13: Withy 3B 84
Margaret's Bldgs.
  BA1: Bath 1A 6 (3B 104)
Margaret's Hill BA1: Bath 2C 104
Margate St. BS3: Wind H 1B 78
Marguerite Rd. BS13: Bis 5B 76
Marigold Wlk. BS3: Bedm 2C 76
Marina Gdns. BS16: Fish 3A 60
Marine Pde. BS20: Pill 1E 53
Mariner's Dr. BS9: Stok B 2F 55
Mariners Path BS9: Stok B 2F 55
  BS20: P'head . . . . . .1A 48 & 5A 34
Mariners Way BS20: Pill 1E 53
Marion Rd. BS15: Han 1D 81
Marion Wlk. BS5: St G 2C 70
Marissal Cl. BS10: Hen 5A 22
Marissal Rd. BS10: Hen 5F 21
Mariston Way BS30: Old C 3E 73
Maritime Heritage Cen. 4D 67
Marjoram Pl. BS32: Brad S 1B 26
Marjoram Way BS20: P'head 1B 50
Marjorie Whimster Ho.
  . . . . .4D 103
Marketgate BS1: Bris 1F 5
Marketside BS2: Bris 5C 68
Market Sq. BS16: Fish 3E 61
Markham Cl. BS11: Shire 4E 37

Marklands BS9: Stok B 3A **56**
Mark La. BS1: Bris 3A **4** (3E **67**)
Marksbury Rd.
  BS3: Bedm, Wind H 2E **77**
Marlborough Av. BS16: Fish 3A **60**
Marlborough Bldgs.
  BA1: Bath 1A **6** (3A **104**)
Marlborough Ct. BA2: Clav D 4A **106**
Marlborough Dr. BS16: Fren 2D **45**
Marlborough Flats *BS2: Bris* 1F **67**
  (off Eugene St.)
Marlborough Hill BS2: Bris 1F **67**
Marlborough Hill Pl. BS2: Bris 1F **67**
Marlborough La. BA1: Bath 3A **104**
Marlborough St. BA1: Bath 2A **104**
  BS1: Bris 1C **4** (1F **67**)
  BS2: Bris 1C **4** (1F **67**)
  BS5: Eastv 3A **60**
Marlepit Gro. BS13: Bis 1A **84**
Marlfield Wlk. BS13: Bis 5A **76**
Marling Rd. BS5: St G 1B **70**
Marlwood Dr. BS10: Bren 5C **22**
Marmaduke St. BS3: Wind H 1B **78**
Marmalade La. BS4: Brisl 3E **79**
Marmion Cres. BS10: Hen 5A **22**
Marne Cl. BS14: Stoc 2F **87**
Marsden Rd. BA2: Bath 2D **109**
Marshall Ho. BS16: Fish 2B **60**
Marshall Wlk. BS4: Know 5F **77**
Marsham Way
  BS30: Bar C, L Grn 4A **72**
Marsh Cl. BS36: Wint 4A **28**
Marshfield Pk. BS16: Down 3E **45**
Marshfield Rd. BS16: Fish 2D **61**
Marshfield Way BA1: Bath 1C **104**
Marsh La. BS3: Bedm 2C **76**
  BS5: Redf 3E **69**
  BS20: Eas 4A **36**
Marsh La. Ind. Est. BS20: Eas 5A **36**
Marsh Rd. BS3: Ash G 1B **76**
Marsh St. BS1: Bris 4B **4** (3F **67**)
  BS11: A'mth 3E **37**
Marston Rd. BS4: Know 2D **79**
Martcombe Rd. BS20: Eas 3C **52**
Martha's Orchard BS13: Bis 5A **76**
Martin Cl. BS34: Pat 5A **8**
Martingale Rd. BS4: Brisl 5F **69**
Martingale Way BS20: P'head 5D **35**
Martins, The BS20: P'head 5F **35**
Martin's Rd. BS15: Han 4E **71**
Martin St. BS3: Bedm 1D **77**
Martock Cres. BS3: Bedm 3E **77**
Martock Rd. BS3: Bedm 3E **77**
  BS31: Key 4C **90**
Marwood Rd. BS4: Know 4A **78**
Marybush La. BS2: Bris 2E **5** (2A **68**)
Mary Carpenter Pl. BS2: Bris 5B **58**
Mary Ct. *BS5: Redf* 1F **69**
  (off Alfred St.)
Marygold Leaze BS30: C Hth 5C **72**
Mary Seacole Cl. *BS2: Bris* 4C **58**
  (off Mercia Dr.)
Mary St. BS5: Redf 1F **69**
Mascot Rd. BS3: Wind H 1F **77**
Masefield Way BS7: Hor 5C **42**
Maskelyne Av. BS10: Hor 4F **41**
Masonpit Pool La. BS36: Wint . . .5E **11**
Masons Vw. BS36: Wint 2B **28**
Matchells Cl. BS4: St Ap 3A **70**
Materman Rd. BS14: Stoc 2A **88**
Matford Cl. BS10: Bren 4F **23**
  BS36: Wint 3A **28**
Matthews Cl. BS14: Stoc 1B **88**
Matthews Rd. BS5: Redf 2E **69**
Maules La. BS16: Ham 1B **44**
Maunsell Rd. BS11: Law W 1D **39**
Maurice Rd. BS6: Bris 4A **58**
Mautravers Cl. BS32: Brad S 1F **25**
Mawdeley Ho. *BS3: Bedm* 5E **67**
  (off Catherine Mead St.)
Maxse Rd. BS4: Know 1D **79**

Maybank Rd. BS37: Yate 4F **15**
Maybec Gdns. BS5: St G 3C **70**
Maybourne BS4: Brisl 2C **80**
Maybrick Rd. BA2: Bath 5F **103**
Maycliffe Pk. BS6: Bris 4B **58**
Mayfield Av. BS16: Fish 4C **60**
MAYFIELD PARK 4C **60**
Mayfield Pk. BS16: Fish 4C **60**
Mayfield Pk. Nth. BS16: Fish 4C **60**
Mayfield Pk. Sth. BS16: Fish 4C **60**
Mayfield Rd. BA2: Bath 5F **103**
Mayflower Ct. BS16: Stap H 1A **62**
May La. BA1: Bath 2D **103**
Maynard Cl. BS13: Hart 2E **85**
Maynard Rd. BS13: Hart 2E **85**
Mayors Bldgs. BS16: Fish 1D **61**
Maypole Sq. BS15: Han 4E **71**
Mays Cl. BS36: Coal H 1F **29**
Maysfield Cl. BS20: P'head 3F **49**
MAYSHILL 4A **14**
Mays Hill BS36: Fram C 4A **14**
May St. BS15: K'wd 5E **61**
Maytree Av. BS13: Bis 5D **77**
Maytree Cl. BS13: Bis 5D **77**
Mayville Av. BS34: Fil 5C **24**
May Tree Wlk. BS31: Key 4E **89**
Maywood Av. BS16: Fish 2D **61**
Maywood Cres. BS16: Fish 2D **61**
Maywood Rd. BS16: Fish 2E **61**
Maze St. BS5: Bar H 3D **69**
Mead, The BS34: Fil 4D **25**
  BS41: Dun 5A **84**
Mead Cl. BA2: Bath 2A **110**
  BS36: Wint 2A **28**
Mead Ct. BS36: Wint 2A **28**
Meade Ho. BA2: Bath 5C **102**
Meadgate BS16: Emer G 4D **47**
Meadlands BA2: Cor 3D **101**
Mead La. BS31: Salt 3B **92**
  BS32: Brad S 2A **26**
Meadow Cl. BS16: Down 4B **46**
Meadow Ct. BA1: Bath 3C **102**
Meadow Ct. Dr. BS30: Old C 1E **83**
Meadowcroft BS16: Down 3C **46**
Meadow Dr. BA2: Odd D 5F **109**
  BS20: Wes 5B **48**
Meadow Gdns. BA1: Bath 1C **102**
Meadow Gro. BS11: Shire 4F **37**
Meadowland Rd. BS10: Hen 4A **22**
Meadow La. BA2: B'ptn 1F **105**
Meadow Mead BS36: Fram C 5D **13**
  BS37: Yate 1A **16**
  (off Leechpool Way)
Meadow Pk. BA1: Bathf 4D **99**
Meadow Rd. BS37: Chip S 4C **16**
Meadows, The BS15: Han 5F **71**
Meadow Side BS37: Iron A 1F **13**
Meadowside Dr. BS14: Whit 4C **86**
Meadow St. BS11: A'mth 2C **36**
Meadowsweet Av. BS34: Fil 5D **25**
Meadowsweet Ct. *BS16: Stap* 1A **60**
  (off Foxglove Cl.)
Meadow Va. BS5: St G 5C **60**
Meadow Vw. BS36: Fram C 1E **29**
Meadow Vw. Cl. BA1: Bath 2C **102**
Meadow Way BS32: Brad S 1A **26**
Mead Ri. BS3: Bris 5B **68**
Mead Rd. BS20: P'head 4E **49**
  BS34: Stok G 2A **26**
  BS37: Chip S 5E **17**
Meads, The BS16: Down 4B **46**
  (not continuous)
Mead St. BS3: Bris 5B **68**
Mead Way BS9: Sea M 5E **39**
Meardon Rd. BS14: Stoc 1A **88**
Mease Rd. BA2: C Down 3B **110**
Mecca Bingo
  Bristol 2D **69**

Mede Cl. BS1: Bris 4A **68**
Media Ho. *BS8: Clif* 2D **67**
  (off Wetherell Pl.)
Medical Av. BS2: Bris 2A **4** (2E **67**)
Medway Cl. BS31: Key 4C **90**
Medway Ct. BS7: B'stn 1F **57**
Medway Dr. BS31: Key 4C **90**
  BS36: Fram C 1D **29**
Meere Bank BS11: Law W 2D **39**
Meg Thatchers Gdns. BS5: St G 2D **71**
Meg Thatcher's Grn. BS5: St G 2D **71**
Melbourne Dr. BS37: Chip S 4D **17**
Melbourne Rd. BS7: B'stn 2F **57**
Melbury Rd. BS4: Know 2B **78**
Melcombe Cl. BA2: Bath 1F **109**
Melcombe Rd. BA2: Bath 5F **103**
Melita Rd. BS6: Bris 3A **58**
Mellent Av. BS13: Hart 4E **85**
Mells Cl. BS31: Key 5C **90**
Melrose Av. BS8: Clif 1D **67**
  BS37: Yate 3B **16**
Melrose Cl. BS37: Yate 3C **16**
Melrose Gro. BA2: Bath 2D **109**
Melrose Pl. BS8: Clif 1D **67**
Melrose Ter. BA1: Bath 5C **96**
Melton Cres. BS7: Hor 3C **42**
Melville Rd. BS6: Redl 5D **57**
Melville St. BS3: Bedm 1E **77**
Melvin Sq. BS4: Know 3A **78**
Memorial Cl. BS15: Han 5D **71**
Memorial Cotts. BA1: W'ton 1E **103**
Memorial Rd. BS15: Han 4D **71**
Memorial Stadium 5B **42**
Mendip Cl. BS31: Key 2F **89**
Mendip Ct. BS16: Fren 2A **44**
Mendip Cres. BS16: Down 4C **46**
Mendip Gdns. BA2: Odd D 5F **109**
Mendip Rd. BS3: Wind H 1F **77**
  BS20: P'head 1C **48**
Mendip Vw. Av. BS16: Fish 3C **60**
Menhyr Gro. BS10: Bren 5D **23**
Mercer Ct. BS14: H'gro 4D **79**
Merchants Academy Community
  Sports & Facilities Cen. 2C **84**
Merchants Cl. BS8: Clif 4C **66**
Merchants Sq. BS20: P'head 5D **35**
Merchants Quay
  BS1: Bris 5B **4** (4F **67**)
Merchants Rest BS2: Bris 2F **5**
Merchants Rd. BS8: Clif 4C **66**
  (Nova Scotia Pl.)
Merchants Rd. BS8: Clif 2C **66**
  (Victoria Sq.)
Merchants Row *BS1: Bris* 4E **67**
  (off Caledonian Rd.)
Merchants Trade Pk. BS2: Bris 2C **68**
Merchant St. BS1: Bris 1D **5** (2A **68**)
Mercia Dr. BS2: Bris 4C **58**
Mercier Cl. BS37: Yate 3B **16**
Meredith Ct. BS1: Bris 4C **66**
Merfield Rd. BS4: Know 2D **79**
Meridian Pl. BS8: Clif 2D **67**
Meridian Rd. BS6: Cot 5E **57**
Meridian Ter. BS7: B'stn 3A **58**
Meridian Va. BS8: Clif 2D **67**
Meriet Av. BS13: Hart 3D **85**
Merioneth St. BS3: Wind H 1B **78**
Meriton St. BS2: Bris 4D **69**
Merlin Cl. BS9: W Trym 3B **40**
Merlin Ct. BS9: W Trym 4D **41**
Merlin Pk. BS20: P'head 2B **48**
Merlin Rd. BS34: Pat 1D **23**
Merlin Way BS37: Chip S 5B **16**
Merrett Ct. BS7: L'lze 5D **43**
Merrick Ct. BS1: Bris 5B **4** (4F **67**)
Merrimans Rd. BS11: Shire 3F **37**
Merritt Way BS16: Mang, Soun 3C **62**
Merryweather Cl. BS32: Brad S 5F **9**
Merryweathers BS4: Brisl 2A **80**
Merrywood Cl. BS3: Bedm 5E **67**

Merrywood Ct. BS4: Know 2D **79**
  (off Maxse Rd.)
Merrywood Rd. BS3: Bedm 5E **67**
Merstham Rd. BS2: Bris 4C **58**
Merton Rd. BS7: Hor 1A **58**
Mervyn Rd. BS7: B'stn 2A **58**
Metford Gro. BS6: Redl 3D **57**
Metford Pl. BS6: Redl 3E **57**
Metford Rd. BS6: Redl 3D **57**
Mews, The BA1: Bath 2C **102**
Mezellion Pl. BA1: Bath 1D **105**
  (off Camden Rd.)
Michaels Mead BA1: W'ton 5D **95**
Michael Tippett Cen., The 5D **101**
Middle Av. BS1: Bris 4B **4** (3F **67**)
Middle Bri. Bus. Pk.
  BS2: P'head 3A **50**
Middleford Ho. BS13: Hart 3E **85**
Middle La. BA1: Bath 1D **105**
Middle Rd. BS15: Soun 3A **62**
Middleton Rd. BS11: Law W 3B **38**
Middleway La. BS41: Dun 5B **84**
Middlewood Cl. BA2: Odd D 3E **109**
Midford Rd. BA2: C Down, Odd D, S'ske
  . . . . .4A **110**
Midland Bri. Rd.
  BA1: Bath 4A **6** (4A **104**)
  BA2: Bath 4A **6** (4A **104**)
Midland M. BS2: Bris 2B **68**
Midland Rd. BA1: Bath 4F **103**
  BA2: Bath 4F **103**
  BS2: Bris 2F **5** (2B **68**)
  BS16: Stap H 2F **61**
Midland St. BS2: Bris 3B **68**
Midland Ter. BS16: Fish 3B **60**
Midsummer Bldgs. BA1: Bath . . .5D **97**
Mildred St. BS5: Redf 2E **69**
Miles Cl. BS20: Pill 3A **54**
Miles Ct. BS8: Clif 5C **56**
  BS30: Bar C 5B **72**
Miles Rd. BS8: Clif 5C **56**
Miles's Bldgs.
  BA1: Bath 2B **6** (3B **104**)
Miles St. BA2: Bath 5D **7** (5C **104**)
Mile Wlk. BS14: H'gro 1C **86**
Milford St. BS3: Bedm 5E **67**
Milk St. BA1: Bath 4B **6** (4B **104**)
Millard Cl. BS10: S'mead 1E **41**
Millar Ho. BS8: Clif 3C **66**
Mill Av. BS1: Bris 4C **4** (3F **67**)
Millbank Cl. BS4: Brisl 1A **80**
Millbrook Av. BS4: Brisl 1B **80**
Millbrook Cl. BS30: Old C 3E **73**
Millbrook Cl. BA2: Bath 5C **104**
  (off Millbrook Pl.)
Millbrook Pl. BA2: Bath . . .5D **7** (5C **104**)
Millbrook Rd. BS37: Yate 3D **15**
Mill Cl. BS20: P'bry 4F **51**
  BS36: Fram C 1E **29**
Mill Cres. BS37: W'lgh 4D **31**
Millennium Cl. BS36: Coal H 1F **29**
Millennium Prom.
  BS1: Bris 5A **4** (4E **67**)
Millennium Sq. BS1: Bris . .5A **4** (4E **67**)
Millers Cl. BS20: Pill 2E **53**
Millers Dr. BS30: Old C 4E **73**
Miller Wlk. BA2: B'ptn 1A **106**
Millfield Dr. BS30: Old C 3E **73**
Millground Rd. BS13: Withy 3A **84**
Mill Ho. BS5: E'tn 5C **58**
Milliman Cl. BS13: Hart 2F **85**
Mill La. BA2: B'ptn 4D **103**
  BA2: B'ptn 5B **98**
  BS3: Bedm 5F **67**
  BS16: Ham 5E **27**
  BS20: P'bry 3A **52**
  BS30: Bit 4F **83**
  BS30: C Hth, Old C 4D **73**
  BS36: Fram C 4D **13**
  BS37: Chip S 4C **16**
  BS37: Old S 2F **33**

Millmead Ho. BS13: Hart 3E **85**
Millmead Rd. BA2: Bath 5E **103**
Millpill Cl. BS9: Stok B 1F **55**
Millpond St. BS5: E'tn 5C **58**
Mill Pool Ct. BS10: S'mead 2D **41**
Mill Rd. BS36: Wint D 4F **27**
Mill Steps BS36: Wint D 5A **28**
Millward Gro. BS16: Fish 2E **61**
Milner Grn. BS30: Bar C 4C **72**
Milner Rd. BS7: Hor 1B **58**
Milsom Pl. BA1: Bath 2B **6** (3B **104**)
Milsom St. BA1: Bath 2B **6** (3B **104**)
  BS5: E'tn 1C **68**
Milton Av. BA2: Bath 1B **110**
Milton Cl. BS37: Yate 3F **15**
Milton Pk. BS5: Redf 2E **69**
Milton Rd. BS7: Hor 5A **42**
  BS37: Yate 3F **15**
Miltons Cl. BS13: Hart 3F **85**
Milverton Gdns. BS6: Bris 4B **58**
Milward Rd. BS31: Key 1A **90**
Mina Rd. BS2: Bris 3C **58**
Minehead Rd. BS4: Know 3B **78**
Minerva Cl. BS41: L Ash 2B **74**
Minerva Ct. BA2: Bath 1D **7**
Minerva Gdns. BA2: Bath 5E **103**
Minor's La. BS10: H'len 1C **20**
Minsmere Rd. BS31: Key 4C **90**
Minster Way BA2: Bath 2E **105**
Minton Cl. BS14: Whit 2D **87**
Minto Rd. BS2: Bris 4B **58**
Minto Rd. Ind. Est. BS2: Bris 4B **58**
Mirage BS20: P'head 5D **35**
Mission Rd. BS37: Iron A 1C **14**
Mitchell Cl. BS1: Bris 4D **5** (3A **68**)
Mitchell La. BS1: Bris 4D **5** (3A **68**)
Mitchell Wlk. BS30: B'yte 2F **73**
Mivart St. BS5: E'tn 4D **59**
Modecombe Gro. BS10: Hen 5B **22**
Mogg St. BS2: Bris 4C **58**
Molesworth Cl. BS13: Withy 3C **84**
Molesworth Dr. BS13: Withy 3C **84**
Monk Rd. BS7: B'stn 2F **57**
Monks Av. BS15: K'wd 1D **71**
Monksdale Rd. BA2: Bath 1F **109**
Monks Ho. BS37: Yate 1F **31**
Monk's Pk. Av. BS7: Hor 2A **42**
Monks Pk. Way BS10: S'mead 3A **42**
MONKTON COMBE 4F **111**
Monkton Rd. BS15: Han 5D **71**
Monmouth Cl. BS20: P'head 2B **48**
Monmouth Ct. BA1: Bath 3A **6**
  (off Up. Bristol Rd.)
  BS20: Pill 1E **53**
Monmouth Hill BS32: Alm 1A **8**
Monmouth Pl. BA1: Bath . . .3A **6** (4B **104**)
Monmouth Rd. BS7: B'stn 2F **57**
  BS20: Pill 1E **53**
  BS31: Key 2F **89**
Monmouth St. BA1: Bath . . .3A **6** (4B **104**)
  BS3: Wind H 1B **78**
Monsdale Cl. BS10: Hen 5C **22**
Monsdale Dr. BS10: Hen 5C **22**
Mont, The BS6: Bris 5A **58**
  (off St Andrew's Rd.)
Montague Cl. BS34: Stok G 3A **26**
Montague Ct. BS2: Bris 1F **67**
  (off Montague Hill Sth.)
Montague Flats BS2: Bris 1F **67**
  (off Eugene St.)
Montague Hill BS2: Bris 1F **67**
Montague Hill Sth. BS2: Bris 1F **67**
Montague Pl. BS6: Bris 1F **67**
Montague Rd. BS31: Salt 5E **91**
Montague St. BS2: Bris 1F **67**
Montgomery St. BS3: Wind H 5B **68**
MONTPELIER 5A **58**
Montpelier BA1: Bath 1B **6**
Montpelier Central BS6: Bris 5A **58**
  (off Station Rd.)
Montpelier Ct. BS6: Bris 4A **58**

Montpelier Station (Rail) 4A **58**
Montreal Av. BS7: Hor 3B **42**
Montrose Av. BS6: Cot 5E **57**
Montrose Cotts. BA1: W'ton 1E **103**
Montrose Dr. BS30: Warm 3D **73**
Montrose Pk. BS4: Brisl 2F **79**
Montroy Cl. BS9: Henle 5E **41**
Moon St. BS2: Bris 1A **68**
Moor Cft. Dr. BS30: L Grn 5B **72**
Moordell Cl. BS37: Yate 4F **15**
MOOREND 1A **46**
Moorend Farm Av. BS11: A'mth . . .3A **20**
Moorend Gdns. BS11: Law W 4B **38**
Moorend Rd. BS16: Ham 5F **27**
Moorfield Ho. BS16: Ham 2E **69**
  (off Church Rd.)
MOORFIELDS 1E **69**
Moorfields Cl. BA2: Bath 1F **109**
  BS5: Redf 2E **69**
Moorfields Dr. BA2: Bath 1F **109**
Moorfields Rd. BA2: Bath 1F **109**
Moor Ga. BS20: P'head 2B **50**
Moor Gro. BS11: Law W 3B **38**
Moorgrove Ho. BS9: C Din 3E **39**
Moorhill St. BS5: E'tn 5D **59**
Moorhouse Cvn. Pk.
  BS11: A'mth 4C **20**
Moorhouse La. BS10: H'len 3B **20**
  BS11: A'mth 3B **20**
Moorings, The BS20: Pill 2E **53**
Moorland Rd. BA2: Bath 5F **103**
  BS37: Yate 4F **15**
MOORLANDS 1F **109**
Moorlands, The BA2: Bath 2F **109**
Moorlands Rd. BS16: Fish 3B **60**
  (not continuous)
Moor La. BS20: Clap G 5A **50**
Moorpark Av. BS37: Yate 4E **15**
Moravian Bus. Pk. BS15: K'wd 1F **71**
Moravian Ct. BS15: K'wd 1F **71**
Moravian Rd. BS15: K'wd 1F **71**
Morden Wlk. BS14: Stoc 5F **79**
Moreton Cl. BS14: Whit 3C **86**
Morford St. BA1: Bath 1B **6** (2B **104**)
Morgan Cl. BS31: Salt 5F **91**
Morgan St. BS2: Bris 5B **58**
Morley Av. BS16: Mang 2C **62**
Morley Cl. BS16: Soun 2F **61**
  BS34: Lit S 1E **25**
Morley Rd. BS3: Bedm 1E **77**
  BS16: Soun 2F **61**
Morley Sq. BS7: B'stn 2A **58**
Morley St. BS2: Bris 5B **58**
  BS5: Bar H 2D **69**
Morley Ter. BA2: Bath 4F **103**
  BS15: K'wd 5F **61**
Mornington Rd. BS8: Clif 4C **56**
Morpeth Rd. BS4: Know 4F **77**
Morris Cl. BA1: Bathf 4D **99**
Morris La. BA1: Bathf 4D **99**
Morris Rd. BS7: L'lze 1C **58**
Morse Rd. BS5: Redf 2E **69**
Mortimer Cl. BA1: W'ton 5D **95**
Mortimer Rd. BS8: Clif 2C **66**
  BS34: Fil 2D **43**
Morton St. BS5: Bar H 2D **69**
Motorway Distribution Cen.
  BS11: A'mth 1E **37**
Mountain Ash BA1: W'ton 1F **103**
Mountain M. BS5: St G 2C **70**
Mountain Wood BA1: Bathf 5E **99**
Mountbatten Cl. BS37: Yate 2F **15**
Mount Beacon BA1: Bath 1C **104**
Mt. Beacon Pl. BA1: Bath 1B **104**
Mt. Beacon Row BA1: Bath 1C **104**
Mount Cl. BS36: Fram C 5B **12**
Mount Cres. BS36: Wint 3A **28**
Mount Gdns. BS15: K'wd 3F **71**
Mount Gro. BA2: Bath 2D **109**
MOUNT HILL 3A **72**
Mount Hill Rd. BS15: Han, K'wd . . .3E **71**

Mt. Pleasant BA2: Mon C 4F **111**
   BS10: H'len 4E **21**
   BS20: Pill 2F **53**
Mt. Pleasant Ter. BS3: Bedm 5E **67**
Mount Rd. BA1: Bath 2B **104**
   BA2: Bath 1C **108**
Mount Vw. BA1: Bath 1C **104**
   (off Beacon Rd.)
   BA2: Bath 2D **109**
Mow Barton BS13: Bis 1B **84**
   BS37: Yate 3F **15**
Mowbray Rd. BS14: H'gro 5E **79**
Mowcroft Rd. BS13: Hart 3E **85**
Moxham Dr. BS13: Hart 3D **85**
Muirfield BS30: Warm 3C **72**
   BS37: Yate 5A **16**
Mulberry Av. BS20: P'head 1A **50**
Mulberry Cl. BS15: K'wd 1A **72**
Mulberry BS20: P'head 1B **50**
Mulberry Cl. BS15: K'wd 5B **62**
Mulberry Gdns. BS16: Soun 3F **61**
Mulberry Wlk. BS9: C Din 3E **39**
Muller Av. BS7: B'stn 2B **58**
Muller Ho. BS7: B'stn 2B **58**
Muller Rd. BS5: Eastv 5B **42**
   (not continuous)
   BS7: Hor 5B **42**
Mulready Cl. BS7: L'lze 5E **43**
Murdoch Sq. BS7: Hor 3B **42**
Murford Av. BS13: Hart 2D **85**
Murford Wlk. BS13: Hart 3D **85**
Murray St. BS3: Bedm 5E **67**
Mus. of Bath at Work 1B **6** (2B **104**)
Mus. of Costume, The . .1B **6** (3B **104**)
Mus. of East Asian Art . . .1A **6** (3B **104**)
Musgrove Cl. BS11: Law W 1E **39**
Myrtle Ct. BS3: Bedm 5D **67**
   (off Exmoor St.)
Myrtle Dr. BS11: Shire 1A **54**
Myrtle Hill BS20: Pill 2E **53**
Myrtle Rd. BS2: Bris 1E **67**
Myrtle St. BS3: Bedm 5D **67**

N

Nags Head Hill BS5: St G 2C **70**
Nailsea Cl. BS13: Bis 5C **76**
Nailsworth Av. BS37: Yate 4A **16**
Naish BS20: Clap G 5B **50**
Naish Ho. BA2: Bath 4C **102**
Napier Ct. BS1: Bris 4D **67**
Napier Miles Rd. BS11: Law W . . .3C **38**
   BS5: Eastv 4D **59**
   BS6: Redl 4D **57**
   BS11: A'mth 2D **37**
Napier Sq. BS11: A'mth 2C **36**
Napier St. BS5: Bar H 3D **69**
Narroways Rd. BS2: Bris 3C **58**
Narrow La. BS16: Soun 3A **62**
Narrow Lewins Mead BS1: Bris . . .2B **4**
Narrow Plain BS2: Bris 3E **5** (3A **68**)
Narrow Quay BS1: Bris 5B **4** (4F **67**)
   (not continuous)
Narrow Quay Ho. BS1: Bris 4B **4**
Naseby Wlk. BS5: S'wll 5B **60**
Nash Cl. BS31: Key 2C **90**
Nash Dr. BS7: L'lze 4E **43**
Neads Dr. BS30: Old C 4E **73**
Neale La. BS11: A'mth 2E **37**
Neate Ct. BS34: Pat 5E **9**
Neath Rd. BS5: W'hall 1F **69**
Nelson Bldgs. BA1: Bath . . .1D **7** (2C **104**)
Nelson Ho. BA1: Bath 3A **104**
   BS1: Bris 2C **4**
   (off Rupert St.)
   BS16: Stap H 1F **61**
Nelson Pde. BS3: Bedm 5F **67**
Nelson Pl. E. BA1: Bath 2C **104**
Nelson Pl. W. BA1: Bath 4A **104**

Nelson Rd. BS16: Stap H 1F **61**
   (not continuous)
Nelson St. BS1: Bris 2C **4** (2F **67**)
   BS3: Bedm 2C **76**
Nelson Vs. BA1: Bath 4A **104**
Neston Wlk. BS4: Know 4B **78**
NETHAM 3F **69**
Netham Ct. BS5: Redf 2F **69**
   (off Netham Rd.)
Netham Gdns. BS5: Redf 2F **69**
Netham Ind. Pk. BS5: Redf 2F **69**
Netham Pk. Ind. Est. BS5: Redf . . .3F **69**
Netham Rd. BS5: Redf 2F **69**
Nettlestone Cl. BS10: Hen 4A **22**
Nevalan Dr. BS5: St G 3C **70**
Nevill Ct. BA2: New L 5D **101**
Neville Rd. BS15: K'wd 4A **62**
Nevil Rd. BS7: B'stn 2A **58**
New Bond St.
   BA1: Bath 3B **6** (4B **104**)
New Bond St. Bldgs. BA1: Bath 3B **6**
   (off New Bond St.)
New Bond St. Pl. BA1: Bath 3C **6**
Newbridge Cl. BS4: Stok G 3C **26**
NEWBRIDGE 2C **102**
Newbridge Cl. BS4: St Ap 3F **69**
Newbridge Ct. BA1: Bath 3D **103**
Newbridge Gdns. BA1: Bath 2C **102**
Newbridge Hill BA1: Bath 2C **102**
Newbridge (Park & Ride) 2B **102**
Newbridge Rd. BA1: Bath 2B **102**
   BA2: Bath 2B **102**
   BS4: St Ap 3F **69**
Newbridge Trad. Est. BS4: St Ap . . .4F **69**
New Brunswick Av. BS5: St G 2D **71**
New Bldgs. BS16: Fish 2B **60**
Newbury Rd. BS7: Hor 4C **42**
New Charlotte St. BS3: Bedm 5F **67**
New Charlton Way BS10: Pat 2C **22**
NEW CHELTENHAM 5A **62**
New Cheltenham Rd.
   BS15: K'wd 5F **61**
Newcombe Dr. BS9: Stok B 2E **55**
Newcombe Rd. BS9: W Trym 4B **40**
Newdown La. BS41: Dun 5D **85**
New Engine Rank BS36: H'fld 5F **29**
Newent Av. BS15: K'wd 2D **71**
New Fosseway Rd. BS14: H'gro . . .1D **87**
Newfoundland Cir.
   BS2: Bris 1F **5** (1B **68**)
Newfoundland Rd. BS2: Bris 1B **68**
Newfoundland St. BS2: Bris 1B **68**
Newfoundland Way BS2: Bris 1B **68**
   BS20: P'head 5D **35**
Newgate BS1: Bris 2D **5** (2A **68**)
New Grove Ends BS6: Fish 2B **60**
Newhaven Pl. BS20: P'head 2A **48**
Newhaven Rd. BS20: P'head 3A **48**
New John St. BS3: Bedm 1E **77**
New Kings Ct. BS7: B'stn 2E **57**
New Kingsley Rd.
   BS2: Bris 3F **5** (3B **68**)
New King St. BA1: Bath 3A **6** (4B **104**)
Newland Dr. BS13: Withy 3C **84**
Newland Rd. BS13: Withy 3C **84**
Newlands, The BS16: Fren 4D **45**
Newlands Av. BS36: Coal H 1E **29**
Newlands Cl. BS20: P'head 1E **49**
Newlands Hgts. BS7: Bris 4B **58**
   (off Hurlingham Rd.)
Newlands Hill BS20: P'head 2E **49**
Newlands Rd. BS31: Key 3F **89**
Newland Wlk. BS13: Withy 4C **84**
NEWLEAZE 1D **43**
New Leaze BS32: Brad S 2E **9**
Newleaze Ho. BS34: Fil 1D **43**
Newlyn Av. BS9: Stok B 1F **55**
Newlyn Wlk. BS4: Know 3D **79**
Newlyn Way BS37: W'lgh 3B **16**
Newman Cl. BS37: W'lgh 4D **31**
Newmarket Av. BS1: Bris . . .2C **4** (2F **67**)

Newmarket Row BA2: Bath 3C **6**
   (off Grand Pde.)
New Mdws. BS14: H'gro 1C **86**
Newnham Cl. BS14: Stoc 5F **79**
Newnham Pl. BS34: Pat 4B **8**
New Orchard St.
   BA1: Bath 4C **6** (4C **104**)
Newport Cl. BS20: P'head 2B **48**
Newport Rd. BS20: Pill 1E **53**
Newport St. BS3: Wind H 1A **78**
Newquay Rd. BS4: Know 3B **78**
New Queen St. BS3: Bedm 5A **68**
   BS15: K'wd 5D **61**
New Rd. BA1: Bathf 5F **99**
   BS20: Pill 2E **53**
   BS34: Fil 5B **24**
   BS34: Fil, Stok G 1E **43**
Newry Wlk. BS4: Know 3A **78**
Newsome Av. BS20: Pill 2E **53**
New Stadium Rd. BS5: Eastv 4D **59**
New Station Rd. BS16: Fish 2C **60**
New Station Way BS16: Fish 2C **60**
New St. BA1: Bath 4B **6** (4B **104**)
   BS2: Bris 1F **5** (2B **68**)
New St. Flats BS2: Bris 1F **5**
New Thomas St.
   BS2: Bris 3F **5** (3B **68**)
Newton Cl. BS15: K'wd 5C **62**
Newton Dr. BS30: C Hth 4C **72**
Newton Mill Camping & Cvn. Pk.
   BA2: New L 4A **102**
Newton Rd. BA2: Bath 5B **102**
   BS30: C Hth 4C **72**
NEWTON ST LOE 4F **101**
Newton St. BS5: E'tn 1C **68**
NEWTOWN 2C **68**
New Tyning Ter. BA1: Bath 1D **105**
   (off Fairfield Rd.)
New Villas BA2: Bath 1C **110**
New Wlk. BS15: Han 4D **71**
New Walls BS4: Wind H 5B **68**
Next Generation Club
   Westbury-on-Trym 3D **41**
Niblett Cl. BS15: K'wd 3B **72**
Niblett's Hill BS5: St G 3B **70**
NIBLEY 4C **14**
Nibley Bus. Pk. BS37: Yate 4C **14**
Nibley La. BS37: Iron A, Yate 2A **14**
   BS37: W'lgh, Yate 4C **14**
Nibley Rd. BS11: Shire 1F **53**
Nicholas La. BS5: St G 3C **70**
Nicholas Rd. BS5: E'tn 5D **59**
Nicholas St. BS3: Bedm 5A **68**
Nicholettes BS30: Old C 4F **73**
Nicholls Ct. BS36: Wint 2A **28**
Nicholls La. BS36: Wint 1A **28**
Nicholl's Pl. BA1: Bath 1B **6**
   (off Lansdown Rd.)
Nichol's Rd. BS20: P'head 1B **48**
Nigel Pk. BS11: Shire 4A **38**
Nightingale Cl. BS4: St Ap 3A **70**
   BS36: Fram C 2C **28**
Nightingale La. BS36: Wint 5C **12**
Nightingale Ri. BS20: P'head 3B **48**
Nightingale Valley BS4: St Ap 4C **70**
Nile St. BA1: Bath 3A **6** (4A **104**)
Nine Tree Hill BS1: Bris 5A **58**
Ninth Av. BS7: Hor 2D **43**
Noble Av. BS30: Old C 5E **73**
Nore Gdns. BS20: P'head 5B **34**
Nore Pk. Dr. BS20: P'head 1B **48**
Nore Rd. BS20: P'head 2A **48**
Norewood Gro. BS20: P'head 1B **48**
Norfolk Av. BS2: Bris 1A **68**
   BS6: Bris 4A **58**
Norfolk Bldgs.
   BA1: Bath 3A **6** (4A **104**)
Norfolk Cres. BA1: Bath . . .3A **6** (4A **104**)
Norfolk Gro. BS31: Key 3E **89**
Norfolk Hgts. BS2: Bris 1A **68**
   (off Norfolk Av.)

Norfolk Pl. BS3: Bedm 1E 77
Norfolk Rd. BS20: P'head 2A 50
Norland Rd. BS8: Clif 1B 66
Norley Rd. BS7: Hor 4B 42
Normanby Rd. BS5: E'tn 5D 59
Norman Gro. BS15: K'wd 4F 61
Norman Rd. BS2: Bris 4C 58
  BS30: Warm 5D 63
  BS31: Salt 4F 91
Normans, The BA2: B'ptn 1B 106
Normans Way BS20: Eas 4A 36
Normanton Rd. BS8: Clif 4C 56
Norrisville Rd. BS6: Bris 5A 58
Northampton Bldgs.
  BA1: Bath 1A 6 (2B 104)
Northampton St.
  BA1: Bath 1A 6 (2B 104)
Northanger Ct. BA2: Bath 2C 6
  (off Grove St.)
Northavon Bus. Cen. BS37: Yate . . .2D 15
Nth. Bristol Pk. BS34: Lit S 3D 25
NORTH COMMON 3F 73
North Contempouris BS8: Clif 2C 66
  (off Merchants Rd.)
NORTH CORNER 4B 12
North Cnr. BS3: Bedm 1D 77
  (off North St.)
Northcote Rd. BS5: St G 1A 70
  BS8: Clif 5B 56
  BS16: Down, Mang 5B 46
Northcote St. BS5: E'tn 5D 59
North Ct. BS32: Brad S 2F 9
North Cft. BS30: Old C 5F 73
Nth. Devon Rd. BS16: Fish 1C 60
NORTH END 2B 98
Northend Av. BS15: K'wd 4F 61
Northend Cotts. BA1: Bathe 2B 98
Northend Gdns. BS15: K'wd 4F 61
Northend Rd. BS15: K'wd 4A 62
Northfield BS37: Yate 5F 15
Northfield Av. BS15: Han 4F 71
Northfield Ho. BS3: Bedm 5E 67
Northfield Rd. BS5: St G 2D 71
  BS20: P'head 3A 48
Northfields BA1: Bath 1B 104
Northfields Cl. BA1: Bath 1B 104
Northgate St. BA1: Bath . . .3C 6 (4C 104)
North Grn. St. BS8: Clif 3B 66
North Gro. BS20: Pill 2E 53
North La. BA2: Clav D 5F 105
Northleach Wlk. BS11: Shire 1B 54
North Leaze BS41: L Ash 2D 75
Northover Cl. BS9: W Trym 2B 40
Northover Rd. BS9: W Trym 2B 40
North Pde. BA1: Bath 4D 7 (4C 104)
  BA2: Bath 4D 7 (4C 104)
  BS37: Yate 3A 16
North Pde. Bldgs. BA1: Bath 4C 6
  (off New Orchard St.)
North Pde. Pas.
  BA1: Bath 4C 6 (4C 104)
North Pde. Rd.
  BA2: Bath 4D 7 (4C 104)
North Pk. BS15: K'wd 5A 62
North Quay BS1: Bris 3E 5
North Rd.
  BA2: Bath, Clav D 1F 7 (3E 105)
  BA2: C Down 4D 111
  BS3: Ash G 5C 66
  BS6: Bris 4F 57
  BS8: L Wds 2E 65
  BS34: Stok G 4A 26
  BS36: Wint 1B 28
  BS37: Yate 1D 15
NORTH STOKE 1E 93
North St. BS1: Bris 1A 68
  BS3: Ash G, Bedm 5C 66
  BS16: Down 1F 61
  BS30: Old C 5E 73
Northumberland Bldgs. BA1: Bath . . .3B 6
  (off Barton St.)

Northumberland Pl.
  BA1: Bath 3C 6 (4C 104)
Northumberland Rd. BS6: Redl . . .4E 57
Northumbria Dr. BS9: Henle 1D 57
North Vw. BS6: Henle 2C 56
  BS16: Soun 2F 61
  BS16: Stap H 1A 62
North Vw. Cl. BA2: Bath 5D 103
NORTHVILLE 2D 43
Northville Ct. BS7: Hor 2B 42
Northville Rd. BS7: Hor 2B 42
North Wlk. BS37: Yate 3A 16
North Way BA2: Bath 5C 102
Northway BS34: Fil 4D 25
Northwell Ho. BS6: Bris 4F 57
  (off Cromwell Rd.)
NORTH WESTON 3E 49
Northwick Rd. BS7: Hor 3B 42
Northwood Pk. BS36: Wint 1C 26
Northwoods Wlk. BS10: Bren 5F 23
Norton Cl. BS15: K'wd 2B 72
Norton Farm Rd. BS10: Hen 5F 21
Norton Ho. BS1: Bris 4A 68
  (off Ship La.)
Norton La. BS14: Whit 5E 87
Norton Rd. BS4: Know 2C 78
Norwich Dr. BS4: St Ap 3A 70
Norwood Av. BA2: Clav D 5A 106
Nottingham Rd. BS7: B'stn 3A 58
Nottingham St. BS3: Wind H 1A 78
Nova Distribution Cen.
  BS11: A'mth 2D 37
Nova Scotia Pl. BS1: Bris 4C 66
Nova Way BS11: A'mth 2D 37
Nover's Cres. BS4: Know 4E 77
Nover's Hill BS3: Know, Wind H . . .3E 77
Nover's Hill Trad. Est. BS3: Bedm . . .3E 77
Nover's La. BS4: Know 4E 77
Nover's Pk. Cl. BS4: Know 3E 77
Nover's Pk. Dr. BS4: Know 3E 77
Nover's Pk. Rd. BS4: Know 4F 77
Nover's Rd. BS4: Know 4E 77
Nugent Hill BS6: Cot 5F 57
No. 1 Royal Crescent 1A 6 (3A 104)
Nunney Cl. BS31: Key 5C 90
Nursery, The BS3: Bedm 1D 77
Nursery Gdns. BS10: Bren 5C 22
Nutfield Gro. BS34: Fil 1D 43
Nutfield Ho. BS34: Fil 2D 43
Nutgrove Av. BS3: Wind H 1A 78
Nuthatch Dr. BS16: B'hll 5B 44
Nuthatch Gdns. BS16: B'hll 5B 44
Nympsfield BS15: K'wd 4A 62

O

Oak Av. BA2: Bath 2E 109
Oak Cl. BS34: Lit S 1F 25
  BS37: Yate 1F 15
Oak Ct. BS14: Whit 1C 86
Oakdale Av. BS16: Down 3F 45
Oakdale Cl. BS16: Down 3A 46
Oakdale Ct. BS16: Down 3F 45
Oakdale Rd. BS14: H'gro 4C 78
  BS16: Down 3A 46
Oakdale Wlk. BS16: Down 4A 46
Oakdene Av. BS5: Eastv 3F 59
Oak Dr. BS20: P'head 2D 49
Oakenhill Rd. BS4: Brisl 2A 80
Oakenhill Wlk. BS4: Brisl 2A 80
Oakfield Bus. Pk. BS15: K'wd 2F 71
Oakfield Cl. BA1: Bath 2F 103
Oakfield Gro. BS8: Clif 1D 67
Oakfield Pl. BS8: Clif 1D 67
Oakfield Rd. BS8: Clif 1C 66
  BS15: K'wd 2F 71
  BS31: Key 4B 90
Oakford La. BA1: Bathe 1C 98
Oak Gro. BS20: Eas 2E 53

Oakhanger Dr. BS11: Law W 2C 38
Oakhill Av. BS30: Bit 2E 83
Oakhill La. BS10: H'len 4E 21
Oakhill Rd. BA2: C Down 3B 110
Oak Ho. BS13: Hart 3F 85
Oakhurst Rd. BS9: W Trym 1B 56
Oakland Bus. Pk. BS37: Yate 2C 14
Oakland Rd. BS5: St G 1A 70
  BS6: Redl 5D 57
Oaklands Cl. BS16: Mang 1D 63
Oaklands Dr. BS16: B'hll 4C 44
  BS30: Old C 2E 83
  BS32: Alm 1C 8
Oaklands Rd. BS16: Mang 1C 62
Oak La. BS5: S'wll 4B 60
Oakleaze BS36: Coal H 1F 29
Oakleigh Av. BS5: W'hall 1F 69
Oakleigh Gdns. BS30: Old C 2E 83
Oakley BA2: Clav D 5A 106
Oakley Rd. BS7: Hor 4B 42
Oak Lodge BS16: Fish 5E 45
  (off Partridge Dr.)
Oakmeade Pk. BS4: Know 2D 79
Oakridge Cl. BS15: K'wd 2C 72
Oak Rd. BS7: Hor 1A 58
Oaks, The BS7: B'stn 2A 58
Oak St. BA2: Bath 5A 6 (5B 104)
Oaktree Cl. BS15: Han 2E 81
Oaktree Ct. BS11: Shire 4A 38
Oaktree Cres. BS32: Brad S 3D 9
Oaktree Gdns. BS13: Withy 2A 84
Oak Tree Wlk. BS31: Key 3F 89
Oakwood Av. BS9: Henle 5D 41
Oakwood Gdns. BA2: Clav D 5F 105
  BS36: Coal H 1A 30
Oakwood Pk. BS16: Fish 3C 60
Oakwood Rd. BS9: Henle 5D 41
Oatlands Av. BS14: Whit 1C 86
Oatley Ho. BS9: W Trym 1C 56
Oberon Av. BS5: S'wll 4A 60
ODD DOWN 4F 109
Odd Down (Park & Ride) 5E 109
Odeon Cinema
  Bath 4A 6 (4B 104)
  Bristol 2C 4 (2F 67)
Odins Rd. BA2: Odd D 4F 109
Okebourne Cl. BS10: Bren 4D 23
Okebourne Rd. BS10: Bren 5D 23
Old Acre Rd. BS14: Whit 4C 86
Old Ashley Hill BS6: Bris 4B 58
Old Barrow Hill BS11: Shire 4F 37
Old Bond St. BA1: Bath . . .3B 6 (4B 104)
Old Bread St. BS2: Bris 3F 5 (3B 68)
Oldbridge Rd. BS14: Whit 4E 87
Old Bristol Rd. BS31: Key 5E 81
Oldbury Chase BS30: Will 2C 82
Oldbury Ct. Dr. BS16: Fish 5D 45
Oldbury Ct. Rd. BS16: Fish 1C 60
Old Farm La. BS5: St G 3D 71
Old Ferry Rd. BA2: Bath 4E 103
Oldfield La. BA2: Bath 1F 109
OLDFIELD PARK 5A 104
Oldfield Park Station (Rail) 4F 103
Oldfield Pl. BA2: Bath 5A 6 (5A 104)
  BS8: Clif 4B 66
Oldfield Rd. BA2: Bath 5A 104
  BS8: Clif 4C 66
Old Fosse Rd. BA2: Odd D 3E 109
Old Frome Rd. BA2: Odd D 3A 110
Old Gloucester Rd.
  BS16: Fren, Ham 2D 45
  BS16: Ham 3D 27
  BS32: Brad S, Wint 3D 27
  BS36: Wint 3D 27
Old King St. BA1: Bath 2B 6 (3B 104)
Old King St. Ct. BS1: Bris . . .1D 5 (2A 68)
OLDLAND 5E 73
OLDLAND COMMON 1E 83
Oldland Common Station
  Avon Valley Railway 5F 73
Oldlands Av. BS36: Coal H 2E 29

Old La. BS16: Emer G 5E **47**
Old Market St. BS1: Bris . .2E **5** (2A **68**)
  BS2: Bris 2F **5** (2A **68**)
Oldmead Wlk. BS13: Bis 5A **76**
Old Midford Rd. BA2: S'ske 5C **110**
Old Mill Cl. BS37: W'lgh 4D **31**
Old Mill Rd. BS20: P'head 5C **34**
Old Newbridge Hill BA1: Bath 2C **102**
Old Orchard BA1: Bath . . .1C **6** (3C **104**)
Old Orchard, The BS16: Mang 1E **63**
Old Orchard St.
  BA1: Bath 4C **6** (4C **104**)
Old Park BS2: Bris 2A **4** (2E **67**)
Old Park Hill BS2: Bris 2A **4** (2E **67**)
Old Park Rd. BS11: Shire 4F **37**
Old Pooles Yd. *BS4: Brisl* 2A **80**
  (off Brookside Rd.)
Old Priory Rd. BS20: Eas 2D **53**
Old Quarry BA2: Odd D 3F **109**
Old Quarry Ri. BS11: Shire 4A **38**
Old Quarry Rd. BS11: Shire 4F **37**
Old School Cl. BS30: Warm 2F **73**
Old School Ho. *BS4: Know* 2D **79**
  (off Maxse Rd.)
Old School La. BS8: Clif 3D **67**
Old Smiths Yd. BS15: Han 4F **71**
Old Sneed Av. BS9: Stok B 2F **55**
Old Sneed Cotts. BS9: Stok B 2F **55**
Old Sneed Pk. BS9: Stok B 2F **55**
Old Sneed Rd. BS9: Stok B 2F **55**
Old Vicarage, The BS6: Bris 4A **58**
Old Vicarage Ct. BS14: Whit 3E **87**
Old Vicarage Grn. BS31: Key 1A **90**
Old Vicarage Pl. BS8: Clif 5C **56**
Old Wellington Rd.
  BS2: Bris 1F **5** (2B **68**)
Old Wells Rd. BA2: Bath 2B **110**
Old Workhouse, The BS5: St G . . .1A **70**
Olveston Rd. BS7: Hor 1A **58**
Olympus Cl. BS34: Lit S 2F **25**
Olympus Rd. BS34: Pat 1F **23**
Onega Cen. *BA1: Bath* 3A **104**
  (off Up. Bristol Rd.)
Onega Ter. BA1: Bath 3A **104**
Oolite Gro. BA2: Odd D 4F **109**
Oolite Rd. BA2: Odd D 4F **109**
Oram Ct. BS30: Bar C 5B **72**
Orange Gro. BA1: Bath . . .3C **6** (4C **104**)
Orange St. BS2: Bris 1B **68**
Orchard, The BA2: C Down 4D **111**
  BA2: Cor 2D **101**
  BS9: W Trym 5C **40**
  BS34: Stok G 3B **26**
  BS36: Fram C 5E **13**
Orchard Av. BS1: Bris 3A **4** (3E **67**)
Orchard Blvd. BS30: Old C 5D **73**
Orchard Cvn. Site, The
  BS14: Whit 3F **87**
Orchard Cl. BS9: W Trym 1B **56**
  BS15: K'wd 1A **72**
  BS20: P'head 1F **49**
  BS31: Key 1E **89**
  BS36: Wint 2A **28**
  BS37: Yate 3B **16**
Orchard Ct. BS1: Bris 3B **4**
  BS5: Redf 2F **69**
  BS9: Stok B 3E **55**
  BS34: Fil 1C **42**
  (off Gloucester Rd. Nth.)
  BS37: Yate 2D **15**
Orchard Cres. BS11: Shire 4F **37**
Orchard Dr. BA2: Odd D 4E **109**
  BS13: Bis 2C **84**
Orchard Gdns. BS15: K'wd 1B **72**
Orchard Ga. BS32: Brad S 3B **9**
Orchard Ho. BS5: St G 1B **70**
Orchard La. BS1: Bris 3A **4** (3E **67**)
  BS9: Stok B 2F **55**
Orchard Lea BS20: Pill 2F **53**
Orchard Lodge BA2: B'ptn 2B **106**
  BS30: Old C 3F **73**

Orchard Rd. BS5: St G 1B **70**
  BS7: B'stn 2A **58**
  BS15: K'wd 1A **72**
  BS36: Coal H 1F **29**
  BS41: L Ash 3B **74**
Orchards, The BS11: Shire 5A **38**
  BS15: K'wd 2B **72**
  BS20: Pill 2E **53**
Orchard Sq. BS5: Redf 2F **69**
Orchard St. BS1: Bris 3A **4** (3E **67**)
Orchard Ter. BA2: Bath 4D **103**
Orchard Va. BS15: K'wd 1B **72**
Oriel Gdns. BA1: Swa 5E **97**
Oriel Gro. BA2: Bath 1D **109**
Orion Dr. BS34: Lit S 2F **25**
Orland Way BS30: L Grn 1C **82**
Orlebar Gdns. BS11: Law W 1D **39**
Ormerod Rd. BS9: Stok B 2A **56**
Ormonds Cl. BS32: Brad S 3A **10**
Ormsley Cl. BS34: Lit S 5E **9**
Orpen Gdns. BS7: L'lze 1D **59**
Orpen Pk. BS32: Brad S 2D **9**
Orpheus Av. BS32: Brad S 2F **25**
Orpheus Cinema 2D **57**
Orwell Dr. BS31: Key 3B **90**
Orwell St. BS3: Wind H 1A **78**
Osborne Av. BS7: Bris 3B **58**
Osborne Cl. BS34: Stok G 4F **25**
Osborne Rd. BA1: Bath 4D **103**
  BS3: Bris 5E **67**
  BS8: Clif 5C **56**
Osborne Ter. BS3: Bedm 2D **77**
Osborne Vs. BS2: Bris 1E **67**
Osprey Ct. BS14: Hart 2F **85**
Osprey Rd. BS5: Redf 2E **69**
Ostlings La. BA1: Bathf 5D **99**
Otago Ter. BA1: Bath 5E **97**
Otterford Cl. BS14: H'gro 2D **87**
Ottery Cl. BS11: Law W 2C **38**
Ottrells Mead BS32: Brad S 2E **9**
OVAL, THE 1E **109**
Oval, The BA2: Bath 1E **109**
OVER 4A **8**
Over Ct. M. BS32: Alm 4A **8**
OVERHILL 3F **53**
Overhill BS20: Pill 3E **53**
Overhill Cl. BS16: Down 1F **61**
Overhill Rd. BS16: Down 1E **61**
Overnhurst Ct.
  BS16: Down 1F **61**
Overton Rd. BS6: Bris 4A **58**
Owen Gro. BS9: Henle 1D **57**
Owen St. BS5: E'tn 1E **69**
Owls Head Rd. BS15: K'wd 3A **72**
Oxbarton BS34: Stok G 3B **26**
Oxenham Ct. BS5: St G 1F **69**
Oxen Leaze BS32: Brad S 3A **10**
Oxford Pl. BA2: C Down 3E **111**
  BS5: E'tn 5D **59**
  BS8: Clif 3B **66**
Oxford Row BA1: Bath 1B **6** (3B **104**)
Oxford St. BS2: Bris 3B **68**
  (Anvil St.)
  BS2: Bris 1E **67**
  (Cotham Rd.)
  BS3: Wind H 5B **68**
  BS5: Redf 2E **69**
Oxford Ter. BA2: C Down 3E **111**
Oxhouse Gdns. BS10: Hen 5A **22**
Oxleaze BS13: Hart 3F **85**
Oxleaze La. BS41: Dun 4A **84**
Ozleworth BS15: K'wd 1C **72**

P

Packgate Rd. BS11: A'mth 4B **20**
Packgate Rdbt. BS11: A'mth 4B **20**
Pack Horse La. BA2: S'ske 5B **110**

Pacquet Ho's. *BS20: Pill* 1F **53**
  (off Underbanks)
Paddock, The BA2: Cor 3D **101**
  BS20: P'head 2F **49**
Paddock Cl. BS16: Emer G 5D **47**
  BS32: Brad S 3F **9**
Paddock Gdn. BS14: Whit 3B **86**
Paddocks, The BA2: C Down 4D **111**
  BS16: Down 2C **46**
Paddock Woods
  BA2: C Down 3F **111**
Padfield Cl. BA2: Bath 5D **103**
PADLEIGH 3C **108**
Padleigh Hill BA2: Bath 3C **108**
Padmore Ct. BS5: St G 2F **69**
Padstow Rd. BS4: Know 4B **78**
Page Cl. BS16: Stap H 2B **62**
Page Ct. BS16: Stap H 2B **62**
Page Rd. BS16: Stap H 2F **61**
Pages Mead BS11: A'mth 3E **37**
Painswick Av. BS34: Pat 5D **9**
Painswick Dr. BS37: Yate 4A **16**
Paintworks BS4: Bris 5D **69**
Palace Yd. M.
  BA1: Bath 3A **6** (4B **104**)
Palmdale Cl. BS30: L Grn 1C **82**
Palmers Cl. BS30: Bar C 3B **72**
Palmers Leaze BS32: Brad S 1C **26**
Palmerston Rd. BS6: Redl 2D **57**
Palmerston St. BS3: Bedm 1E **77**
Palmyra Rd. BS3: Bedm 2D **77**
Panorama Wlk. BS15: Han 5C **70**
Panoramic, The
  BS1: Bris 2A **4** (2E **67**)
Parade, The BA2: Clav D 4A **106**
  BS11: Shire 5A **38**
  BS13: Bis 1C **84**
  BS14: H'gro 4C **78**
  BS34: Pat 4B **8**
  BS37: Chip S 4C **16**
Parade Ct. BS5: S'wll 5B **60**
Paragon BA1: Bath 1C **6** (3C **104**)
Paragon, The BS8: Clif 3B **66**
Parbrook Ct. BS14: H'gro 2D **87**
Parfitts Hill BS5: St G 3B **70**
Parish, The *BS3: Bris* 5D **67**
  (off Park Rd.)
Parish Wharf Leisure Cen. 5D **35**
Park, The BS15: K'wd 1F **71**
  BS16: Fren 2D **45**
  BS20: P'head 1B **50**
  BS30: Will 3D **83**
  BS31: Key 1A **90**
  BS32: Brad S 2E **9**
Park & Ride
  Ashton Vale 2F **75**
  Bath Road 4B **80**
  Lansdown 2E **95**
  Newbridge 2B **102**
  Odd Down 5E **109**
  Portway 4E **37**
Park Av. BA2: Bath 5A **6** (5B **104**)
  BS3: Wind H 1A **78**
  BS5: Eastv 3F **59**
  BS5: St G 1A **70**
  BS32: Alm 3B **8**
  BS36: Fram C 2D **29**
  BS36: Wint 2A **28**
Park Cl. BS15: K'wd 2A **72**
  BS30: C Hth 4D **73**
  BS31: Key 2F **89**
Park Cres. BS5: W'hall 1F **69**
  BS16: Fren 2E **45**
  BS30: C Hth 4D **73**
Park Edge BS5: St G 1A **70**
Parkers Barton BS5: Bar H 3D **69**
Parkers Cl. BS10: Bren 4F **23**
Parker St. BS3: Bedm 1D **77**
Park Farm Ct. BS30: L Grn 5B **72**
Parkfield Av. BS5: St G 2F **69**
Park Gdns. BA1: Bath 2F **103**

Park Gro. BS6: Henle 1D 57
   BS9: Henle 1D 57
Park Hill BS11: Shire 5A 38
Park Ho. BA2: Bath 1A 110
Parkhouse La. BS31: Key 5E 89
   (not continuous)
Parkhurst Av. BS16: Fish 2D 61
Parklands BS15: K'wd 1A 72
Parklands Rd. BS3: Bwr A 5A 66
Park La. BA1: Bath 2F 103
   BS2: Bris 1A 4 (2E 67)
   BS36: Fram C, Wint 4C 28
Park Leaze BS34: Pat 4A 8
Park Mans. BA1: Bath 2A 104
Park Pl. BA1: Bath 2A 104
   BA2: C Down 4D 111
   BS2: Bris 1A 4 (2E 67)
   BS5: Eastv 3A 60
   BS8: Clif 2D 67
Park Rd. BA1: Bath 3D 103
   BS3: Bris 4D 67
   BS7: Hor 2C 42
   BS11: Shire 5A 38
   BS15: K'wd 5F 61
   BS16: Stap 1F 59
   BS16: Stap H 1A 62
   BS30: C Hth 4D 73
   BS31: Key 2A 90
Park Row BS1: Bris 2A 4 (2E 67)
   BS36: Fram C 5C 12
Parkside Av. BS36: Wint 2F 27
Parkside Gdns. BS5: Eastv 2D 59
Parkstone Av. BS7: Hor 5B 42
Park St. BA1: Bath 2A 104
   BS1: Bris 2A 4 (2E 67)
   BS4: Wind H 5C 68
   (not continuous)
   BS5: St G 1B 70
   BS37: Iron A 1F 13
Park St. Av. BS1: Bris 2A 4 (2E 67)
Park St. M. BA1: Bath 2A 104
Park Vw. BA2: Bath 4F 103
   BS15: K'wd 2A 72
Park Vw. Ter. BS5: St G 1A 70
Park Wlk. BS20: Pill 2F 53
Parkwall Cres. BS30: Bar C 5B 72
Parkwall Rd. BS30: C Hth 5B 72
PARKWAY 5A 26
Park Way BS30: C Hth 4D 73
Parkway BS2: Bris 5C 58
   BS5: Eastv 3E 59
   BS16: Fren, Ham 3C 44
Parkway Trad. Est. BS2: Bris 4B 58
Parkwood Cl. BS14: Whit 3B 86
Parliament St. BS4: Wind H 5C 68
Parnall Cres. BS37: Yate 2E 15
Parnall Rd. BS16: Fish 3C 60
Parnall Rd. Ind. Est. BS16: Fish . .3C 60
Parnell Rd. BS16: Stap 4A 44
Parry Cl. BA2: Bath 1D 109
Parry's Cl. BS9: Stok B 1A 56
Parrys Gro. BS9: Stok B 1A 56
Parrys La. BS9: Stok B, W Trym . . .1A 56
Parslows Barton BS5: St G 2C 70
Parsonage Cl. BS20: P'head 2F 49
Parsonage La.
   BA1: Bath 3B 6 (4B 104)
Parsonage Rd. BS41: L Ash 2E 75
Parsons Av. BS34: Stok G 3B 26
Parsons Paddock BS14: H'gro 5C 78
Parson St. BS3: Bedm 2D 77
Parson Street Station (Rail) 2D 77
Parsons Wlk. BS30: B'yte 2F 73
Partis Way BA1: Bath 2C 102
Partition St. BS1: Bris 3E 67
Partridge Cl. BS37: Yate 1B 16
Partridge Dr. BS16: Fren 5E 45
Passage Leaze BS11: Shire 5F 37
Passage Rd. BS9: W Trym 2C 40
   BS10: Hen 3C 22
   BS10: Hen, W Trym 5B 22

Passage St. BS2: Bris 3E 5 (3A 68)
Pasture, The BS32: Brad S 4F 9
Patch Ct. BS16: Emer G 3C 46
PATCHWAY 2E 25
Patchway Sports Cen. 4C 8
Patchway Station (Rail) 2E 25
Patchway Trad. Est. BS34: Pat 5A 8
   (Britannia Rd.)
   BS34: Pat 1F 23
   (Olympus Rd.)
Patterson Ho. BS1: Bris 5D 5
Paulman Gdns. BS41: L Ash 4B 74
Paul St. BS2: Bris 1E 67
Paulton Dr. BS7: B'stn 2E 57
Paultow Av. BS3: Wind H 1A 78
Paultow Rd. BS3: Wind H 1A 78
Pavey Cl. BS13: Hart 3E 85
Pavey Rd. BS13: Hart 3E 85
Pavilion, The 4E 7 (4C 104)
Pavilions, The BS4: Brisl 3E 79
Pawlett Rd. BS13: Hart 4D 85
Pawlett Wlk. BS13: Hart 4E 85
Paxton BS16: Stap 3A 44
Paybridge Rd. BS13: Withy 3B 84
Payne Dr. BS5: E'tn 2D 69
Paynes Orchard Cvn. Pk.
   BS10: Bren 4F 23
Peache Cl. BS16: Down 5A 46
Peache Rd. BS16: Down 5A 46
Peacocks La. BS15: K'wd 1E 71
Pearces Hill BS16: Fren 4D 45
Pearl St. BS3: Bedm 1D 77
Pearsall Rd. BS30: L Grn 2A 82
Pears Cl. BS13: Withy 3A 84
Peart Dr. BS13: Withy 3A 84
Pear Tree Av. BS41: L Ash 4A 74
Peartree Ct. BS13: Hart 3D 85
Peartree Fld. BS20: P'head 1B 50
Pear Tree Hey BS37: Yate 1A 16
Pear Tree La. BS5: St G 3D 71
Peartree La. BS15: Soun 4B 62
Pear Tree Rd. BS32: Brad S 3E 9
Peel St. BS5: E'tn 1B 68
Pegasus Ct. BS20: P'head 1F 49
Pegasus Pk. BS34: Lit S 2D 25
Pegasus Rd. BS34: Pat 1F 23
Peg Hill BS37: Yate 1B 16
Pemberton Ct. BS16: Fish 1D 61
Pembery Rd. BS3: Bedm 1D 77
Pembroke Av. BS11: Shire 5A 38
Pembroke Ct. BA1: W'ton 1E 103
Pembroke Gro. BS8: Clif 2C 66
Pembroke Pl. BS8: Clif 4C 66
Pembroke Rd. BS3: Bris 5E 67
   BS8: Clif 5C 56
   BS11: Shire 5A 38
   BS15: K'wd 3A 62
   BS20: P'head 3A 48
Pembroke St. BS2: Bris 1A 68
Pembroke Va. BS8: Clif 1C 66
Penard Way BS15: K'wd 2B 72
Pendennis Av. BS16: Stap H 1F 61
Pendennis Ho. BS16: Stap H 1F 61
Pendennis Pk. BS4: Brisl 2F 79
   BS16: Stap H 2F 61
Pendennis Rd. BS16: Stap H 1F 61
Pendock Cl. BS30: Bit 3E 83
Pendock Ct. BS16: Emer G 4D 47
Pendock Rd. BS16: Fish 5D 45
   BS36: Wint 3A 28
Penfield Cl. BS16: Emer G 4C 58
Penfield Rd. BS2: Bris 4C 58
Penlea Ct. BS11: Shire 4F 37
Pennant Pl. BS20: P'head 4E 35
Pennard Ct. BS14: Whit 2D 87
Pennard Grn. BA2: Bath 4C 102
Penn Dr. BS16: Fren 2E 45
Penn Gdns. BA1: Bath 2C 102
Penngrove BS30: L Grn 1C 82
Penn Hill Rd. BA1: Bath, W'ton . . .2C 102
Pennine Rd. BS30: Old C 5E 73

Pennlea BS13: Bis 5E 77
Penn Lea Ct. BA1: Bath 2D 103
   (not continuous)
Penn Lea Rd. BA1: Bath 1C 102
Penn St. BS1: Bris 1E 5 (2A 68)
Penny La. BS15: Soun 3B 62
Pennyquick BA2: New L 3E 101
Pennyquick Vw. BA2: Bath 4B 102
Pennyroyal Gro. BS16: Stap 1A 60
Pennywell Ct. BS5: E'tn 1C 68
   (off Pennywell Rd.)
Pennywell Rd. BS5: E'tn 1B 68
Pen Pk. Rd. BS10: S'mead 5E 23
Pen Pk. Sports Pavilion 1F 41
Penpole Av. BS11: Shire 5A 38
Penpole Cl. BS11: Shire 4F 37
Penpole La. BS11: Shire 4F 37
Penpole Pk. BS11: Shire 4A 38
Penpole Pl. BS11: Shire 5A 38
Penrith Gdns. BS10: S'mead 2F 41
   (not continuous)
Penrose BS14: H'gro 5B 78
Penrose Dr. BS32: Brad S 1F 25
Pensfield Pk. BS10: Bren 4F 23
Pensford Ct. BS14: Stoc 2F 87
Pentagon, The BS9: Sea M 5D 39
Penthouse Hill BA1: Bathe 4B 98
Pentire Av. BS13: Bis 1C 84
Pepys Cl. BS31: Salt 5F 91
Pera Pl. BA1: Bath 2C 104
Pera Rd. BA1: Bath 2C 104
Percival Ct. BS8: Clif 1B 66
Percival Rd. BS8: Clif 1B 66
Percy Pl. BA1: Bath 1D 105
Percy St. BS3: Bedm 5F 67
Percy Walker Ct. BS16: Down 5E 45
Perfect Vw. BA1: Bath 1C 104
Pero's Bridge 5B 4 (3F 67)
Perrett Ho. BS2: Bris 1F 5
   (off Redcross St.)
Perretts Ct. BS1: Bris 5A 4 (4E 67)
Perrett Way BS20: Pill 2A 54
Perrinpit Rd. BS36: Fram C, Wint . .1F 11
Perrott Rd. BS15: K'wd 5C 62
Perry Cl. BS36: Wint 3F 27
Perrycroft Av. BS13: Bis 1C 84
Perrycroft Rd. BS13: Bis 1C 84
Perrymans Cl. BS16: Fish 5C 44
PERRYMEAD 2D 111
Perrymead BA2: Bath 1D 111
Perrymead Pl. BA2: Bath 1D 111
Perry Rd. BS1: Bris 2A 4 (2E 67)
   BS41: L Ash 3B 74
Perrys Lea BS32: Brad S 3F 9
Perry St. BS5: E'tn 1C 68
Pesley Cl. BS13: Withy 3C 84
Petercole Dr. BS13: Bis 1C 84
Peterson Sq. BS13: Hart 4E 85
   (not continuous)
Peter's Ter. BS5: Bar H 2D 69
Petersway Gdns. BS5: St G 3C 70
Petherbridge Way BS7: Hor 1C 58
Petherton Cl. BS15: K'wd 2A 72
Petherton Gdns. BS14: H'gro 5D 79
Petherton Rd. BS14: H'gro 4D 79
Petticoat La. BS1: Bris 3E 5 (3A 68)
Pettigrove Gdns. BS15: K'wd 2A 72
Pettigrove Rd. BS15: K'wd 3A 72
Pevensey Wlk. BS4: Know 5F 77
Peverell Cl. BS10: Hen 5B 22
Peverell Dr. BS10: Hen 5B 22
Philippa Cl. BS14: H'gro 5C 78
Philips Ho. BS2: Bris 1A 68
   (off Dove St. Sth.)
Philip St. BS2: Bris 4D 69
   BS3: Bedm 5F 67
Phippen St. BS1: Bris 5D 5 (4A 68)
Phipps Barton BS15: K'wd 1D 71
Phipps St. BS3: Bris 5D 67
Phoenix Bus. Pk. BS3: Bedm 2C 76
Phoenix Ct. BS2: Bris 1F 5

Phoenix Gro. BS6: Henle 1E **57**
Phoenix Ho. BA1: Bath 1A **6**
  BS1: Bris 5C **4** (4F **67**)
  BS5: Bar H 3D **69**
Phoenix St. BS5: Bar H 3D **69**
Phoenix Way BS20: P'bry, P'head . . .4E **35**
Piccadilly Pl. BA1: Bath 1D **105**
Pickwick Rd. BA1: Bath 5C **96**
Picton La. BS6: Bris 5A **58**
Picton M. BS6: Bris 5A **58**
Picton St. BS6: Bris 5A **58**
Pier Cl. BS20: P'head 4D **35**
Pierrepont Pl. BA1: Bath . . .4C **6** (4C **104**)
Pierrepont St. BA1: Bath . . .4C **6** (4C **104**)
Pier Rd. BS20: P'head 4C **34**
Pigeon Ho. Dr. BS13: Hart 3F **85**
Pigott Av. BS13: Withy 3C **84**
PILE MARSH 2F **69**
Pilemarsh BS5: St G 2F **69**
Pilgrims Way BS11: Shire 4E **37**
  BS16: Down 3F **45**
Pilgrims Wharf BS4: St Ap 2A **70**
Pilkington Cl. BS34: Fil 1E **43**
PILL 2E **53**
Pillengers Pl. BS8: Clif 3C **66**
               (off Hotwell Rd.)
Pillengers Gdns. BS6: Redl 4D **57**
Pillengers Rd. BS15: K'wd 2E **71**
Pill Rd. BS8: Abb L 3F **53**
  BS20: Pill 2E **53**
Pill St. BS20: Pill 2E **53**
Pimpernel Mead BS32: Brad S 1A **26**
PINCKNEY GREEN 5F **107**
Pine Ct. BS31: Key 3E **89**
Pinecroft BS14: H'gro 5B **78**
Pine Ct. BS20: P'head 1B **48**
Pine Gro. BS7: Fil 2C **42**
Pine Gro. Pl. BS7: B'stn 3F **57**
Pine Ridge Cl. BS9: Stok B 2E **55**
Pine Rd. BS10: Bren 5D **23**
Pines, The BS9: Stok B 3F **55**
  BS16: Soun 4C **62**
Pines Rd. BS30: Bit 3E **83**
Pines Way BA2: Bath 4A **104**
Pines Way Ind. Est. BA2: Bath 4A **6**
Pinewood BS15: K'wd 5B **62**
Pinewood Cl. BS9: W Trym 4D **41**
Pinhay Rd. BS13: Bis 1D **85**
Pinkers Mead BS16: Emer G 5E **47**
Pinkhams Twist BS14: Whit 2C **86**
Pinnell Gro. BS16: Emer G 4E **47**
Pioneer Av. BA2: C Down 4B **110**
Pioneer Pk. BS4: Brisl 4E **69**
Pipe La. BS1: Bris 3A **4** (3E **67**)
Piper Rd. BS37: Yate 2A **16**
Pippin Cl. BS30: Bar C 5B **72**
Pippins, The BS20: P'head 1B **50**
Pitch & Pay La. BS9: Stok B 3A **56**
Pitch & Pay Pk. BS9: Stok B 3A **56**
Pitchcombe BS37: Yate 1E **31**
Pitchcombe Gdns. BS9: C Din 4F **39**
Pitch La. BS6: Cot 5F **57**
Pithay, The BS1: Bris 2C **4** (2F **67**)
Pithay Ct. BS1: Bris 2C **4** (2F **67**)
Pitlochry Cl. BS7: Hor 2B **42**
Pitman Ct. BA1: Bath 5E **97**
Pitman Ho. BA2: Bath 2F **109**
Pitt Rd. BS7: Hor 1A **58**
Pitville Pl. BS6: Cot 1D **67**
Pixash Bus. Cen. BS31: Key 2D **91**
Pixash La. BS31: Key 2D **91**
Planetarium, The 5A **4** (3E **67**)
Players Cl. BS16: Ham 4D **27**
Playford Gdns. BS11: Law W 3A **38**
Plaza, The BS2: Bris 3B **68**
                (off Anvil St.)
Pleasant Ho. BS16: Stap H 1F **61**
Pleasant Pl. BA1: Bathf 5F **99**
Pleasant Rd. BS16: Stap H 1F **61**
Plimsoll Ho. BS1: Bris 4A **68**
              (off Redcliff Hill)

Plover Cl. BS37: Yate 3E **15**
Plowright Ho. BS15: Han 4D **71**
Plummer's Hill BS5: S'wll, St G . . .1A **70**
Plumpton Ct. BS16: Down 2B **46**
Podgers Dr. BA1: W'ton 5D **95**
Podium, The BA1: Bath . . .2C **6** (4C **104**)
Poet's Cl. BS5: W'hall 1F **69**
Polden Ho. BS3: Wind H 1F **77**
Polden Rd. BS20: P'head 1F **77**
            (not continuous)
Polly Barnes Cl. BS15: Han 4D **71**
Polly Barnes Hill BS15: Han 4D **71**
Polygon, The BS8: Clif 3B **66**
  BS11: A'mth 2F **37**
Polygon La. BS8: Clif 3B **66**
Polygon La. Sth. BS8: Clif 3B **66**
             (off Polygon Rd.)
Polygon Rd. BS8: Clif 3B **66**
Pomfrett Gdns. BS14: Stoc 2A **88**
POMPHREY 1D **63**
Pomphrey Hill BS16: Emer G 1D **63**
Pond Cl. BS34: Pat 4D **9**
Pond Head Ct. BS20: Pill 2F **53**
             (off Eirene Ter.)
Ponsford Rd. BS4: Know 4D **79**
Ponting Cl. BS5: S'wll 5C **60**
Poolbarton BS31: Key 1A **90**
Poole Ct. BS37: Yate 3A **16**
Poole Ct. Dr. BS37: Yate 3A **16**
Poole Ho. BA2: Bath 5B **102**
Poolemead Rd. BA2: Bath 5B **102**
Poole St. BS11: A'mth 3D **37**
Pooles Wharf BS8: Clif 4C **66**
Pooles Wharf Ct. BS8: Clif 4C **66**
Pool Ho. BS34: Pat 5C **8**
Pool Rd. BS15: Soun 3A **62**
Pool Wlk. BA2: New L 5D **101**
Popes Wlk. BA2: Bath 2D **111**
Poplar Av. BS9: Stok B 5F **39**
Poplar Cl. BA2: Bath 1F **109**
  BS30: Old C 3E **73**
Poplar Flds. BS30: Old C 3F **73**
Poplar Pl. BS16: Fish 3C **60**
Poplar Rd. BA2: Odd D 5F **109**
  BS5: S'wll 5B **60**
  BS13: Bis 5B **76**
  BS15: St G 4C **70**
  BS30: Old C 4E **73**
Poplar Rdbt. BS11: A'mth 3A **20**
Poplars, The BS20: Eas 2D **53**
Poplar Ter. BS15: K'wd 1B **72**
Poplar Way E. BS11: A'mth 3A **20**
Poplar Way W. BS11: A'mth 2F **19**
Pople Wlk. BS7: B'stn 3B **58**
Poppy Mead BS32: Brad S 1A **26**
Porlock Rd. BA2: C Down 4C **110**
  BS3: Wind H 1F **77**
PORTBURY 3F **51**
Portbury Comn. BS20: P'head 2A **50**
Portbury Gro. BS11: Shire 5F **37**
Portbury Hundred, The
  BS20: P'bry 2B **50**
Portbury La. BS20: P'bry 4A **52**
Portbury Wlk. BS11: Shire 5F **37**
Portbury Way BS20: P'bry 1F **51**
PORTBURY WHARF 5F **35**
PORTISHEAD 1F **49**
Portishead Bus. Pk.
  BS20: P'head 1F **49**
Portishead Swimming Pool 3B **34**
Portishead Way
  BS3: Ash V, Bwr A 1A **76**
  BS11: Bris 4C **66**
  BS16: Soun 3F **61**
Portland Dr. BS20: P'head 2A **50**
Portland Lofts BS2: Bris 1A **68**
              (off Wilson St.)
Portland Mans. BS2: Bris 1A **68**
             (off Portland Sq.)
Portland Pl. BA1: Bath 2B **104**
  BS16: Stap H 3F **61**

Portland Rd. BA1: Bath 2B **104**
             (off St James's Pk.)
Portland Sq. BS2: Bris 1A **68**
Portland St. BS2: Bris 1E **67**
  BS8: Clif 2B **66**
  BS16: Soun, Stap H 3F **61**
Portland Ter. BA1: Bath 2B **104**
              (off Harley St.)
Portmeirion Cl. BS14: Whit 2D **87**
Port Side Cl. BS5: St G 3B **70**
Port Vw. BS20: Pill 1E **53**
Portview Ho. BS11: A'mth 2D **37**
             (off Portview Rd.)
Portview Rd. BS11: A'mth 2D **37**
Portwall La. BS1: Bris 5D **5** (4A **68**)
Portwall La. E. BS1: Bris . . .5E **5** (4A **68**)
Portway BS9: Sea M, Stok B 5B **38**
  BS11: Shire 3E **37**
Portway La. BS37: Chip S 1C **16**
Portway (Park & Ride) 4E **37**
Portway Rdbt. BS11: Shire 3E **37**
Postal Mus. 2B **6** (3C **104**)
Post Office La. BS5: St G 1A **70**
POTTERSWOOD 2E **71**
Potterswood Cl. BS15: K'wd 2F **71**
Pottery Farm Cl. BS13: Hart 3E **85**
Potts Cl. BA1: Bathe 3B **98**
Pound, The BS32: Alm 1C **8**
Pound Dr. BS16: Fish 1B **60**
Pound La. BS16: Fish 2B **60**
Pound Rd. BS15: K'wd, Soun 4B **62**
Pountney Dr. BS5: E'tn 1D **69**
Powlett Ct. BA2: Bath 1E **7** (3D **105**)
Powlett Rd. BA2: Bath 1E **7** (2D **105**)
Pow's Rd. BS15: K'wd 2F **71**
Poyntz Ct. BS30: L Grn 1B **82**
Poyntz Rd. BS4: Know 4B **78**
Praedium, The BS6: Redl 4D **57**
Prattens La. BS16: Stap H 2F **61**
Preacher Cl. BS5: St G 3D **71**
Precinct, The BS20: P'head 1F **49**
Preddy's La. BS5: St G 3C **70**
Prescott BS37: Yate 5F **15**
Press Moor Dr. BS30: Bar C 5B **72**
Prestbury BS37: Yate 5F **15**
Preston Wlk. BS4: Know 3C **78**
Prestwick Cl. BS4: Brisl 3F **79**
Pretoria Rd. BS34: Pat 5B **8**
Prewett St. BS1: Bris 5D **5** (4A **68**)
Priddy Cl. BA2: Bath 5D **103**
             (not continuous)
Priddy Ct. BS14: Whit 2D **87**
Priddy Dr. BS14: Whit 2D **87**
Priest Path BS31: Q Char 4C **88**
Priestwood Cl. BS10: Hen 5C **22**
Primrose Cl. BS15: K'wd 1E **71**
  BS32: Brad S 3F **9**
PRIMROSE HILL 1F **103**
Primrose Hill BA1: W'ton 1F **103**
Primrose La. BS15: K'wd 5E **61**
Primrose Ter. BS15: K'wd 5E **61**
Princes Bldgs. BA1: Bath 2B **6**
             (off George St.)
  BA2: Bath 5E **7** (5D **105**)
  BS8: Clif 3B **66**
Princes Ct. BS30: L Grn 5B **72**
Prince's La. BS8: Clif 3B **66**
Prince's Pl. BS7: B'stn 3A **58**
Princess Cl. BS31: Key 3A **90**
Princess Gdns. BS16: Stap 5F **43**
Princess Row BS2: Bris 1F **67**
Princess Royal Gdns.
  BS5: Redf 1E **69**
Princess St. BS2: Bris 3C **68**
  BS3: Bedm 5A **68**
Princes St. BA1: Bath 3B **6** (4B **104**)
  BS2: Bris 1B **68**
Princess Victoria St. BS8: Clif 3B **66**
Prince St. BS1: Bris 5B **4** (4F **67**)
Prinknash Cl. BS37: Yate 1F **31**
Prior Pk. Bldgs. BA2: Bath 5D **105**

Prior Pk. Cotts. BA2: Bath 5C **104**
Prior Pk. Gdns.
  BA2: Bath 5E **7** (5D **105**)
Prior Pk. Landscape Garden . . .2E **111**
Prior Pk. Rd. BA2: Bath . . .5E **7** (5D **105**)
Prior's Hill Flats BS6: Bris 5F **57**
Priors Lea BS37: Yate 4F **15**
Priory Av. BS9: W Trym 4C **40**
Priory Cl. BA2: C Down 2D **111**
Priory Cl. BS15: Han 1E **81**
Priory Cl. Rd. BS9: W Trym 4C **40**
Priory Dene BS9: W Trym 4C **40**
Priory Farm Trad. Est.
  BS20: P'bry 3F **51**
Priory Gdns. BS7: Hor 3B **42**
  BS11: Shire 4F **37**
  BS20: Eas 2D **53**
Priory Rd. BS4: Know 2D **79**
  BS8: Clif 1D **67**
  BS11: Shire 5F **37**
  BS20: Eas 2D **53**
  BS20: P'bry 3F **51**
  BS31: Key 5A **82**
Priory Wlk. BS20: P'bry 3F **51**
Pritchard St. BS2: Bris 1E **5** (1A **68**)
Privet Dr. BS13: Hart 2E **85**
Probyn Cl. BS16: B'hll 4C **44**
Pro-Cathedral La. BS8: Clif 2D **67**
Proctor Cl. BS4: Brisl 3F **79**
Proctor Ho. BS1: Bris 5E **5** (4A **68**)
Promenade, The BS7: B'stn 4F **57**
  BS8: Clif 1B **66**
Prospect Av. BS2: Bris 1F **67**
  BS15: K'wd 5D **61**
Prospect Bldgs. BA1: Bathe 2B **98**
Prospect Cl. BS36: Fram C 5B **12**
  BS36: Wint D 4A **28**
Prospect Cres. BS15: Soun 4B **62**
Prospect Gdns. BA1: Bathe 2B **98**
Prospect La. BS36: Fram C 5B **12**
Prospect Pl. BA1: Bath 1C **104**
  (off Camden Rd.)
  BA1: Bathf 5F **99**
  BA1: W'ton 5E **95**
  BA2: Bath 5B **104**
  BA2: C Down 4D **111**
  (off Combe Rd.)
  BS3: Bedm 1E **77**
  (off British Rd.)
  BS5: W'hall 1E **69**
  BS6: Cot 4F **57**
Prospect Rd. BA2: Bath 1E **111**
Prospect Ter. BS3: Bedm 1E **77**
PROVIDENCE 2B **74**
Providence La. BS41: L Ash 1B **74**
Providence Pl. BS2: Bris . . .3F **5** (3B **68**)
  BS3: Bedm 1F **77**
  BS5: Redf 2E **69**
Providence Ri. BS41: L Ash 2B **74**
Providence Vw. BS41: L Ash 3C **74**
Prudham St. BS5: E'tn 5E **59**
Pullin Ct. BS30: Old C 5F **73**
Pulteney Av. BA2: Bath . .4E **7** (4D **105**)
Pulteney Bridge 3C **6** (4C **104**)
Pulteney Bri. BA2: Bath . .3C **6** (4C **104**)
Pulteney Ct. BA2: Bath 5E **7**
Pulteney Gdns.
  BA2: Bath 4E **7** (4D **105**)
Pulteney Gro. BA2: Bath . . .5E **7** (5D **105**)
Pulteney M. BA2: Bath . . .3D **7** (3C **104**)
Pulteney Rd. BA2: Bath . . .5E **7** (5D **105**)
Pulteney Ter. BA2: Bath 4E **7**
  (off Pulteney Av.)
Pump Ho., The BS4: St Ap 4B **70**
Pump Ho. La. BS4: St Ap 4B **70**
Pump La. BA1: Bathf 1D **107**
  BS1: Bris 5D **5** (4A **68**)
Pump Room 3B **6** (4C **104**)
Pump Sq. BS20: Pill 1F **53**
Purcell Wlk. BS30: Hor 5F **77**
Purdown Rd. BS7: Hor 1B **58**

Purdy Ct. BS16: Fish 2C **60**
Purlewent Dr. BA1: W'ton 5E **95**
Pursey Dr. BS32: Brad S 2B **26**
Purton Cl. BS15: K'wd 3A **72**
Purton Rd. BS7: B'stn 4F **57**
Puxley Cl. BS14: Stoc 1A **88**
PYE CORNER 5F **27**
Pye Cft. BS32: Brad S 2A **10**
Pyecroft Av. BS9: Henle 4D **41**
Pylle Hill Cres. BS3: Wind H 5B **68**
Pynne Cl. BS14: Stoc 1B **88**
Pynne Rd. BS14: Stoc 2A **88**
Pyracantha Wlk. BS14: H'gro 1C **86**

Q

QEH Theatre 2D **67**
Quadrangle, The BS37: W'lgh 4E **31**
Quadrant BS32: Brad S 2D **9**
Quadrant, The BS2: Bris 3B **68**
  (off Barton Rd.)
  BS6: Redl 3D **57**
  BS32: Alm 2C **8**
Quadrant E. BS16: Fish 3E **61**
Quadrant W. BS16: Fish 3E **61**
Quakers Cl. BS16: Down 3F **45**
Quakers' Friars BS1: Bris . .1D **5** (2A **68**)
Quakers Rd. BS16: Down 2F **45**
Quantock Cl. BS30: Old C 4E **73**
Quantock Ct. BS16: Fren 2A **44**
Quantock Rd. BS3: Wind H 1F **77**
  BS20: P'head 1D **49**
Quantocks BA2: C Down 4C **110**
Quarrington Rd. BS7: Hor 1A **58**
Quarry Barton BS16: Ham 4E **27**
Quarry Cl. BA2: C Down 4B **110**
Quarry La. BS11: Law W 2E **39**
  BS36: Wint D 4A **28**
Quarrymans Ct. BA2: C Down . . .4D **111**
Quarry Rd. BA2: Clav D 5F **105**
  BS8: Clif 4C **56**
  BS15: K'wd 3F **71**
  BS16: Fren 4D **45**
  BS20: P'head 2E **49**
  BS37: Chip S 4C **16**
Quarry Rock Gdns. Cvn. Pk.
  BA2: Clav D 1F **111**
Quarry Steps BS8: Clif 4C **56**
Quarry Va. BA2: C Down 4D **111**
Quarry Way BS16: Emer G 2C **46**
  BS16: Stap 1A **60**
Quarter Mile All. BS15: K'wd 5F **61**
Quays, The BS1: Bris 5A **4** (4E **67**)
Quays Av. BS20: P'head 1A **50**
Quayside BS1: Bris 3E **5** (3A **68**)
  BS8: Clif 3D **67**
Quayside La. BS5: St G 3B **70**
Quayside Wlk. BS1: Bris 4C **4**
  (off Redcliff Backs)
Quays Office Pk.
  BS20: P'head 1A **50**
Quay St. BS1: Bris 2B **4** (2F **67**)
Quebec BA2: Bath 4C **102**
Quedgeley BS37: Yate 5E **15**
Queen Ann Rd. BS5: Bar H 3D **69**
Queen Charlotte St.
  BS1: Bris 3C **4** (3F **67**)
QUEEN CHARLTON 4C **88**
Queen Charlton La.
  BS14: Whit 4F **87**
  BS31: Q Char 4F **87**
Queen Quay BS1: Bris 4C **4** (3F **67**)
Queens Apartments BS8: Clif . . .2E **67**
  (off Queens Rd.)
Queens Av. BS8: Clif 2D **67**
  BS20: P'head 1E **49**
Queenscote BS20: P'head 1B **50**
Queen's Ct. BS8: Clif 2D **67**
Queensdale Cres. BS4: Know 3C **78**
Queensdown Gdns. BS4: Brisl . . .1E **79**

Queens Dr. BA2: C Down 4C **110**
  BS7: B'stn 2E **57**
  BS15: Han 5D **71**
Queens Ga. BS9: Stok B 1F **55**
Queenshill Rd. BS4: Know 3C **78**
Queensholm Av. BS16: Down 2A **46**
Queensholm Cl. BS16: Down 2A **46**
Queensholm Cres. BS16: Down . .2F **45**
Queensholm Dr. BS16: Down 2A **46**
Queens Pde. BA1: Bath . . .2A **6** (3B **104**)
  BS1: Bris 3D **67**
Queens Pde. Pl.
  BA1: Bath 2B **6** (3B **104**)
Queens Pl. BA2: Bath 5E **7** (5D **105**)
Queen Sq. BA1: Bath 2B **6** (3B **104**)
  BS1: Bris 4B **4** (3F **67**)
  BS31: Salt 4B **92**
Queen Sq. Apartments BS1: Bris 4C **4**
Queen Sq. Av. BS1: Bris . . .4C **4** (3F **67**)
Queen Sq. Pl. BA1: Bath . . .2A **6** (3B **104**)
Queens Rd. BS4: Know 3E **79**
  BS5: St G 1B **70**
  BS7: B'stn 2B **58**
  BS8: Clif 2C **66**
  BS13: Bis, Withy 4B **84**
  BS20: P'head 2A **48**
  BS30: C Hth 5C **72**
  BS31: Key 3F **89**
Queen St. BA1: Bath 3B **6** (4B **104**)
  BS2: Bris 2E **5** (2A **68**)
  BS5: Eastv 3F **59**
  BS11: A'mth 2C **36**
  BS15: K'wd 2D **71**
Queen's Way BS20: P'head 2A **48**
Queensway BS34: Lit S 2E **25**
Queen Victoria Rd. BS6: Henle . . .2C **56**
Queen Victoria St. BS2: Bris 3C **68**
Queenwood Av. BA1: Bath 1C **104**
Quickthorn Cl. BS14: Whit 1C **86**
Quiet St. BA1: Bath 3B **6** (4B **104**)
Quilter Gro. BS4: Know 5F **77**

R

Raby M. BA2: Bath 2E **7** (3D **105**)
Raby Pl. BA2: Bath 2E **7** (3D **105**)
Raby Vs. BA2: Bath 2F **7** (3D **105**)
Rackfield Pl. BA2: Bath 4D **103**
Rackham Cl. BS7: L'lze 5D **43**
Rackhay BS1: Bris 3C **4** (3F **67**)
Radley Rd. BS16: Fish 2D **61**
Radnor Rd. BS7: Hor 1F **57**
  BS9: Henle 1D **57**
Raeburn Rd. BS5: St G 2D **71**
Raglan Cl. BA1: Bath 5C **96**
  (off Raglan La.)
Ragland La. BA1: Bath 5C **96**
Raglan La. BS5: St G 2C **70**
Raglan Pl. BS7: B'stn 3F **57**
Raglan Rd. BS7: B'stn 3F **57**
Raglan St. BA1: Bath 5C **96**
Raglan Ter. BA1: Bath 5C **96**
Raglan Vs. BA1: Bath 1C **104**
Raglan Wlk. BS31: Key 3F **89**
Railton Jones Cl. BS34: Stok G . . .5A **26**
Railway Pl. BA1: Bath 5D **7** (5C **104**)
Railway St. BA1: Bath 5D **7** (5C **104**)
Railway Ter. BS16: Fish 2E **61**
Railway Vw. BS16: Ham 5F **27**
  (off Moorend Rd.)
Rainbow Ct. BS37: Yate 2D **15**
Raja Rammohun Roy Wlk.
  BS16: Stap 2E **59**
Raleigh Cl. BS31: Salt 5E **91**
Raleigh Ri. BS20: P'head 5A **34**
Raleigh Rd. BS3: Ash G, Bris 1C **76**
Ralph Allen Dr.
  BA2: Bath, C Down 1D **111**
Ralph Rd. BS7: B'stn 2B **58**
RAM HILL 3F **29**

Ram Hill BS36: Coal H 3E **29**
Ram Hill Bus. Pk. BS36: Coal H . .3F **29**
Ram Hill Rd. BS36: H'fld 4F **29**
Ramscombe La. BA1: Bathe 1A **98**
Ramsey Rd. BS7: Hor 4B **42**
Ranchway BS20: P'head 2B **48**
Randall Cl. BS15: Soun 4B **62**
Randall Rd. BS8: Clif 3C **66**
Randolph Av. BS13: Hart 2D **85**
⠀⠀⠀⠀BS37: Yate 1F **15**
Randolph Cl. BS13: Hart 2D **85**
Rangers Wlk. BS15: Han 5E **71**
Rannoch Rd. BS7: Fil 1B **42**
Raphael Ct. BS1: Bris 5E **5** (4A **68**)
Ratcliffe Ct. BS2: Bris 4F **5**
Ratcliffe Dr. BS34: Stok G 3A **26**
Rathbone Cl. BS36: Coal H 3E **29**
Ravendale Dr. BS30: L Grn 1D **83**
Ravenglass Cres. BS10: S'mead . .1A **41**
Ravenhead Dr. BS14: H'gro 4D **79**
Ravenhill Av. BS3: Know 2B **78**
Ravenhill Rd. BS3: Wind H 1B **78**
Ravenscourt Rd. BS34: Pat 1D **25**
Ravenswood BS30: L Grn 1C **82**
Ravenswood Rd. BS6: Cot 5E **57**
Rawnsley Ho. BS5: E'tn 5C **58**
Rayens Cl. BS41: L Ash 3B **74**
Rayens Cross Rd. BS41: L Ash . . .3B **74**
Rayleigh Rd. BS9: W Trym 4F **39**
Raymend Rd. BS3: Wind H 1A **78**
Raymend Wlk. BS3: Wind H 2A **78**
Raymill BS4: Brisl 2C **80**
Raymore Ri. BS41: L Ash 4B **74**
Raynes Rd. BS3: Ash G 1C **76**
Reading Ct. BS15: K'wd 1D **71**
Recreation Ground 3D **7**
Rectory Cl. BS37: Yate 2B **16**
Rectory Gdns. BS10: Hen 1A **40**
Rectory La. BS34: Fil 5C **24**
Rectory Rd. BS20: Eas 3D **53**
⠀⠀⠀⠀BS36: Fram C 5C **12**
Redcar Cl. BS16: Down 2B **46**
Redcatch Rd. BS3: Know 1B **78**
⠀⠀⠀⠀BS4: Know 1B **78**
Redcliff Backs BS1: Bris 4D **5** (3A **68**)
Redcliff Cres. BS3: Bris 5A **68**
⠀⠀⠀⠀(off York Rd.)
REDCLIFFE BAY 2A **48**
Redcliffe Cl. BS20: P'head 3A **48**
Redcliffe Pde. E.
⠀⠀⠀⠀BS1: Bris 5C **4** (4F **67**)
Redcliffe Pde. W.
⠀⠀⠀⠀BS1: Bris 5C **4** (4F **67**)
Redcliffe Way BS1: Bris 5C **4** (4F **67**)
Redcliff Mead La. BS1: Bris 5E **5**
Redcliff Quay BS1: Bris 4D **5** (3F **67**)
Redcliff St. BS1: Bris 3D **5** (3A **68**)
Redcross Ct. BS2: Bris 2F **5**
Redcross La. BS2: Bris 1F **5**
Redcross M. BS2: Bris 2F **5** (2B **68**)
Redcross St. BS2: Bris 2F **5** (2B **68**)
Redding Rd. BS5: Eastv 4D **59**
Reddings, The BS15: Soun 4B **62**
REDFIELD 1F **69**
Redfield Hill BS30: Bit, Old C 5F **73**
Redfield Leisure Cen. 2E **69**
Redfield Rd. BS34: Pat 1D **25**
Redford Cres. BS13: Withy 4A **84**
Redford Wlk. BS13: Withy 4B **84**
Redgrave Theatre 1B **66**
Redhill Cl. BS16: Fish 3A **60**
Redhill Dr. BS16: Fish 3A **60**
Red Ho. La. BS9: W Trym 5A **40**
⠀⠀⠀⠀BS32: Alm 1D **9**
REDLAND 4D **57**
Redland Av. BS20: Eas 5B **36**
Redland Ct. Rd. BS6: Redl 3E **57**
Redland Grn. Rd. BS6: Redl 4D **57**
Redland Gro. BS6: Cot, Redl 4E **57**
Redland Hill BS6: Redl 4C **56**

Redland Pk. BA2: Bath 4B **102**
⠀⠀⠀⠀(not continuous)
⠀⠀⠀⠀BS6: Redl 4D **57**
Redland Rd. BS6: Cot, Redl 3C **56**
Redland Station (Rail) 4E **57**
Redland Ter. BS6: Redl 4D **57**
Red Lodge 2A **4** (2E **67**)
Redlynch La. BS31: Key 5D **89**
Redpoll Dr. BS20: P'head 5F **35**
Redshelf Wlk. BS31: Bren 5E **23**
Redwick Cl. BS11: Law W 1E **39**
Redwing Gdns. BS16: B'hll 5A **44**
Redwood Cl. BS30: L Grn 1C **82**
Redwood Ho. BS31: Hart 4F **85**
Redwoods, The BS31: Key 1F **89**
Reed Cl. BS10: Hor 5F **41**
Reed Ct. BS30: L Grn 1B **82**
Reedley Rd.
⠀⠀⠀⠀BS9: Stok B, W Trym 1A **56**
Reedling Cl. BS16: B'hll 5A **44**
Refinery, The BS2: Bris 2F **5**
Regency Dr. BS4: Brisl 2C **80**
Regent Rd. BS3: Bedm 5F **67**
Regents Fld. BA2: B'ptn 2F **105**
Regent St. BS8: Clif 3C **66**
⠀⠀⠀⠀BS15: K'wd 1F **71**
Regina, The BA1: Bath 1B **6**
Remenham Dr. BS9: Henle 1D **57**
Remenham Pk. BS9: Henle 1D **57**
Rene Rd. BS5: E'tn 5D **59**
Repton Hall BS10: Bren 1D **41**
Repton Rd. BS4: Brisl 1E **79**
Reubins, The BS5: S'will 4C **60**
Reynold's Cl. BS31: Key 2C **90**
Reynolds Wlk. BS7: Hor 4C **42**
Rhode Cl. BS31: Key 4C **90**
Rhododendron Wlk. BS10: Hen . . .2A **40**
Richardson Pl. BA2: C Down 4E **111**
Richeson Cl. BS10: Hen 1B **40**
Richeson Wlk. BS10: Hen 1B **40**
Richmond Av. BS6: Bris 4B **58**
⠀⠀⠀⠀BS34: Stok G 3A **26**
Richmond Cl. BA1: Bath 1B **104**
⠀⠀⠀⠀BS20: P'head 1A **50**
⠀⠀⠀⠀BS31: Key 3F **89**
Richmond Ct. BS8: Clif 4C **56**
⠀⠀⠀⠀(off Richmond Dale)
⠀⠀⠀⠀BS34: Pat 4B **8**
Richmond Dale BS8: Clif 4C **56**
Richmond Hgts. BA1: Bath 5B **96**
⠀⠀⠀⠀BS8: Clif 2D **67**
⠀⠀⠀⠀(off Richmond Hill)
Richmond Hill BA1: Bath 1B **104**
⠀⠀⠀⠀BS8: Clif 2D **67**
Richmond Hill Av. BS8: Clif 2D **67**
Richmond La. BA1: Bath 1B **104**
⠀⠀⠀⠀BS8: Clif 2C **66**
Richmond M. BS8: Clif 2C **66**
Richmond Pk. Rd. BS8: Clif 2C **66**
Richmond Pl. BA1: Bath 1B **104**
Richmond Rd. BA1: Bath 5B **96**
⠀⠀⠀⠀BS5: St G 1A **70**
⠀⠀⠀⠀BS6: Bris 5A **58**
⠀⠀⠀⠀BS16: Mang 1C **62**
Richmond St. BS3: Wind H 5B **68**
Richmond Ter. BA1: Bath 1C **104**
⠀⠀⠀⠀(off Claremont Bldgs.)
⠀⠀⠀⠀BS8: Clif 2D **67**
⠀⠀⠀⠀(not continuous)
Richmond Vs. BS11: A'mth 2C **36**
Ride, The BS15: K'wd 4C **62**
RIDGE, THE 3B **16**
Ridge, The BS11: Shire 4A **38**
⠀⠀⠀⠀BS36: Coal H 1E **29**
Ridge Cl. BS20: P'head 2C **48**
Ridge Grn. Cl. BA2: Odd D 5F **109**
Ridgehill BS9: Henle 5E **41**
Ridgemeade BS14: Whit 3D **87**
Ridgemount Gdns. BS14: Whit . . .2D **87**
Ridge Vw. BS41: L Ash 2D **75**

RIDGEWAY 4B **60**
Ridgeway BS36: Coal H 1F **29**
⠀⠀⠀⠀BS37: Yate 3B **16**
Ridgeway, The BS10: W Trym . . .2C **40**
Ridgeway Ct. BS10: W Trym 2C **40**
⠀⠀⠀⠀BS14: Whit 2E **87**
Ridgeway Gdns. BS14: Whit 2E **87**
Ridgeway Ind. Cen.
⠀⠀⠀⠀BS5: S'will 4A **60**
Ridgeway La. BS14: Whit 3D **87**
Ridgeway Pde. BS5: Eastv 3A **60**
Ridgeway Rd. BS16: Fish 3A **60**
⠀⠀⠀⠀BS41: L Ash 3C **74**
Ridgewood BS9: Stok B 4F **55**
⠀⠀⠀⠀BS37: Yate 4B **16**
Riding Cotts., The BS37: Chip S . .3D **17**
Ridingleaze BS11: Law W 2C **38**
Ridings, The BS13: Withy 3A **84**
⠀⠀⠀⠀BS36: Coal H 2E **29**
Ridings Ct. BS37: Chip S 4E **17**
Ridings Rd. BS36: Coal H 2E **29**
Ridley Av. BS16: Soun 3C **62**
Ringswell Gdns. BA1: Bath 1D **105**
Ringwood Cres. BS10: S'mead . . .2E **41**
Ringwood Rd. BA2: Bath 4E **103**
Ripley Rd. BS5: St G 5C **60**
Ripon Ct. BS16: Down 1B **46**
Ripon Rd. BS4: St Ap 3A **70**
Rippleside BS20: P'head 1E **49**
Risdale Rd. BS3: Ash V 3A **76**
Riva Bingo
⠀⠀⠀⠀Knowle 2D **79**
Rivergate BS1: Bris 4F **5** (3B **68**)
Riverland Dr. BS13: Withy 3B **84**
Riverleaze BS9: Sea M 1D **55**
⠀⠀⠀⠀BS20: P'head 1B **48**
River Mead BS37: Yate 2E **15**
River Pl. BA2: Bath 4D **103**
River Rd. BS20: P'bry 2A **36**
⠀⠀⠀⠀BS37: Chip S 4C **16**
Riverside Bus. Pk. BS4: St Ap 3F **69**
Riverside Cl. BS11: Shire 1B **54**
Riverside Ct.
⠀⠀⠀⠀BA2: Bath 5A **6** (4B **104**)
⠀⠀⠀⠀BS4: St Ap 3B **70**
Riverside Gdns. BA1: Bath 4A **6**
Riverside Leisure Cen. 1B **68**
Riverside Leisure Club 1E **25**
Riverside M. BS4: St Ap 3B **70**
Riverside Rd.
⠀⠀⠀⠀BA2: Bath 4A **6** (4A **104**)
Riverside Steps BS4: St Ap 2A **70**
Riverside Wlk. BS5: St G 3B **70**
Riverside Way BS15: Han 1E **81**
Rivers Rd. BA1: Bath 2B **104**
⠀⠀⠀⠀(Mount Rd.)
⠀⠀⠀⠀BA1: Bath 1C **104**
⠀⠀⠀⠀(Perfect Vw.)
Rivers St. BA1: Bath 1A **6** (3B **104**)
Rivers St. M.
⠀⠀⠀⠀BA1: Bath 1A **6** (3B **104**)
Rivers St. Pl. BA1: Bath 1B **6**
River St. BS2: Bris 1F **5** (2B **68**)
River Ter. BS31: Key 2B **90**
River Vw. BS16: B'hll 1A **60**
Riverwood Rd. BS16: Fren 2E **45**
Riviera Cres. BS16: Soun 2A **62**
Riviera Way BS34: Stok G 4C **26**
Roath Rd. BS20: P'head 1F **49**
Robbins Cl. BS32: Brad S 2B **26**
Robbins Ct. BS16: Emer G 5D **47**
Robel Av. BS36: Fram C 5B **12**
Robert Ct. BS8: L Wds 3A **66**
⠀⠀⠀⠀BS16: Emer G 4D **47**
Robertson Dr. BS4: St Ap 3B **70**
Robertson Rd. BS5: E'tn 4D **59**
Robert St. BS5: Bar H 2D **69**
⠀⠀⠀⠀BS5: Eastv 4D **59**
Robin Cl. BS10: Bren 1D **41**
⠀⠀⠀⠀BS14: Stoc 1F **87**

Robin Cousins Sports Cen. 3E 37
Robin Hood La. BS2: Bris . . .1A 4 (2E 67)
Robinia Wlk. BS14: H'gro 5B 78
Robinson Dr. BS5: E'tn 1C 68
Robin Way BS37: Chip S 1B 32
Rochester Rd. BS4: St Ap 4A 70
Rochfort Ct. BA2: Bath 2D 105
Rochfort Pl. BA2: Bath 1D 7 (2C 104)
Rock, The BS4: Brisl 1A 80
Rock Cl. BS4: Brisl 2A 80
Rock Cotts. BA2: C Down 4D 111
Rock Hall Cotts. BA2: C Down . . .4D 111
Rock Hall La. BA2: C Down 4D 111
Rockhill Est. BS31: Key 3B 90
Rock Ho. BS10: Bren 5E 23
Rockingham Gdns.
  BS11: Law W 3C 38
Rockingham Rdbt. BS11: A'mth . . .2E 19
Rockland Gro. BS16: Stap 5F 43
Rockland Rd. BS16: Down 4E 45
Rock La. BA2: C Down 4D 111
  BS34: Stok G 3B 26
Rockleaze BS9: Stok B 4A 56
Rockleaze Av. BS9: Stok B 3A 56
Rockleaze Ct. BS9: Stok B 3A 56
Rockleaze Rd. BS9: Stok B 3A 56
Rockliffe Av. BA2: Bath 2D 105
Rockliffe Rd. BA2: Bath 2D 105
Rock Rd. BS31: Key 2A 90
ROCKS, THE 1B 16
Rockside Av. BS16: Down 3B 46
Rockside Dr. BS9: Henle 5D 41
Rockside Gdns. BS16: Down 3B 46
  BS36: Fram C 5E 13
Rockstowes Way BS10: Bren 5F 23
Rockwell Av. BS11: Law W 2D 39
Rockwood Ho. BS37: Yate 1C 16
Rodborough BS37: Yate 1E 31
Rodborough Way BS15: K'wd 2C 72
Rodbourne Rd. BS10: Hor 4F 41
RODFORD 1F 31
Rodfords Mead BS14: H'gro 5C 78
Rodford Way BS37: Yate 1E 31
Rodmead Wlk. BS13: Withy 3C 84
Rodmoor Rd. BS20: P'head 5C 34
Rodney Av. BS15: K'wd 1C 70
Rodney Cres. BS34: Fil 4C 24
Rodney Ho. BA2: Bath 4C 102
  BS8: Clif 2C 66
  (off Clifton Down Rd.)
Rodney Pl. BS8: Clif 2C 66
Rodney Rd. BS15: K'wd 5C 60
  BS31: Salt 5A 92
Rodney Wlk. BS15: K'wd 5C 60
Rodway Ct. BS16: Mang 5C 46
RODWAY HILL 2C 62
Rodway Hill BS16: Mang 2C 62
Rodway Hill Rd. BS16: Mang 1C 62
Rodway Rd. BS16: Mang 1C 62
  BS34: Pat 1B 24
Rodway Vw. BS15: Soun 3B 62
Roegate Dr. BS4: St Ap 3A 70
Roegate Ho. BS5: S'wll 5B 60
Rogers Cl. BS30: C Hth 4D 73
Rogers Ct. BS37: Chip S 4E 17
Rogers Wlk. BS30: B'yte 2F 73
Rokeby Av. BS6: Cot 5E 57
Roman Baths 4C 6 (4C 104)
Roman Farm Ct. BS11: Law W 1E 39
Roman Farm Rd. BS4: Know 5A 78
Roman Rd. BA2: Eng, Odd D 5E 109
  BS5: E'tn 5D 59
Roman Wlk. BS4: Brisl 1E 79
  BS34: Stok G 3A 26
Roman Way BS9: Stok B 2E 55
Romney Av. BS7: L'lze 1D 59
Romney Gdns. BS7: L'lze 1C 58
  (off Romney Av.)
Romo Ct. BS16: Stap H 2E 61
Ronald Rd. BS16: B'hll 5B 44
Ronaldson BS30: Bit 2E 83

Ronayne Wlk. BS16: Fish 5E 45
Rondo Theatre, The 1E 105
Rookery Rd. BS4: Know 2B 78
Rookery Way BS14: Whit 3B 86
Rooksbridge Wlk. BA2: Bath 4E 103
Rope Wlk. BS1: Bris 3F 5 (3B 68)
Rope Wlk. Ho. BS2: Bris 1F 5
Rosa Parks La. BS6: Bris 5B 58
Rose Acre BS10: Bren 5C 22
Rosebay Mead BS16: Stap 2A 60
Roseberry Pk. BS5: St G 1F 69
Roseberry Pl. BA2: Bath 4F 103
Roseberry Rd. BA2: Bath 4E 103
  BS5: Redf 2E 69
Rosebery Av. BS2: Bris 5C 58
Rosebery Ct. BS2: Bris 5C 58
Rosebery Ter. BS8: Clif 3D 67
Rose Cotts. BA2: Odd D 5E 109
Rose Cl. BS15: K'wd 3F 71
Rosedale Rd. BS16: Fish 3D 61
ROSE GREEN 5A 60
Rose Grn. BS5: Eastv 4F 59
Rose Green Cen. 5F 59
Rose Grn. Cl. BS5: S'wll 4A 60
Rose Grn. Rd. BS5: S'wll 4F 59
Rose Hill BA1: Bath, Swa 5D 97
  (not continuous)
Roseland Cl. BA1: Swa 4E 97
Roseland Gdns. BS15: Warm 1D 73
Rose La. BS36: Coal H 2F 29
Roselarge Gdns. BS10: Bren 1C 40
Rosemary Cl. BS32: Brad S 2B 26
Rosemary Cres. BS20: P'head 1B 50
Rosemary La. BS5: Eastv 4E 59
Rosemead BS7: Hor 4C 42
Rose Mdw. Vw. BS3: Ash V 3A 76
Rosemeare Gdns. BS13: Bis 5A 76
Rosemont Ter. BS8: Clif 3C 66
Rosemount Cl. BS15: K'wd 1D 71
Rosemount La. BA2: Bath 1D 111
Rose Oak Dr. BS36: Coal H 1F 29
Rose Oak La. BS36: Coal H 1F 29
Rose Rd. BS5: St G 2A 70
Rosery, The BS16: Fish 3E 61
Rosery Cl. BS9: W Trym 3C 40
Rose Ter. BA2: C Down 3E 111
Rosevear BS2: Bris 2C 68
Roseville Av. BS30: L Grn 2C 82
Rose Wlk. BS16: Fish 3E 61
Rosewarn Cl. BA2: Bath 1E 108
Rosewell Ct. BA1: Bath . . .3A 6 (4B 104)
Rosling Rd. BS7: Hor 5A 42
Roslyn Rd. BS6: Redl 5E 57
Rossall Av. BS34: Lit S 2E 25
Rossall Rd. BS4: Brisl 1F 79
Ross Cl. BS37: Chip S 4D 17
Rossiter Grange BS13: Withy 3B 84
Rossiter Rd. BA1: Bath 5D 7 (5C 104)
Rossiter's La. BS5: St G 3C 70
Rossiter Wood Ct. BS11: Law W . . .1D 39
Rosslyn Cl. BA1: Bath 3D 103
Rosslyn Rd. BA1: Bath 3D 103
Rounceval St. BS37: Chip S 4C 16
Roundhill Gro. BA2: Bath 2D 108
Roundhill Pk. BA2: Bath 1C 108
Roundmoor Cl. BS31: Salt 4F 91
Roundmoor Gdns. BS14: Stoc 1F 87
Roundways BS36: Coal H 2E 29
Rousham Rd. BS5: Eastv 3C 58
Rowacres BA2: Bath 2D 109
  BS14: H'gro 1B 86
Rowan Cl. BS16: Fish 4C 60
Rowan Ct. BS5: Bar H 2D 69
  BS37: Yate 2E 15
Rowan Ho. BS13: Hart 3F 85
Rowans, The BS16: Fren 2D 45
  BS20: P'head 2D 49
Rowan Wlk. BS31: Key 3E 89
Rowan Way BS15: Han 1D 81

Rowberrow BS14: H'gro 5B 78
Rowland Av. BS16: Stap 2F 59
Rowlands Cl. BA1: Bathf 5E 99
Rowlandson Gdns. BS7: L'lze 5D 43
Rowley St. BS3: Bedm 1E 77
Rownham Cl. BS3: Bwr A 5A 66
Rownham Ct. BS8: Clif 4C 66
Rownham Hill BS8: L Wds 3F 65
Rownham Mead BS8: Clif 4C 66
Royal Albert Rd. BS6: Henle 2C 56
Royal Av. BA1: Bath 1A 6 (3A 104)
Royal Cl. BS10: Hen 5F 21
Royal Crescent 1A 6 (3A 104)
Royal Cres. BA1: Bath 1A 6 (3A 104)
Royal Fort Rd. BS2: Bris . . .1A 4 (2E 67)
Royal Oak Av. BS1: Bris . . .5B 4 (3F 67)
Royal Pde. BS8: Clif 2D 67
Royal Pk. BS8: Clif 2C 66
Royal Pk. M. BS8: Clif 2C 66
Royal Photographic Society, The
  . . . . .1A 110
Royal Portbury Dock 3A 36
Royal Portbury Dock Rd.
  BS20: P'bry 5A 36
Royal Rd. BS16: Mang 5C 46
Royal Victoria Pk. BS10: Bren 1D 41
Royal York Cres. BS8: Clif 3B 66
Royal York M. BS8: Clif 3C 66
Royal York Vs. BS8: Clif 3C 66
Royate Hill BS5: Eastv 4F 59
Roycroft Rd. BS34: Fil 1D 43
Roy King Gdns. BS30: C Hth 3E 73
Royston Wlk. BS10: S'mead 1F 41
Rozel Rd. BS7: Hor 1A 58
Rubens Cl. BS31: Key 2C 90
Ruby St. BS3: Bedm 1D 77
Rudford Cl. BS34: Pat 4D 9
Rudge Cl. BS15: Soun 4B 62
Rudgewood Cl. BS13: Hart 3F 85
Rudgleigh Av. BS20: Pill 2E 53
Rudgleigh Rd. BS20: Pill 2E 53
Rudhall Gro. BS10: Hor 4A 42
Rudmore Pk. BA1: Bath 3C 102
Rudthorpe Rd. BS7: Hor 1A 58
Ruffet Rd. BS36: Coal H 5C 28
Rugby Rd. BS4: Brisl 1F 79
Runnymead Av. BS4: Brisl 3F 79
Runnymede BS15: K'wd 5A 62
Runswick Rd. BS4: Brisl 1E 79
Rupert St. BS1: Bris 2B 4 (2F 67)
  BS5: Redf 2E 69
Rush Cl. BS32: Brad S 3F 9
RUSH HILL 3E 109
Rush Hill BA2: Bath 3D 109
Rushton Dr. BS36: Coal H 1F 29
Rushy BS30: C Hth 5C 72
Rushy Way BS16: Emer G 2C 46
Ruskin Gro. BS7: Hor 3C 42
Russell Av. BS15: K'wd 2A 72
Russell Gro. BS6: Henle 1E 57
Russell M. BS37: Chip S 4D 17
Russell Rd. BS6: Henle 2D 57
  BS16: Fish 4D 61
Russell St. BA1: Bath 1B 6 (3B 104)
RUSSELL TOWN 2D 69
Russell Town Av. BS5: E'tn 1D 69
Russell Town Av. Ind. Cen.
  BS5: Redf 2E 69
  (off Russell Town Av.)
Russets, The BS20: P'head 2D 49
Russ St. BS2: Bris 3F 5 (3B 68)
Rutherford Cl. BS30: L Grn 1C 82
Ruthven Rd. BS4: Know 4A 78
Rutland Av. BS30: Will 2C 82
Rutland Rd. BS7: B'stn 3A 58
Ryde Rd. BS4: Know 2D 79
Rye Cl. BS13: Bis 1A 84
Ryecroft Ri. BS41: L Ash 3D 75
Ryecroft Rd. BS36: Fram C 5E 13
Ryedown La. BS30: Bit 3E 83
Ryland Pl. BS2: Bris 4C 58

Rylestone Cl. BS36: Fram C 5B **12**
Rylestone Gro. BS9: W Trym 1B **56**
Rysdale Rd. BS9: W Trym 5B **40**

S

Sabin Cl. BA2: Bath 2D **109**
Sabrina Way BS9: Stok B 2E **55**
Saco Ho. BA1: Bath 4C **6**
   (off St James's Pde.)
   BS1: Bris 4E **5** (3A **68**)
Sadlers Ct. BS15: K'wd 5F **61**
Sadlier Cl. BS11: Law W 3B **38**
Saffron Cl. BS5: W'hall 1E **69**
Saffron Ct. BA1: Bath 2C **104**
Saffron St. BS5: W'hall 1E **69**
Sage Cl. BS20: P'head 2A **48**
Sages Mead BS32: Brad S 5F **9**
St Agnes Av. BS4: Know 2B **78**
St Agnes Gdns. BS4: Know 2B **78**
St Agnes Wlk. BS4: Know 2B **78**
St Aidans Cl. BS5: St G 3D **71**
St Aidans Rd. BS5: St G 3C **70**
St Albans Rd. BS6: Henle 2D **57**
St Aldwyn's Cl. BS7: Hor 3B **42**
ST ANDREWS 3A **58**
St Andrews BS30: Warm 3D **73**
   BS37: Yate 5A **16**
St Andrews Ga. Rdbt.
   BS11: A'mth 1D **37**
St Andrew's Ho. BS11: A'mth 2C **36**
St Andrew's Rd. BS6: Bris 5A **58**
   BS11: A'mth 1D **37**
St Andrew's Road Station (Rail)
   . . . . .4D **19**
St Andrews Ter.
   BA1: Bath 2B **6** (3B **104**)
St Andrews Trad. Est.
   BS11: A'mth 1E **37**
St Andrew's Wlk. BS8: Clif 3C **66**
ST ANNE'S 4F **69**
St Annes Av. BS31: Key 1F **89**
St Annes Cl. BS5: St G 3B **70**
   BS30: C Hth 5D **73**
St Anne's Ct. BS4: St Ap 4F **69**
   BS31: Key 1F **89**
St Annes Dr. BS30: Old C 2E **83**
   BS36: Coal H 3E **29**
ST ANNE'S PARK 4A **70**
St Annes Pk. Rd. BS4: St Ap 4A **70**
St Anne's Rd. BS4: St Ap 3F **69**
   BS5: St G 3D **71**
St Anne's Ter. BS4: St Ap 4A **70**
St Ann's Pl. BA1: Bath 3A **6**
St Ann's Way BA1: Bath . . .3F **7** (4E **105**)
St Aubin's Av. BS4: Brisl 1B **80**
St Augustine's Cl. BS20: P'head . . .2A **48**
St Augustine's Pde.
   BS1: Bris 3B **4** (3F **67**)
St Augustine's Pl.
   BS1: Bris 3B **4** (3F **67**)
St Barnabas Cl. BS4: Know 3B **78**
   BS30: Warm 2E **73**
St Bartholomew's Rd. BS7: Bris . . .3B **58**
St Bede's Rd. BS15: K'wd 4E **61**
St Bernards Rd. BS11: Shire 5A **38**
St Brelades Gro. BS4: St Ap 4A **70**
St Brendans Rdbt. BS11: A'mth . . .2D **37**
St Brendans Trad. Est.
   BS11: A'mth 1D **37**
St Brendans Way BS11: A'mth . . .2D **37**
St Briavels Dr. BS37: Yate 5F **15**
St Cadoc Ho. BS31: Key 2B **90**
St Catherine's Cl.
   BA2: Bath 3F **7** (4E **105**)
St Catherine's Ct. BS3: Bedm 1F **77**
St Catherines Hospital BA1: Bath . . .4C **6**
St Catherine's Ind. Est.
   BS3: Bedm 5F **67**
   (off Whitehouse La.)

St Catherine's Mead BS20: Pill . . .3F **53**
St Catherine's Pl. BS3: Bedm 5F **67**
St Catherine's Ter. BS3: Bedm . . .1F **77**
   (off Church La.)
St Christopher's Cl. BA2: Bath . . .3E **105**
St Clements Ct. BS2: Bris 1B **68**
   (off Wilson St.)
   BS16: Soun 3F **61**
   BS31: Key 3A **90**
St Clement's Rd. BS31: Key 2A **90**
   (not continuous)
St David's Av. BS30: C Hth 4C **72**
St David's Cres. BS4: St Ap 3B **70**
St Davids M. BS1: Bris 4A **4**
St Dunstans Cl. BS31: Key 1A **90**
St Dunstan's Rd. BS3: Bedm 2E **77**
St Edward's Rd. BS8: Clif 3D **67**
St Edyth's Rd. BS9: Sea M 5D **39**
St Fagans Ct. BS30: Will 2D **83**
St Francis Dr. BS36: Wint 2B **28**
St Francis Rd. BS3: Ash G 5C **66**
   BS31: Key 1E **89**
St Gabriel's Bus. Pk. BS5: E'tn . . .1D **69**
St Gabriel's Rd. BS5: E'tn 1D **69**
ST GEORGE 1C **70**
St Georges Av. BS5: St G 3B **70**
St George's Bristol 3A **4** (3E **67**)
St Georges Bldgs. BA1: Bath 3A **104**
   (off Up. Bristol Rd.)
St Georges Cl. BS20: Eas 3C **52**
St Georges Ga. BS5: St G 1F **69**
   (off Church Rd.)
St Georges Hgts. BS5: Redf 2F **69**
St Georges Hill BA2: B'ptn 2F **105**
   BS20: Eas 3C **52**
St Georges Ho. BS5: St G 1A **70**
St Georges Ind. Est.
   BS11: A'mth 5D **19**
St Georges Pl. BA1: Bath 3A **104**
   (off Up. Bristol Rd.)
St Georges Rd. BS1: Bris . . .4A **4** (3D **67**)
   BS20: P'bry 4A **36**
   BS31: Key 1F **89**
St Gregory's Rd. BS7: Hor 3B **42**
St Helena Rd. BS6: Henle 2D **57**
St Helens Dr. BS30: Old C 2E **83**
St Helen's Wlk. BS5: St G 5C **60**
St Helier Av. BS4: Brisl 5B **70**
St Hilary Cl. BS9: Stok B 1F **55**
St Ivel Way BS30: Warm 3E **73**
St James' Barton
   BS1: Bris 1D **5** (1A **68**)
St James Ct. BS1: Bris 1C **4**
   BS32: Brad S 2E **9**
St James' Pde. BS1: Bris . . .1C **4** (2F **67**)
St James Pl. BS16: Mang 1C **62**
St James's Pde.
   BA1: Bath 4B **6** (4B **104**)
St James's Pk. BA1: Bath 2B **104**
St James's Pl.
   BA1: Bath 1A **6** (2B **104**)
St James's Sq. BA1: Bath 2A **104**
St James's St.
   BA1: Bath 1A **6** (2B **104**)
St James St. BS16: Mang 1C **62**
St Johns BA1: Bath 2D **103**
St Johns Ct. BA2: Bath . . .1C **6** (3C **104**)
   BS16: Fish 3C **60**
   BS31: Key 1A **90**
St John's Cres. BS3: Wind H 2A **78**
St Johns Hospital BA1: Bath 4B **6**
   (off Chapel Ct.)
St John's La. BS3: Bedm, Wind H . . .1E **77**
St John's Pl. BA1: Bath . . .3B **6** (4B **104**)
St John's Rd. BA1: Bath 2D **103**
   BA2: Bath 2C **6** (3C **104**)
   BS3: Bedm 1F **77**
   (East St.)
   BS3: Bedm 1F **77**
   (Lombard St.)
   BS8: Clif 5C **56**

St John's Steep BS1: Bris 2C **4**
   (off All Saints St.)
St John's St. BS3: Bedm 1E **77**
St John's Way BS37: Chip S 3D **17**
St Joseph's Rd. BS10: Bren 5D **23**
St Keyna Ct. BS31: Key 2B **90**
St Keyna Rd. BS31: Key 2A **90**
St Kilda's Rd. BA2: Bath 5F **103**
St Ladoc Rd. BS31: Key 2F **89**
St Laud Cl. BS9: Stok B 1F **55**
St Lawrence Ct. BS11: Law W 3A **38**
St Leonard's Rd. BS5: E'tn 4E **59**
   BS7: Hor 5A **42**
St Loe Cl. BS14: Whit 4B **86**
St Lucia Cl. BS7: Hor 4A **42**
St Lucia Cres. BS7: Hor 4A **42**
St Lukes Cl. BS16: Emer G 4E **47**
St Luke's Ct. BS3: Bedm 5A **68**
St Luke's Cres. BS3: Wind H 5B **68**
St Luke's Gdns. BS4: Brisl 2A **80**
St Lukes Ho. BS16: Emer G 4E **47**
St Luke's M. BS4: Brisl 2A **80**
St Luke's Rd. BA2: Bath 2B **110**
   BS3: Bris, Wind H 5A **68**
St Luke's Steps BS3: Wind H 5A **68**
St Luke St. BS5: Bar H 2D **69**
St Margaret's Cl. BS31: Key 1F **89**
St Margaret's Dr. BS9: Henle 1E **57**
St Mark's Av. BS5: E'tn 4E **59**
St Marks Cl. BS31: Key 1A **90**
St Marks Gdns.
   BA2: Bath 5C **6** (5C **104**)
St Mark's Gro. BS5: E'tn 5D **59**
St Mark's Rd.
   BA2: Bath 5C **6** (5C **104**)
   BS5: E'tn 5D **59**
St Mark's Ter. BS5: E'tn 5D **59**
St Martins BS41: L Ash 3C **74**
St Martin's Cl. BS4: Know 2D **79**
St Martin's Ct. BA2: Odd D 4A **110**
St Martin's Gdns. BS4: Know 3D **79**
St Martins Ind. Pk. BS11: A'mth . . .3B **20**
St Martin's Rd. BS4: Know 2D **79**
St Martin's Wlk. BS4: Know 3D **79**
St Mary Redcliffe Church
   . . . . .5D **5** (4A **68**)
St Mary's Bldgs.
   BA2: Bath 5B **6** (5B **104**)
St Marys Cl. BA2: Bath . . .3F **7** (4D **105**)
   BS30: C Hth 3D **73**
St Mary's Pk. Rd. BS20: P'head . . .2E **49**
St Mary's Rd. BS8: L Wds 3F **65**
   BS11: Shire 4E **37**
   BS20: P'head 2E **49**
St Mary's Wlk. BS11: Shire 5F **37**
St Mary's Way BS37: Yate 3B **16**
St Matthews Av. BS6: Bris 5F **57**
St Matthews Pl. BA2: Bath 5E **7**
St Matthew's Rd. BS6: Bris 1F **67**
St Matthias Ho. BS2: Bris 1F **5**
St Matthias Pk.
   BS2: Bris 1F **5** (2B **68**)
St Michaels Cl. BS7: B'stn 2A **58**
   BS36: Wint 1A **28**
St Michaels Ct. BA2: Mon C 5F **111**
   BS15: K'wd 1D **71**
St Michael's Hill
   BS2: Bris 1A **4** (1E **67**)
St Michael's Pk.
   BS2: Bris 1A **4** (1E **67**)
St Michael's Pl.
   BA1: Bath 4B **6** (4B **104**)
St Michael's Rd. BA1: Bath 3F **103**
   BA2: Bath 5C **102**
St Monica Ct. BS9: W Trym 1C **56**
St Nicholas Ct. BA2: B'ptn 1B **106**
St Nicholas Mkt.
   BS1: Bris 3C **4** (3F **67**)
St Nicholas Pk. BS5: E'tn 5D **59**
St Nicholas Rd. BS2: Bris 5B **58**
   BS14: Whit 3E **87**

St Nicholas St. BS1: Bris . . .3C 4 (3F 67)
St Oswald's Ct. BS6: Redl 3D 57
St Oswald's Rd. BS6: Redl 3D 57
St Patrick's Ct.
  BA2: Bath 3F 7 (4D 105)
  BS31: Key 2A 90
ST PAUL'S 1C 68
St Pauls Pl. BA1: Bath 3A 6
St Paul's Rd. BS3: Bedm 5F 67
  BS8: Clif 2D 67
St Paul St. BS2: Bris 1A 68
St Peters Ct. BS3: Bedm 5F 67
  (off Bedminster Pde.)
St Peter's Cres. BS36: Fram C . . .5D 13
St Peter's Ho. BS8: Clif 3D 67
  (off Jacob's Wells Rd.)
St Peters Lodge BS20: P'head 2F 49
St Peter's Pl. BA2: Bath 4F 103
St Peter's Ri. BS13: Bis 5C 76
St Peter's Rd. BS20: P'head 2F 49
St Peter's Ter. BA2: Bath 4F 103
St Peter's Wlk. BS9: Henle 5D 41
St Philips C'way. BS2: Bris 2C 68
  BS4: Bris 2C 68
  BS5: Bar H 2C 68
St Philips Central Ind. Est.
  BS2: Bris 4C 68
ST PHILIP'S MARSH 4D 69
St Philip's Rd. BS2: Bris 2B 68
St Pierre Dr. BS30: Warm 3D 73
St Ronan's Av. BS6: Cot 5E 57
St Saviours Ho. BS4: Know 2B 78
St Saviours Ri. BS36: Fram C 2D 29
St Saviours Rd.
  BA1: Bath, Swa 1D 105
St Saviour's Ter. BA1: Bath 1D 105
St Saviours Way BA1: Bath 1E 105
St Stephen's Av.
  BS1: Bris 3B 4 (3F 67)
St Stephens Bus. Cen.
  BS30: Old C 4E 73
  (off Poplar Rd.)
St Stephen's Cl. BA1: Bath 1B 104
  BS10: S'mead 1E 41
  BS16: Soun 3A 62
St Stephen's Ct. BA1: Bath 2B 104
St Stephen's Pl. BA1: Bath 2B 104
St Stephen's Rd. BA1: Bath 2B 104
  BS16: Soun 4F 61
St Stephen's St. BS1: Bris . .2B 4 (2F 67)
St Swithin's Pl. BA1: Bath 2C 104
St Swithin's Yd. BA1: Bath 1C 6
St Thomas Pl. BS1: Bris . . .4D 5 (3A 68)
St Thomas St. BS1: Bris . . .3D 5 (3A 68)
St Thomas St. E.
  BS1: Bris 4D 5 (3A 68)
St Vincent's Hill BS6: Redl 4C 56
St Vincents St. BS8: Clif 3C 66
St Vincents Trad. Est. BS2: Bris . .3E 69
Saint Way BS34: Stok G 4C 26
St Werburghs City Farm 3B 58
St Werburgh's Pk. BS2: Bris 4C 58
St Werburgh's Rd. BS2: Bris 4B 58
St Whytes Rd. BS4: Know 4F 77
St Winifred's Dr. BA2: C Down . . .3F 111
St Wulfstan Av. BS10: W Trym 3C 40
Salcombe Rd. BS4: Know 3B 78
Salem Rd. BS36: Wint 1B 28
Salisbury Av. BS15: K'wd 1D 71
Salisbury Dr. BS16: Down 5A 46
Salisbury Gdns. BS16: Down 1A 62
Salisbury Pk. BS16: Down 5A 46
Salisbury Rd. BA1: Bath 5D 97
  BS4: St Ap 4F 69
  BS6: Redl 4F 57
  BS16: Down 5A 46
Salisbury St. BS5: Bar H 3D 69
  BS5: St G 2A 70
Sally Barn Cl. BS30: L Grn 2A 82
Sally Hill BS20: P'head 4D 35
Sally Lunn's House 4C 6 (4C 104)

Sallysmead Cl. BS13: Hart 3D 85
Sallys Way BS36: Wint 1B 28
Salmons Way BS16: Emer G 3C 46
SALTFORD 4A 92
Saltford Cl. BS31: Salt 4A 92
Salthrop Rd. BS7: B'stn 2A 58
Saltmarsh Dr. BS11: Law W 2C 38
Saltwell Av. BS14: Whit 2E 87
Sambourne La. BS20: Pill 1E 53
Samian Way BS34: Stok G 3A 26
Sampson Ho. Bus. Pk.
  BS10: H'len 1F 21
Sampsons Rd. BS13: Hart 3F 85
Samuel St. BS5: Redf 1E 69
Samuel White Rd. BS15: Han 1D 81
Samuel Wright Cl.
  BS30: Old C 4F 73
Sanctuary, The BS20: Pill 2A 54
Sanctuary Gdns. BS9: Stok B 3F 55
Sandbach Rd. BS4: Brisl 5F 69
Sandbed Rd. BS2: Bris 4C 58
Sandburrows Rd. BS13: Bis 1A 84
Sandburrows Wlk. BS13: Bis 1B 84
Sandcroft BS14: H'gro 1B 86
Sanderling Pl. BS20: P'head 5E 35
Sandford Rd. BS8: Clif 4C 66
Sandgate Rd. BS4: Brisl 1F 79
Sand Hill BS4: Brisl 5E 69
Sandholme Cl. BS16: Down 3A 46
Sandholme Rd. BS4: Brisl 5E 69
Sandhurst BS37: Yate 5F 15
Sandhurst Cl. BS34: Pat 4D 9
Sandhurst Rd. BS4: Brisl 5F 69
Sandling Av. BS7: Hor 4C 42
Sandown Cl. BS16: Down 2B 46
Sandown Rd. BS4: Brisl 5F 69
  BS34: Fil 5E 25
Sandringham Av. BS16: Down 3A 46
Sandringham Pk. BS16: Down 3A 46
Sandringham Rd. BS4: Brisl 1F 79
  BS30: L Grn 2B 82
  BS34: Stok G 3F 25
Sands La. BS36: Fram C 4B 12
Sandstone Ri. BS36: Wint 4A 28
Sandwich Rd. BS4: Brisl 5F 69
Sandy Cl. BS32: Brad S 2A 26
Sandy La. BS5: Eastv 3E 59
  BS8: Abb L, Fail . . . .5C 52 & 2A 64
Sandyleaze BS9: W Trym 4A 40
Sandy Lodge BS37: Yate 5A 16
Sandy Pk. Rd. BS4: Brisl 5E 69
Saracens, The BS7: Hor 1A 58
Saracen St. BA1: Bath 2C 6 (3C 104)
Sarah St. BS5: Bar H 2D 69
Sargent St. BS3: Bedm 5A 68
Sarum Cl. BS16: Emer G 5E 47
Sarum Cres. BS10: S'mead 2E 41
Sassoon Ct. BS30: Bar C 4B 72
Satchfield Cl. BS10: Hen 1B 40
Satchfield Cres. BS10: Hen 1B 40
Satellite Bus. Pk. BS5: St G 2F 69
Sates Way BS9: Henle 5E 41
Saunders Rd. BS16: Stap H 2A 62
Saunton Wlk. BS4: Know 4A 78
Savages Wood Rd. BS32: Brad S . . .5F 9
Saville Ga. Cl. BS9: Stok B 2B 56
Saville M. BS6: Bris 1F 67
Saville Pl. BS8: Clif 3C 66
Saville Rd. BS9: Stok B 3B 56
Saville Row BA1: Bath 1B 6 (3B 104)
Savoy Rd. BS4: Brisl 5F 69
Saw Cl. BA1: Bath 3B 6 (4B 104)
Saxon Rd. BS2: Bris 4C 58
Saxon Way BS32: Brad S 4E 9
Say Wlk. BS30: B'yte 2F 73
Scandrett Cl. BS10: Hen 1A 40
Scantleberry Cl. BS16: Down 2F 45
School Cl. BS5: Eastv 3F 59
  BS14: Whit 3B 86
  BS34: Pat 4C 9
School Ct. BS34: Stok G 4C 26

School La. BA1: Bathe 3B 98
  BS16: Stap 1A 60
School Rd. BS4: Brisl 2A 80
  BS4: Wind H 1C 78
  BS15: K'wd 1E 71
  BS30: C Hth 5C 72
  BS30: Old C 1D 83
  BS36: Fram C 5B 12
School Wlk. BS5: W'hall 5F 59
  BS37: Yate 3A 16
Scop, The BS32: Alm 1C 8
Scotland La. BS4: Brisl 4B 80
  BS14: Brisl 1B 88
Scott Ct. BS30: Bar C 4B 72
Scott Lawrence Cl. BS16: B'hll 4C 44
Scott Wlk. BS30: B'yte 2F 73
Scott Way BS37: Yate 5B 16
Sea Bank Rd. BS20: P'bry 3A 36
Seagry Cl. BS10: S'mead 2A 42
SEA MILLS 5E 39
Sea Mills La. BS9: Sea M 2E 55
Sea Mills Station (Rail) 2D 55
Searle Ct. Av. BS4: Brisl 5A 70
Seaton Rd. BS5: E'tn 5E 59
Seaview Rd. BS20: P'head 2B 48
Seawalls BS9: Stok B 4F 55
Seawalls Rd. BS9: Stok B 4F 55
Second Av. BA2: Bath 1F 109
  BS14: H'gro 5D 79
Second Way BS11: A'mth 2F 37
Seddon Rd. BS2: Bris 4C 58
Sedgefield Gdns. BS16: Down 2B 46
Sedgemoor Rd. BA2: C Down . . .4B 110
Sedgemoor Ter. BA2: C Down . . .3C 110
Sedgewick Ho. BS11: Shire 4A 38
Sefton Pk. Rd. BS7: B'stn 3A 58
Selborne Rd. BS7: Hor 1B 58
Selbourne Cl. BA1: Bath 2C 102
Selbrooke Cres. BS16: Fish 5D 45
Selby Rd. BS5: S'wll 5B 60
Selden Rd. BS14: Stoc 2A 88
Selkirk Rd. BS15: K'wd 5E 61
Selley Wlk. BS13: Bis 2C 84
Selworthy BS15: K'wd 2A 72
Selworthy Cl. BS31: Key 2F 89
Selworthy Ho. BA2: C Down 3B 110
Selworthy Rd. BS4: Know 2D 79
Selworthy Ter. BA2: C Down 3B 110
Seneca Pl. BS5: St G 2F 69
Seneca St. BS5: St G 2F 69
Septimus Bldgs. BS14: Hart 2F 85
  (off Hawkfield Cl.)
Serbert Cl. BS20: P'head 1A 50
Serbert Rd. BS20: P'head 1A 50
Serbert Way BS20: P'head 1A 50
Serridge La. BS36: Coal H 4E 29
Seven Acres La. BA1: Bathe 2B 98
Seven Dials BA1: Bath 3B 6 (4B 104)
Seventh Av. BS7: Hor 2D 43
  BS14: H'gro 5C 78
Severn Grange BS10: Hen 5F 21
Severn Ho. BS10: Hen 5F 21
Severn Leigh Gdns. BS9: Stok B . .3B 56
Severnmead BS20: P'head 1B 48
Severn Rd. BS10: H'len 2D 21
  BS11: Chit 1B 20
  BS11: Shire 5F 37
  BS20: P'head 1E 49
  BS20: Pill 1E 53
Severnside Trad. Est.
  BS11: A'mth 3E 19
Severn Vw. BS11: Law W 2E 39
Severn Way BS31: Key 3B 90
  BS34: Pat 4B 8
Sevier St. BS2: Bris 4B 58
Seville Ct. BS20: P'head 4D 35
Seville Rd. BS20: P'head 4D 35
Seymour Av. BS7: B'stn 2A 58
Seymour Pl. BS16: Mang 2B 62
Seymour Rd. BA1: Bath 2C 104
  BS5: E'tn 5C 58

Seymour Rd. BS7: B'stn 2A 58
  BS15: K'wd 5F 61
  BS16: Stap H 2F 61
Seyton Wlk. BS34: Stok G 3A 26
Shackel Hendy M.
  BS16: Emer G 1E 63
Shackleton Av. BS37: Yate 5B 16
Shadwell Rd. BS7: B'stn 3F 57
Shaftesbury Av. BA1: Bath 3E 103
  BS6: Bris 5A 58
Shaftesbury Crusade BS2: Bris . . .3C 68
    (off Union Rd.)
Shaftesbury M. BA2: Bath 5F 103
Shaftesbury Rd. BA2: Bath 5F 103
Shaftesbury Ter. BS5: St G 2F 69
  BS6: Bris 5A 58
    (off Ashley Rd.)
Shaft Rd. BA2: C Down, Mon C . .3F 111
Shakespeare Av. BA2: Bath 1B 110
  BS7: Hor 3C 42
Shaldon Rd. BS7: L'lze 2C 58
Shallows, The BS31: Salt 4B 92
Sham Castle La.
  BA2: Bath 2F 7 (3D 105)
Shamrock Rd. BS5: Eastv 3F 59
Shanklin Dr. BS4: Fil 5D 25
Shannon Ct. BS1: Bris 3C 4
Shannon Wlk. BS20: P'head 5E 35
Shapcott Cl. BS4: Know 3D 79
Shaplands BS9: Stok B 2B 56
Sharland Cl. BS9: Stok B 3A 56
Sharland Gro. BS13: Hart 3E 85
Shaw Cl. BS5: E'tn 1D 69
  BS16: Mang 3D 63
Shaw Gdns. BS14: H'gro 4C 78
Shaws Way BA2: Bath 4B 102
Shearmore Cl. BS7: Hor 4C 42
Shearwater Ct. BS16: B'hll 5F 44
    (off Begbrook La.)
Sheaves Pk. BS10: S'mead 1F 41
Sheene Ct. BS3: Bedm 1E 77
Sheene Rd. BS3: Bedm 1E 77
Sheene Way BS3: Bedm 1E 77
Sheephouse Cvn. Pk. BS20: Eas . . .4A 36
Sheepscroft BS13: Withy 3C 84
SHEEPWAY 1E 51
Sheepway BS20: P'bry, P'head . .2B 50
Sheepway La. BS20: P'bry 1E 51
Sheepwood Cl. BS10: Hen 1C 40
Sheepwood Rd. BS10: Hen 1C 40
Sheldare Barton BS5: St G 2D 71
Sheldrake Dr. BS16: B'hll 5A 44
Shellard Rd. BS34: Fil 1C 42
Shellards Rd. BS30: L Grn 1B 82
Shelley Cl. BS5: St G 1B 70
Shelley Rd. BA2: Bath 5B 104
Shelley Way BS7: Hor 3C 42
Shellmor Av. BS34: Pat 4D 9
Shellmor Cl. BS34: Pat 4E 9
Shepherds Cl. BS16: Stap H 1A 62
Shepherds Wlk. BA2: C Down . . .4B 110
  BS32: Brad S 4F 9
Sheppard Rd. BS16: Fish 5E 45
Sheppards Gdns. BA1: W'ton 5D 95
Shepton Wlk. BS3: Bedm 2E 77
Sherbourne Av. BS32: Brad S 2A 26
Sherbourne Cl. BS15: Soun 4B 62
Sherbourne St. BS5: St G 1A 70
Sheridan Rd. BA2: Bath 5B 102
  BS7: Hor 2C 42
Sheridan Way BS30: L Grn 2C 82
Sherrings, The BS34: Pat 5D 9
Sherrin Way BS13: Withy 3A 84
Sherston Cl. BS16: Fish 1D 61
Sherston Rd. BS7: Hor 3A 42
Sherwell Rd. BS4: Brisl 1A 80
Sherwood Cl. BS31: Key 2A 90
Sherwood Rd. BS15: K'wd 5D 61
  BS31: Key 2A 90
Shetland Rd. BS10: S'mead 2F 41
Shickle Gro. BA2: Odd D 4E 109

Shield Retail Cen. BS34: Fil 5C 24
Shields Av. BS7: Hor 1C 42
Shiels Dr. BS32: Brad S 1F 25
Shilton Cl. BS15: K'wd 2B 72
Shimsey Cl. BS16: Fish 5E 45
Shipham Cl. BS14: Whit 2D 87
Ship Hill BS15: Han 4D 71
Ship La. BS1: Bris 5D 5 (4A 68)
Shipley Mow BS16: Emer G 5D 47
Shipley Rd. BS9: W Trym 3C 40
Shire Gdns. BS11: Shire 3F 37
SHIREHAMPTON 5A 38
Shirehampton Rd.
  BS9: Sea M, Stok B 4D 39
  BS11: Shire 5B 38
Shirehampton Station (Rail) 1F 53
Shirehampton Swimming Pool . . .5A 38
Shires Yd. BA1: Bath 2B 6 (3B 104)
Shire Way BS37: Yate 1E 31
SHOCKERWICK 1F 99
Shockerwick La.
  BA1: Bathf, Sho 3D 99
Shophouse Rd. BA2: Bath 4D 103
Shortfield Rd. BS8: Clif 5C 56
Shorthill Rd. BS37: W'lgh 4E 31
Shortlands Rd. BS11: Law W 2C 38
Short La. BS41: L Ash 2C 74
Short St. BS2: Bris 4C 68
SHORTWOOD 1F 63
Shortwood Hill BS16: Short 1F 63
Shortwood Rd. BS13: Hart 4A 86
Shortwood Vw. BS15: K'wd 1B 72
Shortwood Wlk. BS13: Hart 4A 86
Showcase Cinema
  Bristol 4E 69
Showering Cl. BS14: Stoc 2F 87
Showering Rd. BS14: Stoc 2F 87
Shrubbery, The BA1: Bath 2B 104
Shrubbery Cotts. BS6: Redl 4D 57
Shrubbery Ct. BS16: Stap H 1F 61
Shrubbery Rd. BS16: Stap H 1F 61
Shuter Rd. BS13: Withy 2B 84
Sidcot BS4: Brisl 2C 80
Sideland Cl. BS14: Stoc 1A 88
Sidelands Rd. BS16: Fish 5E 45
Sidings, The BS16: Sis 4D 63
  BS34: Fil 1E 43
Sidmouth Gdns. BS3: Wind H 2F 77
Sidmouth Rd. BS3: Wind H 2F 77
Signal Rd. BS16: Stap H 2A 62
Silas Ct. BS14: Stoc 2E 87
Silbury Ri. BS31: Key 5C 90
Silbury Rd. BS3: Ash V 2A 76
Silcox Rd. BS13: Hart 3E 85
Silklands Gro. BS9: Sea M 5E 39
Silver Birch Cl. BS34: Lit S 1F 25
Silverhill Rd. BS10: Hen 5A 22
Silver St. BS1: Bris 1C 4 (2F 67)
  BS20: Wes 5A 48
Silverthorne La. BS2: Bris 4C 68
Silverthorne Wharf BS2: Bris 3C 68
Silverton Ct. BS4: Know 3B 78
Simmonds Bldgs. BS16: Ham 5E 27
Simmonds Vw. BS34: Stok G 3B 26
Sinclair Ho. BS8: Clif 3D 67
SION HILL 1A 104
Sion Hill BA1: Bath 1A 104
  BS8: Clif 2B 66
Sion Hill Pl. BA1: Bath 1A 104
Sion La. BS8: Clif 2B 66
Sion Pl. BA2: Bath 3F 7 (4D 105)
  BS8: Clif 2B 66
Sion Rd. BA1: Bath 1A 104
  BS3: Bedm 1E 77
Sir John's La. BS5: Eastv 2D 59
    (not continuous)
  BS16: L'lze 2D 59
Siskin Cl. BS20: P'head 5E 35
Siston Cen. BS15: Soun 4C 62
Siston Cl. BS15: Soun 4C 62
SISTON COMMON 4C 62

Siston Comn. BS15: Sis 4C 62
    (not continuous)
  BS30: Sis 4C 62
Siston Hill BS30: Sis 5C 62
    (not continuous)
Siston La. BS30: W Hth 1F 73
Siston Pk. BS15: Soun 4C 62
Sixth Av. BS7: Hor 2D 43
  BS14: H'gro 5C 78
Skippon Ct. BS15: Han 4A 72
Skypark Rd. BS3: Bedm 1E 77
SLADEBROOK 2E 109
Sladebrook Av. BA2: Bath 2E 109
Sladebrook Ct. BA2: Bath 2D 109
Sladebrook Rd. BA2: Bath 1D 109
Slade Rd. BS20: P'head 1F 49
Sleep La. BS14: Whit 4F 87
Slimbridge Cl. BS37: Yate 1B 32
Sloan St. BS5: St G 1F 69
Slymbridge Av. BS10: Bren 5C 22
Small La. BS16: Stap 1A 60
    (not continuous)
Small St. BS1: Bris 2B 4 (2F 67)
  BS2: Bris 4C 68
Smarts Grn. BS37: Chip S 5E 17
Smeaton Rd. BS1: Bris 4B 66
Smithcourt Dr. BS34: Lit S 2E 25
Smithmead BS13: Hart 2D 85
Smoke La. BS11: A'mth, Chit 2E 19
Smoke La. Ind. Est.
  BS11: A'mth 2E 19
Smythe Cft. BS14: Whit 4C 86
Smyth Rd. BS3: Bedm 1C 76
Smyths Cl. BS11: A'mth 2D 37
SNEYD PARK 3F 55
Snowberry Cl. BS32: Brad S 5A 10
Snowberry Wlk. BS5: W'hall 5A 60
Snowdon Cl. BS16: Fish 2B 60
Snowdon Rd. BS16: Fish 1B 60
Snow Hill BA1: Bath 2C 104
Snow Hill Ho. BA1: Bath 2C 104
Soaphouse Ind. Est. BS5: St G 1A 70
Sodbury La. BS37: W'lgh 3A 32
Solsbury Ct. BA1: Bathe 3B 98
  BA2: Clav D 4B 106
Solsbury La. BA1: Bathe 3A 98
Solsbury Vw. BA2: B'ptn 1B 106
Solsbury Way BA1: Bath 5B 96
    (not continuous)
Somerby Cl. BS32: Brad S 1F 25
SOMERDALE 5B 82
Somerdale Av. BA2: Odd D 3E 109
  BS4: Know 4B 78
Somerdale Rd. BS31: Key 1B 90
Somerdale Rd. Nth. BS31: Key . . .5B 82
Somerdale Vw. BA2: Bath 3E 109
Somer La. BS3: Bedm 3E 77
Somermead BS3: Bedm 3E 77
Somerset Av. BS37: Yate 2B 16
Somerset Cres. BS34: Stok G 3B 26
Somerset Ho. BA2: Bath 2F 109
  BS2: Bris 2B 68
    (off Lawfords Ga.)
Somerset La. BA1: Bath 1A 104
Somerset Pl. BA1: Bath 1A 104
Somerset Rd. BS4: Know 1C 78
  BS20: P'head 1B 48
Somerset Sq. BS1: Bris 5D 5 (4A 68)
Somerset St. BA1: Bath . . .5B 6 (5C 104)
  BS1: Bris 5E 5 (4A 68)
  BS2: Bris 1F 67
Somerset Ter. BS3: Wind H 1F 77
Somerton Cl. BS15: K'wd 2A 72
Somerton Rd. BS7: Hor 5A 42
Somerville Cl. BS31: Salt 5A 92
Somerville Rd. BS6: Bris 3B 58
  BS7: B'stn, Bris 3A 58
Sommerville Rd. Sth. BS6: Bris . . .4B 58
  BS7: Bris 4B 58
Soper Gdns. BS4: Know 5F 77
Sorrel Gdns. BS20: P'head 1B 50

SOUNDWELL 3B 62
Soundwell Rd. BS15: K'wd 5E 61
  BS16: Soun 5E 61
Southampton Gdns. BS7: B'stn . . .1B 58
Southampton M. BS7: B'stn 1B 58
South Av. BA2: Bath 5F 103
  BS20: P'head 5C 34
  BS37: Yate 4D 15
Southblow Ho. BS3: Ash G 1C 76
Southbourne Gdns. BA1: Bath . . .1D 105
Southbourne Mans.
  BA2: Bath 4D 7 (4C 104)
Sth. Bristol Bus. Pk.
  BS4: Know 5A 78
Sth. Bristol Crematorium & Cemetery
  BS13: Bis 4B 76
Sth. Bristol Retail Pk.
  BS3: Ash G 1B 76
Sth. Bristol Trade Pk.
  BS3: Ash V 1B 76
Southcot Pl. BA2: Bath . . .5D 7 (5C 104)
South Cl. BS32: Brad S 2F 9
South Cft. BS9: Henle 4E 41
South Dene BS9: Stok B 5A 40
SOUTH DOWN 2D 109
Southdown Av. BA2: Bath 2D 109
Southdown Rd. BA2: Bath 1D 109
  BS9: W Trym 3B 40
Southdowns BS8: Clif 5C 56
Southernhay BS8: Clif 3D 67
    (off Cliftonwood Cres.)
  BS16: Stap H 2E 61
Southernhay Av. BS8: Clif 3D 67
Southernhay Cres. BS8: Clif 3D 67
Southey Av. BS15: K'wd 5A 62
Southey Ct. BS15: K'wd 5F 61
Southey St. BS2: Bris 4B 58
Southfield Av. BS15: K'wd 5A 62
Southfield Ct. BS9: W Trym 4C 40
Southfield Rd. BS6: Cot 5F 57
  BS9: W Trym 4C 40
Southfield Way BS37: Yate 1C 16
Southgate BA1: Bath 4C 6 (5C 104)
    (not continuous)
South Grn. St. BS8: Clif 3B 66
South Gro. BS6: Henle 1E 57
  BS20: Pill 2E 53
South Hayes BS5: Eastv 2D 59
Southlands BA1: W'ton 5C 94
    (not continuous)
  BS4: Know 3D 79
Sth. Lea Rd. BA1: Bath 2C 102
Southleigh Rd. BS8: Clif 1D 67
Sth. Liberty La.
  BS3: Ash V, Bedm 3A 76
South Lodge BS9: Stok B 5F 39
SOUTH LYNCOMBE 2B 110
SOUTHMEAD 2E 41
Southmead Rd.
  BS10: S'mead, W Trym 4E 41
  BS34: Fil 4E 41
Southmead Way BS10: S'mead . . .3F 41
Southover Cl. BS9: W Trym 3C 40
South Pde. BA2: Bath 4D 7 (4C 104)
  BS8: Clif 1D 67
  BS37: Yate 4A 16
South Pde. Cotts.
  BA2: C Down 4E 111
    (off Tyning Rd.)
South Quay BS1: Bris 3E 5 (3A 68)
South Rd. BS3: Bedm 1E 77
  BS6: Redl 4E 57
  BS15: K'wd 1F 71
  BS20: P'head 4C 34
Southsea Rd. BS34: Pat 1C 24
Southside Cl. BS9: C Din 3D 39
SOUTH STOKE 5B 110
Southstoke La. BA2: S'ske 5B 110
Southstoke Rd. BA2: C Down 4B 110
South St. BS3: Bedm 1D 77
South Ter. BS6: Redl 4D 57

SOUTH TWERTON 5F 103
South Vw. BA1: Bath 1C 104
    (off Camden Rd.)
  BA2: Mon C 4F 111
  BS2: Bris 1F 67
    (off Marlborough Hill Pl.)
  BS16: Stap H 1A 62
  BS20: P'head 4C 34
  BS36: Fram C 1D 29
South Vw. Cres. BS36: Coal H 2F 29
South Vw. Pl. BA2: Odd D 5E 109
South Vw. Ri. BS36: Coal H 2E 29
South Vw. Rd. BA2: Bath 4F 103
SOUTHVILLE 5E 67
Southville Pl. BS3: Bedm 5F 67
Southville Rd. BS3: Bedm 5E 67
Southville Ter. BA2: Bath 1D 111
South Wlk. BS37: Yate 4A 16
Southway Dr. BS30: Old C 4F 73
Southwell St. BS2: Bris 1A 4 (1E 67)
Southwood Av. BS9: C Din 3E 39
Southwood Dr. BS9: C Din 4D 39
Southwood Dr. E. BS9: C Din 3E 39
Space BS3: Bedm 3D 77
Spa La. BA1: Swa 5E 97
Spalding Cl. BS7: Eastv 3C 58
Spar Rd. BS37: Yate 3F 15
Spartley Dr. BS13: Bis 1B 84
Spartley Wlk. BS13: Bis 1B 84
Spa Vis. Cen. 4B 6
Spectrum Ho. BS2: Bris . .1E 5 (1A 68)
SPEEDWELL 5C 60
Speedwell Av. BS5: S'wll 2F 69
Speedwell Rd. BS5: S'wll 5B 60
  BS15: K'wd 5B 60
Speedwell Swimming Pool 5B 60
Spencer Ho. BS1: Bris 4A 68
    (off Mede Cl.)
Spencers Belle Vue BA1: Bath . . .2B 104
Spinney, The BS20: P'head 2E 49
  BS32: Brad S 1A 26
  BS36: Fram C 1D 29
Spinney Cft. BS13: Withy 2B 84
Spires Vw. BS16: Stap 1A 60
Sprigg Dr. BS20: Wes 5B 48
Spring Cres. BA2: Bath 4D 7 (4C 104)
Springfield Av. BS7: Hor 1B 58
  BS11: Shire 5F 37
  BS16: Mang 5C 46
Springfield Cl. BA2: Bath 5D 103
  BS16: Mang 4C 46
Springfield Gro. BS6: Henle 1D 57
Springfield Ho. BS6: Cot 1E 67
Springfield Lawns BS11: Shire 5F 37
Springfield Pl. BA1: Bath 1B 104
Springfield Rd. BS6: Bris 5F 57
  BS16: Mang 4C 46
  BS20: P'head 1D 49
  BS20: Pill 2E 53
Springfields BS34: Fil 1C 42
Springfields Rd. BS4: Know 3C 78
Spring Gdns. Rd.
  BA2: Bath 3D 7 (4C 104)
    (Argyle St.)
  BA2: Bath 4D 7 (5C 104)
    (Ferry La.)
Spring Hill BS2: Bris 1F 67
    (not continuous)
  BS15: K'wd 4A 62
Spring La. BA1: Bath 5D 97
Springleaze BS4: Know 3C 78
  BS16: Mang 4C 46
Springly Ct. BS15: K'wd 1C 72
Spring Ri. BS20: P'head 3E 49
Spring St. BS3: Bedm 5A 68
Spring St. Pl. BS3: Bedm 5A 68
Spring Va. BA1: Bath 5D 97
Springville Cl. BS30: L Grn 1C 82
Springwater Pk. Trad. Est.
  BS5: St G 2A 70
Springwood Dr. BS10: Hen 5F 21

Spruce Way BA2: Odd D 5A 110
  BS34: Pat 1A 24
Square, The BA2: Bath 5A 6 (5B 104)
  BS1: Bris 4F 5 (3B 68)
  BS4: Brisl 2F 79
  BS16: Stap H 2A 62
Squires Ct. BS3: Bedm 5A 68
  BS30: L Grn 5B 72
Stable Yd. BA2: Bath 4F 103
Stackpool Rd. BS3: Bris 5D 67
Stadium Rd. BS6: Henle 1E 57
Stafford Rd. BS2: Bris 4C 58
  BS20: P'head 2A 50
Staffords Cl. BS30: C Hth 3C 72
Stafford St. BS3: Bedm 5F 67
Stainer Cl. BS4: Know 1F 85
Stall St. BA1: Bath 4C 6 (4C 104)
STAMBRIDGE 4B 98
Stambrook Pk. BA1: Bathe 2B 98
Stanbridge Cl. BS16: Down 5B 46
Stanbridge Rd. BS16: Down 5B 46
Stanbury Av. BS16: Fish 1E 61
Stanbury Rd. BS3: Wind H 1A 78
Standfast Rd. BS10: Hen 5B 22
Standish Av. BS34: Pat 4D 9
Standish Cl. BS10: Hen 2B 40
Standon Way BS10: S'mead 1E 41
Stane Way BS11: A'mth 4E 37
Stanfield Cl. BS7: L'lze 5D 43
Stanford Cl. BS36: Fram C 5B 12
Stanford Pl. BS4: Know 5F 77
Stanhope Pl.
  BA1: Bath 3A 6 (4A 104)
Stanhope Rd. BS30: L Grn 2B 82
Stanier Cl. BS3: Bris 4C 68
Stanier Rd. BA1: Bath 4A 104
  BA2: Bath 4A 104
  BS16: Mang 3D 63
Stanley Av. BS7: B'stn 3A 58
  BS34: Fil 1D 43
Stanley Chase BS5: S'wll 4F 59
Stanley Cres. BS34: Fil 1D 43
Stanley Gdns. BS30: Old C 5D 73
Stanley Hill BS4: Wind H 5C 68
Stanley Mead BS32: Brad S 3A 10
Stanley Pk. BS5: E'tn 5E 59
Stanley Pk. Rd. BS16: Soun 3A 62
Stanley Rd. BS6: Redl 4E 57
  BS15: Warm 1D 73
Stanley Rd. W. BA2: Bath 5F 103
Stanley St. BS3: Bedm 1E 77
Stanley St. Nth. BS3: Bedm 1E 77
Stanley St. Sth. BS3: Bedm 1E 77
Stanley Ter. BS3: Bedm 2E 77
Stanley Vs. BA1: Bath 1C 104
    (off Camden Rd.)
Stanshaw Cl. BS16: B'hll 4C 44
STANSHAWE 5A 16
Stanshawe Cres. BS37: Yate 4A 16
Stanshawes Ct. Dr.
  BS37: Yate 5A 16
Stanshawes Dr. BS37: Yate 4F 15
Stanshaw Rd. BS16: B'hll 4C 44
Stanshaws Cl. BS32: Brad S 3D 9
Stanton Cl. BS15: K'wd 5B 62
Stanton Rd. BS10: S'mead 2F 41
Stanway BS30: Bit 3E 83
Stanway Cl. BA2: Odd D 4F 109
Staple Gro. BS31: Key 2F 89
Staplegrove Cres. BS5: St G 2C 70
STAPLE HILL 2F 61
Staple Hill Rd. BS16: Fish 2D 61
Staples Rd. BS37: Yate 3F 15
STAPLETON 1E 59
Stapleton Cl. BS16: Stap 1F 59
Stapleton Rd. BS5: Eastv 4D 59
  BS5: E'tn, Eastv 1C 58
Stapleton Road Station (Rail) 5D 59
Star Apartments BS16: Fish 3B 60
Star Av. BS34: Stok G 4C 26

Star Barn Rd. BS36: Wint 1A 28
Star La. BS16: Fish 3B 60
  BS20: Pill 2E 53
Starveall Cl. BS5: S'wll 5C 60
Station App. Rd.
  BS1: Bris 5F 5 (4B 68)
Station Av. BS16: Fish 2C 60
Station Av. Sth. BS16: Fish 2C 60
Station Cl. BS15: Warm 1E 73
  BS37: Chip S 5F 17
Station Ct. BA1: Bath 3E 103
Station La. BS7: Hor 2C 58
Station Rd. BA1: Bath 3E 103
  BA2: B'ptn 5B 98
  BS4: Brisl 2F 79
  BS4: St Ap 4A 70
  BS6: Bris 4F 57
  BS7: B'stn 2B 58
  BS10: Hen 1A 40
  BS11: Shire 1F 53
  BS15: Soun 2A 62
  BS16: Fish 2C 60
  BS20: P'bry 3F 51
  BS20: P'head 5C 34
  BS20: Pill 2E 53
  BS30: Warm 2E 73
  BS31: Key 1A 90
  BS34: Fil 5D 25
  (not continuous)
  BS34: Lit S, Pat 5D 9
  BS36: Coal H 3E 29
  BS37: Iron A 2F 13
  BS37: Yate 3E 15
Station Rd. Bus. Cen.
  BS15: Soun 3C 62
Station Rd. Workshops
  BS15: Soun 3C 62
Station Yd. BS36: Wint 4A 28
Staunton Flds. BS14: Whit 4E 87
Staunton La. BS14: Whit 3E 87
Staunton Way BS14: Whit 4F 87
Staveley Cres. BS10: S'mead . . .1E 41
Staverton Cl. BS34: Pat 4D 9
Staverton Way BS15: K'wd 2C 72
Staynes Cres. BS15: K'wd 1A 72
Stean Bri. Rd. BS32: Brad S 2F 25
Steel Cl. BS30: L Grn 1B 82
Steel Mills BS31: Key 3B 90
Stella Gro. BS3: Bedm 2C 76
Stephen's Dr. BS30: Bar C 4B 72
Stephen St. BS5: Redf 1E 69
Stepney Rd. BS5: W'hall 5E 59
Stepney Wlk. BS5: W'hall 5E 59
Stepping Stones, The
  BS4: St Ap 3A 70
Steps, The BS41: Dun 5A 84
Sterncourt Rd. BS16: B'hll 4C 44
Steven's Cres. BS3: Wind H 5B 68
Stevens Wlk. BS32: Brad S 5F 9
Stewart Ct. BS16: Fish 2B 60
  (off Wharf Rd.)
Steway La. BA1: Bathe 2C 98
Stibbs Ct. BS30: L Grn 5B 72
Stibbs Hill BS5: St G 2C 70
STIDHAM 2E 91
Stidham La. BS31: Key 1D 91
Stile Acres BS11: Law W 2C 38
Stillhouse La. BS3: Bedm 5F 67
Stillingfleet Rd. BS13: Hart 2E 85
Stillman Cl. BS13: Withy 3A 84
Stinchcombe BS37: Yate 4A 16
Stirling Cl. BS37: Yate 1F 15
Stirling Rd. BS4: Brisl 5E 69
Stirling Way BS31: Key 3A 90
Stirtingale Av. BA2: Bath 2E 109
Stirtingale Rd. BA2: Bath 2E 109
Stockton Cl. BS14: Whit 3B 86
  BS30: L Grn 1D 83
Stockwell Av. BS16: Mang 5C 46

Stockwell Cl. BS16: Mang 4B 46
Stockwell Dr. BS16: Mang 5C 46
Stockwell Glen BS16: Mang 4B 46
STOCKWOOD 2A 88
Stockwood Cres. BS4: Know . . .2B 78
Stockwood Hill BS31: Key 5E 81
Stockwood La. BS14: Key, Stoc . .3A 88
  BS14: Whit 3F 87
  BS31: Key 1B 88
Stockwood M. BS4: St Ap 4B 70
Stockwood Open Space Nature Reserve
  . . . . .5A 80
Stockwood Rd. BS4: Brisl 3B 80
  BS14: Stoc 2F 87
STOCKWOOD VALE 1E 89
Stockwood Va. BS31: Key 2D 89
STOKE BISHOP 2A 56
Stoke Bri. Av. BS34: Lit S 2F 25
Stoke Cotts. BS9: Stok B 2A 56
STOKE GIFFORD 4B 26
Stoke Gro. BS9: W Trym 5A 40
Stoke Hamlet BS9: W Trym 4B 40
Stoke Hill BS9: Stok B 2A 56
Stoke La. BS9: W Trym 1A 56
  BS16: B'hll, Stap 4A 44
  BS34: Pat 5D 9
Stokeleigh Wlk. BS9: Sea M 1E 55
Stokemead BS34: Pat 5E 9
Stoke Mdws. BS32: Brad S 4F 9
Stoke Paddock Rd. BS9: Stok B . .5F 39
Stoke Pk. Rd. BS9: Stok B 3A 56
Stoke Pk. Rd. Sth. BS9: Stok B . .3A 56
Stoke Rd. BS9: Stok B 3B 56
  BS20: P'head 1F 49
Stokes Cl. BS30: Bar C 5C 72
Stokes Cft. BS1: Bris 1A 68
Stoke Vw. BS34: Fil 5C 24
Stoke Vw. Bus. Pk. BS16: Fish . .3B 60
Stoke Vw. Rd. BS16: Fish 3B 60
Stoneberry Rd. BS14: Whit 4D 87
Stonebridge Pk. BS5: Eastv 4F 59
Stonechat Gdns. BS16: B'hll 5A 44
Stonechat Grn. BS20: P'head . . .5F 35
Stone Cl. BS36: Wint D 4A 28
STONE HILL 5A 72
Stonehill BS15: Han 5F 71
  BS30: L Grn 5F 71
Stonehouse Cl. BA2: C Down . . .3D 111
Stonehouse La. BA2: C Down . . .3D 111
Stone La. BS36: Wint D 5B 28
Stoneleigh Cl. BA1: L'dwn 4A 96
Stoneleigh Cres. BS4: Know 2C 78
Stoneleigh Dr. BS30: Bar C 4B 72
Stoneleigh Ho. BS8: Clif 2D 67
  (off Jacob's Wells Rd.)
Stoneleigh Rd. BS4: Know 2C 78
Stoneleigh Wlk. BS4: Know 2C 78
Stones Cotts. BS10: H'len 4E 21
Stoneyfield Cl. BS20: Eas 2D 53
Stoneyfields BS20: Eas 2D 53
Stoney Hill BS1: Bris 2A 4 (2E 67)
Stoney La. BS7: B'stn 3B 58
Stoney Steep BS20: P'head 5B 34
Stony La. BA2: New L 4A 102
Stothard Rd. BS7: L'lze 4D 43
Stottbury Rd. BS7: Eastv 3C 58
Stoulton Gro. BS10: Bren 5C 22
Stourden Cl. BS16: B'hll 4C 44
Stourton Dr. BS30: Bar C 5B 72
STOVER 3D 15
Stover Rd. BS37: Yate 3D 15
Stover Trad. Est. BS37: Yate 3D 15
Stow Ho. BS11: Shire 1A 54
Stowick Gdns. BS11: Law W 2E 39
Stradbrook Av. BS5: St G 2D 71
Stradling Rd. BS11: Law W 1E 39
Stradlings Yd. BS2: Bris 1E 67
  (off Lit. Paul St.)
Straight St. BS2: Bris . . .3F 5 (3B 68)
Straits Pde. BS16: Fish 1D 61
Stratford Cl. BS14: Whit 4B 86

Stratford Mill 2A 40
Strathearn Dr. BS10: Bren 1D 41
Strathmore Rd. BS7: Hor 5A 42
Stratton Cl. BS34: Lit S 1E 25
Stratton Pl. BS30: L Grn 2B 82
Stratton Rd. BS31: Salt 4F 91
Strawberry Cres. BS5: St G 2A 70
Strawberry La. BS5: St G 2A 70
  BS13: Withy 4A 84
  BS41: Dun 4A 84
Strawbridge Rd. BS5: Bar H 2D 69
Stream, The BS16: Ham 1D 45
Stream Cl. BS10: Bren 5F 23
Streamleaze BS16: Mang 5B 46
Streamside Rd. BS37: Chip S 4C 16
Streamside Wlk. BS4: Brisl 1A 80
Stretford Av. BS5: W'hall 1F 69
Stretford Rd. BS5: W'hall 1F 69
Stroud Rd. BS11: Shire 1A 54
  BS34: Pat 5A 8
Stuart Pl. BA2: Bath 4F 103
Stuart St. BA5: Redf 2E 69
Studios 58 BS1: Bris 1F 67
  (off Dighton St.)
Studland Ct. BS9: Henle 5D 41
Sturden La. BS16: Ham 5E 27
Sturdon Rd. BS3: Bedm 1C 76
Sturmer Cl. BS37: Yate 1A 16
Sturmey Way BS20: Pill 3A 54
Sturminster Cl. BS14: Stoc 1F 87
Sturminster Lodge BS14: Stoc . .1F 87
Sturminster Rd. BS14: Stoc 4E 79
Sulis Mnr. Rd. BA2: Odd D 5E 109
Sullivan Cl. BS4: Know 1F 85
Summer Ct. BS8: Clif 2C 66
  (off Triangle Sth.)
Summerfield Cotts. BA1: Bath . .1D 105
  (off Tyning La.)
Summerfield Rd. BA1: Bath 1C 104
Summerfield Ter. BA1: Bath 1C 104
Summer Ground Dr. BS13: Bis . . .2C 84
Summerhayes BS30: Old C 4F 73
Summer Hill BS4: Wind H 5C 68
Summerhill Rd. BA1: Bath 1F 103
  BS5: St G 1A 70
Summerhill Ter. BS5: St G 2B 70
Summer Ho. Way BS30: Warm . .2D 73
Summer La.
  BA2: C Down, Mon C 4D 111
Summerlays Ct.
  BA2: Bath 4E 7 (4D 105)
Summerlays Pl. BA2: Bath 4E 7
Summerleaze BS16: Fish 3E 61
  BS31: Key 5A 82
Summers Mead BS37: Yate 1A 16
Summers Rd. BS2: Bris 5C 58
Summers Ter. BS2: Bris 5C 58
Summer St. BS3: Bedm 5E 67
Summit Cl. BS15: K'wd 1A 72
Sundays Hill BS32: Alm 1C 8
Sunderland Pl. BS8: Clif 2D 67
Sunderland St.
  BA2: Bath 2D 7 (3C 104)
Sundridge Pk. BS37: Yate 1A 32
Sunningdale BS8: Clif 1D 67
  BS37: Yate 5A 16
Sunningdale Dr. BS30: Warm 3D 73
Sunny Bank BS15: K'wd 5D 61
Sunnybank BA2: Bath 1D 111
  BS16: Down 5A 46
  BS37: W'lgh 5C 30
Sunny Bank M. BS16: Down 5A 46
Sunnybank Way BS16: Down 5F 69
Sunny Hill BS9: Sea M 4D 39
Sunnymead BS31: Key 5A 38
Sunnyhill Ho. E. BS11: Shire 5A 38
  (off Sunnyhill Dr.)
Sunnyhill Ho. W. BS11: Shire . . .5A 38
  (off Sunnyhill Dr.)
Sunnymead BS31: Key 4B 90
Sunnyside BS9: Stok B 1A 56
  BS36: Fram C 1D 29

Sunnyside La. BS16: Ham 1E 45
 BS37: Yate 4E 15
Sunnyvale Dr. BS30: L Grn 1D 83
Sunny Wlk. BS15: K'wd 5D 61
Sunridge BS16: Down 5F 45
Sunrise Gro. BS4: Brisl 5F 69
Surrey Rd. BS7: B'stn 3A 58
Surrey St. BS2: Bris 1A 68
Suspension Bri. Rd. BS8: Clif 2B 66
Sussex Pl. BA2: Bath 5D 7 (5C 104)
 BS2: Bris 5B 58
Sussex St. BS2: Bris 3C 68
Sutcliffe Ho. BA1: Bath 2D 105
Sutherland Av. BS16: Down 4A 46
 BS37: Yate 1F 15
Sutherland Pl. BS8: Clif 4C 56
Sutton Av. BS4: Brisl 5F 69
 (not continuous)
Sutton St. BA2: Bath 1E 7 (3D 105)
SWAINSWICK 2E 97
Swainswick BS14: H'gro 1B 86
Swainswick Gdns. BA1: Swa 5E 97
Swainswick La. BA1: Swa 2E 97
Swaish Dr. BS30: Bar C 5B 72
Swallow Ct. BS14: Key 1C 88
Swallow Dr. BS34: Pat 5A 8
Swallows Ct. BS34: Stok G 4A 26
Swallow St. BA1: Bath 4C 6 (4C 104)
Swancombe BS20: Clap G 5A 50
Swane Rd. BS14: Stoc 1B 88
Swan Fld. BS37: Yate 3B 16
Swan La. BS36: Wint 4D 11
Swanmoor Cres. BS10: Bren 4C 22
Sweets Cl. BS15: K'wd 4A 62
Sweets Rd. BS15: K'wd 4A 62
SWINEFORD 1C 92
Swiss Cl. BS3: Ash V 2B 76
Swiss Dr. BS3: Ash V 2B 76
Swiss Rd. BS3: Ash V 2B 76
Sycamore Cl. BS5: W'hall 5A 60
 BS15: Han 1D 81
Sycamore Ct. BS7: B'stn 3A 58
Sycamore Dr. BS34: Pat 1A 24
Sycamore Ho. BS16: Fish 5E 45
 (off Partridge Dr.)
Sydenham Bldgs. BA2: Bath 5A 104
Sydenham Hill BS6: Cot 5F 57
Sydenham La. BS6: Bris 5F 57
Sydenham Pl. BA2: C Down 4E 111
 (off Alexandra Pl.)
Sydenham Rd.
 BA2: Bath 4A 6 (4A 104)
 BS4: Know 1C 78
 BS6: Bris, Cot 5F 57
Sydenham Ter. BA2: C Down 4E 111
Sydenham Way BS15: Han 1E 81
Sydney Bldgs. BA2: Bath . . .3F 7 (4D 105)
Sydney Ct. BA2: New L 5D 101
Sydney M. BA2: Bath 2E 7 (3D 105)
Sydney Pl. BA2: Bath 1E 7 (3D 105)
Sydney Rd. BA2: Bath 2F 7 (3D 105)
Sydney Row BS1: Bris 4D 67
Sydney Wharf
 BA2: Bath 3F 7 (4D 105)
Sylvan Way BS9: Sea M 5D 39
Sylvia Av. BS3: Wind H 1B 78
Symes Pk. BA1: W'ton 5C 94
Symington Rd. BS16: Fish 1D 61
Syston Vw. BS15: K'wd 1C 72
Syston Way BS15: K'wd 5F 61

Talgarth Rd. BS7: B'stn 2B 58
Tallis Gro. BS4: Know 1F 85
Tamar Dr. BS31: Key 3C 90
Tamarisk Vs. BS5: W'hall 5A 60
 (off Snowberry Wlk.)
Tamar Rd. BS2: Bris 3E 69
Tamsin Ct. BS31: Key 2A 90
Tamworth Rd. BS31: Key 3A 90
Tan Ct. BS4: Brisl 5F 69
Tankard's Cl. BS2: Bris 1A 4
 BS8: Clif 1A 4 (2E 67)
Tanner Cl. BS30: Bar C 4B 72
Tanner Ct. BS30: Bar C 4B 72
Tanners Cl. BS16: Fren 2D 45
Tanners Wlk. BA2: Bath 5B 102
Tanorth Cl. BS14: Whit 4C 86
Tanorth Rd. BS14: Whit 4B 86
Tansy La. BS20: P'head 1B 50
Tanyard, The BS30: Will 2D 83
Tapsters BS30: C Hth 5C 72
Tara Cl. BS36: Fram C 4B 12
Tarn Ho. BS34: Pat 5C 8
Tarnock Av. BS14: H'gro 5B 78
Tarragon Pl. BS20: P'head 1B 50
 BS32: Brad S 1B 26
Taunton Wlk. BS7: Hor 4C 42
Taverner Cl. BS4: Know 5F 77
Tavistock Rd. BS4: Know 3B 78
Tavistock Wlk. BS4: Know 3B 78
Taylor Cl. BS15: K'wd 1B 72
Taylor Gdns. BS13: Withy 3B 84
Tayman Cl. BS10: Hor 5A 42
Tayman Ridge BS30: Bit 4F 83
Taynton Cl. BS30: Bit 2E 83
Teal Cl. BS32: Brad S 3F 9
Teal Way BS20: P'head 6E 35
Teasel Mead BS32: Brad S 1A 26
Teddington Cl. BA2: Bath 1E 109
Teewell Av. BS16: Stap H 2A 62
Teewell Cl. BS16: Stap H 2A 62
Teewell Ct. BS16: Stap H 2A 62
Teewell Hill BS16: Stap H 2A 62
Teignmouth Rd. BS4: Know 3B 78
Telephone Av. BS1: Bris . . .3B 4 (3F 67)
Telford Ho. BA2: Bath 2F 109
Telford Wlk. BS5: St G 5C 60
Tempera BS5: E'tn 2D 69
Templar Rd. BS37: Yate 2A 16
Temple Bk. BS1: Bris 3E 5 (3A 68)
Temple Bk. E. BS1: Bris 4F 5 (3B 68)
Temple Cir. BS1: Bris 4E 5 (3A 68)
Temple Ct. BA2: New L 5D 101
 BS31: Key 2A 90
Temple Ga. BA2: New L 5E 5 (4A 68)
Temple Ga. District Cen.
 BS3: Bris 4B 68
Temple Ga. Ho. BS1: Bris . . .5E 5 (4A 68)
Templeland Rd. BS13: Withy 2B 84
Temple Quay Ho.
 BS1: Bris 4F 5 (3B 68)
Temple Rose St.
 BS1: Bris 4E 5 (3A 68)
Temple St. BS1: Bris 3D 5 (3A 68)
 (not continuous)
 BS3: Bedm 2D 77
 BS31: Key 2A 90
Temple Trad. Est. BS2: Bris 4E 69
Temple Way BS1: Bris 4E 5 (3A 68)
 BS2: Bris 4E 5 (3A 68)
Templeway Ho.
 BS1: Bris 3E 5 (3A 68)
Temple Way Underpass
 BS1: Bris 2F 5 (2B 68)
 BS2: Bris 2F 5 (2B 68)
Tenby Rd. BS5: St G 3F 89
Tenby St. BS5: Bar H 2D 69
Tennessee Gro. BS6: Henle 1E 57
Tenniscourt Rd. BS15: K'wd 5C 62
Tennis Rd. BS4: Know 2C 78
Tennyson Cl. BS31: Key 1B 90
Tennyson M. BS10: Bren 1D 41

Tennyson Rd. BA1: Bath 3F 103
 BS7: Hor 1A 58
Tenth Av. BS7: Hor 2D 43
Tereslake Grn. BS10: Bren 4F 23
Terrace Wlk. BA1: Bath . . .4C 6 (4C 104)
Terrell Gdns. BS5: St G 2F 69
Terrell St. BS2: Bris 1B 4 (1F 67)
Terrill Ct. BS8: Clif 5C 56
Terris Ct. BS34: Stok G 4A 26
Terry Ho. BS1: Bris 2A 4
Tetbury Cl. BS34: Lit S 5E 9
Tetbury Rd. BS15: K'wd 1D 71
Teviot Rd. BS31: Key 3C 90
Tewkesbury Rd. BS2: Bris 4C 58
Tewther Rd. BS13: Hart 4E 85
Teyfant Rd. BS13: Hart 3A 86
Teyfant Wlk. BS13: Hart 3A 86
Thackeray BS7: Hor 3C 42
Thanet Rd. BS3: Bedm 2D 77
Thatcher Cl. BS20: P'head 2F 49
Thatchers Cl. BS5: St G 2D 71
The . . . .
 Names prefixed with 'The' for
 example 'The Academy' are
 indexed under the main name
 such as 'Academy, The'
Theatre Royal 3B 4 (3F 67)
Theatre Royal (Ustinov Studio) 3B 6
There & Back Again La.
 BS8: Clif 2E 67
Theresa Av. BS7: B'stn 2A 58
Thermae Bath Spa 4B 6
Theynes Cft. BS41: L Ash 3C 74
Thicket Av. BS16: Fish 4D 61
Thicket Rd. BS16: Fish 2E 61
Thiery Rd. BS4: Brisl 2E 79
Thingwall Pk. BS16: Fish 3A 60
Third Av. BA2: Bath 5F 103
 BS7: Hor 2C 42
 BS14: H'gro 5D 79
Third Way BS11: A'mth 1D 37
Thirlmere Ct. BS30: Old C 3F 73
Thirlmere Rd. BS34: Pat 5C 8
Thistle St. BS3: Bedm 1D 77
Thomas Av. BS16: Emer G 3D 47
Thomas Cl. BS1: Bris 4D 5
Thomas La. BS1: Bris 4D 5 (3A 68)
Thomas Pring Wlk. BS5: St G 5C 60
Thomas St. BA1: Bath 2C 104
 BS1: Bris 5B 58
 BS2: Bris 5B 58
 BS5: Bar H 2D 69
Thomas St. Nth. BS2: Bris 5F 57
Thomas Way BS16: Stap 4A 44
Thompson Rd. BS14: Stoc 1A 88
Thomson Rd. BS5: E'tn 1D 69
Thornbank Gdns.
 BA2: Bath 5A 6 (5B 104)
Thornbank Pl. BA2: Bath . .5A 6 (5A 104)
Thorn Cl. BS37: Yate 4F 15
Thorndale BS8: Clif 1C 66
Thorndale Cl. BS8: Clif 5C 56
Thorndale M. BS8: Clif 1C 66
Thorneycroft Cl. BS7: L'lze 4D 43
Thornhayes Cl. BS36: Fram C 5C 12
Thornhills, The BS16: Fish 5D 45
Thornleigh Rd. BS7: Hor 1A 58
Thornmead Gro. BS10: Bren 5C 22
Thorns Farm BS37: Yate 4A 16
Thorpe Lodge BS6: Bris 5F 57
 (off St Matthew's Rd.)
Three Brooks La. BS32: Brad S . . .5A 10
Three Brooks Local Nature Reserve
 . . . . .5B 10
Three Kings Ct., The
 BS1: Bris 2B 4 (2F 67)
Three Oaks Cl. BS16: Fish 2E 61
Three Queens' La.
 BS1: Bris 4D 5 (3A 68)
Three Wells Rd. BS13: Withy 3B 84
Thrissell St. BS5: E'tn 1C 68

Tabernacle Rd. BS15: Han 3E 71
Tackley Rd. BS5: Eastv 3D 59
Tadwick La. BA1: Up Swa 1B 96
Tailor's Ct. BS1: Bris 2C 4 (2F 67)
Talavera Cl. BS2: Bris 2C 68
Talbot Av. BS15: K'wd 5D 61
Talbot Rd. BS4: Brisl, Know 2D 79

Throgmorton Rd. BS4: Know 4B 78
Thunderbolt Sq. BS1: Bris 4B 4
Thunderbolt Steps BS4: Wind H . . .5C 68
Thurlestone BS14: H'gro 1B 86
Thurlow Rd. BS5: E'tn 4E 59
Thurston's Barton BS5: W'hall 5A 60
Thyme Cl. BS20: P'bry, P'head 1B 50
Tibberton BS15: K'wd 1C 72
Tibbott Rd. BS14: Stoc 2F 87
Tibbott Wlk. BS14: Stoc 2E 87
Tichborne Rd. BS5: Redf 2E 59
Tide Gro. BS11: Law W 3C 38
Tidenham Way BS34: Pat 4B 8
Tiffany Cl. BS31: Key 5E 5 (4A 68)
Tilley Cl. BS31: Key 5C 90
Tilling Rd. BS10: Hor 4A 42
Tilling Wlk. BS10: Hor 4A 42
Timber Dene BS16: Stap 2F 59
Timberscombe Wlk.
 . . . BS14: Whit 2D 87
Timsbury Rd. BS3: Know 2A 78
Timsbury Wlk. BS3: Know 2A 78
Tindell Ct. BS30: L Grn 5B 72
Tintagel Cl. BS31: Key 3F 89
Tintern Av. BS5: St G 1F 69
Tintern Cl. BS30: Bar C 3B 72
Tippetts Rd. BS15: K'wd 3F 71
Titan Barrow BA1: Bathf 5E 99
Tiverton Wlk. BS16: Fish 4C 60
Tobacco Factory, The 5C 66
Tobias Gdns. BS37: Yate 4F 15
Toddington Cl. BS37: Yate 5F 15
Toll Bri. Rd. BA1: Bathe 4A 98
Toll Ho. Ct. BS3: Ash G 5C 66
Tormarton Cres. BS10: Hen 4B 22
Toronto Rd. BS7: Hor 3B 42
Torpoint Rd. BS3: Wind H 3F 77
Torrance Cl. BS30: Old C 3F 73
Torridge Rd. BS31: Key 3C 90
Torrington Av. BS4: Know 4B 78
Tortworth Rd. BS7: Hor 1A 58
Totshill Dr. BS13: Hart 4A 86
Totshill Gro. BS13: Hart 3A 86
Tottenham Pl. BS8: Clif 2D 67
TOTTERDOWN 5B 68
Totterdown Bri. Trad. Est.
 . . . BS2: Bris 5C 68
Touchstone Av. BS34: Stok G 3B 26
Tourist Info. Cen.
 . . . Bath 4C 6 (4C 104)
 . . . Bristol, Anchor Sq. . . .4A 4 (3E 67)
 . . . Bristol, The Galleries
 . . . . .2D 5 (2A 68)
 . . . Bristol, Trenchard St.
 . . . . .2B 4 (2F 67)
 . . . Bristol, University Rd. 2E 67
 . . . Chipping Sodbury 4D 17
Tower, The BS1: Bris 3D 5 (3A 68)
Tower Hill BS2: Bris 3E 5 (2A 68)
Tower La. BS1: Bris 2C 4 (2F 67)
 . . . . (not continuous)
 . . . BS30: Warm 3C 72
Tower La. Bus. Pk. BS30: Warm . . .3D 73
Towerleaze BS9: Stok B 3F 55
Tower Rd. BS15: K'wd 5E 61
 . . . BS20: P'head 2C 48
Tower Rd. Nth. BS30: Warm 2D 73
Tower Rd. Sth. BS30: C Hth 2D 73
Tower St. BS1: Bris 4E 5 (3A 68)
Townsend BS32: Alm 1B 8
Townsend Cl. BS14: Stoc 2B 88
Townsend La. BS32: Alm 1B 8
Townsend Rd. BS14: Stoc 2B 88
Toynbe Rd. BS4: Know 4A 78
Tozer's Hill BS4: Know 2E 79
Tracy Cl. BS14: H'gro 5B 78
 . . . . (not continuous)
Trafalgar Rd. BA1: W'ton 1D 103
Trafalgar Ter. BS3: Bedm 2D 77
Tralee Wlk. BS4: Know 3F 77

Tramshed, The
 . . . BA1: Bath 2C 6 (3C 104)
Tramway Rd. BS4: Brisl 1E 79
Tranmere Av. BS10: Bren 4C 22
Tranmere Gro. BS10: Bren 5C 22
Transom Ho. BS1: Bris 4E 5
Tratman Wlk. BS10: Hen 5B 22
Travers Cl. BS4: Know 1F 85
Travers Wlk. BS34: Stok G 3B 26
Tredegar Rd. BS16: Fish 3D 61
Treefield Pl. BS2: Bris 4C 58
Treeleaze BS37: Yate 3B 16
Tregarth Rd. BS3: Ash V 3B 76
Trelawney Av. BS5: St G 1F 69
Trelawney Pk. BS4: Brisl 1F 79
Trelawney Rd. BS6: Cot 5E 57
Trellick Wlk. BS16: Stap 3A 44
Trenchard Rd. BS31: Salt 4F 91
Trenchard St. BS1: Bris 2B 4 (2E 67)
Trench La. BS32: Alm 3A 10
 . . . BS36: Wint 3A 10
Trendlewood Pk. BS16: Stap 2A 60
Trent Gro. BS31: Key 3C 90
Tresco Ho. BS2: Bris 4C 58
Trescothick Cl. BS31: Key 1F 89
Trescothick Dr. BS30: Old C 5F 73
Tresham Cl. BS32: Brad S 3F 9
Trevelyan Wlk. BS10: Hen 5B 22
 . . . BS34: Stok G 3C 26
Trevenna Rd. BS3: Ash V 3B 76
Treverdowe Wlk. BS10: Hen 5F 21
Trevethin Cl. BS15: K'wd 2E 71
Trevisa Gro. BS10: Bren 4E 23
Trewint Gdns. BS4: Know 4B 78
Triangle, The BS20: P'head 1D 49
Triangle E. BA2: Bath 5F 103
Triangle Nth. BA2: Bath 4F 103
Triangle Sth. BS8: Clif 2D 67
Triangle Vs. BA2: Bath 5F 103
Triangle Wlk. BS8: Clif 2D 67
 . . . . (off Triangle Sth.)
Triangle W. BA2: Bath 5F 103
 . . . BS8: Clif 2D 67
Trident Cl. BS16: Down 2C 46
Trim Bri. BA1: Bath 3B 6 (4B 104)
Trim St. BA1: Bath 3B 6 (4B 104)
Trinder Rd. BS20: Eas 2D 53
Trinity Cl. BA1: Bath 4A 6 (4B 104)
Trinity Ct. BS15: K'wd 1A 72
Trinity La. BS37: Chip S 3E 17
Trinity M. BS2: Bris 2F 5
Trinity Pl. BA1: Bath 3A 6 (4A 104)
 . . . BS8: Clif 3C 66
 . . . .(off Charles Pl.)
Trinity Quay BS2: Bris 3F 5 (3B 68)
Trinity Rd. BA2: C Down 3D 111
 . . . BS2: Bris 2C 68
Trinity St. BA1: Bath 4B 6 (4B 104)
 . . . BS1: Bris 4A 4 (3E 67)
 . . . BS2: Bris 2C 68
Trinity Theological College 2A 56
Trinity Wlk. BS2: Bris 2B 68
Trin Mills BS1: Bris 5C 4 (4F 67)
Tripps Row BS41: L Ash 3C 74
Troon BS37: Yate 5A 16
Troon Dr. BS30: Warm 3D 73
Trooper's Hill Rd. BS5: St G 3B 70
Trossachs Dr. BA2: Bath 2F 105
Trowbridge Rd. BS10: S'mead 2E 41
Trowbridge Wlk. BS10: S'mead 2E 41
Trubshaw Cl. BS7: Hor 5B 42
Trumpet La. BS5: St G 2D 71
Truro Rd. BS3: Ash G 1D 77
Trym Cross Rd. BS9: Sea M 1E 55
Trym Leaze BS9: Sea M 1E 55
Trym Rd. BS9: W Trym 3C 40
Trym Side BS9: Sea M 1E 55
Trymwood Cl. BS10: Hen 1B 40
Trymwood Pde. BS9: Stok B 5F 39
Tuckett Ho. BS16: Fren 4E 45
Tuckett La. BS16: Fren 4E 45

Tudor Cl. BS30: Old C 1E 83
Tudor Rd. BS2: Bris 5B 58
 . . . BS5: E'tn 5E 59
Tudor Rd. BS15: Han 4E 71
 . . . BS20: P'head 2A 50
Tuffley Rd. BS10: W Trym 3E 41
Tufton Av. BS11: Law W 3C 38
Tugela Rd. BS13: Bis 5B 76
Tumps Nature Area, The 4B 8
Tunbridge Way BS16: Emer G 3C 46
Tunstall Cl. BS9: Stok B 2A 56
Turley Rd. BS5: E'tn 5F 59
Turnberry BS30: Warm 3D 73
 . . . BS37: Yate 5A 16
Turnberry Wlk. BS4: Brisl 3F 79
Turnbridge Cl. BS10: Bren 5E 23
Turnbridge Rd. BS10: Bren 5E 23
Turner Cl. BS31: Key 2C 90
Turner Dr. BS37: Yate 4D 15
Turner Gdns. BS7: L'lze 5D 43
Turners Ct. BS30: L Grn 5B 72
Turner Wlk. BS30: B'yte 2F 73
Turnpike Cl. BS37: Yate 3A 16
Turnstone Av. BS20: P'head 5E 35
Turtlegate Av. BS13: Withy 3A 84
Turtlegate Wlk. BS13: Withy 3A 84
Turville Dr. BS7: Hor 5C 42
Tuscany Ho. BS6: Redl 3C 56
Tweeny La. BS30: Old C 3F 73
Twenty Acres Rd. BS10: S'mead . . .1D 41
TWERTON 5F 103
Twerton Farm Cl. BA2: Bath 4D 103
TWERTON HILL 2C 108
Twerton Pk. 5D 103
Twickenham Rd. BS6: Henle 1E 57
Twinnell Ho. BS5: E'tn 1C 68
Two Acres Rd. BS14: H'gro 4C 78
Two Mile Ct. BS15: K'wd 1D 71
TWO MILE HILL 1D 71
Two Mile Hill Rd. BS15: K'wd 1C 70
Two Stones La. BS37: Chip S 5E 17
Twynings, The BS15: K'wd 4A 62
Tybalt Way BS34: Stok G 3A 26
Tydeman Rd. BS20: P'head 1B 50
Tydings Cl. BS41: L Ash 3C 74
Tyler Cl. BS15: Han 4A 72
Tylers Farm BS37: Yate 1B 16
Tylers La. BS16: Stap H 1F 61
Tyler St. BS2: Bris 3C 68
Tylers Way BS37: Yate 1B 16
Tyndale Av. BS16: Fish 2D 61
 . . . BS37: Yate 2F 15
Tyndale Ct. BS6: Redl 5D 57
 . . . .(off Chertsey Rd.)
Tyndale Rd. BS15: Soun 4A 62
Tyndall Av. BS8: Clif 1A 4 (2E 67)
Tyndall Ho. BS2: Bris 1F 5
Tyndall Rd. BS5: E'tn 1D 69
TYNDALL'S PARK 2D 67
Tyndall's Pk. Rd. BS8: Clif 1D 67
Tyndalls Way BS10: S'mead 3A 42
Tyne Gro. BS20: P'head 5E 35
Tyne Path BS7: B'stn 4F 57
Tyne Rd. BS7: B'stn 3F 57
Tyne St. BS2: Bris 4C 58
Tyning, The BA2: Bath 5F 7 (5D 105)
Tyning Cl. BS14: H'gro 5C 78
 . . . BS37: Yate 3A 16
Tyning End BA2: Bath 5F 7 (5D 105)
Tyning La. BA1: Bath 1D 105
Tyning Pl. BA2: C Down 3E 111
Tyning Rd. BA2: B'ptn 5B 98
 . . . BA2: C Down 3E 111
 . . . BS3: Wind H 1B 78
 . . . BS31: Salt 5A 92
Tynings, The BS20: Wes 5B 48
Tyning's La. BS36: Wint 3E 11
Tyning Ter. BA1: Bath 1D 105
 . . . .(off Fairfield Rd.)
Tynte Av. BS13: Hart 4F 85

Tyntesfield Rd. BS13: Bis 5C 76
Tyrone Wlk. BS4: Know 4A 78
Tyrrel Way BS34: Stok G 3A 26

U

Ullswater Cl. BS30: Old C 3F 73
　BS37: Yate 2A 16
Ullswater Dr. BA1: Bath 5C 96
Ullswater Rd. BS10: S'mead 2D 41
Underbanks BS20: Pill 2F 53
Underdown Ho. BS1: Bris . . .5C 4 (4F 67)
Underwood Rd. BS20: P'head 3E 49
Unicorn Bus. Pk. BS4: Brisl 4F 69
Unicorn Pk. Av. BS4: Brisl 4E 69
Union Pas. BA1: Bath 3C 6 (4C 104)
Union Rd. BS2: Bris 3C 68
　(not continuous)
Union St. BA1: Bath 3C 6 (4C 104)
　BS1: Bris 1C 4 (2F 67)
Unite Ho. BS1: Bris 3A 4
Unity Ct. BS31: Key 2C 90
Unity Rd. BS31: Key 2C 90
　(not continuous)
Unity St. BS1: Bris 3A 4 (3E 67)
　BS2: Bris 2F 5 (2B 68)
　BS15: K'wd 1E 71
University Cl. BS9: Stok B 2B 56
University Hall BS9: Stok B 2B 56
University of Bath 5A 106
University of Bath Sports
　Training Village 5B 106
University of Bristol
　Cantock's Cl. 1A 4 (2E 67)
　Canynge Hall 1E 67
　　(off Whatley Rd.)
　Cobham House 1E 67
　Dorothy Hodgkin Building
　 . . . . .1C 4 (1F 67)
　Graduate School of Education
　 . . . . .2E 67
　Hampton House 1E 67
　Queen's Rd. 2A 4 (2E 67)
　School of Medical Sciences
　 . . . . .1E 67
　The Victoria Rooms 2D 67
　Woodland Rd. 1D 67
University of Bristol Botanic Garden
　 . . . . .2B 56
　　(off Hollybush La.)
University of Bristol Library 1A 4
University of the West of England
　Bower Ashton Campus 5F 65
　Frenchay Campus 3A 44
　Glenside Campus 1A 60
　St Matthias Campus 1C 60
University Rd. BS8: Clif . . .1A 4 (2E 67)
University Wlk. BS8: Clif . . .1A 4 (2E 67)
Uphill Dr. BA1: Bath 5D 97
Uphill Rd. BS7: Hor 1B 58
Upjohn Cres. BS13: Hart 4F 85
Uplands Dr. BS31: Salt 5B 92
Uplands Rd. BS16: Fish 3E 61
　BS31: Salt 5A 92
Up. Belgrave Rd. BS8: Clif 4C 56
Up. Belmont Rd. BS7: B'stn 3A 58
Up. Berkeley Pl. BS8: Clif 2D 67
Up. Bloomfield Rd. BA2: Odd D . . .5E 109
Up. Borough Walls
　BA1: Bath 3B 6 (4B 104)
Up. Bristol Rd.
　BA1: Bath 2A 6 (3E 103)
Up. Byron Pl. BS8: Clif 2D 67
Up. Camden Pl. BA1: Bath 2C 104
Up. Chapel La. BS36: Fram C 1E 29
Up. Cheltenham Pl. BS6: Bris 5A 58
Up. Church La. BS2: Bris . .2A 4 (2E 67)
Up. Church St.
　BA1: Bath 1A 6 (3B 104)

Up. Cranbrook Rd.
　BS6: Henle, Redl 2D 57
Up. East Hayes BA1: Bath 1D 105
UPPER EASTON 1D 69
UPPER EASTVILLE 3A 60
Up. Hedgemead Rd.
　BA1: Bath 2B 104
UPPER KNOWLE 1D 79
Up. Lambridge St. BA1: Bath 5E 97
Up. Lansdown M. BA1: Bath 1B 104
Up. Maudlin St. BS2: Bris . . .1B 4 (2F 67)
UPPER SOUNDWELL 3F 61
Up. Station Rd. BS16: Stap H 2E 61
Up. Stone Cl. BS36: Fram C 1E 29
Upper St. BS4: Wind H 5C 68
UPPER SWAINSWICK 2D 97
Up. Sydney St. BS3: Bedm 1D 77
Up. Wells St. BS1: Bris 2A 4 (2E 67)
UPPER WESTON 4D 95
Up. York St. BS2: Bris 1A 68
Upton La. BS41: Dun 5B 84
Upton Rd. BS3: Bris 5D 67
Urfords Dr. BS16: Fish 5E 45

V

Vale Foundry La. BS3: Ash V 2B 76
Vale La. BS3: Bedm 4E 77
Valentine Cl. BS14: H'gro 2D 87
Valerian Cl. BS11: Shire 5B 38
Vale St. BS4: Wind H 1C 78
Vale Vw. Pl. BA1: Bath 1D 105
Vale Vw. Ter. BA1: Bathe 4B 98
Valley Gdns. BS16: Down 3B 46
Valley Hgts. BS13: Bis 5C 76
Valley Rd. BS8: L Wds 2E 65
　BS13: Bis 4C 76
　BS16: Mang 1C 62
　BS20: P'head, Wes 3A 48
　BS30: Old C 3F 73
Valley Vw. Cl. BA1: Bath 5D 97
Valley Vw. Rd. BA1: Charl 4D 97
Valls, The BS32: Brad S 2B 26
Valma Rocks BS5: St G 3C 70
Vanbrugh La. BS16: Stap 4A 44
Van Diemen's La. BA1: L'dwn 5A 96
Vandyck Av. BS31: Key 1B 90
Vane St. BA2: Bath 2E 7 (3D 105)
Vantage Pk. BS32: Brad S 2C 26
Vassall Cl. BS16: Fish 1D 61
Vassall Rd. BS16: Fish 1D 61
Vaughan Cl. BS10: Hen 5B 22
Vauxhall Av. BS3: Bris 5C 66
Vauxhall Ter. BS3: Bris 5C 66
Vayre Cl. BS37: Chip S 4E 17
Vellore La. BA2: Bath 2F 7 (3D 105)
Ventnor Av. BS5: St G 1B 70
Ventnor Rd. BS5: S'will, St G 5B 60
　BS34: Fil 5D 25
Venton Cl. BS15: Han 4D 71
　　(off Henbury Rd.)
Venue, The BS10: Pat 2E 23
Vera Rd. BS16: Fish 4B 60
Verdigris BS2: Bris 2F 5
Vernham Gro. BA2: Odd D 4E 109
Vernhamwood Cl. BA2: Odd D 4E 109
Vernon Cl. BS31: Salt 4F 91
Vernon Pk. BA2: Bath 4E 103
Vernon St. BS4: Wind H 5B 68
Vernon Ter. BA2: Bath 4E 103
Vernslade BA1: W'ton 5C 94
Verona Ho. BS16: Fish 2D 61
Verrier Rd. BS5: Redf 2E 69
Verwood Dr. BS30: Bit 3E 83

Vibe BS2: Bris 2C 68
　　(off Waterloo Rd.)
Vicarage Ct. BS5: Redf 2E 69
　　(off Victoria Av.)
　BS15: Han 4D 71
Vicarage Rd. BS3: Bris 5D 67
　BS5: E'tn 1E 69
　BS8: L Wds 3F 65
　BS13: Bis 1B 84
　BS15: Han 4D 71
　BS36: Coal H 3E 29
Vicars Cl. BS16: Fish 2D 61
Victor Ho. BS34: Lit S 1E 25
Victoria Art Gallery 3C 6 (4C 104)
Victoria Av. BS5: Redf 2E 69
Victoria Bri. Ct. BA1: Bath 3A 104
　　(off Victoria Bri. Rd.)
Victoria Bri. Rd. BA1: Bath 4A 104
　BA2: Bath 4A 104
Victoria Bldgs. BA2: Bath 4F 103
Victoria Cl. BA2: Bath 5E 103
　BS20: P'head 1F 49
Victoria Cres. BS6: Redl 4C 56
　BS20: P'head 1F 49
Victoria Gdns. BA1: Bathe 4B 98
　BS6: Cot 5F 57
Victoria Gro. BS3: Bedm 5A 68
Victoria Ho. BA1: W'ton 2F 103
Victoria Pde. BS5: Redf 1E 69
VICTORIA PARK 1D 67
Victoria Pk. BS15: K'wd 1F 71
　BS16: Fish 1C 60
Victoria Pk. Bus. Cen.
　BA1: Bath 3F 103
Victoria Pk. Ct. BS3: Wind H 1B 78
　　(off St Johns La.)
Victoria Pl. BA1: Bath 1E 105
　　(off St Saviours Rd.)
　BA2: C Down 4E 111
　BS3: Bedm 5E 67
　BS5: St G 2F 69
　　(off Pilemarsh)
Victoria Rd. BA2: Bath 4F 103
　BS2: Bris 4C 68
　　(not continuous)
　BS11: A'mth 3D 37
　BS15: Han 4E 71
　BS30: Old C 4E 73
　BS31: Salt 4F 91
Victoria Sq. BS8: Clif 2C 66
　BS20: P'head 1F 49
Victoria St. BS1: Bris 3D 5 (3A 68)
　BS16: Stap H 2F 61
Victoria Ter. BA2: Bath 4F 103
　BS2: Bris 4D 69
　BS8: Clif 3B 66
Victoria Wlk. BS6: Bris, Cot 5F 57
Victor Rd. BS3: Bedm 1E 77
Victor St. BS2: Bris 5C 68
　BS5: Bar H 3D 69
Vigor Rd. BS13: Hart 2D 85
VILLA FIELDS 2D 105
Village, The BS16: Emer G 4E 47
Village Cl. BS37: Yate 4F 15
Villiers Rd. BS5: E'tn 5D 59
Vimpany Cl. BS10: Hen 5B 22
Vincent Cl. BS11: Law W 1E 39
Vincent Ct. BS16: Soun 3F 61
Vine Acres BS7: Hor 1C 58
Vineyards BA1: Bath 1C 6 (3C 104)
Vining Wlk. BS5: E'tn 1D 69
Vinny Av. BS16: Down 4C 46
VINNY GREEN 4C 46
Vintery Leys BS10: W Trym 4D 41
Virginia Cl. BS37: Chip S 4C 16
Vivian St. BS3: Wind H 1F 77
Vivian Cl. BS13: Withy 3D 85
Voyager Cl. BS34: Stok G 4C 26
Vue Cinema
　Cribbs Causeway 2E 23
　Kingswood 4A 72

Vulcan Ho. BA2: Bath 1D **7** (3C **104**)
Vyvyan Rd. BS8: Clif 2C **66**
Vyvyan Ter. BS8: Clif 2C **66**

W

Wadehurst Ind. Pk. BS2: Bris 2C **68**
Wade Rd. BS37: Iron A 2C **14**
Wades Rd. BS34: Fil 5D **25**
Wade St. BS2: Bris 1F **5** (1B **68**)
Wadham Dr. BS16: Fren 2D **45**
Wadham Gro. BS16: Emer G 1D **63**
Wainbrook Dr. BS5: Eastv 4F **59**
Wakeford Rd. BS16: Down 4C **46**
Wakeford Way BS30: B'yte 2F **73**
Walcot Bldgs. BA1: Bath 2C **104**
Walcot Ct. BA1: Bath 2C **104**
Walcot Ga. BA1: Bath 1C **6** (2C **104**)
Walcot Ho. BA1: Bath 2C **104**
Walcot Pde. BA1: Bath 2C **104**
(off London Rd.)
Walcot St. BA1: Bath 2C **6** (3C **104**)
Walcot Ter. BA1: Bath 2C **104**
Waldegrave Rd. BA1: Bath 1A **104**
Walden Rd. BS31: Key 3C **90**
Walker Cl. BS5: E'tn 1D **69**
BS16: Down 4C **46**
BS37: Yate 4D **15**
Walker St. BS2: Bris 1E **67**
Wallace Rd. BA1: Bath 1D **105**
Wallcroft Ho. BS6: Redl 3C **56**
Wallingford Rd. BS4: Know 5F **77**
Walliscote Av. BS9: Henle 5E **41**
Walliscote Rd. BS9: Henle 5E **41**
Wallis Est. BS2: Bris 3B **58**
Wallscourt Rd. BS34: Fil 1D **43**
Wallscourt Rd. Sth. BS34: Fil 2D **43**
Walmsley Ter. BA1: Bath 1D **105**
(off Snow Hill)
Walnut Av. BS37: Yate 3C **16**
Walnut Cl. BS15: K'wd 5B **62**
(not continuous)
BS20: Eas 3C **52**
BS31: Key 3E **89**
BS36: Coal H 2E **29**
Walnut Cres. BS15: K'wd 1B **72**
Walnut Dr. BA2: Bath 1A **110**
Walnut La. BS15: K'wd 1C **72**
Walnut Wlk. BS13: Bis 1C **84**
BS31: Key 3E **89**
Walsh Av. BS14: H'gro 5C **78**
Walshe Av. BS37: Chip S 4E **17**
Walsingham Rd. BS6: Bris 4A **58**
Walter St. BS3: Bris 5C **66**
Waltining La. BA2: New L 4F **101**
Walton Av. BS4: St Ap 4F **69**
Walton Cl. BS30: Bit 3E **83**
BS31: Key 3F **89**
Walton Heath BS37: Yate 4B **16**
Walton Ri. BS9: W Trym 3C **40**
Walton Rd. BS11: Shire 5F **37**
Walton St. BS5: E'tn 5D **59**
Walwyn Cl. BA2: Bath 4C **102**
Walwyn Gdns. BS13: Hart 4F **85**
Wansbeck Rd. BS31: Key 3C **90**
Wanscow Wlk. BS9: Henle 5D **41**
Wansdyke Bus. Cen. BA2: Bath ...1F **109**
Wansdyke Ct. BS14: Whit 2D **87**
Wansdyke Rd. BA2: Odd D 4E **109**
Wansdyke Workshops BS31: Key ...1C **90**
WAPLEY 4A **32**
Wapley Bushes Local Nature Reserve
...........................2A **32**
Wapley Hill BS37: W'lgh 3A **32**
Wapley Rank BS37: W'lgh 3F **31**
Wapley Rd. BS37: Cod, W'lgh ...5B **32**
Wapping Rd. BS1: Bris 5B **4** (4F **67**)
Warden Rd. BS3: Bedm 5E **67**
Wardour Rd. BS4: Know 4F **77**
Ware Ct. BS36: Wint 3F **27**

Waring Ho. BS1: Bris 4F **67**
WARLEIGH 5E **107**
Warleigh Dr. BA1: Bathe 4C **98**
Warleigh La. BA1: Warl 2D **107**
Warman Cl. BS14: Stoc 1B **88**
Warman Rd. BS14: Stoc 1B **88**
Warmington Rd. BS14: H'gro 4E **79**
Warminster Rd.
BA2: Bath, B'ptn, C'ton
...........................1F **7** (2E **105**)
BS2: Bris 4C **58**
WARMLEY 1D **73**
WARMLEY HILL 1B **72**
Warner Cl. BS15: K'wd 3B **72**
Warns, The BS30: C Hth 5C **72**
Warren Cl. BS32: Brad S 2F **9**
Warren Gdns. BS14: Stoc 2B **88**
Warren La. BS41: L Ash 3A **74**
Warren Rd. BS34: Fil 5D **25**
Warren Way BS37: Yate 2A **16**
Warrington Rd. BS4: Brisl 2F **79**
Warwick Av. BS5: E'tn 5D **59**
Warwick Cl. BS30: Will 2D **83**
Warwick Rd. BA1: Bath 3D **103**
BS5: E'tn 5D **59**
BS6: Redl 5D **57**
BS31: Key 3F **89**
Warwick Vs. BA2: Bath 5E **103**
Washingpool La. BS11: Chit 1A **20**
Washing Pound La. BS14: Whit ...3D **87**
Washpool La. BS5: E'tn 5E **59**
Washpool La. BA2: Eng 3B **108**
Watch Elm Cl. BS32: Brad S 2A **26**
Watch Ho. Pl. BS20: P'head 4D **35**
Watch Ho. Rd. BS20: Pill 2F **53**
Watchill Av. BS13: Bis 1B **84**
Watchill Cl. BS13: Bis 1B **84**
Waterbridge Rd. BS13: Withy 2B **84**
Watercress Rd. BS2: Bris 3B **58**
Waterdale Cl. BS9: Henle 4E **41**
Waterdale Gdns. BS9: Henle 4E **41**
Waterford Rd. BS9: Henle 5D **41**
Waterhouse La. BA2: Lim S 5F **111**
Water La. BS1: Bris 3E **5** (3A **68**)
BS3: Wind H 1B **78**
BS4: Brisl 3F **79**
(not continuous)
BS20: Pill 2E **53**
Waterloo Bldgs. BA2: Bath 4D **103**
(not continuous)
Waterloo Ho's. BS20: Pill 1E **53**
(off Underbanks)
Waterloo Pl. BS2: Bris 2C **68**
Waterloo Rd. BS2: Bris 2B **68**
Waterloo St. BS2: Bris 2B **68**
BS8: Clif 2B **66**
Watermead Cl. BA1: Bath 4A **6**
(off Kingsmead W.)
Watermore Cl. BS36: Fram C 1C **29**
Watermore Gdns. BS36: Fram C ...5F **13**
Waters Edge BS20: P'head 1E **35**
Watershed Media Cen. 4B **4** (3F **67**)
Waterside Cl. BA2: Bath 4E **103**
Waterside Dr. BS32: Alm 4C **8**
BS34: Pat 4C **8**
Waterside Pk. BS20: P'head 2A **48**
Water's La. BS9: W Trym 4C **40**
Waters Rd. BS15: K'wd 1E **71**
Waters Rd. Bus. Pk. BS15: K'wd ...1E **71**
Watery La. BA2: Bath 4C **102**
BS37: Yate 1E **15**
Wathen Rd. BS6: Bris 3B **58**
Wathen St. BS16: Stap H 1F **61**
Watkins Yd. BS9: W Trym 3C **40**
Watley's End Rd. BS36: Wint 1A **28**
Watling Way BS11: Shire 4E **37**
Watson Av. BS4: Brisl 5F **69**
(not continuous)
Watson's Rd. BS30: L Grn 1B **82**
Watters Cl. BS36: Coal H 2F **29**

Watts La. BS15: K'wd 5A **62**
Wavell Cl. BS37: Yate 2F **15**
Waveney Rd. BS31: Key 4C **90**
Waverley Ho. BS1: Bris 5A **4**
Waverley Rd. BS6: Cot 5E **57**
BS11: Shire 5A **38**
BS37: Yate 3D **15**
Waverley St. BS5: E'tn 5C **58**
Wayfield Gdns. BA1: Bathe 3B **98**
Wayford Cl. BS31: Key 4C **90**
Wayland Ct. BS16: Fish 2C **60**
(off Guinea La.)
Wayleaze BS36: Coal H 1F **29**
Wayside Cl. BS36: Fram C 1D **29**
Weal, The BA1: W'ton 5D **95**
Weare Ct. BS1: Bris 4C **66**
Weatherley Dr. BS20: P'head 3B **48**
Weatherly Av. BA2: Odd D 3F **109**
WEBBS HEATH 1F **73**
Webbs Heath BS30: W Hth 5F **63**
Webb St. BS5: E'tn 1C **68**
Webbs Wood Rd. BS32: Brad S ...2B **26**
Wedgewood Rd. BS16: Down 2F **45**
Wedgwood Cl. BS14: Whit 2D **87**
Wedgwood Rd. BA2: Bath 5B **102**
Wedlock Way BS3: Ash G 1B **76**
Wedmore Cl. BA2: Bath 2C **108**
BS15: K'wd 2B **72**
Wedmore Pk. BA2: Bath 2C **108**
Wedmore Pl. BS3: Know 2A **78**
Wedmore Rd. BS31: Salt 3F **91**
Wedmore Va.
BS3: Know, Wind H 2A **78**
Weedon Cl. BS2: Bris 4C **58**
Weight Rd. BS5: Redf 2E **69**
Weir La. BS8: Fail 3A **64**
Welland Rd. BS31: Key 3B **90**
Well Cl. BS41: L Ash 3D **75**
Wellesley M. BS10: W Trym 3E **41**
Wellgarth Ct. BS4: Know 2C **78**
Wellgarth Rd. BS4: Know 2C **78**
Wellgarth Wlk. BS4: Know 2C **78**
Well Ho. Cl. BS9: Stok B 4A **56**
Wellington Av. BS6: Bris 5A **58**
Wellington Bldgs. BA1: W'ton ...5D **95**
Wellington Cres. BS7: Hor 5A **42**
Wellington Dr. BS9: Henle 5F **41**
BS37: Yate 3D **15**
Wellington Hill BS7: Hor 5A **42**
Wellington Hill W. BS9: Henle 4E **41**
Wellington La. BS6: Bris 5A **58**
Wellington M. BS11: Shire 1F **53**
Wellington Pk. BS8: Clif 5C **56**
Wellington Pl. BS16: Fren 2D **45**
Wellington Rd. BS2: Bris 1B **68**
BS15: K'wd 4F **61**
BS37: Yate 1A **16**
Wellington Ter. BS8: Clif 3B **66**
Wellington Wlk. BS10: W Trym ...4E **41**
Wells Cl. BS14: Whit 2E **87**
Wells Rd. BA2: Bath 5A **6** (5A **104**)
BA2: Cor, New L 4A **100**
BS4: Know, Wind H 5B **68**
BS14: H'gro, Whit 4D **79**
BS41: Dun 5B **84**
Wells St. BS3: Ash G 5C **66**
Wellstead Av. BS37: Yate 4F **15**
Wellsway BA2: Bath, Odd D 5F **109**
BS31: Key 2B **90**
Wellsway Cl. BA2: Odd D 4F **109**
Wellsway Pk. BA2: Odd D 5F **109**
Welsford Av. BS16: Stap 2F **59**
Welsford Rd. BS16: Stap 2E **59**
Welsh Bk. BS1: Bris 4C **4** (3F **67**)
Welsh Back Squash and Health Club
...........................4C **4** (3F **67**)
Welton Wlk. BS15: K'wd 4E **61**
Wenmore Cl. BS16: Down 2F **45**
Wentforth Dr. BS15: K'wd 4E **61**
Wentworth BS30: Warm 3C **72**
BS37: Yate 4A **16**

Wentworth Rd. BS7: B'stn 3F 57
Wescott Gro. BS11: Law W 1E 39
Wesley Av. BS15: Han 4F 71
Wesley Cl. BS5: W'hall 5F 59
   BS16: Soun 3F 61
Wesley Hill BS15: K'wd 5F 61
Wesley La. BS30: C Hth 4D 73
Wesley Pl. BS8: Clif 4C 56
Wesley Rd. BS7: B'stn 2A 58
Wesley St. BS3: Bedm 1E 77
Wessex Av. BS7: Hor 4B 42
Wessex Ct. BS7: Hor 4B 42
Wessex Ho. BS2: Bris 3E 5 (3A 68)
               (Cheese La.)
  BS2: Bris 2B 68
         (off Lawfords Ga.)
Westacre Cl. BS10: Hen 1C 40
West Av. BA2: Bath 5E 103
West Bath Riverside Path 4D 103
Westbourne Av. BS31: Key 2A 90
Westbourne Gro. BS3: Bedm 1E 77
Westbourne Ho.
  BA2: Bath 4D 7 (4C 104)
Westbourne Pl. BS8: Clif 2D 67
Westbourne Rd. BS5: E'tn 1D 69
  BS16: Down 3B 46
Westbourne Ter. BS16: Fren 4D 45
West Broadway BS9: Henle 5F 41
Westbrooke Ct. BS1: Bris 4C 66
Westbrook Pk. BA1: W'ton 5C 94
Westbrook Rd. BS4: Brisl 4F 79
Westbury College Gatehouse . . .4C 40
Westbury Ct. BS9: W Trym 4C 40
Westbury Ct. Rd. BS9: W Trym . . .4B 40
Westbury Hill BS9: W Trym 4C 40
Westbury La. BS9: Sea M 4D 39
Westbury M. BS9: W Trym 4C 40
      (off Westbury Hill)
WESTBURY-ON-TRYM 4C 40
WESTBURY PARK 2C 56
Westbury Rd. BS6: Henle 2C 56
  BS9: W Trym 2C 56
West Cl. BA2: Bath 5C 102
West Coombe BS9: Stok B 5F 39
West Cotts. BA2: C Down 4E 111
West Country Water Pk. 3B 10
Westcourt Dr. BS30: Old C 5D 73
West Cft. BS9: Henle 4E 41
West Dene BS9: Stok B 5A 40
W. Dundry La. BS41: Dun 5A 84
West End BS2: Bris 1F 67
  BS3: Bris 4E 67
Westering Cl. BS16: Mang 1C 62
WESTERLEIGH 4D 31
Westerleigh Bus. Pk.
  BS37: Yate 5D 15
Westerleigh Cl. BS16: Mang 4B 46
Westerleigh Hill BS37: W'lgh 5E 31
Westerleigh Rd. BA2: C Down . . .4D 111
  BS16: Down 5A 46
  BS36: H'fld 2D 47
  BS37: W'lgh 2D 31
  BS37: Yate 1E 31
Western Av. BS36: Fram C 4C 12
Western Ct. BS34: Stok G 4C 26
Western Dr. BS14: H'gro 5A 78
Western Rd. BS7: Hor 5A 42
Westfield Cl. BA2: Bath 2A 110
  BS15: Han 4F 71
  BS31: Key 2E 89
Westfield La. BS34: Stok G 5A 26
Westfield Pk. BA1: Bath 3C 102
  BS6: Redl 5D 57
Westfield Pk. Sth. BA1: Bath . . .3C 102
Westfield Pl. BS8: Clif 2B 66
Westfield Rd. BS9: W Trym 3C 40
Westfield Way BS32: Brad S 3F 9
Westgate BS1: Bris 4D 67
Westgate Bldgs.
  BA1: Bath 3B 6 (4B 104)

Westgate St. BA1: Bath . . .3B 6 (4B 104)
West Gro. BS6: Bris 5B 58
Westhall Rd. BA1: Bath 3F 103
WEST HILL 1D 49
West Hill BS20: P'head 1D 49
W. Hill Ct. BS20: P'head 5B 34
W. Hill Gdns. BS20: P'head 1E 49
Westland Av. BS30: Old C 5E 73
W. Lea Rd. BA1: Bath 2C 102
W. Leaze Pl. BS32: Brad S 2A 26
Westleigh Cl. BS10: S'mead 2F 41
  BS37: Yate 4E 15
Westleigh Ct. BS37: Yate 4E 15
Westleigh Pk. BS14: H'gro 4C 78
Westleigh Rd. BS10: S'mead 2E 41
West Mall BS8: Clif 2B 66
Westmead Gdns. BA1: W'ton 5C 94
Westmead Rd. BS5: St G 2D 71
Westminstere Ct. BS9: W Trym . . .4C 40
Westminster Rd. BS5: W'hall 1F 69
Westmoreland Dr. BA2: Bath 4A 104
Westmoreland Rd.
  BA2: Bath 5A 6 (5A 104)
  BS6: Redl 3D 57
Westmoreland Sta. Rd.
  BA2: Bath 5A 6 (5A 104)
Westmoreland St. BA2: Bath 5A 104
Westmorland Ho. BS6: Redl 3C 56
WESTON 1D 103
Weston Av. BS5: St G 2F 69
Weston Big Wood Nature Reserve
                  . . . .4C 48
Weston Cl. BS9: Sea M 4E 39
Weston Cres. BS7: Hor 5A 42
Weston Drove BS20: Wes 5B 48
Weston Farm La. BA1: W'ton 5D 95
Westonian Ct. BS9: Stok B 2E 55
WESTON IN GORDANO 5B 48
Weston La. BA1: W'ton 1E 103
Weston Lock Retail BA2: Bath . . .4D 103
WESTON PARK 1E 103
Weston Pk. BA1: W'ton 1E 103
Weston Pk. Ct. BA1: W'ton 1F 103
Weston Pk. E. BA1: W'ton 2E 103
Weston Pk. W. BA1: W'ton 1E 103
Weston Rd. BA1: Bath, W'ton 2F 103
  BS41: L Ash 4A 74
  BS48: Flax B 4A 74
Westons Brake BS16: Emer G 2C 46
Westons Hill Dr. BS16: Emer G . . .3C 46
Westons Way BS15: K'wd 3B 72
Weston Wood Rd. BS20: P'head . .3E 49
Westover Cl. BS9: W Trym 2B 40
Westover Dr. BS9: W Trym 3C 40
Westover Gdns. BS9: W Trym 3B 40
Westover Ri. BS9: W Trym 2C 40
Westover Rd. BS9: W Trym 2B 40
West Pde. BS9: Sea M 4E 39
West Pk. BS8: Clif 1D 67
West Pk. Rd. BS16: Stap H 1A 62
W. Point Row BS32: Brad S 2E 9
Westpoint Trad. Est.
  BS15: K'wd 2F 71
W. Priory Cl. BS9: W Trym 4C 40
West Ridge BS36: Fram C 1E 29
W. Rocke Av. BS9: Stok B 4F 39
West Shrubbery BS6: Redl 4D 57
West St. BS2: Bris 2F 5 (2B 68)
  BS3: Bedm 2D 77
  BS15: K'wd 1F 71
  BS30: Old C 5E 73
W. Town Av. BS4: Brisl 3F 79
W. Town Ct. BS4: Brisl 2A 80
W. Town Dr. BS4: Brisl 3F 79
W. Town Gro. BS4: Brisl 4F 79
W. Town La. BS4: Brisl 4E 79
  BS14: H'gro 4E 79
W. Town Pk. BS4: Brisl 3F 79
W. Town Rd. BS11: A'mth, Shire . . .4E 37
        (not continuous)
West Vw. BS16: Mang 5C 46

West Vw. Rd. BA1: Bathe 4C 98
  BS3: Bedm 1D 77
  BS31: Key 2A 90
West Wlk. BS37: Yate 4A 16
Westward Dr. BS20: Pill 2E 53
Westward Gdns. BS41: L Ash 2D 75
Westward Rd. BS13: Bis 5B 76
West Way BS10: Bren 4F 23
  BS34: Bren 4F 23
Westwood BA2: Clav D 4A 106
Westwood Cres. BS4: St Ap 4B 80
Westwood Rd. BS4: Brisl 4F 79
Westwoods BA1: Bathf 4D 99
Westwood Vw. BA2: Odd D 4E 109
Wetherby Cl. BS16: Down 2B 46
Wetherby Gro. BS16: Down 2B 46
Wetherell Pl. BS8: Clif 2D 67
Wetlands La. BS20: P'head 3E 49
Wexford Rd. BS4: Know 4F 77
Weymouth Ct. BA1: Bath 2D 105
       (off Weymouth St.)
Weymouth Rd. BS3: Wind H 2F 77
Weymouth St. BA1: Bath 2D 105
Wharf La. BS20: P'bry 5F 35
Wharf Rd. BS16: Fish 2B 60
Wharnecliffe Cl. BS14: H'gro 2D 87
Wharnecliffe Gdns. BS14: H'gro . .2D 87
Whartons BS4: Brisl 3F 79
Whatley Ct. BS8: Clif 5D 57
Whatley Rd. BS8: Clif 5D 57
Wheatfield Dr. BS32: Brad S 4F 9
Wheathill Cl. BS31: Key 2E 89
Wheelers Patch BS16: Emer G . . .1D 63
Whimbrel Av. BS20: P'head 5E 35
Whinchat Gdns. BS16: B'hll 5B 44
Whippington Ct.
  BS1: Bris 1D 5 (2A 68)
Whistle Rd. BS16: Sis 4D 63
Whitby Rd. BS4: Brisl, St Ap 5E 69
        (not continuous)
WHITCHURCH 3E 87
Whitchurch District Cen.
  BS14: Whit 2C 86
Whitchurch La. BS13: Bis 1C 84
        (not continuous)
  BS13: Hart 2E 85
  BS14: Hart, Whit 2F 85
Whitchurch Rd. BS13: Bis 1C 84
Whitchurch Sports Cen. 2B 86
Whitebeam Ct. BS5: St G 1A 70
Whitebeam Ho. BS16: Fish 5E 45
Whitecroft Way BS15: K'wd 2C 72
Whitecross Av. BS14: H'gro 1E 87
Whitefield Av. BS5: S'wll 5C 60
  BS15: Han 4F 71
Whitefield Cl. BA1: Bathe 3D 99
Whitefield Rd. BS5: S'wll 5B 60
Whitefields BS37: Chip S 4E 17
Whitefriars BS1: Bris 1B 4 (2F 67)
WHITEHALL 5F 59
Whitehall Av. BS5: W'hall 5A 60
Whitehall Gdns. BS5: W'hall 5F 59
Whitehall Rd. BS5: E'tn, W'hall . . .1D 69
Whitehall Trad. Est. BS5: Redf 1E 69
White Hart Steps BS8: Clif 3D 67
Whitehaven BA1: Bathf 5E 99
Whitehouse La. BS3: Bedm 1F 77
Whitehouse Pl. BS3: Bedm 5A 68
Whitehouse St. BS3: Bedm 5A 68
Whiteladies Ga. BS8: Clif 5D 57
Whiteladies Rd. BS8: Clif 5D 57
Whiteleaze BS10: W Trym 3E 41
White Lodge Pk. BS20: P'head . . .5C 34
White Lodge Rd. BS16: Stap H . . .2B 62
Whitemead Ho. BS3: Ash G 1C 76
Whitemore Ct. BA1: Bathe 3C 98
WHITE'S HILL 3C 70
WHITESHILL 5F 27
White's Hill BS5: St G 3C 70
Whiteshill BS16: Ham 5F 27
Whiteshill Ho. BS16: Ham 5E 27

White St. BS5: E'tn 1B 68
Whitethorn Va. BS10: Bren 5E 23
White Tree Rd. BS9: Henle 2D 57
WHITEWAY
   BA2 .5B 102
   BS5 . . . . .1C 70
Whiteway Cl. BS4: St Ap 3A 70
   BS5: St G 1C 70
Whiteway Cl. BS5: St G 1C 70
Whiteway M. BS5: St G 1C 70
Whiteway Rd. BA2: Bath 5A 102
   BS5: S'wll, St G 1B 70
WHITE WELLS 5D 97
Whitewells Rd. BA1: Bath 5C 96
Whitewood Rd. BS5: S'wll 5B 60
Whitfield Cl. BS16: Soun 3F 61
Whiting Rd. BS13: Withy 3C 84
Whitland Av. BS13: Hart 2D 85
Whitland Rd. BS13: Hart 2D 85
Whitley Cl. BS37: Yate 2E 15
Whitley Mead BS34: Stok G 5A 26
Whitmead Gdns. BS13: Hart 3E 85
Whitmore Av. BS4: Brisl 1C 80
Whitson Ho. BS2: Bris 1F 5
Whitson St. BS1: Bris 1C 4 (1F 67)
Whittington Rd. BS16: Fish 5E 45
Whittock Rd. BS14: Stoc 2F 87
Whittock Sq. BS14: Stoc 5F 79
Whittucks Cl. BS15: Han 5F 71
Whittucks Rd. BS15: Han 1E 81
Whitwell Rd. BS14: H'gro 4D 79
Wholesale Fruit Cen. BS2: Bris . . .5C 68
Whytes Cl. BS9: W Trym 3C 40
Wick Cres. BS4: Brisl 1F 79
Wicket, The BS5: St G 1F 69
Wickets, The BS15: K'wd 4F 61
Wicketts, The BS7: Fil 2B 42
Wickham Cl. BS37: Chip S 5F 17
Wickham Ct. BS16: Stap 1A 60
Wickham Glen BS16: Stap 1F 59
Wickham Hill BS16: Stap 1F 59
Wickham Theatre 2A 4 (2E 67)
Wickham Vw. BS16: Stap 2F 59
Wick Ho. Cl. BS31: Salt 4F 91
Wicklow Rd. BS4: Know 4A 78
Wickwar Rd. BS37: Chip S, Yate . . .1C 16
Wick Wick Cl. BS16: Emer G 1C 46
WIDCOMBE 5E 7 (5D 105)
Widcombe BS14: H'gro 1C 86
Widcombe Cl. BS5: St G 2C 70
Widcombe Cres. BA2: Bath 5D 105
Widcombe Hill
   BA2: Bath, Clav D . .5E 7 (5D 105)
Widcombe Manor 1D 111
Widcombe Pde. BA2: Bath 5D 7
Widcombe Ri. BA2: Bath 5D 105
Widcombe Ter. BA2: Bath 1D 111
Widmore Gro. BS13: Hart 2D 85
Wight Row BS20: P'head 5E 35
Wigton Cres. BS10: S'mead 2E 41
Wilbye Gro. BS4: Know 5F 77
Wilcox Cl. BS15: K'wd 3E 71
Wild Country La. BS41: L Ash 4A 74
   BS48: Bar G 4A 74
Wildcroft Ho. BS9: Henle 1D 57
Wildcroft Rd. BS9: Henle 1D 57
Wilder Ct. BS2: Bris 1A 68
Wilder St. BS2: Bris 1A 68
Willada Cl. BS3: Bedm 2D 77
Willcock Ho. BS30: Old C 4F 73
William Mason Cl. BS5: Bar H 2D 69
Williams Cl. BS30: L Grn 1B 82
Williamson Rd. BS7: Bris 3B 58
Williamstowe BA2: C Down 4E 111
William St. BA2: Bath 2D 7 (3C 104)
   BS2: Bris 5B 58
                                   (Carr Ho.)
   BS2: Bris 5B 58
                               (Princess St.)
   BS3: Bedm 5A 68

William St. BS3: Wind H 5B 68
   BS5: Redf 1E 69
   BS16: Fish 3D 61
Willinton Rd. BS4: Know 5B 78
Willis Rd. BS15: Soun 4B 62
Willment Way BS11: A'mth 2F 37
Willmott Cl. BS14: Whit 4B 86
Willoughby Cl. BS13: Bis 5C 76
Willoughby Rd. BS7: Hor 1A 58
Willowbank BS10: W Trym 4E 41
Willow Bed Cl. BS16: Fish 5D 45
Willow Cl. BA2: Odd D 5F 109
   BS20: P'head 2E 49
   BS30: Old C 3F 73
   BS34: Pat 1A 24
   BS41: L Ash 3B 74
Willow Falls, The BA1: Bathe 4A 98
Willow Grn. BA2: Bath 1A 110
Willow Gro. BS16: Fish 4E 61
Willow Ho. BS13: Hart 3F 85
Willow Rd. BS15: Han 1E 81
Willows, The BS16: Fren 2D 45
   BS31: Key 1A 90
   BS32: Brad S 5F 9
   BS37: Yate 3F 15
Willow Shop. Cen., The
   BS16: Down 5F 45
Willow Wlk. BS10: Bren 5D 23
   BS31: Key 3F 89
Willow Way BS36: Coal H 2E 29
WILLSBRIDGE 2C 82
Willsbridge Hill BS30: Will 2C 82
Willsbridge Ho. BS30: Will 2C 82
Willsbridge Mill Countryside Cen.
   . . . . .2C 82
Willsbridge Valley Nature Reserve
   . . . . .2D 83
Wills Dr. BS5: E'tn 1C 68
Wills Hall BS9: Stok B 2B 56
Wills Way BS13: Bis 1F 85
Willway St. BS2: Bris 2F 5 (2B 68)
   BS3: Bedm 5F 67
Wilmot Cl. BS30: C Hth 3C 72
Wilmots Way BS20: Pill 2F 53
Wilshire Av. BS15: Han 4F 71
Wilson Av. BS2: Bris 1B 68
Wilson Pl. BS2: Bris 1B 68
Wilson St. BS2: Bris 1B 68
Wiltshire Cl. BS10: S'mead 3E 41
Wiltshire Av. BS37: Yate 2C 16
Wiltshire Pl. BS15: Soun 3A 62
Wiltshire Way BA1: Bath 5C 96
Wilverley Ind. Est.
   BS4: Brisl 3B 80
Wimbledon Rd. BS6: Henle 1E 57
Wimborne Rd. BS3: Bedm 3E 77
Winash Cl. BS14: Stoc 5F 79
Wincanton Cl. BS16: Down 2B 46
Winchcombe Gro. BS11: Shire 1B 54
Winchcombe Rd. BS36: Fram C . . .5D 13
Winchcombe Trad. Est.
   BS2: Bris 5C 68
Winchester Av. BS4: Brisl 1F 79
Winchester Rd. BA2: Bath 5F 103
   BS4: Brisl 1F 79
Wincroft BS30: Old C 5E 73
                             (not continuous)
Windcliff Cres. BS11: Law W 3A 38
Windermere Rd. BS10: S'mead 1F 41
Windermere Rd. BS34: Pat 5C 8
Windermere Way BS30: Old C 3F 73
Windmill Farm Bus. Cen.
   BS3: Bedm 5F 67
WINDMILL HILL 1A 78
Windmill Hill BS3: Wind H 1F 77
Windmill Hill City Farm 5F 67
Windmill La. BS10: Hen 5F 21
Windrush Cl. BA2: Bath 1B 108
Windrush Grn. BS31: Key 3C 90
Windrush Rd. BS31: Key 3C 90

Windsor Av. BS5: St G 3D 71
   BS31: Key 3A 90
Windsor Bri. Rd. BA1: Bath 4F 103
   BA2: Bath 4F 103
Windsor Castle BA1: Bath 3F 103
                       (off Up. Bristol Rd.)
Windsor Cl. BS34: Stok G 3A 26
Windsor Ct. BA1: Bath 3F 103
   BS8: Clif 3B 66
   BS16: Down 4A 46
Windsor Cres. BS10: H'len 4E 21
Windsor Dr. BS37: Yate 3F 15
Windsor Gro. BS5: E'tn 1D 69
Windsor Pl. BA1: Bath 3E 103
   BS8: Clif 3B 66
   BS16: Mang 1C 62
Windsor Rd. BS6: Bris 4A 58
   BS30: L Grn 2B 82
Windsor Ter. BS3: Wind H 5B 68
   BS8: Clif 3B 66
Windsor Vs. BA1: Bath 3E 103
Wineberry Cl. BS5: W'hall 5F 59
Wine St. BA1: Bath 4C 6 (4C 104)
   BS1: Bris 2C 4 (2F 67)
Winfield Rd. BS30: Warm 2E 73
Winford Cl. BS20: P'head 2A 50
Winford Gro. BS13: Bis 4C 76
Winford Rd. BS31: Know 2A 78
Winifred's La. BA1: Bath 1A 104
Winkworth Ho. BS1: Bris 4A 4
Winkworth Pl. BS2: Bris 5B 58
Winsbury Way BS32: Brad S 5E 9
Winscombe Cl. BS31: Key 1F 89
Winsford St. BS5: E'tn 1C 68
Winsham Cl. BS14: Whit 2D 87
Winsley Rd. BS6: Cot 5F 57
Winstone Ct. BS2: Bris 1A 4
                     (off St Michael's Hill)
WINTERBOURNE 2F 27
WINTERBOURNE DOWN 4A 28
Winterbourne Hill BS36: Wint 3F 27
Winterbourne Rd. BS32: Brad S . . .3C 26
   BS34: Stok G 2A 26
Winterstoke Cl. BS3: Bedm 2D 77
Winterstoke Ho. BS3: Ash G 1C 76
Winterstoke Rd.
   BS3: Ash V, Bedm 1B 76
Winterstoke Underpass
   BS3: Bwr A 5B 66
Winter Wlk. BS14: H'gro 1E 87
Winton St. BS4: Wind H 5B 68
Wiseman Apartments BS8: Clif 1B 66
Wisemans Ho. BS8: Clif 1C 66
Wisteria Av. BS37: Chip S 4C 16
Witchell Rd. BS5: Redf 2E 69
Witch Hazel Rd. BS13: Hart 4A 86
Witcombe BS37: Yate 1E 31
Witcombe Cl. BS15: K'wd 5A 62
Witham Rd. BS31: Key 4C 90
Withey Cl. E. BS9: W Trym 5B 40
Withey Cl. W. BS9: W Trym 1A 56
Witheys, The BS14: Whit 3E 87
Withington Cl. BS30: Bit 2E 83
Withleigh Rd. BS4: Know 2D 79
Withypool Gdns. BS14: Whit 2D 87
Withys, The BS20: Pill 2F 53
WITHYWOOD 3B 84
Withywood Gdns. BS13: Withy 2B 84
Withywood Rd. BS13: Withy 3B 84
Witney Cl. BS31: Salt 4F 91
Witney Mead BS36: Fram C 5D 13
Woburn Cl. BS30: Bar C 4B 72
Woburn Rd. BS5: Eastv 3D 59
Wolferton Rd. BS7: Bris 4B 58
Wolfridge Gdns. BS10: Bren 4C 22
Wolseley Rd. BS7: B'stn 3F 57
Woodacre BS20: P'head 4D 35
Woodbine Rd. BS5: W'hall 1F 69
Woodborough St. BS5: E'tn 5D 59
Woodbridge Rd. BS4: Know 2C 78
Woodbury La. BS8: Clif 4C 56

Woodchester BS15: Soun 3A **62**
  BS37: Yate 1A **32**
Woodchester Rd. BS10: W Trym ..4E **41**
Woodcote Rd. BS15: Han 3F **71**
Woodcote Rd. BS16: Fish 3D **61**
Woodcote Wlk. BS16: Fish 4D **61**
Woodcroft Av. BS5: W'hall 5F **59**
Woodcroft Cl. BS4: Brisl 5A **70**
Woodcroft Rd. BS4: Brisl 5A **70**
Woodend BS15: K'wd 3F **71**
Woodend Rd.
  BS36: Coal H, Fram C 1D **29**
Wood End Wlk. BS9: Sea M 5E **39**
Woodfield Rd. BS6: Redl 5D **57**
Woodgrove Rd. BS10: Hen 1F **39**
Woodhall Cl. BS16: Mang 5B **46**
WOODHILL 4C **34**
Woodhill Av. BS20: P'head 4C **34**
Wood Hill Pk. BS20: P'head 4C **34**
Woodhill Pl. BA2: Clav D 5F **105**
Woodhill Rd. BS20: P'head 5C **34**
Woodhouse Gro. BS7: Hor 5A **42**
Woodhouse Rd. BA2: Bath 4C **102**
Woodington Ct. BS30: Bar C 5B **72**
Woodland Av. BS15: K'wd 4F **61**
Woodland Cl. BS15: K'wd 4E **61**
Woodland Ct. BS8: Clif 1D **67**
  BS9: Stok B 3E **55**
  BS16: Fish *5E **45***
    (off Partridge Dr.)
Woodland Gro. BA2: Clav D ...5A **106**
  BS9: Stok B 5F **39**
Woodland Pl. BA2: Clav D 5F **105**
Woodland Ri. *BS8: Clif* *2A **4***
    (off Cantock's Cl.)
Woodland Rd. BS8: Clif ...1A **4** (1E **67**)
WOODLANDS 2E **9**
Woodlands BS16: Down 5A **46**
  BS32: Brad S 2F **9**
Woodlands Ct. BS32: Brad S 2D **9**
Woodlands La. BS32: Alm 1A **10**
  BS32: Brad S 3D **9**
    (not continuous)
Woodlands Pk. BA1: Bath 5E **97**
  BS32: Brad S 2E **9**
Woodlands Ri. BS16: Down 5F **45**
Woodlands Rd. BS20: P'head 4C **34**
Woodland Ter. BS6: Redl 4D **57**
  BS15: K'wd 1A **72**
Woodland Way BS15: K'wd 4E **61**
Wood La. BS20: Clap G 5A **50**
Wood Leaze BS37: Yate 4B **16**
Woodleaze BS9: Sea M 5D **39**
Woodleigh Gdns. BS14: H'gro ...1E **87**
Woodmancote BS37: Yate 5F **15**
Woodmancote Rd. BS6: Bris ...5A **58**
Woodmans Cl. BS37: Chip S 5D **17**
Woodmans Rd. BS37: Chip S ...5D **17**
Woodmans Va. BS37: Chip S ...5E **17**
Woodmarsh Cl. BS14: Whit 3C **86**
Woodmead Gdns. BS13: Hart 3E **85**
Woodnock, The BS10: S'mead ...1E **41**
Wood Rd. BS15: K'wd 1F **71**
Woodside BS9: Stok B 3F **55**
Woodside Cotts. BA2: Eng 5E **109**
Woodside Gdns. BS20: P'head ...1A **48**
Woodside Gro. BS10: Hen 5F **21**
Woodside Rd. BS4: St Ap 3A **70**
  BS15: K'wd 2E **71**
  BS16: Down 4E **45**
  BS36: Coal H 1F **29**
WOODSTOCK 2A **72**
Woodstock Av. BS6: Cot 5E **57**

Woodstock Cl. BS15: K'wd 1B **72**
Woodstock Rd. BS6: Redl 4D **57**
  BS15: K'wd 1B **72**
Wood St. BA1: Bath 3B **6** (4B **104**)
  BA2: Bath 5A **6** (5B **104**)
  BS5: E'tn 4D **59**
Woodview BS11: Shire 4A **38**
Woodview Ter. BA2: Bath 4B **102**
Woodward Av. BS37: Yate 4D **15**
Woodward Dr. BS30: Bar C 5B **72**
Woodwell Rd. BS11: Shire 5A **38**
    (not continuous)
Woodyleaze BS15: Han 3E **71**
Woodyleaze Dr. BS15: Han 3E **71**
Woolcot St. BS6: Redl 4D **57**
Woollard La. BS14: Whit 4F **87**
WOOLLEY 1B **96**
Woolley La. BA1: Charl, W'ly 2B **96**
Woolley Rd. BS14: Stoc 2A **88**
Wootton Cres. BS4: St Ap 3A **70**
Wootton Pk. BS14: H'gro 3D **79**
Wootton Rd. BS4: St Ap 3A **70**
Worcester Bldgs. BA1: Bath 5D **97**
Worcester Cl. BS16: Fish 4D **61**
Worcester Ct. *BA1: Bath* *5D **97***
    (off Worcester Pk.)
Worcester Cres. BS8: Clif 1C **66**
Worcester Pk. BA1: Bath 5D **97**
Worcester Pl. BA1: Bath 5D **97**
Worcester Rd. BS8: Clif 1C **66**
  BS15: K'wd 1B **72**
Worcester Ter. BA1: Bath 1D **105**
  BS8: Clif 1C **66**
Worcester Vs. BA1: Bath 5D **97**
Wordsworth Rd. BS7: Hor 5C **42**
Worlds End La. *BS8: Clif* *3D **67***
    (off Southernhay Av.)
  BS31: Key 2E **91**
Worrall M. BS8: Clif 4C **56**
Worrall Rd. BS8: Clif 4C **56**
Worrell's La. BS16: Ham 5F **27**
Worsley St. BS5: Redf 2F **69**
Worthing Rd. BS34: Pat 5B **8**
Worthsworth Ho. BS34: Pat 5C **8**
Worthy Cl. BS15: K'wd 3B **72**
Worthy Rd. BS11: Chit 1F **19**
Worthys, The BS32: Brad S 2C **26**
Wotton Rd. BS37: Iron A 1A **14**
Wraxall Gro. BS13: Bis 4C **76**
Wraxall Rd. BS30: C Hth, Warm ..3C **72**
    (not continuous)
Wrenbert Rd. BS16: Stap H 1F **61**
Wren Cl. BS16: Stap 3A **44**
    (not continuous)
Wren Dr. BS16: B'hll 5B **44**
Wright Way BS16: Stap 3A **44**
Wrington Cl. BS34: Lit S 1E **25**
Wrington Cres. BS13: Bis 5C **76**
Wroughton Dr. BS13: Hart 3F **85**
Wroughton Gdns. BS13: Hart ...3F **85**
Wroxham Dr. BS34: Lit S 5E **9**
Wyatt Av. BS13: Bis 2B **84**
Wyatt Cl. BS13: Bis 2B **84**
Wyatts Vw. BS4: St Ap 3A **70**
Wychwood BS15: K'wd 3A **72**
Wyck Beck Rd. BS10: Hen 4B **22**
Wycliffe Row BS3: Wind H 5B **68**
Wycliffe Rd. BS9: Henle 4D **41**
Wyecliffe Rd. BS10: Bren 5F **23**
Wyedale Av. BS9: C Din 4D **39**
Wykis Ct. BS15: Han 4A **72**
Wymbush Cres. BS13: Hart 2E **85**

Wymbush Gdns. BS13: Hart 2E **85**
Wyndham Ct. BS2: Bris 1E **5**
Wyndham Cres. BS4: Brisl 5B **70**
  BS20: Eas 2D **53**
Wyndham Way BS20: P'head ...5C **34**
Wyndham Way Retail Pk.
  BS20: P'head 1A **50**
Wynstones, The BS15: K'wd 2E **71**
Wytherlies Dr. BS16: B'hll 5B **44**

Y

Yalland Cl. BS16: Fish 2C **60**
Yanleigh Est. BS41: L Ash 4D **75**
YANLEY 4D **75**
Yanley La. BS41: L Ash 2D **75**
Yard, The BS2: Bris 3C **58**
YATE 4A **16**
Yate Heritage Cen. 3A **16**
Yate Leisure Cen. 3A **16**
Yate Outdoor Sports Complex ...1E **15**
Yate Rd. BS37: Iron A, Yate 2A **14**
Yate Station (Rail) 3E **15**
Yatton Cl. BS13: Bis 4B **76**
Yeaman's Ho. BS1: Bris 4A **68**
Yelverton Rd. BS4: Brisl 3A **80**
Yeo La. BS41: L Ash 3B **74**
Yeomans Cl. BS9: Stok B 1F **55**
Yeomanside Cl. BS14: H'gro 2E **87**
Yeomeads BS41: L Ash 3B **74**
Yewcroft Cl. BS14: Whit 3C **86**
Yew Tree Cl. BS14: H'gro 2D **87**
Yew Tree Dr. BS15: Soun 3A **62**
Yew Tree Gdns. BS20: Eas 2E **53**
Yomede Pk. BA1: Bath 2C **102**
York Av. BS7: B'stn 2B **58**
York Bldgs. BA1: Bath ...2B **6** (3B **104**)
  BS3: Bris 5A **68**
York Cl. BS16: Down 2B **46**
  BS34: Stok G 4F **25**
  BS37: Yate 1A **16**
York Ct. BS2: Bris 1A **68**
York Gdns. BS8: Clif 3B **66**
  BS36: Wint 5B **12**
York Pl. BA1: Bath 2D **105**
  BS1: Bris 3E **67**
  BS8: Clif 2D **67**
York Rd. BS3: Bris 5F **5** (5A **68**)
  BS5: E'tn 5E **59**
  BS6: Bris 5A **58**
  BS16: Stap H 2A **62**
York St. BA1: Bath 4C **6** (4C **104**)
  BS1: Bris 1D **5** (1A **68**)
  BS2: Bris 1D **5** (1A **68**)
    (Bond St.)
  BS2: Bris 4B **58**
    (Sevier St.)
  BS5: Redf 2E **69**
  BS8: Clif 4C **56**
Youngs Ct. BS16: Emer G 3D **47**

Z

Zed All. *BS1: Bris* *2B **4***
    (off Host St.)
Zenith BS5: St G 2F **69**
Zetland Rd. BS6: Redl 4F **57**
Zig Zag BS8: Clif 3B **68**
Zone, The BS5: St G 1C **70**

HOSPITALS, WALK-IN CENTRES and HOSPICES covered by this atlas.

N.B. Where it is not possible to name these facilities on the map,
the reference given is for the road in which they are situated.

BATH BMI CLINIC 3F **111**
Claverton Down Road
Combe Down
BATH
BA2 7BR
Tel: 01225 835555

BLACKBERRY HILL HOSPITAL 1B **60**
Manor Road
Fishponds
BRISTOL
BS16 2EW
Tel: 0117 9656061

BRISTOL DENTAL HOSPITAL 1B **4** (2F **67**)
Lower Maudlin Street
BRISTOL
BS1 2LY
Tel: 0117 9284383

BRISTOL EYE HOSPITAL 1C **4** (2F **67**)
Lower Maudlin Street
BRISTOL
BS1 2LX
Tel: 0117 9230060

BRISTOL GENERAL HOSPITAL 5C **4** (4F **67**)
Guinea Street
BRISTOL
BS1 6SY
Tel: 0117 9286223

BRISTOL HAEMATOLOGY & ONCOLOGY CENTRE
. . . . .1B **4** (2F **67**)
Horfield Road
BRISTOL
BS2 8ED
Tel: 0117 9282416

BRISTOL HOMOEOPATHIC HOSPITAL (OUTPATIENTS)
. . . . .1E **67**
Cotham Hill
BRISTOL
BS6 6JU
Tel: 0117 9731231

BRISTOL NUFFIELD HOSPITAL AT ST MARY'S 2D **67**
Upper Byron Place
BRISTOL
BS8 1JU
Tel: 0117 9872727

BRISTOL NUFFIELD HOSPITAL AT THE CHESTERFIELD
. . . . .3C **66**
3 Clifton Hill
BRISTOL
BS8 1BP
Tel: 0117 9730391

BRISTOL PRIORY GRANGE HOSPITAL 2D **59**
Heath House Lane
Stapleton
BRISTOL
BS16 1EQ
Tel: 0117 9525255

BRISTOL ROYAL HOSPITAL FOR CHILDREN
. . . . .1B **4** (2F **67**)
Upper Maudlin Street
BRISTOL
BS2 8BJ
Tel: 0117 342 8461

BRISTOL ROYAL INFIRMARY 1B **4** (1F **67**)
Marlborough Street
BRISTOL
BS2 8HW
Tel: 0117 9230000

BRISTOL SPIRE HEALTH CLINIC 5C **56**
116 Pembroke Road
Clifton
BRISTOL
BS8 3EW
Tel: 0117 3171300

BRISTOL SPIRE HOSPITAL 4C **56**
Redland Hill
Redland
BRISTOL
BS6 6UT
Tel: 0117 9804000

CALLINGTON ROAD HOSPITAL 3E **79**
Marmalade Lane
BRISTOL
BS4 5BJ
Tel: 0117 919 5600

COSSHAM MEMORIAL HOSPITAL 4E **61**
Lodge Road
BRISTOL
BS15 1LF
Tel: 0117 9671661

FRENCHAY HOSPITAL 3D **45**
Frenchay Park Road
BRISTOL
BS16 1LE
Tel: 0117 9701212

FROMESIDE 1B **60**
Blackberry Hill
Stapleton
BRISTOL
BS16 1EG
Tel: 0117 958 3678

GROVE ROAD DAY HOSPITAL 4C **56**
12 Grove Road
Redland
BRISTOL
BS6 6UJ
Tel: 0117 9730225

NHS WALK-IN CENTRE (BATH) 3A **6** (4A **104**)
Riverside Health Centre
James Street West
BATH
BA1 2BT

Hospitals, Walk-in Centres and Hospices

NHS WALK-IN CENTRE (BRISTOL - CITY GATE)
. . . . .2C **4** (2F **67**)
33 Broad Street
BRISTOL
BS1 2EZ
Tel: 0117 903 9610

NHS WALK-IN CENTRE (BRISTOL - SOUTH) 3F **77**
5 Knowle West Health Park
Downton Road
Knowle
BRISTOL
BS4 1WH
Tel: 0117 903 0000

ROBERT SMITH UNIT DAY HOSPITAL 2C **66**
12 Mortimer Road
BRISTOL
BS8 4EX
Tel: 0117 9735004

ROYAL NATIONAL HOSPITAL FOR RHEUMATIC DISEASES
. . . . .3B **6** (4B **104**)
Upper Borough Walls
BATH
BA1 1RL
Tel: 01225 465941

ROYAL UNITED HOSPITAL 2D **103**
Combe Park
BATH
BA1 3NG
Tel: 01225 428331

ST MARTIN'S HOSPITAL .4A **110**
Midford Road
BATH
BA2 5RP
Tel: 01225 831500

ST MICHAEL'S HOSPITAL 1A **4** (1E **67**)
Southwell Street
BRISTOL
BS2 8EG
Tel: 0117 928 5325

ST PETERS HOSPICE 2C **78**
St. Agnes Avenue
BRISTOL
BS4 2DU
Tel: 0117 9159200

ST PETERS HOSPICE (BRENTRY) 1D **41**
Charlton Road
Brentry
BRISTOL
BS10 6NL
Tel: 01179 159400

SOUTHMEAD HOSPITAL 3F **41**
Southmead Road
Westbury-on-Trym
BRISTOL
BS10 5NB
Tel: 0117 9505050

SAFETY CAMERA INFORMATION

Safety camera locations are publicised by the Safer Roads Partnership who operate them in order to encourage
drivers to comply with speed limits at these sites. It is the driver's absolute responsibility to be aware of and

By showing . . . . s' A-Z Map Company Ltd., to encourage
safe c . . . . Data accurate at time of printing.